CHARLES LASALLE.

The Autobiography of

WILL ROGERS

The Autobiography of

WILL ROGERS

selected and edited by
DONALD DAY

with a foreword by
BILL and JIM ROGERS

PEOPLES BOOK CLUB, CHICAGO

To Will's Friends
Which Means You

FOREWORD

FATHER would like this book.

He was stubborn about some things, especially that every man had the right to speak his own piece.

In 1933 in his weekly column he begged "Please don't write my life!" He said in part:

Every guy that has a pencil and some old fools cap paper is going to put my life right in between the kivers of a dime novel (maybe nickle). I guess it is the same in each state. The disappointed writers of Kansas are perhaps after notorious characters up there. The unpublished writers of Texas are perhaps telling the early life struggles of some old Texas highbinder. That these gentlemen dident know you, or maby had just met you once or twice in their lives never seemed to hinder their idea that they was the one to do your life.

What kinder hurt me about all this life writing epidemic is that no one that knows me has ever suggested writing one (that kinder hurt my pride).

Most of my life has been lived alone. I never run with a pack. In my later years Mrs. Rogers could perhaps give you a few details, but no one of my various authors has ever seen or asked her.

Besides I havent even started living. I am going to cut loose here some day and try to get some life into my life and even then it wont be fit to tell about. The first part will be uninteresting and the last part will be too scandalous.

I am just tipping the boys off to sharpen their pencils and go after somebody else. Why dont they pick on Governor Bill Murray? Bill has done more, lived more in a year than I ever did or will. So Bill, I hereby pass on a batch (I think it is a dozen) of amateur Carl Sandbergs. Give em a chance, they are all fine boys. I got nothing against em. But let em practice writing your life. Yours can stand it. But my poor little life Bernard Shaw couldent make it look like anything.

Henry Carr once wrote that Dad's column "was the day-by-day story of his life, a life-story of singular completeness and self-revelation." Donald Day believes this. For months he has been going through Dad's writings, selecting those that would in a limited space give to you just what Dad was trying to do and say.

For years Father was billed as "the Poet Lariat" of the United States. In this book he certainly throws his own rope in lassoing himself and you.

BILL and JIM ROGERS

Beverly Hills, California

CONTENTS

Letting Will Rogers
Lasso Himself

LIKE AMERICA, when Will Rogers started out, a wad of gum in his jaw, twirling a rope, a grin on his face, he didn't know where he was going. His was no planned, educated, groomed, scientifically test-tubed existence. That's why it is so American."

So far, so good. Then Charles Collins, who wrote this, went on to say, as has almost every writer who has written about Will, that he was "as a type, the average American, as that theoretical figure likes to imagine himself if incarnated." One writer even went so far as to say that "he was America."

Now let's see what Will himself said. On February 22, 1925, he wrote:

When an Office Holder, or one that has been found out, can't think of anything to deliver a speech on, he always falls back on the good old subject, AMERICANISM. Now that is one thing that I have never delivered an Essay on, either written or spoken. So now I am going to take up the subject and see what I can wrestle out of it. Let's get our rope ready and turn it out, and we will catch it and see really what brand it has on it. Here it comes out of the Corral. We got it caught, now it's throwed and Hog tied; and we will pick the brands and see what they are.

The first thing I find out is there ain't any such animal. This American Animal that I thought I had there is nothing but the big Honest Majority, that you might find in any Country. *He is not a Politician, he is not a 100 per cent American. He is not any organization, either uplift or down fall. In fact I find he don't belong to anything. He is no decided Political faith or religion. I can't even find out what religious brand is on him. From his earmarks he has never made a speech, and announced that he was an American. He hasn't denounced anything.* It looks to me like he is just an Animal that has been going along, believing in right, doing right, tending to his business, letting the other fellows alone.

He don't seem to be simple enough minded to believe that everything is right and he don't appear to be Cuckoo enough to think that everything is wrong. He don't seem to be a Prodigy, and he don't seem to be a Simp. In fact, all I can find about him is that he is just NORMAL. After I let him up and get on my Horse and ride away I look around and I see hundreds and hundreds of exactly the same marks and Brands. In fact they so outnumber the freakly branded ones that the only conclusion I can come to is that this Normal breed is so far in the majority that there is no use to worry about the others. They are a lot of Mavericks and Strays.

Honestly, I could spout for forty volumes and not lasso Will Rogers better than that. If any one thing runs through what he wrote and said like a drumbeat it is that if you give "the big Honest Majority" a chance, you don't have to worry about the freaks. On the other hand he was not simp enough to think that "the big Honest Majority" is always given a chance. Because this is true, Will tried to become both the watchdog and the spokesman for this inarticulate group.

Will didn't go to the Mount to speak his sermon nor did he speak in parables. Like a folk song, fresh from the heart of the people, he said things that they want to say but do not know how to put into words. Their inarticulate voice has spoken many times in the verities of Christ and Lincoln and Woodrow Wilson and many others. Their immovable courage kept these men going. Nevertheless, Will's phrasings of their longings was even closer because he was more a part of them. He knew only too well that the granite fibers out of which democracy has been built came from them.

Perhaps that is the reason why, without any hullabaloo or advertising, over twelve hundred people a day drop their tears at the Will Rogers Memorial at Claremore, Oklahoma, and thousands of others leave his old ranch house at Santa Monica, California, stilled and hushed.

Will is "their" man because he came right out of "the big Honest Majority" and he never departed their ways. He grew up with them both historically and personally.

As the American frontier moved westward, the settlers listened more and more to horse-sense humorists. This was a natural and necessary development. The men who sought out new homes were not as a rule skilled in group associations, particularly governmental. They had to build their own institutions out of the rawest material. And their efforts were more often ludicrous than profound. If they could not have laughed at their bumbling, their crude structures would have come tumbling in ruins about their ears. The first American symposium met around the cracker barrels and stoves in the country stores when crops were laid by. Some of the group gathered there said more pertinent things and said them better. A few of these developed into spokesmen for the region. A handful rose to national prominence. Unlike politicians, they were fired in a crucible that tempered them to a minute fineness.

Beginning in 1835 with Major Jack Downing until the death of Will Rogers America was not without its cracker-box philosopher who often possessed power approaching or exceeding that of the President. Unlike the President, if they abused or failed to exercise their power, they were "recalled" instantly. Sut Lovingood, Artemus Ward, Petroleum V. Nasby, Bill Arp, Mark Twain, Josh Billings, Mr. Dooley — What an array!

Will was born on the last frontier as it was passing out of existence. At his very doorsteps this unbelievable task of conquering a continent and building a great nation, in nothing flat as the lives of nations go, was being completed. His father was a man of influence in the community and in the affairs of the Cherokee Indian tribe. Will probably heard politics discussed earlier than he began roping things — which was about the time that he learned to walk. When he was ten the huge free range that his father had used for ranching was cut up and given out as homesteads. That ended Will's early dream of becoming a big rancher. At about the same time his mother died. That blasted his home ties. These two events turned him both inward and outward. From then on his eager spirit — urged on by three sixteenths Cherokee Indian blood — kept him mentally and physically on the move, but always with his feet still planted firmly in the soil from which he came.

Chance, no doubt, took him into the show business. Wild West performances — riding and roping contests — were coming much into the public eye, particularly after Teddy Roosevelt and his rough riders flashed their meteoric career across the horizon. These contests gave Will's restless spirit a chance to keep unlimbered without too great a break with the past. From a mere entertainer he developed, slowly and gradually, into a commentator who "was liable to talk about anybody or anything." By the time he had finished his first stretch in Ziegfeld's Follies in 1919 he had become a full-fledged cracker-box philosopher. But with differences from any that had gone before.

He had started out pretty much as the rest of them — as an oral humorist — and had graduated to the printed word. But instead of stopping there, he went on to other mediums as they developed, as no doubt many of his predecessors would have done. When he was killed he was the top moving-picture box-office attraction, radio entertainer, newspaper columnist, after-dinner speaker and lecturer in the United States. And, even more important, he was without a doubt first in the affections of his countrymen.

Of course this last attribute was his crowning achievement. It was made possible by his greatest difference from the other cracker-box philosophers. All of them had been one person in private life and another in their character as a horse-sense humorist. Will just ambled out in whatever medium he chose as Will, one and inseparable in his person and in his character as a humorist. In this way he could and did become the prototype of "the big Honest Majority." His humor, his comments, his sarcasms were just as much a part of him as his big ears, his shuffling gait, his grin and his unruffled good nature. He was as real as a mule wiggling its ears on a hot summer day.

As a prototype of "the big Honest Majority" Will was more than just an American. He was one of the great internationalists of all times — as all real democrats are. His "big Honest Majority," as he said, crosses all national boundaries, all creeds and colors. His was not Jingo Internationalism with a solution by force backed up by bayonets or atom bombs. When he went abroad, he went to see folks from the highest to the humblest, and he went to see them *for what they were and not for what he could change them into or do them out of*. He didn't want to Americanize Mexico, he wanted that country to develop as it wanted to. He didn't want us to send missionaries to China, he pointed out rather tellingly that China might well send missionaries to us. He said over and over, even though he didn't phrase it in those words, "I never visited a nation I didn't like."

When all of Will's writings are published they will constitute the best *blow-by-blow* history of a period ever written (chiefly from December 31, 1922, to August 15, 1935). For the first time "the big Honest Majority" will have a history not written by a propagandist or a pedant; for the first time the people will have a history written as they would write it if articulate. And what a history, how penetrating, how lucid, how critical, but brimming over with eternal hope! If two hundred great dailies, two thousand country newspapers, half of the leading magazines, twenty-five percent of the time and efforts of the radio and moving-picture studios, were for two years devoted to publishing and telling about just such a contemporary history, domestic differences could be ironed out and national boundaries broken down so that a people's peace would be possible — the only real democratic peace. Atom bombs and germ warfare can accomplish no more than bayonets and block-busters have in the past.

It is obvious then that Will was not a freak spewed out of American life like Minerva came from the brain of Zeus. His was the flowering of the "big Honest Majority," particularly its sense of humor, an indivisible and indispensable attribute of democracy. He could have been replaced at his death only by one that came out of the same crucible as he. As Bob Wagner phrased it, "we might find some one to fill his space, but not his place." And none has. Maybe the crucible has cooled. God help us if it has. Will's life, as a lot of ours, encompassed a span as broad as the nation's: from a self-sufficing rural economy (his of the cowman) to the collectivism of the New Deal. Yet Will, like America, at the time of his death didn't know where we were going, and didn't want to. That is the dynamics of democracy that forever pounds against and clings to the unchangeableness of "the big Honest Majority" in spite of the efforts of dictators and planners to trap and mould things to their wishes. And in spite of those who claim democracy only because it permits them to become little autocrats and dictators in their personal affairs. Will thoroughly hated them as he hated any effort, Platonic or Hitlerian or Stalinistic or Ku Klux Klan, to set up an ideal out of their own conjuring of what constituted perfection. If individuals thought right, believed right and did right there would be little need to worry about the group. Well, the ambling Will is dead but the Will that fused itself with the people, like Lincoln, just keeps a drawlin' on as what he said insistently becomes a part of democratic folklore, the marrow and bone of the hope for the future.

The selection of Will's writings has been made with two ideas in view: (1) to let Will tell you how he became the spokesman and watchdog for the inarticulate public (although he'd never admit that he was), and (2) for him to say again to you the pertinent things he said during probably the most critical period of change in American life.

The chute is open, here he comes his horse a-pitchin', lasso a-swingin'. He's going to catch himself and you with the same rope.

Adios,
DONALD DAY

Claremore, Oklahoma
Beverly Hills, California

The Autobiography of

WILL ROGERS

CHAPTER ONE

It Was Just a Habit

IN ALL the Autobographys I ever read the first line was I was born at So-and-so on Such-and-such a Date. That is the accustomed first line of any Autubiography. Now the thing that struck me was if a fellow could give a reason why he was born you'd be a novelty. Now that is what has been holding me up on this Autobography, I was born, but why? Now I've got it.

I was born because it was a habit in those days, people dident know anything else. In those days they dident put a Bounty on you for being born. Nowadays, the income Tax allows you 200 dollars for each child. Just removing his adanoids cost more than that, to say nothing about his food, Tonsils and Fraternoty pins. In those days a Doctor would bring you into the World for two

1

Dollars a visit and make good money at it. Everything you was born with was supposed to be buried with you, but nowadays when you die about all you have left at the funeral is Scars and stitches.

If you had the stomack Ache the Doctor cured it; if you have it nowadays they remove it.

Ether has replaced pills as our national commodity.

So I just figured out I was born as a Martyr to the ignorance of old time Drs. It was the law of averages that put me here. I beat Race Suicide by just one year, I arrived when childbirth was not grounds for divorce. If a family dident have at least 8 children in those days the Father was either in jail or deceased.

MOTHER and Baby doing well was our National yell.

It falls to the lot of few to be born on National Holidays. A Child born on the Fourth of July, as my good friend George Cohan was, has to spend the rest of his life waving a flag. A child born on Xmas uses the Chimney for an entrance even after he is married. The New Years child arrived with wonderful resolutions and passes out by electrocution.

I am the only known child in History who claims Nov. 4th as my Birthday, that is election day. Women couldent vote in those days so My Mother thought she would do something, so she stayed home and gave birth to me. The men were all away. I decided to get even with the Government. Thats why I have always had it in for politicians.

I was the only child born on our beat that day. The news had to cross the Country by Pony Express, so it was two years later that it reached Washington, so Garfield was shot.

I was born on the Verdigris river, one mile below where Spencer Creek enters the river. Rutherford B. Hayes was President at the time of my birth.

I was the youngest and last of 7 Children. My folks looked me over and instead of the usual drowning procedure, they said, "This thing has gone far enough, if they are going to look like this, we will stop."

I was born at our old Ranch 12 miles north of Claremore, Okla (the home of the best Radium Water in the World). It was a big two story Log House, but on the back we had three rooms made of frame. Just before my birth my mother, being in one of these frame rooms, had them remove her into the Log part of the House. She wanted me to be born in a log House. She had just read the life of Lincoln. So I got the Log house end of it OK. All I need now is the other qualifications.

It is customary in most Auto biographies to devote a couple of paragraphs to the parents. Now in my case the parents should have the Article devoted to them and the couple of Paragraphs to me.

My father was Clem V. Rogers, a Part Cherokee Indian, who was a Captain under Stan Waitie during the Civil War. He afterwards freighted from St Joe, Mo., to Dallas, Texas. The Covered Wagon went West and got into Pictures. He went South. If he had gone West instead of South, he might have got into "The Covered Wagon," or maybe the "10 Commandments."

He did that for years until he found out that St. Joe, Missouri, dident have anything that Dallas, Texas, dident have (outside of the James Boys). Under the circumstances I think my Father was pretty wise in quitting hauling from St. Joe to Dallas. He went into the Cattle Business and settled on the Ranch we have in the family yet. They drove a bunch of Cattle from down there up to Kansas City, and unlike the Story of North of 36, there was no Girl with the outfit, no Negro Maids. They just took Cattle. Well, when they got to KC they couldent sell them. There was no celebration when they drove into town, so they said what other Town have you got around here that want 3 thousand cattle. They said, why St. Louis, Lemp and Anhauser Busch had just moved into St. Louis so Papa and his gang lit out for there, only 590 miles. Now if I wanted to make a scenario out of this instead of the truth, I would tell you that they couldent sell in St. Louis and had to go on to Chicago, but such is not the truth. They dident happen to meet any one with a sense of humor to tell em that. They only lost one Steer. He jumped off the Boat crossing the Mississippi going over to East St. Louis and tried to swim back to Missouri. He really committed suicide rather than enter Illinois. He went on down the river and I dont know at that if he ever drowned. Mark Twain just liable to picked him up with one of those Mississippi Steam shovels of his, on down the river some place. Then they all had to ride back home to the Indian Territory Horseback. They dident by the way have to go back by KC. Jim Reed had just begin practicing law there in KC then and they knew that he would figure out some way to take this money away from them.

Papa rode a Mule on the whole trip, not much romance in that, thats why he come back single.

Mamas name was Mary and if your Mother was an old-fashioned Woman and named Mary you dont need to say much for her, everybody knows already.

Most men in their Auto Biographies after they are born kinder skip over a lapse of time, and they dont seem to be able to remember anything until they get up able to hold political office. Now that is the only thing remarkable about me, I looked em all over the next day after arrival and sized the whole thing up and says this Life is going to be a lot of Apple Sauce. Being born on election day, it kinder gave me the advantage of seeing the Bunk in it all. I arrived amid a day of crooked Ballotts. I could read when I was a year old. I was not a Child Prodigy, because a Child Prodigy is a child who knows as much when it is a Child as it does when it grows up.

Well, the next year, 1880, why Garfield was elected President on my first Birthday. I dident vote but they voted my name every year up to 18.

The East River in NY froze over that year and people walked over without paying Subway fare. Garfield was Assassinated in a Depot in Washington waiting for the Baltimore and Ohio Railroad train. He is the first man ever assassinated waiting for one of those trains but he is not the first casualty, as thousands have starved to death waiting for em. I can remember the day of the Assassination. I cried that day, well I cried the day before and the day after too, but I remember that particular day well.

I was named by an Indian Chief, William Penn Adair. He says, "Mary, I want another young Chief named for me. I name him Will Penn Adair Rogers." The River was up and he had to stay there a week, so he got paid for his name. I just looked at him when he named me and thought by the time I get to be big enough to be Chief we wont have any more Country than a Jay Bird.

All Auto Biographies have pictures of the person being autobied. Now I have some taken at the age of three in a group at a Circus. Of course I havent got many with prominent men taken at the opportune time because at that time I did not know that I would ever have an Autobiography.

Well, Claremore is the county seat of Rogers County, which was named for my father. My family had lived there for over fifty years. My father was one-eighth Cherokee Indian and my mother was a quarter-blood Cherokee. I never got far enough in arithmetic to figure out just how much "Injun" that makes me, but there's nothing of which I am more proud than my Cherokee blood. My father was a senator in the tribe for years, and was a member of the convention that drafted the constitution of the State of Oklahoma.

My father was pretty well fixed, and I being the only male son he tried terribly hard to make something out of me. He sent me to about every school in that part of the country. In some of them I would last for three or four months. I got just as far as the fourth reader when the teachers wouldn't seem to be running the school right, and rather than have the school stop I would generally leave.

Then I would start in at another school, tell them I had just finished the third reader and was ready for the fourth. Well, I knew all this fourth grade by heart, so the teacher would remark:

"I never see you studying, yet you seem to know your lessons." I had that education thing figured down to a fine point. Three years in McGuffey's Fourth Reader, and I knew more about it than McGuffey did.

But I don't want any enterprising youth to get the idea that I had the right dope on it. I have regretted all my life that I did not at least take a chance on the fifth grade. It would certainly come in handy right now, and I never go through a day that I am not sorry for the idea I had of how to go to school and not learn anything.

I was just a thinking what I would have to do if I was to start out to help out my old schools. "Drumgoul" was a little one-room log cabin four miles east of Chelsea, Indian Territory (where I am right now writing). It was all Indian kids went there and I being part Cherokee had enough white in me to make my honesty questionable.

There must have been about thirty of us in that room that had rode horseback and walked miles to get there, and by the way it was a Co Ed Institution. About half of em was Coo-Coo Eds. We graduated when we could print our full names and enumerate to the teacher, or Principle or Faculty (well, whenever we could name to her), the nationality of the last Democratic President.

But as I say the school went out of business. We wasent able to get games which was profitable. It seems that other school grabbed off all the other good dates, and got the breaks in the newspapers. We couldent seem to ever be accused of professionalism. I could see the finish even as far back as when I was there along in 1887.

Why I can remember when the Coach couldent get enough out of us 15 Boys out to make a team. We got to running Horse Races instead. I had a little chestnut mare that was beating everything that any of them could ride to school and I was losing interest in what we was really there for. I was kinder forgetting that we was there to put the old school on a Paying basis by seeing how many times we could get through that Goal with that old pigskin.

I got to thinking well Horseracing is the big game, thats where the money is, thats what the crowds pay to see. But as years went along it showed that I was a Lad of mighty poor foresight. Little did I dream that it was football that was to be the real McCoy. Course we had no way of hardly telling it then, for we was paid practically nothing at all. In fact we had what I would call a Real Simon Pure Amateur Team. Course we got our side line (Schooling) free. The Cherokee Nation (we then had our own Government and the name Oklahoma was as foreign to us as a Tooth Paste), well, the Cherokee Nation paid the Teacher.

But anyhow there was a mighty few of us that was there under any kind of a guarantee. Course I will admit one of the Alumni got me to go there. He had spent three weeks there and couldent get along with the Teacher and he wanted to do what he could for the old School so he procured me. I looked like a promising End. I could run pretty fast. In fact my nickname was and is to this day among some of the old-timers "Rabbit." I could never figure out if that referred to my speed or my heart.

Mind you, you wouldent believe it, but we dident even have a Stadium. Think of that in this day and time! Thousands and Thousands of acres surrounded us with not a thing on it but Cows and not a concrete seat for a spectator to sit on. Well you see as I look back on it now, a school like that dident have any license to exist. It had to perish. It just staid with books such as Rays Arithmetic and McGuffy 1st, 2nd, and 2 pupils in the 3rd Readers. We had a Geography around there but we just used it for the pictures of the cattle grazing in the Argentine and the wolves attacking the sleighs in Russia.

Well you see they just couldent see what was the future in Colleges. They just wore out the old books instead of wearing out some footballs. We had Indian Boys that could knock a Squirrel out of a Tree with a rock. But do you think the Regents knew enough to get a Pop Warner and teach em how to hide a Ball under their Jerseys? No. They just had the old-fashioned idea that the place must be made self-sustaining by learning alone, and you see where their ignorance got them. Now the weeds is higher there than the School house was and thats what is happening in a few places in this country. We got those same "Drumgoul" ideas. Course not many but a few. They wont switch and get to the new ideas that its open field running that gets your old College somewhere and not a pack of spectacled Orators or a mess of Civil Engineers. Its better to turn out one good Coach than Ten College Presidents. His name will be in the papers every day and it will always be referred to where he come from. But with the College Presidents, why as far as publicity is concerned they just as well might have matriculated in Hong Kong. So dont let your school be another Drumgoul.

Well, back to my autobography. You see, the lariat-slinging business drifted into my system when I was pretty young. My father would send me out on the ranch, but instead of riding the

range I'd go off into a shady place and there spend the time practicing with the rope — cutting curliques and things in the prairie
breeze or lassoing prairie dogs and things not made to be lassoed.

Then he hired me out to other ranch-men, but I was so fond of
using the lariat when there was no call for it that I couldn't hold a
job. In a fit of bad temper the old gent decided to make a preacher
of me, and he sent me to a school up in Missouri. When I lassoed
the stone gal — goddess of something — off the top of the water
fountain and broke all her limbs, the old gent paid the bill rather
than have me sent back to the nation, because he didn't need me on
the ranch, but when I got the string around the Professor's neck —
by accident — my career on the road to the ministry ended.

My old daddy — Uncle Clem, they called him — then sent me
to a military school at Boonville, Mo., Kemper, thinking the dis-
cipline might tame me.

*Will arrived there on January 13, 1897, dressed in a ten-gallon hat, with
a braided horsehair cord, flannel shirt with a red bandana handkerchief,
highly colored vest, and high-heeled red top boots with spurs and his
trousers legs tucked in the boot tops. He carried coiled ropes outside his
luggage.*

Me and Ben Johnson, down at Chickasha, Oklahoma, were bud-
dies together at Kemper, just a couple of poor ornery Indian boys.
But the fact is we were sent to the Missouri State reformatory which
is located near the same town and through somebody's mistake,
they enrolled us at the Kemper Military Academy instead.

Col. Johnson — the head man — didn't run Kemper in accord-
ance with the standards that I thought befitting a growing intellect.
I was spending my third year in the fourth grade and wasn't being
appreciated, so I not only left them flat during a dark night, but
quit the entire school business for life.

Billy Johnston of Canadian, Texas, was also an inmate, and a
ranch boy like I had been in Oklahoma, so he advised me of a
friend's ranch at Higgins, Texas. I, not wanting to face my father
with what little I knew, lit a shuck for there.

When I got there, the outfit had gone away, boss and all. Just a
cook and two or three old broke-down cowboys was left.

I stayed around until the boss, Mr. Ewing, and his son Frank came back and they give me a job. We took a trail herd to Kansas and I worked with them for some time. He was a great fellow, funny as they make em. I got enough money to buy me an old horse and lit out for Amarillo, Texas.

This country was thinly settled then — only passed three ranches on the way in. They'd let me cook up a lot of biscuits and some jerky — dried beef — and then that old skate and I would amble on.

One night I staked him out in good grass and hit the old sougans, as I was dead tired. During the night a thunder storm come up. I'd never seen such lightning and heard such noise in my life. A big bunch of range horse got frightened and run smack into that rope I'd staked my old horse out with. When it come another flash of lightning, I couldent see him and thought he'd been killed.

I was wet as a drowned rat and hit out back for a line camp I'd passed and hadn't gone in. I knocked and yelled, "Hello! Hello!" and nobody answered. I went in and as my matches was all wet — fumbled around in the dark till I found a table and went to sleep on it. When I woke the sun was shining bright and there just six feet away was a good warm bunk with blankets and everything. There was coffee and a side of bacon and I made a fire in the stove and cooked up a bait. After I got the wrinkles out of my belly I lit out on foot. About a mile from the camp I went up on a little hill and there on the other side was my horse grazing away on the grass as good as ever.

When I finally got into Amarillo the whole country around was covered with trail herds waiting for cars to ship them away. There was plenty of grass and water everywhere.

I hit up every trail boss I could find for a job, but they didn't want me. At night I'd go out a piece from town, stake out my horse, and sleep, then the next morning go back.

While I dident have anything else to do, I got to watching an old spotted dog. He was just an ordinary dog, but when I looked at him close, he was alert and friendly with everyone. Got to inquiring around and found out he'd been bumped off a freight train and seemed to have no owner. He made himself at home and started right in business. When a crowd of cowboys would go into a saloon, he would follow em in and begin entertaining. He could do all kinds of tricks — turn somersaults, lay down and roll over, sit up on his hind feet, and such like.

He would always rush to the door and shake hands with all the newcomers. The boys would lay a coin on his nose, and he'd toss it high in the air and catch it in his mouth and pretend to swallow it. But you could bet your life he dident swallow it — he stuck it in one side of his lip and when he got a lip full of money, he'd dash out the back door and disappear for a few minutes. What he really done was hide his money. As soon as he worked one saloon, he would pull out and go to another place.

I got to thinking while watching this old dog, how much smarter he is than me. Here I am out of a job five hundred miles from home, and setting around and cant find a thing to do, and this old dog hops off a train and starts right in making money, hand over fist.

Me and some boys around town tried to locate his hidden treasure, but this old dog was too slick for us. He never fooled away no time on three or four of us boys that was looking for work. He seemed to know we was broke, but he was very friendly. As he was passing along by me, he'd wag his tail and kinda wink. I must a looked hungry and forlorn. I think he wanted to buy me a meal.

When times was dull and he got hungry, he would mysteriously disappear. Pretty soon he'd show up at a butcher shop with a dime in his mouth and lay it on the counter and the butcher would give him a piece of steak or a bone. He always paid for what he got in the line of grub. Pretty soon he seemed to get tired of the town, and one morning he was gone. A railroad man told us later that he seen this same dog in Trinidad, Colorado.

One morning a merchant told me a trail boss had sent him word to hire him a hand, but that he already spoke to another boy. He told me to go see him just in case he dident want the other boy. I was on the spot, you bet.

Right then I seen a feller talk himself out of a job. He started in telling the boss what a good hand he was. The old cowman listened to him till he had had his say, then he told him, "I'm in need of a hand all right, but I think you'd suit me too well."

I just told him maby I could do the work. He told me to get on my horse and come out to his camp. Them was the happiest words I ever heard in my life.

I got to the chuck wagon just in time for dinner. The boys setting around grinned as I stowed away helping after helping of beans. But when I finished there wasent a wrinkle left in my belly.

The boss put me to wrangling ponies. We moved on up to Panhandle City crossing the Canadian River at a Famous Ranch, where Remington had painted some of his pictures, the old "L.X." Ranch. We went on over to the boss' ranch near Woodward, Oklahoma, where I worked through the roundup and helped brand the calves.

Finally, I got tired and another boy and I went to California with a shipment of cattle and up to Frisco, and that night something happened. He says he didn't blow the gas out, maybe there was a leak. I was asleep when he came in — anyhow they dug us out of there next morning and hauled us to a hospital, and believe me I didn't know a fighting thing until late that night and that was just bull luck. The main doctors gave me up, but a lot of young medical students just by practicing on me happened to light on some nut remedy that no regular doctor would ever think of and I come alive.

Well I landed back home pretty badly buggered up. This stuff had located in my system. I went to Hot Springs to boil it out and when I would get in a hot room they would all think the gas was escaping some place.

Well, my old dad called me off a few weeks later and told me, "If you're bound to punch cows, there's no need for you to leave home. You're the only child I have at home now, as your sisters are married and have homes of their own. I'm a going to give you this Dog Iron Ranch, lock, stock and barrel. It's yours and you can run it the way you want to, for I'm going to move to Claremore."

Well, I dident exactly run it to suit him. I danced all my young life to the music of old country fiddlers and I dident drag a bad bow myself. Between dances and roping contests, I dident have time for much serious ranching business.

I had a little cream-colored pony with a white mane and tail, name Comanche. He was about the best horse wrapped up in that much hide. I used to race horses with some Negroes lived next to us. One of the boys owned his horse. Couldent ever beat him so swapped him my horse and ten dollars to boot for him.

Well, I remember when we was out at a steer roping and bronc busting contest at the Elks' Carnival at Springfield, Missouri. A cowboy that I let ride Comanche roped a steer and threw him right in front of the grand stand. When he jumped off to tie the steer, the old cuss rolled over and got to his feet and charged straight at him, cutting him off from his horse. But old Comanche, when the steer crossed the rope, turned and busted him all by himself. The cowboy dident lose over three seconds time in tying him.

A wealthy New Yorker come down from the grandstand and wanted to buy the pony. He finally got up to five hundred dollars. "A dollar looks as big to me as a wagon wheel," I told him, "but I just don't want to sell him."

He came back, "He can be bought for some price, name it, and I'll ship him to Long Island, New York."

"Mister," I told him, "I don't know how much money you got, but there ain't money enough in that grand stand to buy old Comanche."

Well, I kept going to these steer-roping contests. I learned a lot from men like Clay McGonagill, Tom Vest, Abe Wilson, and the rest of the top-notchers who'd be there. Shortly after the Spanish-American War, the Rough Riders held a reunion at Oklahoma City. When I got there the fair grounds was full of horses and cowboys. These contestants were cowboys right off the ranches that done roping work every day. They come from Texas, New Mexico, Arizona, Colorado, Wyoming, and, of course, Indian Territory.

Colonel Theodore Roosevelt was there, mixing in with us boys. Old Booger Red was there from San Angelo, Texas. I broke my rope and old Jim O'Donnell won. He'd of beat me anyhow.

My real show career kinder dates from the time I first run into the Col. Zack Mulhall. It was in 1899 at the St. Louis fair (not the Worlds fair) just the big St. Louis fair they held every year. They had decided as an attraction that they would put on a Roping and Riding Contest. They were not called Rodeo's or Stampedes, in those days they were just what they are, a "Roping and Riding Contest." Well I was pretty much of a Kid, but had just happened to have won the first and about my only Contest at home in Claremore, Okla., and then we read about them wanting entries for this big contest at St. Louis.

Well some one sent in my name, and the first thing I knew I was getting transportation for myself and pony to the affair. Well I went, and Col. Zack Mulhall had charge of it. I dident get very far in this St. Louis Contest. I made the serious mistake of catching my steer and he immediately jerked me and my Pony down for our trouble.

But that gave me a touch of "Show business" in a way, so that meant I was ruined for life as far as actual employment was concerned. He had a couple of Daughters, Miss "Bossy" and Lucille. Bossy was quite a good rider but she never took it up in the professional way that little Lucille did. Lucille was just a little kid when we were in St. Louis that year, but she was riding and running her Pony all over the place, and that was incidentally her start too. It was not only her start, but it was the direct start of what has since come to be known as the Cowgirl. There was no such a thing or no such word then as Cowgirl. But as Col. Mulhall from that date drifted into the professional end of the Contest and show business, why Lucille gradually come to the front, and you can go tell the world that his youngest Daughter Lucille Mulhall was the first well-known Cowgirl.

She become a very expert roper, and was the first girl that could rope and tie a Steer, not only do it but do it in such time that it would make a good roper hustle to beat her.

Colonel Mulhall was at the time general stock agent for the Frisco Railroad. He got together a Cowboy Band of about sixty musicians. They was dressed in ten-gallon hats, jackets, chaps, boots and spurs. We made all the State Fairs through the Middle West. As those musicians could not ride in a wagon unless their shirt tails was nailed to the floor, Colonel Zack thought it would help to have a few cowboys along.

He advertised he could pick out boys in the band that would ride any old outlaw horse in the State. He offered to bet that we could rope and tie a steer in less time than anybody they could produce. Me and Jim O'Donnell had to produce — mostly Jim. There we'd sit with the band, me with a trombone which I couldn't make a sound on.

Well, once we got invited down to the Fair at San Antone. That time we needed help so we wired old Clay McGonagill and little Joe Gardener. It wasent like it is now — a little runty calf. You roped steers. Them big boogers was given a hundred foot start and when the flag dropped, the roper's rope was tied to his saddle. All he had to do was to take down his rope, build a loop, rope the steer, throw him and tie his legs. When you finished, you held up your hands. In ten minutes, the judge would look that steer over and if he was still tied properly, you got your time. You had to tie em good and tight. The judge was old John Blocker, who knew more about a calf than her mother did. Boy, we sure needed old Clay and Joe that time.

Those Texas folks liked our band and took us in. They give us the town. Then they had a barbecue for us and while I was stacking in the grub, someone asked me to speak. I guess I sorter blinked and scratched my head and finally stammered, "Well, folks, this is a mighty fine dinner, what there is of it." That surprised them and me too. I saw I wasent going so good, so I said, trying to cover up, "Well, there is plenty of it, such as it is."

Maby that was my first after-dinner speech because that was all there was of it.

We had a lot of visitors at the Mulhall and amongst them once was a big raw-boned Irishman. He was the sheriff of Marshall, Oklahoma. The election was coming up soon, so he decided to give a big barbecue at Bart Murphy's Ranch. As he was a great friend of Col. Mulhall, we decided to go over and put on a show for him.

Well, when we got there it looked like everybody that lived in the country was there to spend the night. The barns and corrals was all filled with horses and mules, and the house was crammed full of women. All the men had to sleep out of doors, or in the barns.

When we left camp, there wasn't much money amongst any of us. Tom Mix and I had five dollars between us. We couldn't get change and, as you'd suspect, it was in Tom's pants. It was hot and Tom pulled off his pants. During the night, those pants and my hat fell down into a stall where there was a big old Missouri mule. He et both of em. The next morning I went bareheaded and Tom had nothing to wear but his chaps. Guess that old mule digested that five dollars, we dident spend it. Anyhow, we had a big day with a barbecue and danced that night till three o'clock. I dont remember, but I'll bet that big Irishman was re-elected sheriff.

CHAPTER TWO

A Rambling I Did Go

I HAD HEARD that the Argentine Republic was a great Ranch country so I sold a bunch of my cattle and took a boy named Dick Parris with me and we hit the trail for South America. We went down to New Orleans, but they said, "No boat here; you must go to New York." We come to New York. There they told us, "This year's boat for Buenos Aires has just left; but you go to England, as they appreciate the South American trade, and have regular boats running there." We landed up in a little hotel down by the battery.

We was here a week and never got further up town than the City Hall. If we had ever got as far up as 42nd Street we would of thought we was in Albany. We sailed on the *Philadelphia*. Well, I

broke all records for seasickness. I just lasted on deck long enough
to envy the Statue of Liberty for being in a permanent position and
not having to rise and fall with the tide. I dident even last to see
Sandy Hook — Oh, Doctor, I sho was sick and, say, talk about
boats doing things, say Bub this baby cut some capers. A bucking
horse, why this thing did ever thing but rare up and fall back.

I couldent have any luck eating and I layed on my broad back
that whole trip. My diet consisted of a small part of two lemons on
the whole trip. When I come on deck the last day they thought a
new passenger had got on board. Well after not having luck enough
to die we finally unloaded. When I landed in England my sole
purpose was to become a naturalized citizen until some enterprising
party built a bridge back home.

We went up to London and wanted to see everything and noticed
that Piccadilly Circus was billed bigger than anything else on all
the busses, but when we got there we soon learned it wasent much
of a show, but I'll give the Picadilly's credit — they got a great
location if they ever want to put on a show.

We happened to ooze our way into an Opera House and saw an
awful funny little guy. I dident know he amounted to much. I
saved my programme and afterwards learned it was Dan Leno, and
he was a topmounter on all the show bills and was as big a man in
England as Bill Fields is in New York.

We stood a good chance getting beheaded there once down by
the Headquarter Ranch where his Royal Liftiness hangs out. They
have planted around what they call "the Kings Own Lifeguards."
They set back on a big truckhorse in a little covered coop and wear
a high lambs wool muff on their knob for a hat and enough swords
and capes and harness to put out a No. 2 show. My pardner
thought the first one we eased into was a statue. Then we saw he
still wore all this and lived. Dick asked him to gouge this old
bobtail Clydesdale in the ribs and see if he couldent get him to
buck. Then a London Robert directed us to drive on down the
boulee.

But we was safe from that Geezer on the horse cause you would
have to give him three days notice to shed some of that wardrobe

so he could handle his artillery. Can you imagine a flock of these located in front of the White House when Teddy Roosevelt was there. But different nations have different ideas of humor.

Little did we think in those days, looking at the King's palace, that some day a Democrat would get to sleep in it. But I guess at that it wasn't near as big a surprise to us as it was to the Republicans.

I know from the tough time we had over there making ourselves understood with the American language, that we were certainly fortunate in having President Wilson represent us. He is the only one we could have sent over that spoke good enough English for them to understand.

We mooched on up around the Bank of England and Dick discovered that we were being watched. That made us feel sorter important. You see our dress was not what you would call decidedly English. I guess they figured we looked tough enough to croak His Nobs or crack the bank — but we dident even know the king and couldent even count English money — we had seen so little of it.

The old village was pretty busy just getting ready to top off King Edward so we went out to the Tower of London to get a peek at this Skypiece they were going to ornament His Muchness with and it was what you would call considerable Headgear.

Well, when I got over remembering the trip across, we took another steamer, touching at Lisbon, Portugal, and at Vigo, Spain. Saw what was left of Spain's emergency fleet corporation. It consisted of the same number that Hog Island turned out during the war — *one*. We then crossed the equator and then to Rio Janeiro. That trip dealt me another mess of misery for 23 days. Just seem like I was right on the verge of dying and then not do it, and the other guy, no matter if that old tub did a neck spin he could set right on the rail over the backend and chew old Star Navy and spit in the ocean and ever time they ring a bell to change the watch he thought it was a dinner bell and stampeded for the Chuck Box, and to rub it in ever time he would come into where I lay he would be eating.

Well I breezed around Argentina for 5 months till I was plum busted. In the meantime Dick had lit a shuck for Old Glory. I layed around a lot of those ranches. Those good native Gauchos or Pulers down there get 15 dollars a month in rag money — thats 42 cents on the dollar of regular money. Well I dident bother to do much good down there.

I was sorter itching to show these Gauchos how we could rope and tie down a steer, so one day they wanted to catch one to pick the brand on him, so I takes me down my little manila rope, and I even goes so far as to pick out the exact bit of earth where I will lay this brute down.

Well, I hadn't even got close enough to start swinging my rope when I heard something go whizzing over my head. A guy running about twenty feet behind me had thrown clear over my head and caught the steer. I couldn't speak much Spanish outside of asking for something to eat and cussing, but I took off my hat to that hombre and took my rope and tied it all up again my saddle with knot after knot, to give them the impression that I didn't have any more use for it down there.

They savvied the humor all right. I says to myself: "I'll get fat showing *these* birds how to rope! They can rope an animal further than I could hit him with a rock."

When I went to check up to leave the country I found I dident have enough dough to make the first payment on a soda cracker.

Well, I was plum busted, sho nuff. I slept in a park one night and the next morning, hungrier than a she-wolf, went down to the stockyards. There was some gauchos over in a corrall trying to rope mules that they was loading on a big steamer to take to South Africa. I tried to let em know I wanted a job, but couldent make em savvy. There was an old gaucho trying to rope a mule and missing every lick. I grabbed that rope and slipped the noose over that old hardtail's neck. The boss of the gauchos offered me 25 cents for every one I roped. Say, I stayed with em without any time for breakfast and dinner. They offered me a job on that boat chaperonning them mules and she cows to Africa. Figuring I might get a chance to eat I took it.

Well, I worked my way out of there on that cowship. Had ever old kind of animal on there — horses, hardtails — mules — cows and, away up high where the crow's nest ought to be, was wooly sheep. Now if there's anything I hate worse than being on early at Hammersteins opening shop, its *sheep* — Add to this conglomeration 90 Honyocks of all nationalities — not a one could spit a word of English — and we were to act as waiters for this 3 thousand head. A German ship crew, an Irish Vetenarian who spent most of his time working on me, but last and not least of this zoo was an Englishman that owned the whole layout — he was a regular legit. Well I couldent wrastle with a bale of hay and a dose of seasickness at the same time, and they couldent fire me so I was appointed night watchman on the deck with the cows. Well after I did get so I could eat things without a return ticket on it why we dident have anything to eat. I reckon that Englishman figured we could graze on that baled alfalfa. I finally figured out a way to land some extra nourishment, some of those cows had calves. Well I got a rope and tied em off and later on would go and milk these old wild cows. They were harder to get too than the back end of a sixth floor loft is. After bearfighting them old snaky heifers around there and getting kicked over till pretty near daylight, I would get my little pint cup ⅔ full. Well I haven't drank milk since I was a papoose so I would take it up to the cook who was tickled to get fresh milk in the middle of that ocean to use in his cooking. Well he would load me up with a bunch of truck that looked like Dowlings lunch counter at noon — everything that this Englishman couldent eat the night before. I would leave a call with him and go back on watch.

This little perfumed luxury jaunt only consumed thirty-one days. When we got to Durban, Natal, the military authorities greeted us with the glad news that no one could land in the country without he had one hundred pounds — which is five hundred bucks — as they wanted no paupers. And he looked right at me when he said it. Well, I was just as near having five hundred dollars as our friend Bryan is to the White House.

Guess it wouldn't be any harm to tell it now, as the case would

he outlawed, but I got ashore anyway, drifted down around Lady-
smith and got a job breaking horses for the British army.

You know these American and Australian horses killed and crippled more soldiers than the Boers. Why they were Western
Bronchos that had never been broke and then they expect some of
those yeomanry that had never rode anything worse than a 'Ansom
Cab, and couldent ride in a box car without the door ceiled up, to
crawl up in the middle of these old snuffy Bronks in a little Pan Cake
Saddle. Why, it was nothing less than suicide.

When a whole company would get new horses and they would
holler Company Mount, in 10 seconds you couldent see nothing but
loose horses and Tommies coming up digging the dirt out of their
eyes and wondering if the Boers was after them. Those fellows had
as much chance staying on top of some of those Renegades as a man
would have sneezing against a cyclone. But you have to slip it to
those old Tommies for nerve, they would come right up clawing
mud out of their eyes and want to take another fall out of the Bloomin
Bleeder, but sometimes nerve can be taken for darn foolishness.

There was one regiment of Highcollars from London that had
more money than war ability — that became known as De Wet
Remounts. De Wet was the Boer General. After having tea and
their nails manicured they would start out with all these fancy uniforms and good horses. De Wet would catch em and take their
horses and part of their wardrobe and guns and turn em loose and
let em go get mounted and then get em again. They were about as
handy around a war as a she bear in a drug store.

They never could get this old De Wet. The Boers traveled and
eat and slept just like the Mexicans. When they was hungry, they
just reached back and untied the leg of a sheep and eat their breakfast, lunch and Dinner while they kept moving. Every time the
English would get close to him why it would be Tea Time and they
would all have to stop to pour.

When the war stopped I joined Texas Jacks Wild West Show at
Johannesburg. I showed him my little tricks with a rope and he
put me in that night. That was my first shot at the show business
and I was sho scared bleary-eyed. I thought a fellow to do roping

in a show just had to be a curly wolf and do all sorts of curious things with a rope, or set up and fan a Bronk with one hand and roll a cigarette with the other like you've all heard of but nobody ever has seen. And dont let any four carder pick that load in you cause there is some high Weavers in some of those contests out west that good men cant set on and say Cigarette.

When I got in that ring that night I couldent slip up on the bank and throw a rope in the creek. I couldent a-doubled that rope up and hit the ground with it. I tangled myself up in that rope so I guess they thought I was doing a Houdini. Finally, when Jack saw I wasent going to be able to choke myself he come in and drove me out. Then it come time to show how real Wild Cowboys conquer untamed Mustangs Buck Jumpers.

I told Jack I better not take out a stack in this Bronk affair cause he was liable to get the top of his tent punctured with an aviating rough neck cause I havent got a single medal on my person for remaining on the hurricane deck of any outlaw Cayouse. I told him to bring out some nice little crowhopper and if the saddle horn was on solid I'd try cause I sho did need the job. Out trots a big old Walleyed Muckle Dun Australian Bronk. He certainly did look the part, but I found out afterwards they considered him a joke and he couldent throw a wet saddle blanket.

Well I screwed that old Kak down on him and got a death grip on that old apple and away we went — him just hitting a high lope around this little ring and me hanging on three quarters like a monk but I wasent going to turn loose of that horn cause I dident know what minute this old bronk might bog his head and I couldent set on a fence and not pull leather. All he did was run into a long tent pole at the edge of the ring and break it and the gas pipe that lit the whole ran up this pole. It bent the pipe and throwed the whole works in the dark. This turned on a half-breed panic. When the lights finally come on that skate was standing there asleep and me hanging on to that horn like an actor to his top money contract.

Say, you couldn't have pried me loose from that old Kak with a jimmy. They told me to get off so they could get the horse out of there but not this old rumdum. I was riding for a job, or rather hanging on for a job, and the ramrod had told me to stay on top so I was staying there until I got orders from headquarters. I wouldn't move until Jack came to tell me to get off.

It must of been a big hit cause everybody laughed.

But there was another American boy there that was some Bronk-eating poor boy. Anytime that old Ranahan took a setting on one of those buzzard heads, that skate was in for a fine cleaning because this boy was some tamer of ferocious animals. He could pluck the wild hairs out of their tails every jump. He rode em with paws in the air, feet free and a scratchin. Anytime this old wooly screwed his centerfire down on some sunfisher and the old wampus hoss started burning his sides, the old cattler would just take another wrap on his hackings strap and rare back and do the hooch on him. Us other punks dident have any license to even watch him ride.

Well, I throwed in with the layout and stuck for almost a year and we showed everywhere down there. I took a shot at everything. I did a clown in the leaps and did a coon-song and blackface in the concert. Of course I thought to be a regular Wild Wester I had to have a name so I christened myself "The Cherokee Kid" and had letterheads made.

Texas Jack was one of the smartest showmen I ever met. It was him who gave me the idea for my original stage act with my pony. I learned a lot about the show business from him. He could do a bum act with a rope that an ordinary man couldent get away with, and make the audience think it was great, so I used to study him by the hour and from him I learned the great secret of the show business — learned when to get off. It's the fellow that knows when to quit that the audience wants more of.

Then I began to feel a longing for seasickness, so I started in alphabetically and found Australia. After a year's steady toil — to give you an idea of my salary — I had enough to go to Australia second class; and the fare was not so much at that, as the Government was not running the line at that time.

By this time I was a full-fledged circus performer and wanted to join a big circus. Jack give me a letter to Wirth Bros.

Well I payed for the privilege of spending another 20 days of agony on another ocean. This time it was the Indian Ocean, and it sho was on the war path when I breezed over it. Well all that peeved me was that I had to go "American" instead of "European." That old company certainly made some coin off of me. I didn't think it was possible to be so sick and still live. That little passover was 20 days bounding agony.

It was my extreme good fortune to be on a boat that did not touch Australia but went right on to New Zealand 5 days further, and there re-loaded you on another old seagoing hack and I had the pleasure of a small matter of 5 days to be back to where I had almost been 10 days previous — a very wonderful transportation arrangement, especially for a Jasper that gives up going to Hoboken on a ferryboat.

Well again fate was cruel to me and I survived the trip and joined the Wirth Bros circus in Sidney, Australia. I did my roping act and a trick riding act. The circus was like a vaudeville show, they only had one act at a time, one show a day, no Sundays. It was a nice little frameup. We toured thru Australia and I was overstuffed with pleasure when I heard they were going to sail for New Zealand. Well the only consolation I had was, they said even the Captain got sick.

Say that little New Zealand is just what I would call a regular country. The best system of government in the world, the greatest scenery and natural resources of the country are great. I again christened myself, "The Cherokee Kid," a name that I used until I got back to America and realized what a fine joke it was. Then I immediately applied the tinware to it.

At a racing meet in Australia, I hooked my toes around the saddle horn and with my pony hitting the breeze, leaned back over his rump and picked up three handkerchiefs on the ground. The governor-general sent a man over to ask me to do it again.

"Tell him I'll do it for $150," I said.

The man squalled like a wildcat.

"You tell the governor-general if he'll do it cheaper, I'll loan him my horse and handkerchief," I said.

Well, he didn't tell that to his nibs, but that crowd made up a pot of $150 and I did it again.

A man come to try to get me to go in a show that made all the coast towns in India, Straight Settlement, China and Japan. Said he would pay me good straight salary all the time — had me all excited till he said it was easy as we only showed about a third of the time and we were on the boat traveling most all the time. Well, I dont know till plum yet what kept me from hitting him right then. Those old "coolies" over there aint never going to see me unless Mr. McAdoo stretches out one of his tunnels further than he ever has yet, believe me. And I would sorter like to get amongst them once too cause they say they raise em over there that can throw a rope up in the air and climb up it. That woulden't be a bad trick to get — would do to open with.

Funny some manager dont snake one of those guys out of there and bring him over here if they do all we hear they do.

Well, needless to say, I joined no Salt Water circus.

The show had finished New Zealand, was going back to Australia. Well I couldent see any luck in having another boat ride going further away from home again, so I left them — like so many have left the Barnum show — *Flat* and I headed for America.

Well now comes the crowning trick of all this seasick stuff — and I hope to chew up my best rope if it aint just as recorded. Made a day trip by train and had to take a boat for just one nights run to get to Auckland where I was to get the boat coming to Frisco. Well our train pulled up side of this little skiff that night and we all stacked out of there into the boat which was tied to the dock. Well I figured the way to do is to go right to bed. There was no stateroom thing — the men had one big room full of bunks — I dident take time to take off my clothes, I hit the alfalfa but I prepared myself — I got one of those cute little tin lunch baskets that you hang on the side of your bunk. Well I layed there and rolled around and commenced to feel uneasy in certain parts and finally I couldent wait longer and Man I was sick. Well this had been going on for some distance when some old Wooly said to another one — "I wonder whats the matter, aint this boat going to go?"

Well that shows you just what a big mess of imagination will do for you. But then too there's a curious sort of a smell on all boats that if I get a whiff of it in the middle of the Mohave Desert I sho would take ill. If they would make more of those men use their time shooting coal into that scoundrel and make it get yonder faster instead of having whole herds of em painting and varnishing all the time, wouldent be so many people seasick.

Well I got back to Frisco after being gone most three years during which time I had made complete circuit of the world in such way that I had traveled over 50 thousand miles. I had started out 1st class (yes, and put on the old double-barrel behavior for dinner too). You ought to have got me floating down the main aisle of this dining saloon with this Hart, Schaffner, Marks hand-me-down wedding suit on. I was late getting in cause I couldent get that high collar fastened and I got my white tie dirty putting it on and I had to wear gallowses and I do hate em. I must of been a hit when I come in cause everybody laughed. Then I traveled 2nd class, then 3rd class, then when I was companion to those she cows was what might be called no class at all. It took me three years to get enough money to get back home on and say, George Cohans trade mark [Old Glory] sho looked good when I sighted it outside Golden Gate.

I was so broke some of the boys told my dad, "Well, Willie got back from his trip around the world and he's wearing overalls for drawers."

CHAPTER THREE

There Is Nothing Like the
Show Business

I LANDED back here just before the World's Fair in St. Louis and worked there with Col. Mulhall that year. I lived with the family at Mulhall (town named for the Colonel). The Col had always kinder seemed to like me, and I thought a lot of the family.

Lucille was grown by now but she never dressed like the Cowgirl you know today, no loud colors, no short leather skirts, and great big hats, no sir, her skirt was divided, but long, away down over her patent-leather boot tops, a whip-cord grey, or grey broadcloth, small stiff brim hat, and always white silk shirt waist. They were received by the best people in every place. The Girls could have had a Society career if they had preferred.

We were in St. Louis during the whole summer of the fair, with

27

the "Cummings and Mulhall Wild West Show on the Pike."

Well I had the stage fever and another boy and I got a job for a week at the old Standard in St. Louis with a stock burlesque. I showed the act to old Col. Hopkins and he liked it and wrote to Murdock in Chicago and he finally gave me a week at the Chicago Opera House for 30 dollars. Well I went to Chicago and found I was not to be there cause I had failed to send Billing and Photos. Well I figured that was about the limit of honriness when I dident have any pictures and dident know what billing was. He dident need much billing for 30 dollars.

Well I was laying around there and starting in to see a show at Cleveland Theatre on Wabash Avenue and as I was buying my ticket he was talking over the phone and wanting an act right now, and I told him I had an act, and he said how long before you could get to doing it. I said just as long as it will take me to run to the hotel a few blocks away. Well in 5 minutes I was opening up his troop. I dident have time to get scared. Well this was Thursday and I lasted the week out. One show during the act, a speckled pup from a dog act run across the stage and I was lucky enough to hang a loop on him as he breezed by and say that was a riot. Well that gave me the tip so instead of trying to keep on with this single roping act I decided people wanted to see you catch something, so I went back home and got me out a plot of ground about as big as a stage and started to work on the horse act.

Along back late in 1904, or about that time, the 101 Ranch put on a Wild West show in Kansas City Convention Hall for a week following the Horse Show. The outfit comprised such representative gentlemen as Henry Starr, Lon Seeley, Shorty Purviance, Rocky Mountain Hank, Dick Paris and me.

Naturally we attracted some attention on the street and elsewhere. In the lobby of the Baltimore a gentleman introduced to Dick a lady of inquisitive mind. After a little approach talk, she said:

"Mr. Paris, possibly I am too inquisitive in asking you something I should not, but really Mr. Paris I am curious. I understand you are part Indian. Mr. Paris, how much Indian are you?"

Dickie, with his well known smile replied: "Eighty acres worth, ma'am, — just figure it out."

At the Dantzinger Bottling Works, — the home of Harvest King whiskey, a half dozen of the boys were being shown through the works by Dan Dantzinger. As the bunch stood before the bottling machine Dan turned to a porter and said: "Bring each of the gentlemen a bottle of Harvest King."

Dickie stepped forward and pointing to the machine squirting whiskey into quart bottles, said: "Mister, you can save one bottle, hook me onto that machine. I hold just a quart."

Dick used to relate a story of a big six foot half-blood Cherokee who was serving on the City Council in Bartlesville. One night the Councilman, all stimulated up, left the Elks Club and at two A.M. proceeded up the main street of Bartlesville. About every twenty steps he would halt, lift his face to the moon and let off a long-drawn wolf howl. Then announce in a loud voice:

"I am a wolf — look out. Give me room to howl."

A policeman drawn by the whooping and howling recognized the howler as one on whom he depended for a job; nevertheless he felt he must stop the noise. The policeman detoured a block, placed himself in a dark stair-way, and as the howler passed, he paused and announced himself again. The policeman sprang out, caught him around the upper arms and pinioned him. Shaking him to show he had him fast, he said:

"So you are a wolf — are you?"

The Councilman looked over his shoulder, saw the Law, relaxed in his frame and a broad sociable smile replaced his wolf expression, then in a mild explanatory manner he said:

"Yes, I am a wolf — but hell I'm just a pet wolf, can't you see my chain a draggin?"

Then, the following year, about 1905, Colonel Zach Mulhall brought a bunch of us boys to New York from the West to give an exhibition in Madison Square Garden.

The Col. was a natural showman, loved the spectacular but never had any fakes. Every boy was a real one. His shows were of the very best. Neatness was one of his hobbys. His life was miserable trying to keep me presentable. "Look at the Injun (he always called me Injun), he wont wear a silk shirt and I have bought him a dozen!" He was generous to a fault. When Col Mulhall had money, we were nigger rich. When he dident, well you wouldent hardly know it. He never hollered; he never squealed; he took the misfortune with a smile.

Tom Mix was with us. That was his first start on his Wild West Career. We dident get much money; in fact our salary was supposed to be $20 a week. Tom was in the Theatre the other night and I told him that was the only time we were ever paid just about what we were worth. That was one time we were not overpaid Actors, because we dident even get that twenty.

But he was a great old fellow, Mulhall, a typical old-time west erner. We would touch him so much at odd times we never had anything coming. He was a very liberal fellow and in those days of Bar Rooms would always order drinks for everybody in the place and hand the Bar Tender a Bill of perhaps $20 to pay for what was $5 or 6 dollars check and my great habit was to edge in next to him when the man put the change back in front of him, and I would grab it and duck with it. Well he thought that was a great joke, and so did I. In fact I think it was one of the best jokes I ever pulled. He would laugh and that would make a good fellow out of him with the crowd, and incidentally keep from making a Tramp out of me. I was perfectly willing that they could have the drinks as long as I got the change.

I was doing the roping in the show. We had some wild steers, and one jumped over the railing and ran up the stairs among the audience. The other boys followed him up, but I saw he was going around and come out on the other side. So I headed him off and roped him, and we led him down, and no one was hurt.

Well, that didn't do me any harm from a newspaper standpoint, so I figured out I could stay here when the others went back, and with my pony do the roping act on a stage. I was the first one ever to rope a horse on the stage. Managers wouldn't believe it was possible, and I hung around several weeks trying to get on, till finally one day I heard one of the booking men ring up Keith's Union Square and say (he didn't know I heard him), "Put this nut and his pony on at one of your supper shows and just get rid of him." Keith's was the big New York vaudeville theatre in those days.

Buck McKee was the cowboy that used to work with me in a vaudeville set and rode the horse, or little cowpony rather, Teddy. He trained the pony for the stage. He wasent any trick pony, he just worked on a smooth board stage, with felt-bottom boots buckled on his feet like goloshes, and run for my fancy roping catches. But Buck trained him to do on a slick stage just about what a good turning cowpony can do on the ground.

Supper show meant that all the big acts did two shows a day, and the littler ones an extra one at supper time between about six and eight, when nobody that had a home or somewhere to eat would be in a theatre. So we came on and the sign, "Extra Act." They knew we were doing a trial show, and I think they took pity on that poor pony and figured that if we didn't make good, both of us would have to ride him back to Oklahoma. So to the surprise of everybody and the disgust of the manager, we were pretty good, and I didn't know enough to act and the people sorter liked it.

But it was at the Theatre where they sent me the second week where I made my best hit and stayed at it all Summer. That was at the greatest Vaudeville theatre of that and all time. That was Hammerstein's. I stayed on the roof one whole summer. The first night, I couldent get the old pony to go in the elevator. He thought thats acting too high for me.

We played on the roof at nights and down stairs at Matinee. We have never produced another showman like Willie Hammerstein, and the old man himself was living in those days and with what that theatre made he was able to indulge in presenting Opera.

I only had a roping act then. The idea of using any talk hadn't occurred to me. During the first week I had a trick where I threw two ropes at once and caught the horse and rider separately. Some actor told me I ought to announce it, as the audience didn't know what I was going to do. I dident think up my speech beforehand. I just stopped the orchestra and said:

"Ladies and gentlemen, I want to call your sho nuff attention to this next little stunt I am going to pull on you, as I am going to throw about two o' these ropes at once, catching the horse with one and the rider with the other. I don't have any idea I'll get it, but here goes." Well, they laughed and believe me, I was mad when I come off. I thought I hadn't said anything for them to laugh at, and I told the manager I was through. It was quite a while before I would open my trap again on the stage; but the other actors and the manager kept telling me to do it the same way again. And that's how I got to putting talk into my act. The first gag I ever pulled was when I got my rope all tangled up and says, "A rope ain't bad to get tangled up in if it ain't around your neck."

As it panned out, it was the luckiest thing I ever did; but I can't claim much credit for grabbing that chance. It took all of my friends to drive me to it.

The next laugh that come was one night when I was missing a lot and told the audience I was a bit handicapped up there, because the manager wouldn't allow a fellow to cuss when he misses.

One instance I remember. Ernest Hogan, famous Negro comedian, was playing there and my first night I went fine and took a bow and started to my room. Hogan grabbed me and pushed me out in front of the curtain, and as I came off he apologized and said, "Boy, don't overlook any of them, they aint bows," he says, "thems curtain calls and there is damn few of them up here."

One Summer Hammerstein had an old Lady that he dug up. They called her Sober Sue. She was supposed to never laugh. He sat her in the Box every night and the Vaudeville act among us who made her laugh was supposed to get a raise in salary.

We tried all summer and never got a wrinkle out of her.

On the last night after the roof closed she confided to us that she was Deaf, and was short sighted, and had never seen or heard any of us all summer. She laughed when she told us this, but that was too late to do us any good. She was one afflicted person after this that I could never seem to sympathise with.

The old act went pretty well and Mr. Hammerstein was paying me $125 a week. I had to board my horse, pay booking agent and a salary to my cowboy and take care of myself. I waited week after week mustering up courage enough to ask Willie Hammerstein for a raise, and then the raise I asked for was $10.00.

I made two trips to Europe, the first in the Spring of 1906, where I played the Winter Garden in Berlin. I used to go riding in the Tier Garten on my pony every afternoon, as there was no matinee, and I always met a lot of officers. One day I met a guy riding ahead of the others. He nodded, and turned and looked at my Western outfit, but I never paid him any attention. A little farther on, some man stopped me and said, "You didn't salute him." I said, "Salute who?" "Why, the Kaiser; don't you know that was him you just met on the bridle path?" I said, "I'm sorry; but if he's so great why don't he have his own path and stay off mine?" I met him lots of days after that, and he always seemed pretty good and would nod at me. I guess he was kinder sorry for me 'cause I wasn't a German. I never did salute him. I just nodded back. I didn't know anything about saluting. I might have used the wrong hand or something.

In the theatres in Germany there's a fireman stands right in the wings on duty, and you have to climb over him to get on or off the stage. So one night I thought it would be a big laugh if I roped him and pulled him on the stage. So I did. Say, there was 'most a panic! I had interfered with his dignified position. They liked to have called out the whole army. They were going to invade me like they did Belgium. The manager had to come out and tell 'em that my rope slipped. In America I have done that stunt, and it's a yell. But in Germany they have cultivated everything they got but their humor.

I played in England two years. I did the old act with the horse for almost six years; then I tried the act without the horse, just doing tricks, and trying all the time to develop the comedy end of the act. I wasn't any headliner, but they played me steady all the time, and I kept practicing new tricks, as I love roping better than anything else in the world. I work out lots of tricks that I never do on the stage, but I have them for my personal satisfaction. And lots of days yet I go to the theatre and rope for six or eight hours, just because I like to.

In my early vaudeville days I used to get out and see a lot of ball games, or see part of em. (Depending when I was on the bill.) Then the players were great theatre goers. They always come to the leading vaudeville theatre, generally in bunches, and I would know they were there and generally kid about them from the stage, and lots of times I would be stopping at the same hotel. They were a great bunch.

Then I have had on a uniform and "Shagged" flys at practice in the mornings with the home team. I knew all the old players. That was back in 1905–6–7–8. From then on I got out of my country ways, and was too lazy to get up and practice in the mornings. I was a "Regular" actor by then.

One summer they turned all the ball parks into open-air summer vaudeville. They would put in a movable stage about where home plate is, and they put in great lights, and the show would be held right there. Well I was booked on the whole circuit, Pittsburg, and the Red Sox Park in Boston, and Philadelphia, and as we only showed at night we had nothing to do all day but be around with the ball players, then get my pony out at night, and Buck McKee who rode him for me, and run him by and I would rope him. And it was great to get to do it on the ground, and not on a stage, we had so much more room outdoors. I liked that work but the thing dident go so good, and of course all of us acts were just transferred back into the theatres instead, but I met and become acquainted with many a fine fellow.

Once, when I was playing on the Orpheum Circut, I popped through Kansas City jumping to Seattle, Washington, to do my little act. Well, in those days every man that traveled any farther than from the House to the Barn thought he had to have an Alligator Bag, with big warts on the side of it, that would rub Bunions on the side of your Legs if you carried it over a block. That and a Diamond Ring, were the first things you were supposed to buy, especially if you were a traveling man or in the Theatrical Business.

So I had just worked long enough to have both. One Toothbrush, a Couple of shirts, and five Ropes, were nestling in this Crocodile-bound inclosure, with not only big warts but Horns on the side of it. I had to buy a ticket, and in those days it took an Agent longer to make out a Ticket to Seattle, than it did to go there. It sold by footage, One Foot to the Mile. The Excess Baggage on your Ticket cost you more than your Fare. He handed it to you neatly folded in Yard lengths. You only had to sign it for each Town you went through.

Well the Afternoon I spent buying my Ticket, I forgot to keep one foot solidly implanted on my deceased Crocodile. Some lover of Animals kindly annexed my prosperous Trade Mark, and when I turned around the one year's savings I had invested in Hides was just passing over the Kaw River. I went to relate my unhappy ending to a Policeman, and found a line longer than a Congressional Investigation Committee witnesses, all trying to find out where their Grips had gone to. I didn't even get a chance to tell him about mine. And if I had not been for that long Ticket to the Coast and back, I would not have had a clean thing to put on every morning till I got there.

And, by the way, coming back I played Butte, and lost the Diamond Ring. So it took two Thieves to at least TRY and give me the appearance of a Gentleman. Now when I see a Man wearing either a Diamond Ring, or an Alligator Valise, I offer up thanks to the two men who robbed me.

On November 25, 1908, I was married to Betty Blake of Rogers, Arkansas. When I roped her that was the star performance of my life. For a wedding present, I took her to hear Caruso sing.

Years later, as toastmaster at a dinner honoring the famous tenor, Will described this experience:

I never met this bird Caruso but I hear he is a regular fellow and cant help it because he is a tenor singer.

I have seen Caruso twice, once when I took my wife to hear him as a wedding present and once on a bet.

My wife wanted to see two things in NY, one was Caruso and the other was Grants Tomb.

Well I hustled around and got two seats from a Spec. I noticed him laughing, I thought he was laughing at me, I dident know he was laughing at the seats.

Well the wife said I had to put on my wedding suit, that spoiled it even if it had been a good show. I had to crawl into that Montgomery Ward. WE were living just across the street from the Met, at the Albany Hotel, but she said everyone went in a cab to the opera so we got a cab and crossed the street. My wife was right about the cab, we should of kept it till we found our seats. I dident know a seat could be so far away and still be in the same theatre, we could just see the drummer, my wife was worried about how we could tell Caruso and I told her he would be the fellow that sing, my lord thats all all of them did. My wife wanted to know who was in the boxes, I dident know but they all looked about as miserable as we did.

WELL we stuck it out till intermission and then I went up to Hammersteins to see the three Keatons and a good show.

Well we stayed awake till the early editions of the morning papers come out to see who besides ourselves were there. Well we found out Caruso was the fellow who had played the part of a clown but I could not think of a funny thing that he did, I hate to say it but I enjoyed Grants Tomb more cause I stayed outside while my wife went in.

I dont think that show Caruso was in was much of a hit as I passed there next day and they had a different show billed.

CHAPTER FOUR

I Froliced and I Follied

I<small>N</small> 1915 I went up on Mr. Ziegfeld's roof in the Midnight Frolic show. I got two-fifty a week, and got my first car, an Overland, and drove it out on Long Island every night about two thirty. It got to knocking so much that one night the cop arrested me. "Hey, you can go down the road at night, Rogers, but you got to leave that thing. You're like an alarm clock at three A.M."

Ever know how the Midnight Shows started? Well I can tell you for I was in the first one.

The Midnight Frolic was the start of all this Midnight and late style of entertainment. That has since degenerated into a drunken orgy of off-colored songs, and close-formation dancing. It was the first midnight show. It started right on the stroke of twelve, it could have 50 or 75 people in the cast, bigger than all the modern day shows given at regular hours. It had the most beautiful girls of any show Ziegfeld ever put on, for the beautiful ones wouldent work at a matinee for they never got up that early.

We used to have a time getting em up for the midnight show. I dont mean I did, I dident have to go round waking any of em up but somebody did.

The same bunch of folks, that is about 50 per cent of the main ones, were up there every night.

It was for folks with lots of money. And plenty of insomnia. He would have great big musical numbers, all written especially for the show, maby 40 girls in em, led by some well known local Broadway star at that time.

We would put on a new show about every four months. Costumes and all. There has never been anything to equal it since then.

My act at that time consisted generally of the same jokes each night, all pertaining to the place or to the other acts in the show. Then Mr. Ford started his memorable peace trip. Well, I doped out a lot of gags on it, and the first one I used turned out to be about the best one I ever had.

"If Mr. Ford had taken this bunch of girls, in this show, and let 'em wear the same costumes they wear here, and marched them down between the trenches, believe me, the boys would have been out before Christmas!"

After that line of stuff died out, I wished somebody else would start something, but I thought at that time there would never be anything as funny as that. One day my wife said:

"Why don't you talk about what you read? Goodness knows! you're always reading the papers!"

So I started to reading about Congress; and, believe me, I found they are funnier three hundred and sixty-five days a year than anything I ever heard of.

Now here's the point: if I had been in a regular show where they have a different audience every night, I wouldn't have had to change my stuff; but on the roof we got a lot of repeaters each night, and a man won't laugh at the same joke more than once. So that was what made me dig. I would read the papers for hours, trying to dope out a funny angle to the day's news, and I found that they would laugh easiest at the stuff that had just happened that day. A joke don't have to be near as funny if it's up to date.

So that's how I learned that my own stuff, serving only strictly fresh-laid jokes, as you might say, goes better than anything else.

I use only one set method in my little gags, and that is to try and keep to the truth. Of course you can exaggerate it, but what you say must be based on truth. And I have never found it necessary to use the words "hell" or "damn" to get a laugh, either.

Personally, I don't like the jokes that get the biggest laughs, as they are generally as broad as a house and require no thought at all. I like one where, if you are with a friend, and hear it, it makes you think, and you nudge your friend and say; "He's right about that." I would rather have you do that than to have you laugh — and then forget the next minute what it was you laughed at.

I like all kinds of audiences excepting the convention kind, the lodge brand, the sort of crowd that wants itself praised. That kind gives me a pain. There's always some fellow sends you a note framing your gag for you, asking you to mention this and that and not to forget a certain name. It's sure to be the name of the fellow that writes the note — some modest business guy that wants to get his name incorporated in the libretto of the Follies. It is usually a great pleasure to pan him — if only you can remember his unknown name, which mostly you can't.

We played for President Wilson and I used one joke which he repeated in his Boston speech on his return from France. He said:

"As one of our American humorists says [up to that time I had only been an ordinary rope thrower], Germany couldn't understand how we could get men over there and get them trained so quick. They didn't know that in our manual there's nothing about retreating! And when you only have to teach an army to go one way, you can do it in half the time."

Of course you know how much truth there was in that. See Pershing's reports.

President Wilson was my best audience. I have played to him five times, and always used lots of things about him. I want to speak and tell of him as I knew him for he was my friend. We of the stage knew that our audiences are our best friends, and he was the greatest Audience of any Public Man we ever had. I want to tell of him as I knew him across the footlights. A great many Actors and Professional people have appeared before him, on various occasions in wonderful high-class endeavors. But I don't think that any person met him across the footlights in exactly the personal way that I did.

Every other Performer or Actor did before him exactly what they had done before other audiences on the night previous, but I gave a great deal of time and thought to an Act for him, most of which would never be used again and had never been used before.

It just seemed by an odd chance for me every time I played before President Wilson that on that particular day there had been something of great importance that he had just been dealing with. For you must remember that each day was a day of great stress with him. He had no easy days. So when I could go into a Theatre and get laughs out of our President by poking fun at some turn in our National affairs, I don't mind telling you it was the happiest moments of my entire career on the stage.

The first time I shall never forget, for it was the most impressive and for me the most nervous one of them all. The Friars Club of New York one of the biggest Theatrical Social Clubs in New York had decided to make a whirlwind Tour of the Principal Cities of the East all in one week. We played a different City every night. We made a one-night stand out of Chicago and New York. We were billed for Baltimore but not for Washington. President Wilson came over from Washington to see the performance. It was the first time in Theatrical History that the President of the United States came over to Baltimore just to see a Comedy.

It was just at the time we were having our little Set Too, with Mexico, and when we were at the height of our Note Exchanging career with Germany and Austria. The house was packed with the Elite of Baltimore.

The Show was going great. It was a collection of clever 'Skits, written mostly by our stage's greatest Man, George M. Cohan, and even down to the minor bits was played by Stars with big Reputations. I was the least-known member of the entire aggregation, doing my little specialty with a Rope and telling Jokes on National Affairs, just a very ordinary little Vaudeville act by chance sandwiched in among this great array.

I was on late, and as the show went along I would walk out of the Stage door and out on the Street and try to kill the time and nervousness until it was time to dress and go on. I had never told Jokes even to a President, much less about one, especially to his face. Well, I am not kidding you when I tell you that I was scared to death. I am always nervous. I never saw an Audience that I ever faced with any confidence. For no man can ever tell how a given Audience will ever take anything.

But here I was, nothing but a very ordinary Oklahoma Cowpuncher who had learned to spin a Rope a little and who had learned to read the Daily Papers a little, going out before the Aristocracy of Baltimore, and the President of the United States, and kid about some of the Policies with which he was shaping the Destinies of Nations.

How was I to know what the audience would rise up in mass and resent it? I had never heard, and I don't think any one else had ever heard of a President being joked personally in a Public Theatre about the Policies of his administration.

The nearer the time came the worse scared I got, George Cohan, and Willie Collier, and others, knowing how I felt, would pat me on the back and tell me, "Why he is just a Human Being; go on out and do your stuff." Well if somebody had come through the dressing room and hollered "Train for Claremore Oklahoma leaving at once," I would have been on it. This may sound strange but any who have had the experience know, that a Presidential appearance in a Theatre, especially outside Washington, D.C., is a very Rare and unique feeling even to the Audience. They are keyed up almost as much as the Actors.

At the time of his entrance into the House, everybody stood up, and there were Plain Clothes men all over the place, back stage and behind his Box. How was I to know but what one of them might not take a shot at me if I said anything about him personally?

Finally a Warden knocked at my dressing-room door and said: "You die in 5 more minutes for kidding your Country." They just literally shoved me out on the Stage.

Now, by a stroke of what I call good fortune (for I will keep them always), I have a copy of the entire Acts that I did for President Wilson on the Five times I worked for him. My first remark in Baltimore was, "I am kinder nervous here tonight." Now that is not an especially bright remark, and I don't hope to go down in History on the strength of it, but it was so apparent to the audience that I was speaking the truth that they laughed heartily at it. After all, we all love honesty.

Then I said, "I shouldn't be nervous, for this is really my second Presidential appearance. The first time was when Bryan spoke in our town once, and I was to follow his speech and do my little Roping Act." Well, I heard them laughing, so I took a sly glance at the President's Box and sure enough he was laughing just as big as any one. So I went on, "As I say, I was to follow him, but he spoke so long that it was so dark when he finished, they couldn't see my Roping." That went over great, so I said, "I wonder what ever became of him." That was all right, it got over, but still I had made no direct reference to the President.

Now Pershing was in Mexico at the time, and there was a lot in the Papers for and against the invasion. I said "I see where they have captured Villa. Yes, they got him in the morning Editions and the Afternoon ones let him get away." Now everybody in the house before they would laugh looked at the President, to see how he was going to take it. Well, he started laughing and they all followed suit.

"Villa raided Columbus New Mexico. We had a man on guard that night at the Post. But to show you how crooked this Villa is, he sneaked up on the opposite side." "We chased him over the line 5 miles, but run into a lot of Government Red Tape and had to come back." "There is some talk of getting a Machine Gun if we

can borrow one. The one we have now they are using to train our
Army with in Plattsburg. If we go to war we will just about have
to go to the trouble of getting another Gun."

Now, mind you, he was being criticized on all sides for lack of
preparedness, yet he sat there and led that entire audience in laughing at the ones on himself.

At that time there was talk of forming an Army of 2 hundred
thousand men, so I said, "we are going to have an Army of 2 hundred thousand men. Mr. Ford makes 3 hundred thousand Cars
every year. I think, Mr. President, we ought to at least have a Man
to every Car." "See where they got Villa hemmed in between
the Atlantic and Pacific. Now all we got to do is to stop up both
ends." "Pershing located him at a town called Los Quas Ka
Jasbo. Now all we have to do is to locate Los Quas Ka Jasbo." "I
see by a headline that Villa escapes Net and Flees. We will never
catch him then. Any Mexican that can escape Fleas is beyond
catching." "But we are doing better toward preparedness now,
as one of my Senators from Oklahoma has sent home a double portion of Garden Seed."

After various other ones on Mexico I started in on European
affairs which at that time was long before we entered the war. "We
are facing another Crisis tonight, but our President here has had so
many of them lately that he can just lay right down and sleep beside
one of those things."

Then I first pulled the one which I am proud to say he afterwards repeated to various friends as the best one told on him during
the war. I said, "President Wilson is getting along fine now to
what he was a few months ago. Do you realize, People, that at one
time in our negotiations with Germany that he was 5 Notes behind?"

How he did laugh at that! Well, due to him being a good fellow
and setting a real example, I had the proudest and most successful
night I ever had on the stage. I had lots of Gags on other subjects
but the ones on him were the heartiest laughs with him, and so it was
on all the other occasions I played for him. He come back Stage at
intermission and chatted and shook hands with all.

For a long time after the war we always had so many returned
men at the shows that I used something about them like:

"I see where they are going to muster all you boys out as soon as they investigate the morale of your homes."

"The reason they leave some of our boys over there so long is so they can get the mail that was sent to them during the war."

"If they had divided up all the money they spent on parades for you boys, you wouldent have to be looking for a job."

"If they really wanted to honor the boys, why dident they let them sit on the stands and have the people march by?"

Lots of good subjects would be in the papers for days [1] and I couldnt think of a thing on them. Some of the best things came to me when I was out on the stage. I figured out the few subjects that I would touch on and always had a few gags on each one, but the thing I went out to say might fall flat, and some other gag I just happened to put in out there went great. For instance here is an example! "Mr. Edison is perfecting a submarine destroyer. Well they say he only sleeps three or four hours out of the twenty-four. That gives him plenty of time to invent . . ." That was only a little laugh, but I used it to show the audience that I had read about the invention which had only been announced that day. It happened that at this time New York cafés were closed at one o'clock so I casually added to the remark my sudden thought: "Suppose Mr. Edison lived in New York and Mayor Mitchell made him go to bed at one o'clock; where would our invention come from?" And that was the big laugh.

This illustrates my work. I had to have my idea — all extemporaneous speakers do — but my laugh came quickly and apparently out of nowhere.

Another thing I read, was that submarines could not operate in the Warm Gulf Stream — so I said: "If we can only heat the ocean we will have them licked." That didn't get much of a laugh and I was kinda stuck — but happened to add, "Of course, that is only a rough idea. I haven't worked it out yet." This last went big and covered up the other.

I was talking of the income tax and how hard it hit our girls in

---

[1] Much of the following was taken from an interview reported by George Martin, "Wit of Will Rogers," *American Magazine,* November, 1919.

the show, and just happened to mention, "A lot of them have figured out it would be cheaper to lay off."

I would start on a subject and if it was no good then I would switch quick and lots of times when I come off the stage I would have done an entirely different act from what I intended when I went on. Sometimes an audience is not so good and my stuff that night might not have been very good, so it is then you would see the old ropes commence to do something. It got their mind off the bum stuff I was telling and as I often said to the folks in the show, "I reach away back in my hip pocket and dig up a sure-fire gag, as I always try to save some of my best gags — just like a prohibition State man will his last drink."

In the four years I was with Mr. Ziegfeld in his Follies and Midnight Frolic where we played to a great many repeaters, I never did the same act any two nights. I always changed parts of it and in the Frolics a great many times I did an entirely new act.

Another thing, I think I did the shortest act of any monologue man and that recommended it. On the Amsterdam Roof I never did over six minutes and in the Follies nine or ten, generally eight.

Picking out and talking about distinguished people in the audience I used quite a little, but never unless I knew them personally and knew that they would take a joke as it was meant. The late Diamond Jim Brady I always spoke of, as I knew him and he always seemed to take an interest in my act. Once at a big banquet Mr. Brady recited a little poem which he had written himself. I learned the piece and shortly afterwards one night when he was in the audience I did his poem. This made a great hit with Mr. Brady. My best one on him was: "I always get to go to all the first nights, yes I do. I go with Mr. Brady. He sits in the first row and I stand at the back and if anybody cops a diamond I am supposed to rope 'em before they get away with it."

On opening night of a New Midnight Frolic Lieut. Vernon Castle had just returned from France and was then with Mrs. Castle. Vernon and I had played polo together and he was a regular fellow. I walked over to them, shook hands and said: "Here is one old Tango Bird that has made good," and then I told about how Fred

Stone and I got Vernon on a bucking horse once and that was where he got his idea of aviating. I said: "Vernon, we worried about you when you were out there at the front, but not half as much as we worried about Irene in the pictures. Boy you don't know what war is, you should see what your wife has been giving them in 'Patria'!"

A few months later when Vernon was killed at Fort Worth, Texas, in a plane crash, Will said in the Follies:

Now I will tell you I knew he was game before he enlisted. He and Fred Stone had a polo team, and had been playing quite a while — at least, they knew the rules. Well, the first day I played I didn't know a polo ball from Bollo Pasha. I could ride, but I couldn't hit the ball with a rake. I was in everybody's way, missing the ball farther each lick.

Finally I came a-tearing across at right angles at Castle, thinking I would scare this dancer off the ball. It was a foul, as I was crossing him. But say, that Englishman didn't scare worth a darn, he kept a-coming at me too. Well we hit, and there were dancers, horses and rope throwers scattered all over Long Island. What did he say when he got up?

"That's all right. I did that, too when I was learning."

We all had many a tilt with him and he never flinched.

At a big benefit one night on the Manhattan Opera House stage, Castle, Sloane, Tinney, Carillo, and I put on a wild west act called "The Horse Thief." Castle was the only one game enough to volunteer to play the thief. In the act, as he was running away on the horse I was to rope him from another horse, have the rope tied to my saddle, drag him off at a dead run, and then drag him around the stage.

Well, I put it on real and he went through with it, and I'll tell the world he was game.

He was the most skillful and fearless driver of a car I ever saw.

Now I just want to say to you people who didn't know him, he was a regular guy, and I was mighty hurt to hear of his death, because he was doing his bit just as much as if he had been killed trying to drop a bomb on that kaiser's bean.

Few men gave up more to enlist and it should teach us all a lesson that no matter how frail or small or physically unfit, and no matter what kind of work he has been doing, if the old heart is in the right place he is there.

And still a lot of folks thought it was pretty soft for a cowboy to get paid for stuff like that. But they didn't figure that lots of comedians go through a whole year with one act. But because I had set myself this job of trying to give em something new they wouldn't stand for old stuff from me, as they would from lots of others, because I was expected to keep up with the times. And I tell you it was sure hard digging.

With the Follies on the road I carried two horses and a man on the road, though I never used them in my act. I went to the riding academies in the various cities and practiced fancy catches from horseback. If I ever get a vacation I want to go to some big ranch and rope all the time.

In towns on the road I always used lots of local things. New York is too big for local things, as half of your audience comes from out of town. The smaller the city the better the local gags go. In Detroit I used stuff about Mr. Ford, but I always gave him the best of it. I spent a whole day with him, telling him jokes that I had used on him and he said: "You must just lie awake nights thinking up jokes on me." He is a great fellow.

When I'm in Indianapolis, I used stuff on Abe Martin. That's Kin Hubbard. They know Kin personally out there. I'll use some of his jokes, like maby, "As Abe Martin says, women is just like elephants: I like to look at em, but I'd sure hate to own one."

In Columbus, Ohio, I was just ahead of the Methodist Centennary Celebration in 1919. "It's a terrible thing for the saloons of this town that they'll have to close just before this great gathering of Methodists," I told em. "But there are other terrible things. A man told me there'll be one band of eighty trombonists — it's almost impossible to listen to one, but think of eighty. A trombonist is like a vice — he ought to be segregated. And they say there'll be seventy thousand preachers. Why, you can't hardly keep awake listening to one. What will seventy thousand of em do to you?"

"Yes, I like the stage," *Will said in 1917*, "and as long as I can hang and rattle with it, some farmer is losing about a twenty-eight-per-cent efficient farmhand. If I can keep on my friendly relations with the audience and not have them suffer, I will stick to my job on what is in the newspapers, and not try to put over any outside propaganda as von Bernstorff did; and when I do get my papers — in the nature of the audience not liking my little act — I will not pull one of those strategic victories, by saying the people don't know a good act when they see one. I will bundle up my wife and three little Cherokees and burn the breeze for the tall grass of Oklahoma, get me one of those long-distance shooting guns, that some of our boys will have captured and brought home from Berlin, and point it down the main road. If ever I see a man coming down the road with a newspaper I will cut the gun loose and just keep on living in ignorance." [1]

[1] Karl Schmidt, "The Philosopher with the Lariat," *Everybody's*, October, 1917.

CHAPTER FIVE

When I Write Em They Go as They Lay

*W*ILL *first broke into print in 1918 when he reported for the* New York American *a big stampede which he and Fred Stone had promoted on Long Island. Paula Stone says the first thing that she remembers was when Will took her on his horse to ride ahead of him in the Grand Entry. Of this writing Will said:*

I was asked to write for a paper — like those great authors and writers, Christy Mathewson and Ty Cobb.

I am going to lay my chips a little different from what they say those birds do. I am not only going to sign my name, but I am going to take a shot at the whole works myself, and I want it to go as she lays, even if the guy that has to set up the type has to get drunk to do it.

49

I know a lot of you will say, well, Will, why aren't you out there showing us something? Say, I don't see any of you fellows fighting Willard. My "rep" as a rope tangler was mostly east of the Hudson River and it started vanishing today.

Besides acting a fool in one show [*Follies*] and trying to keep New Yorkers awake the rest of the night in another one [*Midnight Frolic*], and day herding three young Rogerses in a yard to keep 'em from catching this disease [*influenza*] — I can't even spell it — a man don't get a whole lot of time to practice.

* * * * *

I finally left the arena and went around up in the grandstand, and there's where I step on a mule's shoe and have me some luck. I am invitationed to join Miss Mary Pickford and Mr. Douglas Fairbanks and a lot of other poor struggling moving-picture actors.

Say, I lost quite a bit of interest in that show, as much as I love it. How Ziegfeld overlooked that Pickford part, I don't know.

Well, the big feature of the day, the one that the crowd seemed to enjoy most, was the bulldogging. You know, tossing the old he-oxen has long been the favorite pastime of New York, but here was a brand new way to do it. Those boys sure did do some fine work throwing them old steers, but I think Fairbanks and I held our own doing the same thing right there in the box.

I didn't know how easy it was to improve on another man's work until I sat and watched it. Why, we rode bucking horses and roped steers all over the box for Miss Pickford's benefit. I have to say it, but I believe she enjoyed the work in the arena as much as she did ours.

* * * * *

When Russia dropped out of World War One Will wrote this for the Chicago Examiner:

Now they've asked me to write about Russia.

That's fine! There's some sense to that. I can write about Russia for I know that my readers don't know any more about Russia than I do; even as great a man as President Wilson passed up mention of it in his last speech.

There is always this to look forward to with Russia. Pick up the morning paper and look for Russian news and have a fear of reading the worst; you won't be disappointed.

I will give the Russians credit for one thing: They didn't sign a peace with Germany. They said: "What's the use of signing something? We just quit."

You see, Germany was willing to treat for peace as long as Russia did all the treating.

Now they have given German freedom to some province called Ukrainia; sounds like ukulele, and I doubt if it will flourish even as long as that short-lived instrument.

* * * * *

The ukulele had this advantage: Not even a trained musician could tell if you were playing on it or just monkeying with it, but the Ukrainian liberty can't fool anybody; those poor independents have "Made in Germany" stamped all over it.

You see, the Kaiser has the dope on it this way: It is better to be surrounded by a lot of small nations than by a couple of regular ones; they come in handier to go through.

Germany wants to make peace with Roumania. She says, "We will take a chunk off you and give it to Bulgaria, as we promised them something. After looking it all over they seem to like your country best. But for what we give Bulgaria of yours, we will take a small hunk out of Russia and you all can have that."

* * * * *

You see, if Russia's land holds out long enough, Germany should be able to make a very generous peace with her eastern foes. One thing I will say for the Germans, they are always perfectly willing to give somebody else's land to somebody else.

Of course, we will admit that they (Russia) were handicapped by not having a national anthem to fight by; it's hard to fight without a good anthem.

If we had only known it, we could have loaned them "Poor Butterfly," but only on one condition, that is, that they keep it.

* * * * *

I guess that old nut monk [*Rasputin*] over there had about the only right dope on Russia. He could throw sticks in the water and make any of them go out and get them. Some bird over there shot at this guy, Lenine, the other day, and missed him.

In 1918, Will wrote the "War of Washington" (which might have been written more recently):

The War of Washington

Want to speak about the training of these officers in this war of Washington, or how to get a higher Commission. In all my gags I like to take the part of the private against the officers as it is always more popular to uphold the few against the many.

First thing is to come to Washington. Thats the most essential thing. Then try to get a room, thats the hardest thing. No previous experience necessary to be an officer unless it is that you are in danger of being drafted as a private by your own board. Then pick out the branch of service whose office hours are the shortest. Then get your home senators address. Await your turn in line and if you draw only a Capt. dont feel discouraged. You may meet a cabinet officer and be promoted before night.

Next the most essential thing is your uniform. Without it you wouldent want the office. Then decide whether you want to take your savings of years and get an officers equipment or pay a weeks room rent with it. They both cost the same. Unfortunately, our uniforms are mostly alike. When we have had as many wars as the European countries we can remedy that to the satisfaction of our officers. Your only chance of ranking above your fellow officers is to get a more expensive grade of cloth. Now you wont have time to have this made to order AS Foch is holding up this war now waiting till you get in. Besides you have a date at the photographers at four o'clock so go to the best ready-made store. He will fit you till you can have a suit made and will show you what insignia to put on your shoulder and which end of your putees to go on top. If you decide as most of them do to get boots and spurs be sure to get spurs without the rowels or sharp things in them, as you may cut your boots up with them. Besides they are more apt to catch in your clutch and you cant shift your gears as well with them.

Now when you have found a coat that is uncomfortably tight and pants with the necessary bigness above the knees the clerk for a small extra fee will show you how to salute as you may in going out meet a cadet who has only been in West Point three years and you as a superior officer must return his humble salute. Now with the salute learned you are a full-fledged American Officer in the Great War of Washington, D.C.

Now try and think of some humble unpatriotic friend whom you used to know before you entered this awful conflict who is toiling trying to make enough to pay his taxes and meet his payments on his Liberty Bonds and ask him out to dinner with you. You cant afford to go in any but the best now as you may be humiliated by being next to a lot of non-com officers. Now be sure and tell your friend confidentially that you got it straight but he must not mention where it come from that Turkey was about through and that the only thing you are sore about is that it may end before you get across. Now the Follies are playing in town so you take your friend. Now its perfectly proper for an army Washington officer to admit that ignorance of the war but its gross negligence to admit he is not acquainted with at least five of the girls. When the usher comes back and says there is no answer, bawl him out before your friend and tell him you bet he gave it to the wrong girl and was he sure he told her it was Captain Jasbo.

From now on you pan the show. Its the worst you've ever seen and you've seen them all.

Now its tomorrow morning and you are to start in as the deciding factor in this war. When you get to your office building your hardest war work is trying to find a place to park your car.

Now make sure of one thing and that is as to where you are to be located. The saddest case that has happened in this war was a fellow dident notice how his appointment read and he found he had been put with a regiment that was to go to the European War. But that was the only case.

You spend your first day being introduced to your typewriters. By night you will begin to realize what a tremendous war this is. Now its time to dress for dinner so you return to your rest billets.

Brush your new suit, see that your shoulder tags are on straight and make for a café, get a table where you can get a good view of all these new officers who have only been appointed today.

Tonight you start in on your military training. You attend a school for twelve lessons to learn how to dance with a girl without catching your spurs in her dress.

Carry a French book in your pocket. You know you are not going to use it but it lends a certain amount of atmosphere.

Youve now been in about long enough to commence figuring on a promotion. By this time you should be receiving the paper from home. That is one of the most anxious moments of your entire military career, wondering how the picture will turn out and if its on the front page.

You know one of the most unfortunate cases in this war was a boy after sacrificing a good home and all his social standing to enlist as a 2nd Lieutenant in this civil conflict returned home on a furlough and dident look well in his uniform. Well his people were just simply killed about it. Now they dont know whether to try and get him out of the army or get another Tailor. You know the ordinary person dont realize the chances these men take when they enlist in this service. Why I have seen them pouring out of those government buildings after a hard days struggle with three Austrian notes and the ink on their hands up to their wrists.

Why the casualty list in one day out of a million and a half officers in Washington was ten wounded getting in and out of Taxicabs. Two choked through their collars being too tight, 61 hurt through typewriters choking up, 500 prostrated when they heard war was over and they would have to go back to work.

It will take two years to muster all of them out of Willard Hotel Lobby. It will take all the Drawing Room space on McAdoos Railroad for years to get them home again.

Then people at home will have to listen for another year why they dident go over. The hardest part of it is trying to look like an officer, and how to act in the presence of someone who has been across. Also how to properly thank the staff officer for past performances and ask for future ones.

I met one officer here who could tell me what he was doing without explaining. Most of them had their hardest jobs trying to make their uniforms look worn somewhere else besides the trouser seat.

They are allowed to keep their uniforms to show their children and grand children the desk marks on them. One officer has been recommended for gallantry. He has only missed one show and no dances since the war started.

In 1919 Will broke out in "serious" print by publishing two books: The Cowboy Philosopher on The Peace Conference *and* The Cowboy Philosopher on Prohibition, *both published by Harper and Brothers, New York, 1919. In them, in short, pithy paragraphs he printed the best gags that had come out of his Frolic and Follies routines. For instance, in the book on the peace conference, which is still timely, he said:*

"The war was too serious a subject. I could not write on it. But the Peace Feast, that seemed to offer a better field of humor provided you stick to the facts."

Now for the Number 2 Peace Trip. This Peace trip is not an original Idea (it was originated by some obscure Manafacturer of Knick Knacks, from some lake town, I cant think of that Birds name). [*Ford's Peace ship.*]

Of Course this No 2 Company used better Judgment than the first one. This one waited till the war was over to Go.

This is the only case in Theatrical History where the No 2 Company was better than the original.

I wanted to go along as JESTER. Pres. Wilson will miss his comedy when he gets away from Congress.

Mr Creel went along to suppress any SCANDAL that may crop up.

Col House was there to meet the Boat in a listening capacity. Lot of men have fought their way into fame and talked their way into fame but Col House is the only man that ever just LISTENED HIMSELF IN.

* * * * *

Peace table is turning out like all banquets, the speeches are too long.

Everybody at the Table wants a second helping, And Germany the cook hasent got enough to go around.

They agreed on one of the 14 points, that was that America went in for nothing and expects nothing, they are all UNANIMOUS WE GET IT.

* * * * *

Best time to have formed this league of Nations was during the war when all these Nations needed each other.

One thing we got to be thankful for our Soldiers can win wars faster than our Diplomats can talk us into them.

One thing about this League, The last war there were only 10 or 15 nations in it, now if they all sign this, they can all be in the next one. It wont be near so exclusive.

Well they finally handed Germany the Peace terms, 80 thousand words, only thing ever written longer than a Lafolette Speech.

Had to be that long to tell the Germans what they thought of them.

Imagine what a document for Lawers to pick flaws in.

Could have settled the whole thing in one sentence, "IF YOU BIRDS START ANYTHING AGAIN WE WILL GIVE YOU THE OTHER BARREL."

I thought the Armistace terms read like a second Mortgage, but this reads like a FORECLOSURE.

Now Folks, with all this kidding and foolishness aside, for I just say in here whatever I think anybody might laugh at, But of Course my real sentiments are the same as everybody else, If He puts this thing through and there is no more wars, His address will be WHITE HOUSE WASHINGTON DC till his whiskers are as long as the Peace Treaty. If it should be a Fliv (which it wont) Why then a letter would reach him at ALABI NEW JERSEY. So all Credit to Pres. Wilson, it took some game Guy to go through with it.

CHAPTER SIX

I Horn into Hollywood

I HAVE BEEN ASKED to tell something of these bucking pictures and as I have been in only one I know all about it. I horned into this El Dorado a little different from most of them. I had been going along peacefully working for a living on the stage and really felt a little hurt that I had never been offered a job in them.

One day Mrs. REX Beach, who you hear very little of but who is really the Ram Rod of the Beach outfit, Mrs. Beach, after a late supper consisting of a Rarebit, had a very bad night and thought of some terrible things. She arose early and commanded James to taxi out the favorite Limouzine and give it the gun for where I was bedded down for the mosquieto season on Long Island.

I had just started in licking on my third Kid and I was a little vexed at being thrown behind in my daily routine.

Well, she climbed out of this royalty on the "Spoilers" and chirped above the wail of young rope throwers, "Will, you are going into the Flickering photos." Now I live at the same town and its not a coincidence on the island where the Asylum is located, so I winked at her chouffer and said, "You brought this Woman to the wrong house."

Now, I tried to tell the lady that I had never bothered anybody and never annoyed over one Audience at a time and that these were war times and a man could be arrested for treason as treason meant any thing that causes pain to our people thereby giving aid to the enemy. But she still insisted that the people of OOlagah, Okla, and Higgens, Texas would grow up in ignorance if I did not enlighten them with my Art on the old muslin, said education for which they could obtain for a jitney and tax.

I told her that I couldent afford to earn any more, that I was just on the verge of the Income Tax now, all that saved me was that the Gov allowed two hundred for each child and my children and my income just come out even, and that I would have to speak to my wife and see if we could afford to increase our income.

I told her that I had heard that some of these Movable Actors sometimes appeared personally at the Theatre where their pictures were showing. She said, yes, some of them do but most of them dont or wont. She says you wont have to and I would advise you not to let them know even where you live.

Of course she had one corking good argument, that Caruso and myself were the last two singers to go in and look what it would mean to Caruso when someone, after looking at his picture, asked him why he went in. He could say, "Well, Will went in, us artists have to stick together." I showed her that Caruso had used up his only means of publicity getting married and was going into the movies and that the first thing you know he would be back singing again. I wanted time to think it over but she kept insisting she must know at once as she said if it got nosed around Fairbanks and Chaplin might get to me with a bigger offer.

Will's first picture was Laughing Bill Hyde, *made in the summer of 1918 at Goldwyn's old Fort Lee Studio in New Jersey, while he was still with the Follies. That Fall Goldwyn put him under exclusive contract and the following spring sent him to California. The family later moved out and California became their permanent home. Will wrote about his first experience there.*

* * * * *

First Day on the Set.

When a big burly nabbed me by the coat tail and yanked me back and said, "You poor boob, I saved your life. Thats Miss Geraldine Farrar taking close ups for the hell cat." I had heard what she did to Caruso one time and I thanked him. I watched her a while in hopes she would sing, but I tell you what she did have, she had an orchestra playing appropriate music in all of her scenes.

This man said he would show me where I belong, so we passed through an Irish farmhouse of Tom Moores, stopped to see May Marshes Propagander picture choking the Kaiser. We passed through Metropolitan Opera House and Cheyenne Joes saloon on the way to my gang. By the time I got there they thought I had given up the picture and gone back home.

It was now ten thirty and I thought I was late. We took the first scene at exactly three forty five in the afternoon. The Director says, "Now, Will, we are going to take the scene where your old pal dies. You have broken out of jail and he gets hurt and you are bringing him into the Doctors office at night to get him treated and he dies. Its the dramatic scene of the whole opera." I says, "But I havent got out of Jail yet." He says, "No, you wont for a couple of weeks yet. Besides the Jail is not built yet."

Thats the first time I learned that they just hop around any old way. We took a scene the start of a fellow and I fighting out doors and a lot of rainy weather come and a week later he knocked me down in the same fight. I thought we were trying to beat the European war record.

The Director says, "Have you ever had any Camera experience?" I said only with a little Brownie No 2 I used to have. He says, "Any moving Picture experience." I told him I worked with Miss

Norman once but I dident know how it turned out. He warned me that if I was thinking a thing the camera would show it. I told him I would try and keep my thoughts as clean as possible.

Telegram sent when Sam Goldwyn wanted to change the name of Jubilo:

OCTOBER 17, 1919

SAMUEL GOLDWYN

469 FIFTH AVENUE

NEW YORK CITY NY

THOUGHT I WAS SUPPOSED TO BE A COMEDIAN BUT WHEN YOU SUGGEST CHANGING THE TITLE OF JUBILO YOU ARE FUNNIER THAN I EVER WAS. I DONT SEE HOW LORIMER OF THE POST EVER LET IT BE PUBLISHED UNDER THAT TITLE. THAT SONG IS BETTER KNOWN THROUGH THE SOUTH BY OLDER PEOPLE THAN GERALDINE FARRAR'S HUSBAND. WE HAVE USED IT ALL THROUGH BUSINESS IN THE PICTURE BUT OF COURSE WE CAN CHANGE THAT TO "EVERYBODY SHIMMIE NOW." SUPPOSED IF YOU HAD PRODUCED THE MIRACLE MAN YOU WOULD HAVE CALLED IT A QUEER OLD GUY. BUT IF YOU REALLY WANT A TITLE FOR THIS SECOND PICTURE I WOULD SUGGEST JUBILO. ALSO THE FOLLOWING:

A POOR BUT HONEST TRAMP

HE LIES BUT HE DONT MEAN IT

A FARMERS VIRTIOUS DAUGHTER

THE GREAT TRAIN ROBBERY MYSTERY

A SPOTTED HORSE BUT HE IS ONLY PAINTED

A HUNGRY TRAMP'S REVENGE

THE VAGABOND WITH A HEART AS BIG AS HIS APPETITE

HE LOSES IN THE FIRST REEL BUT WINS IN THE LAST

THE OLD MAN LEFT BUT THE TRAMP PROTECTED HER

WHAT WOULD YOU HAVE CALLED THE BIRTH OF A NATION?

WILL ROGERS

Ad for Jubilo:

Now I was asked to write my own add, Now that is a pretty tough job Cause after my telling you what a picture we have you will think I am a little egotistical, At that I am glad they asked me to write it instead of paying for it. Jubilo means a song, an old-time Negro Camp Meeting song IN THE LAND OF JUBILO, I sing this song but fortunately the voice dont register on the film so you need not stay away on that account. ˉ

It was originally before we got ahold of it a very good story and appeared in the Saturday Evening Post (I get nothing extra for mentionning their name) This character Jubilo is a tramp, Well after Mr Goldwyn saw me several times in my street clothes he said there is the fellow to play the tramp.

Now this picture is just as long as any other 5-reel picture and takes up just as much time as a regular picture does, Another thing exibitors need have no fear of it conflicting with anything else on their programs, As it cant interfere with anything and nothing can hurt it, In one respect our picture is as good as lots of others, We have a Cast that can act and a Star that can not, an unusual combination in this business. We only have one Villain in the picture so you have no trouble telling who is doing all the dirty work. You know come to think of it it aint such a bad picture at that, it has Father, Girl, Villain who makes play for girl, Tramp Hero, dirty but honest. Pickford, Fairbanks and all of them have the same layout and get real doe for theirs, Story, theres no use telling you wise Birds. Same as usual. Looks bad for the Hero right up to the last Close Up, First reel introduces Hero dividing last crum of bread with dog, which they all do in the movies but nobody ever did in real life, Second reel looks bad for hero, Third reel looks even worse for Hero, Fourth reel evidence all point to Hero being the robber, Villain looks slick and satisfied, End Reel 5 the winners, The tramp wins 100 percent HERO, Villain 2 and three quarters.

The directions was very good when you consider the director wore no Puttees or riding breeches.

The Photography was mostly shot in focus, the Camera used was a Brownie No 2.

The Sets, Goldwyn really spread themselves in this picture, there is one scene with mountains in the background that if you had to build it would have cost a million dollars, To give you an Idea we traveled over 2 miles from the studio to get it.

Interior Sets there is a Barn showing real hay, No fake stuff but real Hay and a Kitchen Scene that I'll bet dident cost a cent under 25 dollars but very realistic dirty dishes in the sink and everything. Theres an eating scene. (Well to give you an idea how good I did it we had to wait for the war to be over or Hoover would never let such eating pass.)

* * * * *

In "Jubilo" Ben Ames Williams wrote the finest story it was ever my privilege to work in. It was the only Story ever made out here where there was no Scenario made. We just shot the scenes from the various paragraphs in the Story in the Saturday Evening Post. When we took a Scene we just marked it off and went on to the next. I think, and Williams verified it, that it was the only story ever made that was absolutely filmed as it was written, and here is the big Novelty to it. We dident change his main Title either. They will film the Lords Supper and when it is made, figure out that it is not a good release Title and not catchy enough, so it will be released under the heading, "A Red Hot Meal," or "The Gastronomical Orgy."

In 1919 one of Will's movie fans sent him twenty-five cents in stamps to pay for a photograph. About six weeks later when Will happened to read the letter he returned the stamps with this note:

My dear Sir:

I thank you for the use of your money. I havent got a picture of myself. If I did have it wouldent be worth two-bits. If I did have one, I'd give you two bits to keep it.

Yours,

Will Rogers

* * * * *

In 1919 Will wrote his famous fourteen points on the moving picture business in Wid's Yearbook, *published by the* Film Daily.

President Wilson and I each have fourteen points. He took his to Paris where they not only saw his fourteen but raised him twelve more, I brought my fourteen points to the coast. The first five and principal of mine a wife and four children in itself constitutes a novelty in this business, that is provided you still live with them.

Point number six: I heard there was a movement on to revive moving pictures.

Point Number seven: Producers decided to make fewer and worse pictures. They may make fewer but they will never make worse.

Point number eight: I hold the distinction of being the ugliest man in pictures.

Point number nine: Caruso and I and Jesse Willard were the last to go in.

Point number ten: Goldwyn figured by getting a good cast and a great story, it would about offset the action of the star.

Point number eleven: I can't roll a cigarette with one hand and can't whip but one man at a time (and he must be littler than I am).

Point number twelve: I made a picture last year and some theatres bought it. So they figured if I made another one they could double the sale on this one. Get two to use it.

Point number thirteen: Moving pictures are the only way in the world that you can play and tour and not have to worry about hotels.

Point number fourteen: It's the only business where you can sit out front and applaud yourself.

Will Rogers

In 1920 Will wrote his suggestions on how to improve the Moving Picture industry. His suggestions might be read with profit, from time to time, by the industry. Here they are:

Use your audience for a Press Agent instead of hiring one.

Don't tell your audience what your picture cost, they know what they were stung by the price of admission.

How can you make five movies a year of over four million different pictures each when it took Rembrandt five years to make one still?

You hear it asked, Are Movie audiences getting smarter? The answer is No. Ain't more people going to Movies than there ever was?

There is only one thing that can kill the Movies, and that is education.

What Movies need is another name for an All-Star Cast.

What the Picture business needs is a picture.

What the Movie audience needs is endurance.

What the Movie actor needs is better doubles (so they can do better stunts).

What the weeping Movie heroine needs is glycerine that won't stay in one place, but will run down the face.

What the entire industry needs is a sense of humor.

If the Movies want to advance, all they have to do is not to get new stories but do the old ones over as they were written.

Producers say Pictures have improved, but they haven't. It's only audiences have got used to them.

You can't spring a new plot on an audience the first time and expect it to go. It takes a Movie audience years to get used to a new plot.

Moving Picture audiences are just like an old gold miner, they will keep on going and going for years hoping against hope to eventually some day strike a picture.

The finish of the Movies will be when they run out of suggestive titles.

Movie Patron coming out of Theatre was asked, How's the feature? "I guess it's good, but I didn't see one."

A plot that will make money and that could be elaborated by an imaginative director into a big feature is a little Bo-Peep.

Some say, What is the salvation of the Movies? I say run em backwards. It can't hurt 'em and it's worth a trial.

Some Cinics ask, Is Movies really an Art yet? Yes, selling them is. Will the industry live? Not unless a Mid-Wife comes. We can't tell yet, it's like a newly born cat, we've got to wait nine days to see if it will open it's eyes.

Which one of the Arts will it supplant? It must have been Literature, as there hasn't been any in a long time (if it hadn't been for my book).

Pictures are getting so long that the life of a moving Picture fan is four features.

The average life of the movie is till it reaches the critic.
The average life of the movie hero is till he is found out.

* * * * *

One time out here in the old silent day pictures, it was in 1919,
we made about three pictures up at a place near Mohave, Called-
darnsburg. It has a big old mine, and Irene Rich was with us.
She was just a breaking in as a leading lady. In those days I was
one of the love interest. (Nowadays I just have to fix it for some
young ones. They wont let me have anything to do with it personally. I guess its just as well, I never was so hot as a screen lover.)
But in those days your age never mattered. Audiences figured that
old people fall in love too, but now thats all out. Modern audiences think that old folks are just to be the fathers and mothers of
the young ones. And too in one of those same pictures was Margaret
Livingston, who is now Paul Whitemans's wife. She is the one
that made him quit eating so much. The way she did it she would
let him order whatever he wanted and then she had a string tied
to it and she would pull it away from him, and he got thin grabbing
at it. I was one time to rescue her out of the water.

Well we had to go another two hundred miles to find a stream.
You know this water thing out here aint just water, its gold. Well
I was supposed to swim in on a horse and rescue her, and as I
dragged her ashore pull her up on my horse and run to the doctors
with her. Well say you get on dry land and try to stay up on your
horse and pull a fair size old gal up on there with you, when she
is supposed to be plum dead, and then wet to boot! Say, she had
to reduse before I could get her up there. There is nothing heavier
than a person that is wet, even a little person. You dip one of
Singers Midgets in the water and let him soak awhile, and I bet
you Dempsey wouldent lift him up in front of him.

Another time I was supposed to get on a bucking horse in a
corral and he was supposed to buck out of the gate and down to
the creek, where he was to throw me off into the water. Then
the leading lady was supposed to come up and see me as I was
crawling out of the water, and I was to register embarrassment and

try to conceal my wetness at the same time. It was in the winter-time when we took it. The fellow that wrote this little byplay in the scenario did so in a nice warm dry room.

Well, I got on the horse and got almost to the gate, when he bucked me off. We caught him and did it over again. And the next time I stayed with him until he got out of the gate and that was all.

The director said, "That's no good. You'll have to try it again. You are supposed to stay on until you get to the creek and then get bucked off."

I says, "Say, listen, if you want me to do this scene, you get a corral that's nearer the creek; or better still, find some creek that's nearer a corral."

Under his contract with Sam Goldwyn Will made the following moving pictures: Laughing Bill Hyde; Almost a Husband; Water, Water Everywhere; Jubilo; The Strange Boarder; Jes' Call me Jim; Cupid, the Cowpuncher; Honest Hutch; Guile of Woman; Boys will be Boys; An Unwilling Hero; Doubling for Romeo; *and*, A Poor Relation.

CHAPTER SEVEN

I Bark for my Dinner

*T*HE *motion picture business went through violent reorganizations in 1920. Will's pictures had been only moderately successful. When he asked Sam Goldwyn for a raise, Goldwyn decided to let him go. Will went into production for himself.* He made three pictures: Fruits of Faith, The Roping Fool *and* One Day in 365. *They broke him. Will wrote* The Roping Fool *himself. By the use of a white rope and his black pony, Dopey, he showed all of the rope tricks and catches that he had used for so long. This picture is still being shown.*

Broke, with nothing to do in Hollywood, Will went back to New York to the stage. He began on November 8 on Shubert's Winter Garden but was soon back with the Follies. The highest-paid entertainer in the city, his income was still not enough to pay off his debts and support himself and his family. Through engagements arranged by an agent he began "barking around town" to various meetings.   *He wrote:*

I have spoken to many Banquets during the year. A great many will think that it is dispepsia that is driving me away from the old Banquet Table. But it is not. There is only one way a Person can survive a year of Banquets and not wind up with a Burlesque stomach — that is not to eat there at all.

Now I tell you what I did. There is a little Chili Joint on Broadway and 47th street where there is just a counter and a few stools, but, Comrades, what Chili!! Well, on any night I had to go to a Banquet, I would go in there and play about two rounds of Enchilades, and a few encores of the Chili, and I want to tell you that I was fortified, not only to refuse anything that might be offered to me at the Dinner, but I would just set through almost any kind of speeches.

I tell you that is what has made Texas. Did you ever listen to a Texan make a speech? Now, you thought it sounded terrible, didn't you? That was because you had not eaten Chili.

Now, you take a man on that Banquet routine, and you ain't in any shape to listen to the words.

We will, just as the old Doctor says, diagnose the Banquet Menu; they are all alike. It starts with a little Fruit Cocktail (they call it). I don't know where they got the Cocktail part of the name.

Then comes Thin Consome in Cups (you know you never want to give a man too much Consome, hot water ain't food for you before you eat). Then, thirdly, comes the Fish (generally weakfish). That's to match the speeches. Then comes that inevitable Chicken, broiled of course. It was broiled before the Guests were even invited to the affair, so naturally it's dry. That is so there will be no grease to splatter on your white Shirt which you had such a time getting the button into.

Sorter what they call garnishing, or in the same corral with this Chicken, is always 5 little saratoga Chips. They have been balling from a box in the grocery store for months to you. Then on the side where the Bottle used to set, is a quarter of a head of Lettuce, swamped by Bolsheviki, or Russian Dressing. Nobody but a Russian on a Revolution could have ever thought of a concoction like that.

Now for the big surprise! I bet you can't guess what it is. It's Ice Cream. It's different colors (that's a novelty) and if it's a big Banquet and they have spared no expense, it be in shape of whatever the organization represents. For instance for the Bankers, it was a Black Jack or Billy.

After the Ice Cream, of course, comes the Coffee, served Demitasse. That's to prevent any possibility of drinking out of the saucer.

Now, you know a man can't listen to good heavy speeches on a diet like that, especially if the Speaker is a man with a Message. You know, a man with a Message is a whole lot harder to listen to than any other species of Speaker. That is why I recommend Chili. It's the only thing I have ever found that will strengthen a man up to listen to all he hears.

* * * * *

Speech to International Bankers Association New York, 1922

Loan Sharks and Interest Hounds, I have addressed every form of organized Graft in the U.S. excepting Congress. So its naturally a pleasure for me to appear before the biggest.

You are without a doubt the most disgustingly rich Audience I ever talked to, With the possible exception of the Bootleggers Union Local No 1, combined with the enforcement officers.

Now I understand you hold this Convention every year to announce what the annual Jip will be.

I have often wondered where the Depositors hold their Convention.

I had an account in a Bank once and the banker asked me to withdraw, that they used up more red ink on my account than it was worth.

I see your Wives come with you, You notice I say Come, not Were Brought.

I see where your Convention was opened by a Prayer, and you had to send outside your ranks to get somebody that could pray.

You should have had one Creditor there, he would have shown you how to pray.

I noticed that in the prayer Clergyman announced to the Almighty that the Bankers were here. Well, it wasent exactly an announcement, It was more in the nature of a warning.

He dident tell the Devil, he figured he knew where you all were all the time.

I see by your speeches that you are very optimistic of the business conditions of the coming year. I dont blame you, if I had your dough I would be optomistic too.

Will you please tell me what you do with all the Vice Presidents a Bank has? I guess thats to get you more discouraged before you can see the President. Why, the United States is the biggest Business institution in the World and they only have one Vice President and nobody has ever found anything for him to do.

I have met most of you as I come out of the stage door of the Follies every night. I want to tell you that any of you that are capitalized under a million dollars needent hang around there. Our Girls may not know their Latin and Greek but they certainly know their Dunn and Bradstreet.

You have a wonderful organization, I understand you have 10 thousand here, and with what you have in the various Federal Prisons brings your Membership up to around 30 thousand.

So, Goodbye Paupers, You are the finest bunch of Shylocks that ever foreclosed a Mortgage on a Widows home.

*   *   *   *   *

Settling the Corset Problem of this Country

If a Man is called on to tell in a Public Banquet room what he knows about Corsets, there is no telling what other Ladies' wearing apparel he might be called on to discuss. So me back to the Morals of Hollywood before it's too late.

I was, at that, mighty glad to appear at a dinner given by an essential industry. Just imagine, if you can, if the flesh of this country were allowed to wander around promiscuously! Why, there ain't no telling where it would wind up. There has got to be a gathering or a get-together place for everything in this world, so, when our human Bodies get beyond our control, why we have to call on some mechanical force to help assemble them and bring back what might be called the semblance of a human frame.

These Corset Builders, while they might not do a whole lot to help civilization, are a tremendous aid to the Eyesight. They have got what you would call a Herculean task as they really have to improve on nature. The same problem confronts them that does the people that run the Subways in New York City. They both have to get so many pounds of human flesh into a given radius. The subway does it by having strong men push and shove until they can just close the door with only the last man's foot out. But the Corset Carpenters arrive at the same thing by a series of strings.

They have what is known as the Back Lace. This is known as a One Man Corset.

Now the Front Lace can be operated without a confederate. By judiciously holding your breath and with a conservative intake on the Diaphragm you arrange yourself inside this. Then you tie the strings to the door knob and slowly back away. When your speedometer says you have arrived at exactly 36, why, haul in your lines and tie off.

We have also the Side Lace that is made in case you are very fleshy, and need two accomplices to help you congregate yourself. You stand in the middle and they pull from both sides. This acts something in the nature of a vise. This style has been known to operate so successful that the victims' buttons have popped off their shoes.

Of course, the fear of every fleshy Lady is the broken Corset String. I sat next to a catastrophe of this nature once. We didn't know it at first, the deluge seemed so gradual, till finally the Gentleman on the opposite side of her and myself were gradually pushed off our Chairs. To show you what a wonderful thing this Corseting is, that Lady had come to the Dinner before the broken string episode in a small Roadster. She was delivered home in a Bus.

They have also worked out a second line of control, or a place to park an extra string on the back. You can change a string now while you wait, and they have demountable strings.

Now, of course, not as many women wear Corsets as used to but what they have lost in women they have made up with men.

When corsets were a dollar a pair they used to be as alike as two Fords. A clerk just looked you over, decided on your circumference and wheel base and handed you out one. They come in long Boxes and you were in doubt at first if it was a Corset or a Casket.

Nowadays with the Wraparound and the Diaphragm-Control, and all those things a Corset Manufacturer uses more rubber than a Tire co.

Imagine me being asked to talk at a Corset Dinner anyway; Me, who has been six years with Ziegfeld Follies and not a corset in the Show.

Men have gone down in History for shaping the destinies of Nations, but I tell you this set of Corset Architects shape the Destinies of Women and that is a lot more important than some of the shaping that has been done on a lot of Nations that I can name off hand. Another thing makes me so strong for them, if it wasn't for the Corset Ads in Magazines men would never look at a Magazine.

Will loved nothing better than kidding New Yorkers. "When a boy is born and brought up in the middle west," Will said, "he either decides one or two things. If he is industrious and honest and wants to work for a living, he either stays home or goes further west. But if he has a bit of the sharper or an underlying current of Graft in his nature he comes East — generally to New York."

Once Will had come to New York his audience loved this. But Will tried to keep to what he was in the Middle West. A friend in New York once invited him to have dinner with him.

"No, thanks," Will said, "I've already et."

"You shouldn't say 'et,' Will," the friend chided. "You should say 'have eaten.'"

"Yeah . . ." Will grinned. "Well, I know a lot of fellers who say 'have eaten' who ain't et."

Seriously, though, he did feel that a New York audience lacked the first-hand experience which many out in the "sticks" had. In writing about one of his speaking engagements, he said:

I have played to audiences all over the country, cities, towns, and right on the bald prairies, and lots of swell charity affairs in New York, and if you talk about International or political affairs a fashionable New York audience is the dumbest one you can assemble anywhere in the Country. Small town people will make a sucker out of em for reading and keeping up with the news.

I will never forget one time I went over to Sherrys, a fashionable restaurant, after the Follies show one night to play a charity affair for one of the Vanderbilt ladies, and I thought I had some good material at the time. The League of Nations was in the height of its argument, Ireland and England was fussing, disarmament was a headline topic. William Randolph Hearst was sitting with a party of friends at one of the tables. Well he had heard these same little jokes of mine over at the Follies show, and I breezed out there rather cocky thinking I had some sure fire material. Well you never saw jokes hit a ball room floor and slide off like those did. Those old dowagers, and those young debutantes had no more read a paper than I had Shakespeare. Mr. Hearst was dying laughing, but not at the jokes. He was laughing at me out there dying. He had heard these get big laughs with an out of town audience at the Follies, and he got a kick out of em laying an egg there with that bunch.

They dident know who was on or off the gold. They knew they were on velvet was all.

Then two nights later after that fiasco I went to Sing Sing and did a show for them and I never had as well read audience in my life. They dident muff a gag. Ever since then I have always felt we had the wrong bunch in there.

In June of 1923 Will returned to California and remained nearly a year doing short comedies for Hal Roach. He starred in the following: Jus' Passin' Through; Hustlin' Hank; Gee Whiz Genevieve; Two Wagons, Both Covered; The Cowboy Sheik; The Cake Eater; Big Moments From Little Pictures; Highbrow Stuff; Going to Congress; No Parking There; Our Congressman; *and,* A Truthful Liar.

In June 1924 he returned to the Follies and played a solid year in New York. But in the meantime he had taken, next to his marriage, perhaps the most important step in his career.

CHAPTER EIGHT

The Fifth Estate Got Me

IN DOZENS of newspapers over the United States on the last day of 1922 appeared this notice:

The famous cowboy monologist, Will Rogers, has undertaken to write for this paper a weekly article of humorous comment on contemporary affairs. The Literary Digest recently quoted an editorial from the New York Times thus: "Not unworthily is Will Rogers carrying on the tradition of Aristophanes on our comic stage."

Instead of an audience of two thousand daily, as Will had had in New York on the stage, from now on his "autobiography" became an important part of the life and thoughts of practically everyone in the United States and began to spill over to other parts of the world. As Harry Carr said, he wrote his own story in these newspaper articles which, in 1926, became daily

*in addition to the weekly ones. The basis for selection has been those that
keep up with his amazing life and his reaction to the crucial period from
1920 to 1935 — during which time the United States did a complete flip-flop
in its economic, political and social thinking.*

* * * * *

December 31, 1922:
Being in Ziegfeld Follies for almost a solid year in New York
has given me an inside track on some of our biggest men in this
country, who I meet nightly at the stage door.

So I am breaking out in a rash here. I will cite an example to
prove to you what you are going to get. Not long ago there was a
mess of Governors here from various Provinces. And a good friend
of mine brought back to the stage and dressing room Governor
Allen of Kansas. Well, I stood him in the wings, he was supposed
to be looking at my act, but he wasn't. He was watching what
really is the Backbone of our Show. He anyway heard some of
my Gags about our Government and all who are elected to mis-
run it.

So at the finish of my act I dragged him out on the stage and
introduced him to the audience. He made a mighty pretty little
speech and said he enjoyed Will's Impertinences, and got a big
laugh on that. Said I was the only man in America who was able
to tell the truth about our Men and Affairs.

When he finished I explained to the audience why I was able to
tell the truth. It is because I have never mixed up in Politics.
So you all are going from time to time to get the real Low Down on
some of those Birds who are sending home the Radish Seed.

January 14:
There is a mess of conferences going on, but they are just like
the poor and the Democrats, they will always be with us.

England wants to settle one way with Germany and France has
a different plan. Now, as Germany owes both of them, there
is no reason why each couldn't settle in their own way. But no,
that's too easy. Nations don't do things that way. If they did

they would be no Diplomats, and Diplomats are nothing but high class Lawyers (some aint even high class).

* * * * *

These other Nations have got it on us. They can play half a dozen Conferences at once, while with us, if we can find a man to send to one, why, we are lucky, and we always feel uneasy till he gets home.

They always bring a Pack of Experts and Technical men along to advise. I have always noticed that any time a man can't come and settle with you without bringing his Lawyer, why, look out for him.

February 4:

A Liberal is a man who wants to use his own ideas on things in preference to generations who, he knows, know more than he does.

Mr. Harding has had quite a little sick spell lately from which he is recovering. I sorter think it's these Doctors these Presidents have. They are promoted from a Horse and Buggy trade in the country to an Admiral in the U.S. Navy, or a Major General in the U.S. Army so quickly that I really believe they have to give so much time trying to learn to salute and to getting their uniform on proper side forward that they haven't the time to devote to our President's health. So, with our next President, I hereby start a movement to let his Doctor keep his bagged-kneed breeches and his ole slouch hat.

February 18:

The way to judge a good Comedy is by how long it will last and have people talk about it. Now Congress has turned out some that have lived for years and people are still laughing about them.

Girls win a little State Popularity Contest that is conducted in some Newspaper; then they are put into the Movies to entertain 110 million people who they never saw or know anything about. Now that's the same way with the Capitol Comedy Company of Washington. They win a State Popularity Contest backed by a

Newspaper and are sent to Washington to turn out Laws for 110 million people they never saw.

They have what they call Congress, or the Lower House. That compares to what we call the Scenario Department. That's where somebody gets the idea of what he thinks will make a good Comedy Bill or Law, and they argue around and put it into shape.

Then it is passed along, printed, or shot, or Photographed, as we call it; then it reaches the Senate or the Cutting and Titling Department. Now, in our Movie Studios we have what we call Gag Men whose sole business is to just furnish some little Gag, or Amendment as they call it, which will get a laugh or perhaps change the whole thing around.

Now the Senate has what is considered the best and highest priced Gag men that can be collected anywhere. Why, they put in so many little gags or amendments that the poor Author of the thing don't know his own story.

They consider if a man can sit there in the Studio in Washington and just put in one funny amendment in each Bill, or production, that will change it from what it originally meant, why, he is considered to have earned his pay.

Now, Folks, why patronize California-made Productions? The Capitol Comedy Co. of Washington, D.C. have never made a failure. They are every one, 100 percent funny, or 100 percent sad.

March 11:

A Comedian is not supposed to be serious nor to know much. As long as he is silly enough to get laughs, why, people let it go at that. But I claim you have to have a serious streak in you or you can't see the funny side in the other fellow. Last Sunday night a Young Girl who had made a big hit in the Salvation Army preaching on the Street in New York, decided to go out and give religious Lectures of her own. So on her first appearance I was asked by her to introduce her. She said she would rather have me than a Preacher, or a Politician, or any one else. Well, I could understand being picked in preference to a Politician, as that is one Class us Comedians have it on for public respect, but to be chosen in preference to a Preacher was something new and novel.

April 15:

I read a chart showing that over 50 percent of all Rugs and Tapestries were bought by women and Girls between the ages of 18 and 30. Now any man knows that that is the Boob Age. A woman will do either one of two things between 18 and 30. She will either get married or buy a rug: and, if she is extra feeble minded, she may do both.

May 6:

Mr. Harding wants to see the Follies, but, on account of the humorous relations between the White House and myself being rather strained, he naturally feels a kind of hesitancy about coming, for, at the present time, you can't see the American Girl being glorified without being annoyed by a jarring presence among them, which I am free to admit is myself.

So, on the first of June, I am leaving; not because I want to (for, speaking candidly, it's not the worst position in the World, as my surroundings here have been most beautiful). But even though you wouldn't judge it by my writings or Grammar, I have some politeness and courtesy, and, being a fair American Citizen (I won't say "good" as I think I have heard that used before) I certainly have a high regard for the Chief Executive of this great Commonwealth and I won't do a thing to stand in the way of any pleasure that he may wish to enjoy, no matter how small. So I am willing to get out and sacrifice a living wage.

* * * * *

May 20:

Well, they had another big Convention here this week — the Chambers of Commerce from all over the U.S. Being big sound business men, they wanted some good conservative business man to address them, and also wanted some frivolous or light talker that would sound amusing but mean nothing.

So Herb. Hoover drew this last frothy or care-free assignment. He had those BABBITS just rolling off their seats telling them about the prosperous conditions of this Country.

Then he knocked 'em Coo Coo with a gag for the Government not to go into business. He said the standard of living had advanced so far in this country that we could lay off two million men from work and the rest of the people would live just as good as they did 10 years ago.

He didn't say what would become of the 2 Millions he laid off. But you take a busy man like that, he can't stop to worry about trifles like a couple of million men.

Well, the next night after Mr. Hoover spoke, why, they were ready for some real conservative business talk. So I went over and instructed them.

You know what the Chamber of Commerce is, don't you? You remember the Old Ladies' sewing circle in towns years ago that knew everybody's business and were into everything. Well, this is the Male end of that same organization. They fix everything from the local Marble Championship to the next War. The minute a fellow gets into the Chamber of Commerce he quits mowing his own lawn.

June 3:

Politicians, after all, are not over a year behind Public Opinion.

I understand the type of man you all want for President. We want a man in there who can handle men, a man who when his Hired Help gets to acting up, down at the other end of Pennsylvania Avenue, can hop in his car, go down there and tell 'em who is Boss and where to head in. Don't confer with them — just sock 'em.

You see the class of help a President gets in the Senate and Congress since immigration has been restricted, you can't treat them with kindness. A Congressman or Senator is not used to kind treatment, even at home, so you have got to be rough with those Birds.

June 10:

Our Public men are speaking every day on something, but they ain't saying anything. But when Mr. Harding said that, in case of another war that capital would be drafted the same as men, he put over a thought that, if carried out, would do more to stop

Wars than all the International Courts and Leagues of Nations in the World.

When that Wall Street Millionaire knows that you are not only going to come into his office and take his Secretary and Clerks, but, that you come in to get his dough, say Boy, there wouldn't be any war. You will hear the question, "Yes, but how could you do it?"

Say, you take a Boy's life, don't you? When you take Boys away you take everything they have in the World, that is, their life. You send them to war and part of that life you don't lose you let him come back with it. Perhaps you may use all of it. Well, that's the way to do with wealth. Take all he has, give him a bare living the same as you do the Soldier. Give him the same allowance as the Soldier — all of us that stay home. The Government should own everything we have, use what it needs to conduct the whole expenses of the war and give back what is left, if there is any, the same as you give back to the Boy what he has left.

There can be no Profiteering. The Government owns everything till the war is over. Every Man, Woman and Child, from Henry Ford and John D. down, get their Dollar and a Quarter a day the same as the Soldier. The only way a man could profiteer in war like that would be raise more Children.

But, no, it will never get anywhere. The rich will say it ain't practical, and the poor will never get a chance to find out if it is or not.

June 24:

Well, folks, I am writing my little Swan Song to New York. I have been for 52 weeks, one solid year, telling my mangy little jokes to Broadway.

So me for Los Angeles and the Movies for at least a year and perhaps two. It seems that Rudolph Valentino can't get his troubles straightened out so I am going out to take his place.

Los Angeles, July 1:

Poverty drove me out of this Paradise. I was living fine on the climate out here but those kids of mine have no sense of value of Climate and Beauty. They demanded meat and bread. Colum-

bus Day has rather an added significance to Los Angeles, as they
want to celebrate the good fortune of his landing on the Atlantic
instead of the Pacific side, because if he landed out here he never
would have gone back even to tell the Queen. He would have
stayed tight here and nobody would have even known it but him.

July 15:

Say, we have discovered out here in California, A Dr. House,
of Texas, who has invented a Serum called Scopalamin, a thing
that when injected into you will make you tell the truth, at least
for a while. They tried it on a Male Movie Star in Hollywood and
he told his right Salary and his Press Agent quit him. They then
tried it on a Female Movie Staress and she recalled things back as
far as her first Husband's name. The only failure to date has been
a Los Angeles Real Estate Agent. They broke three needles trying
to administer the stuff to him and it turned black the minute it
touched him. He sold Dr. House three lots before he got out of
the operating room.

It really is a wonderful thing and if it could be brought into
general use it would no doubt be a big aid to Humanity. But it
will never be, for already the Politicians are up in arms against it.
It would ruin the very foundation on which Political Government
is run. If you ever injected truth into politics you have no politics.

July 22:

Well, all I read in the papers now is about some fellow named
Edward Bok offering 100 thousand dollars for someone to suggest
a plan where they stop wars. Now he is receiving serious editorial
mention for his idea and philanthropy. People that praise his idea
laughed at Henry Ford's for trying to just stop one war, while this
fellow offers just 100 thousand dollars to stop all of them.

I claim that both men were equally sincere, but, on the other
hand, if there is to be ridicule, I claim they should equally share
in that, too. The very terms of this make it ridiculous. He is to
give half the money when the Trustees accept the plan, and the
other half when the Senate accepts and passes it.

Now, I am no Philanthropist. I am hard to separate from

money; if I killed two Birds with one stone I would want the stone back. But I will just raise Mr. Bok's offer 100 thousand dollars. I will hereby make a Bona Fide offer of 200 thousand dollars to any man in the World who can draw up any kind of a Bill or Suggestion, I don't care on what subject, no matter how meritorious, and send it to the Senate of the United States and send this paper a copy of the Bill submitted, and, if the United States Senate passes the bill as you sent it in, you get the 200 thousand.

Talk about stopping War, I will bet any man in the United States 5 thousand even that there ain't a man in this Country that can draw up a bill that the Senate themselves won't go to war over while they are arguing it.

Can you imagine the bunch of Multi-Millionaires made by the last war agreeing to stop all chances of a future war for 100 thousand dollars? I am only an ignorant Cowpuncher but there ain't nobody on earth, I don't care how smart they are, ever going to make me believe they will ever stop wars.

We ain't as smart as the Generations ahead of us and they tried to stop them and haven't been able to.

The only way to do is just stay out of them as long as you can, and the best way to stay out of them for quite a while, instead of teaching a Boy to run an Automobile, teach him to fly, because the Nation in the next war that ain't up in the Air, is just going to get something dropped on its Bean.

Mr. Harding has the plan, "Draft Capital as well as men," but you see if Congress passes it.

September 30:

See where the Prince of Wales is up in Canada on his Ranch. When he was up in Calgary the time before, a very wealthy old Ranchman who I have known for years, and who originally come from Texas but now owns the biggest ranch up there, decided that the Prince ought to have a Canadian ranch. So, as there was one adjoining his, he got them to buy it, saying that if it was too big he would take part of it and let the Prince have the other part.

Now half of this Ranch was very good, and he had been wanting it for years to add to his big one, but he couldn't buy the good half and not take the bad. But when his Majesty graciously come along, he was able to obtain the half for himself that he had so long desired. And, incidentally, to have only a Barb wire fence separating you and the future Viceroy of India don't hurt the value of your land any to speak of. Can you imagine what he could have rented his Ranch for this fall to some old Newport Matron with a couple of empty Bob-headed Girls of marriageable age?

This same old Gentleman, who is a Great Character, and known and liked by all the Notables that ever visit western Canada, was present a few years ago when the Duke of Connaught and Princess Patricia were in Calgary at a big Rodeo Celebration in their honor.

Charley Russell, the great Cowboy Artist, and the finest Painter of the West we have, had an exhibition there and the Duke saw them and bought some, and wanted to meet this Cowboy who painted them. So he asked Mr. Lane, this old Ranchman, and a lifelong friend of Russell's where he could find Russell.

So Mr. Lane says, "You won't find him around here with these white folks; he will be over back of the Fair Grounds with them Injuns. Come on Duke and we will hunt him up." He never called him anything but just Duke.

Well, he dragged him through the dust over till they found Charley. Then he said, "Charley, I want you to meet Duke," and Charley, who is also like Mr. Lane, one of our Characteristic Americans, said, "Howdy, Duke."

The Duke said, "I have enjoyed your wonderful Paintings. Mr. Russell, you are a Genius."

Charley said, "No, I am just an ordinary Dobber."

The Duke said, "Dobber? Dobber? What is a Dobber?" He turned to Mr. Lane and said, "What does he mean — Dobber?"

Lane thought a minute, he didn't know what Charley was kidding himself about, but he wasn't going to be stuck by any question the Duke might ask, so he said, "Well, if Charley says he was that, you can depend on it, Duke, he wouldn't lie to anybody."

Charley was telling me about painting old Man Lane a Picture of a bunch of Cowboys around the Chuck Wagon in the morning, some of them eating and some getting on their Horses and one

Horse bucking through the Camp fire. Near by was an Axe and Wood for the fire. It was a Big Picture with lots of People and action in it.

Well, he sent for Mr. Lane to come down to Great Falls, Montana, where Charley lives to see the Picture. Lane looked at it quite a while and Charley said he began to feel that there was something terrible wrong with it. He knew the old man knew for he had been a Cowpuncher all his life.

Finally he said, "Charley, you ain't got that Axe handle wrapped with rawhide. You know them Cooks was Hell for breaking Axe handles in them days."

Charley picked up a brush and wrapped the Axe handle with it, and the old Gentleman handed over his paltry ten thousand Bucks for it and took his Axe handle back to Canada.

When the Prince was up there before, he went out to Lane's Ranch where they were rounding up a Big Herd and was riding around on a Horse. Finally Lane yelled at him, "Hey, Prince, get out of there. You are getting in the way of my Cowboys' working."

This Prince seems to be a mighty fine kind of Guy and it is a shame that he should have been handicapped by birth, for there is a Boy who would have made something out of himself.

*　*　*　*　*

I guess that the King of Spain will be buying a Ranch in Canada or Mexico or some place. Spain just pulled off a bloodless Revolution. You known those bloodless Revolutions are the ones that hurt the King Business worse than a fighting one does. A king can stand people's fighting but he can't last long if people start thinking.

October 14:
One-third of the people in the United States promote, while the other two-thirds Provide.

October 21:
I don't want any White Robed Gentlemen leading me forth in

the middle of the night and massaging me with any Tar, and sprinkling feather on me for a chaser.

I'm not going to express any opinion even for Political purpose on the Klan fight in Oklahoma. I live down there and know a lot of those Birds. "Rest in Peace" covers many a man's head down there who spoke out of his turn.

There are old Guys down there who have an old Squirrel Rifle laying up over the door on some deer Horns, and if they shoot at you and don't hit you in the eye, why, they call it a miss. I want to conduct myself so that when I go back home to Oklahoma I can shake hands with all my friends — not just have to wave at 'em as I am running.

I ain't going to tell some people 2 thousand miles away how they should conduct their business. I am like a Song that Bert Williams used to sing in the Follies, "I ain't got much education but I got good common sense."

*　*　*　*　*

There's the one thing no Nation can ever accuse us of and that is Secret Diplomacy. Our Foreign dealings are an Open Book, generally a Check Book.

October 28:

I had heard so much of late years of self-made men that I was anxious to see what one looked like. I think the same fellow who started that Self-Made Gag started that other assinine expression, "100 percent American."

A Made Man is a finished Man and I doubt if we have one in this Country now. If we have, for the Lord's sake let's find him!

A real Self-Made Man would have to be one who had received no learning or knowledge, or assistance from any Person or Source. The woods are full of those Birds. Every Toastmaster at every 75 cent Luncheon introduces from 3 to 5 Self-Made ones every day.

December 30:

My opinion on the bonus is based on what I heard uttered to

soldiers in the days when we needed them, when they were looked on not as Political organization with a few votes to cast, but as the pick of One Hundred Million People, the Saviors of Civilization.

You promised them everything but the Kitchen Stove if they would go to War. We promised them EVERYTHING, and all they got was $1.25 a day and some knitted Sweaters and Sox.

They got a Dollar and a quarter a day. Out of the millions of bullets fired by the Germans every day, statistics have proven that an average of 25 Bullets were fired at each Man each day. That figures out at the rate of 5 cents a Bullet. Now, the boys in this Bonus want the Salary at least doubled. And I don't think that 10 cents a Bullet is an exorbitant price.

Now the only way to arrive at the worth of anything is by comparison. Take Shipbuilding, Wooden ones, for instance. Statistics show that the Men working on them got, at the lowest, $12.50 per day, and, by an odd coincidence, Statistics also show that each Workman drove at the rate of 25 Nails a day — the same number of Nails as Bullets stopped or evaded by each Soldier per day. That makes 50 cents a Nail.

Now I don't think that there is 45 cents per Piece difference. I know that Bullet stopping comes under the heading of Unskilled Labor, and that Ship Building by us during the War was an Art. But I don't think that there is that much difference between skilled and unskilled, while I claim he is only 5 times as good.

Now, as I say, while the Soldiers got no overtime, the Nail Experts got Time and a Half for overtime, up to a certain time, then Double Time after that. Of course, he lost some time in the morning selecting which Silk Shirt he should Nail in that day. And it was always a source of annoyance as to what Car to go to work in.

Now I may be wrong, for these Rich Men who are telling you that the Nail is 10 times harder to handle than the Bullet know, for they made and sold both of them to the Government.

Everybody's Alibi for not giving them the Bonus is, "We Can't commercialize the Patriotism of our Noble Boys." "They didn't go to War for Money, they went for Glory."

I have a plan for raising this Bonus which I haven't heard brought up. That is, raise it by a Tax on all Tax-Exempt Securities. These Boys helped their Country in a time of need. Tax-Exempt Bond Buyers knowingly hindered it in a time of need by cheating it out of Texas.

In 1916 there was 1296 men whose income was over $300,000 and they paid a Billion in Taxes. This year there was only 246 whose income was supposed to be over 3 hundred thousand, and they only paid 153 million.

You mean to tell me that there are only 246 men in this Country who only make 300 thousand? Why, say, I have spoken at Dinners in New York where there was that many in one Dining Room, much less the United States.

That old Alibi about the Country not being able to pay is all Apple Sauce. There is no debt in the World too big for this Country to pay if they owe it. If we owed it to some Foreign Nation you would talk about honor and then pay it. Tax exempt Securities will drive us to the Poor House, not Soldiers' Bonuses.

Now if a Man is against it why don't he at least come out and tell the real truth. "I don't want to spare the Money to pay you Boys." I think the best Insurance in the World against another War is to take care of the Boys who fought in the last one. YOU MAY WANT TO USE THEM AGAIN.

CHAPTER NINE

Prosperity Remained With Them That Had

1924 — Republicanism rode high. **The** Saturday Evening Post
printed the gospel. *America was rapidly lapsing back into its traditional
isolationism.* *For political reasons the Republican Party brought in the
World Court as a sort of back-door answer to the Democrat's League of
Nations.* *Time payment was fast becoming a national habit.*

*The Tea-Pot Dome Scandal started the year off with gushing hopes for
the Democrats.* *Woodrow Wilson died.* *General Pershing was retired
on half-pay.* *Coolidge preached economy.* *Walter Johnson zipped his fast
ball over.*

*Then there was the presidential election which showed the Democrats
that their gusher was a duster.* *The country decided to "keep cool with
Coolidge."* *What time United States had to get away from Main Street
she spent fiddling with Wall Street — while the fires burned beneath the deck.*

January 6:

I think Mr. Ford is wrong when he says "90 percent of the people are satisfied." 90 percent of the people in this Country are not satisfied. Its just got so that 90 percent of the People in this Country don't Give a Damn.

There is millions of people in this Country that know the Color of Mary Pickford's hair, but think the Presidential office is heireditary. There is more Mortgages in this country than there is Votes. This Country right now is operating on a Dollar down and a Dollar a Week.

It ain't Taxes that is hurting this Country; it's Interest.

The only way to solve the Traffic problems of this Country is to pass a law that only paid-for Cars are allowed to use the Highways. That would make traffic so scarce we could use our Boulevards for Children's play grounds.

No, it's not politics that is worrying this Country; it's the Second Payment.

January 27:

Young John D. Rockefeller says: "Love is the greatest thing in the World." You take a few words of affection and try and trade them to him for a few Gallons of Oil, and you will discover just how great Love is.

February 10:

Tea started one War we had, but nobody ever thought that a Tea Pot would boil over enough to scald some of our most Honorable Financiers. [*Tea Pot Dome Scandal.*]

Now I see only one way out of this lamentable Scandal. That is to do as the Movies did, appoint a Will Hays to Wet Nurse the Oil Industry, and see if he can keep their Nose clean. When you come to think of it there is a great similarity between the two Industries. Neither one is a Public necessity.

The great criticism of the Movies is that People are suddenly thrown into possession of Money who never were accustomed to handle it before, and that they lose their heads. Did you ever think of Oil People? Why, they are rich so quick they are Million-aires before they have time to get the grease off their hands. They jump from a Ford to a Rolls Royce so fast that they try to crank the Rolls through force of habit.

So you take the two industries, Scandal for Scandal, and Bribe for Bribe, Oil has blackened the reputations of 99 percent more people than the Movies.

Our History honors many names whose Morals would not stand the Acid Test, but our History Honors no man who betrayed, or attempted to betray a Government Trust.

I sympathize with their Industry. I can remember when the Movies looked bad and it was thought we would never be able to show our heads again. So if they can just get a Will Hays to chaperone them back into decency again, we may yet be able to save some of our Oil for what is left of our Navy.

February 17:

Some of the most glowing and deserved tributes ever paid to the memory of an American have been paid to our past President Woodrow Wilson. They have been paid by learned men of this and all Nations, who knew what to say and how to express their feelings. They spoke of their close association and personal contact with him. Now I want to add my little mite even though it be of no importance.

Just think there were hundreds of millions of Human Beings interested directly in that terrible War, and yet out of all of them he stands, 5 years after it's over, as the greatest man connected with it. What he stood for and died for, will be strived after for years.

But it will take time for with all our advancement and boasted Civilization, it's hard to stamp out selfishness and Greed. For after all, Nations are nothing but Individuals, and you can't stop even Brothers from fighting sometimes. But he helped it along a lot. And what a wonderful cause to have laid down your life for! "The World lost a Friend." The Theatre lost its greatest sup-porter. And I lost the most distinguished Person who ever laughed

at my little nonsensical jokes. I looked forward to it every year.
Now I have only to look back on it as my greatest memory.

March 30:

The Oil Investigation has been transferred to Los Angeles. Mr.
Doheny arrived here in three Private cars — two and a half Cars
of Lawyers and a half Car of Evidence.

Well, they unloaded the first Car just at daybreak. They were
just little ones. Chances are there was not one in that Car whose
Fee run any higher than of maybe 40 thousand a Case. In fact
they were just kinder engaged to carry the Brief Cases.

It was at the second Car load that we commenced to prick up our
Ears, for we were now getting into the Big Money.

Lawyers came out of that car who wouldn't argue even a speed-
ing case in a Traffic Court for less than a Hundred thousand. And
then maybe you would have to give them a retainer in case you
got pinched again.

There were men in there who had procured Divorces for every
one of the 400.

Well, when they had unpacked this second Car and got them
safely away to Individual Private Suites at our Home Talent Bilt-
more, why, then come the real Headliners. Just a few big ones
that were in real touch with Mr. Doheny personally. Real Lawyers!
Men who, on a Case like this which involved perhaps about 400
Million Dollars, why they consider that slumming.

Well after seeing this wonderful Pagentry of Lawyers arrive I
thought, well, now me for the Station to see Uncle Sam's Battalion
of Justice arrive. For the United States of America is not to be
outdone in Marshaling of Legal Talent. So if these people have
three Cars, what will Uncle Sam have?

So I go down to the Station next day and finally a Local pulled
in. Who do you think Emerged? Why Atlee Pomerene and a
Mr. Roberts. They came crawling out of a Day Coach where they
had been Sleeping on the back of their Necks from Cheyenne.
They didn't even have a Caddy to carry the legal proofs.

Well, I just looked at them and then visioned what I had beheld the day before. And I thought to myself, "Uncle Sam, no wonder you never get anywhere."

Of course there is one Silvery lining on the Navy's fuel. That is that the other side has so many Lawyers they may get to Fighting amongst themselves and we would win Accidentally.

But they are well fortified against every emergency. They have Expert Technicality Lawyers. That is, a Lawyer that don't know or have to know Anything at all about the Case, but who, if it goes against his side, why he can point out that Witness So and So had on the Wrong Color Tie when he Testified, and that in signing his Name he had failed to dot one of his i's, and that Therefore that rendered the whole of his testimony Null and Void.

He is a Man who could take W. J. Bryan and show you on Technicalities how he is entitled to be President.

Then they have one Car load of just Postponement Lawyers. Men who can have the Falls of Niagara put back on account of the water not being ready to come over. Men who on the last Judgment Day will be arguing that it should be postponed on account of Lack of Evidence.

April 27:

Just been reading about the great Amalgamation and buying and selling and combining of New York Newspapers. The Congressional Record has been trying for weeks to amalgamate with my Exposure retaining the best features of each.

For instance, the Editorial Policy of The Exposure would be retained. But this monotony of just reading Common Sense would be broken up by also retaining the Humorous angles of the Congressional Record. I wouldn't consider it for a minute as The Exposure is breaking into fields where the Record could never hope to ascend.

But, on the other hand, one must consider the names and Class of Writers who contribute to the Record. Just think of being sandwiched in between a Humorous Paragraph on Taxes by Henry Cabot Lodge, and a pastoral scene on Cows Returning Laden with Milk by Magnus Johnson. And then maybe an occasional little Personal Advice by Calvin Coolidge. You see the Record has never been a paying Proposition. They are anxious to link it with something that is on its feet Financially.

Heretofore it has been a Periodical that Statesmen mailed out to their Voters free. Now that has got to be stopped. Men are gradually Realizing that a thing that is free is of no earthly Importance. And, besides, it has lost Men more votes than it has gained for them. All one has to do to get his Speech reprinted in the Record is to find a Stenographer that can stay awake long enough to take it. Then you mark in the "Applause" and "Laughter" parts yourself.

But just between us two I would rather tie up with the Police Gazette than the Congressional Record. The Old Gazette may be yellow, but her Soul is White.

May 11:

You wire the State or the Federal Government that your Cow or Hog is sick and they will send out experts from Washington and appropriate money to eradicate the Cause. You wire them that your Baby has the Diphtheria or Scarlet Fever and see what they do. All you will do is hire your own Doctor if you are able, and there will be a Flag put up on your front Gate. Where Children that don't know can still go in and perhaps be exposed to certain Death, the Government won't have Guards at every Entrance to keep you back from that Exposed House.

If your Hog has the Cholera the whole State knows it and everybody is assisting in Stamping it out. You can have 5 Children down with the Infantile Paralysis, more deadly 10 times over than any Foot and Mouth disease, and see how many Doctors they send out from Washington to help you.

There is more Money spent on Hogs' sickness by State and Federal Governments than there is on Children, when one child's life is worth all the Hogs and Cows that ever had a Disease. If you want the Government to help you, don't tell them it is any Human Sickness. Tell them it is Boll Weevil or Chinch Bugs, and they will come a running, because they have big appropriations and men paid for that.

How many Children die every day from some contagious disease, that would be Living if we exercised the same vigilance over a Child that we do over a Cow?

I fully believe that every sane Precaution that is being exercised is necessary, but while we are all thinking of it, why can't we get the Government to at least do for a Child's protection, what they do for a Cow or a Hog?

May 25:

New York: That City from which no weary Traveler returns without drawing again on the Home Town Bank. That City of Skyscrapers, where they have endeavored to make the height of their Building keep pace with their prices. That City of Booze, Boobs and Bankrolls where the Babbitts from Butte and Buffalo can pay the Speculators $8.80 for a $2.20 show, view the Electric Signs until 12 o'clock and then write home of the Bacchanalian Revels.

I am going back to join the new Ziegfield Follies which will open in the early part of June. This is a Political Year as some of the Candidates might have told you, and I thought it better that I be near the heat of Battle.

We are now nearing Kansas City and I am branching off and going down for a few days to my Home around Claremore, Oklahoma. I am mighty happy I am going home to my people, who know me as "Willie, Uncle Clem Rogers' boy who wouldn't go to school but just kept running around the Country throwing a Rope, till I think he finally got in one of them Shows."

I'll not do any talking but listen and see all my old friends and hear 'em call me WILLIE, and they will give me some Political opinions that will beat all your Lodges or Borahs, and maybe I will tell 'em a little about Hollywood and the night life. For I want to keep on the good side of them. They don't know how I make a living. They just know me as Uncle Clem's Boy. They are my real friends and when no one else will want to hear my measly old Jokes, I want to go home. It won't make no difference to them.

June 1:

Ed Wynn, the Comedian, and his Wife were on the same train with us. And when I say comedian, I mean Comedian. He of the Perfect Fool Fame. Ed and I spent three days on that Train trying out jokes on our Wives that we were going to use in New York this year. I just looked at Mrs. Wynn, who is a lovely Woman, and perfectly sane, and at Mrs. Rogers, who if I do say it myself, after sixteen years of forced laughter, is bearing up remarkably, and under happier surroundings might retain her faculties for years. In a kind of abstract moment I just looked at both of them, and thought what have these Women done in their lifetime that they should be subjected to this brand of jokes, not only for three days, but for life. Truly providence acts in a strange manner and justice is sometimes long delayed.

June 8:

I am to go into Ziegfeld's new Follies and I have *no* Act. So I thought I will run down to Washington and get some material. Most people and Actors appearing on the Stage have some Writer to write their material, or they reproduce some Book or old masterpiece, but I don't do that; Congress is good enough for me.

Why should I go and pay some famous Author, or even myself, sit down all day trying to dope out something funny to say on the Stage! No Sir, I have found that there is nothing as funny as things that have happened, and that people know that have happened. So I just have them mail me every day the Congressional Record. It is to me what the Police Gazette used to be to the fellow who was waiting for a Hair Cut, it is a life saver.

Besides, nothing is so funny as something done in all seriousness. The material on which the Congressional Record is founded is done there every day in all seriousness. Each State elects the most serious man it has in the District, and he is impressed with the fact that he is leaving Home with the expressed idea that he is to rescue his District from Certain Destruction, and to see that it receives its just amount of Rivers and Harbors, Post Offices, and Pumpkin

Seeds. Naturally you have put a pretty big load on that Man.
I realize that it is no joking matter to be grabbed up bodily from
the Leading Lawyer's Office of Main Street and have the entire
Populace tell you what is depending on you when you get to Washington. The fellow may be all right personally and a good fellow,
but that Big League Idea of Politics just kinder scares him.

Now, they wouldn't be so serious and particular if they only
had to vote on what they thought was good for the Majority of the
people of the U.S. That would be a Cinch. But what makes it
hard for them is every time a Bill comes up they have a million
things to decide that have nothing to do with the merit of the Bill.
They first must consider is, or was, it introduced by a member of
the opposite Political Party. If it is, why then something is wrong
with it from the start, for everything the opposite side does has a
catch in it. Then the principal thing is of course, "what will this
do for me personally back home?" If it is something that he thinks
the folks back home may never read, or hear of, why then he can
vote any way he wants to, but Politics and Self-Preservation must
come first, never mind the majority of the people of the U.S. If
Lawmakers were elected for Life I believe they would do better.
A man's thoughts are naturally on his next term, more than on his
Country.

Outside the Congress Hall, they are as fine a bunch of men as
any one ever met in his life. They are full of Humor and regular
fellows. That is, as I say, when you catch them when they haven't
got Politics on their Minds. But the minute they get in that im-
mense Hall they begin to get Serious, and it's then that they do
such Amusing Things. If we could just send the same bunch of
men to Washington for the Good of the Nation, and not for Political Reasons, we could have the most perfect Government in the
world.

August 31:
I am just an old country boy in a big town trying to get along.

I have been eating Pretty Regular, and the reason I have been is because I have stayed an old country boy.

September 14:

80 thousand people paid 800 thousand dollars to see twelve rounds of wrestling between Wills and Firpo [*for the heavyweight boxing championship of the world*]. On the same day those alleged Fighters received 150 thousand Dollars cash for 36 minutes embracing why we released on half salary General Pershing who had spent 42 years fighting for his Country. During 42 years his whole total Salary paid to him by (what is sometimes humorously referred to as a liberal Government) never amount to what these men received in 36 minutes, and there were no Boxing gloves on the hands of any enemy he ever fought. All these men could lose was their Reputation. All he could lose in his fights for us was his Life.

So if you are thinking of taking up fighting as a career why be sure and FIGHT FOR YOURSELF INSTEAD OF FOR YOUR COUNTRY.

August 3:

Mr. J. P. Morgan just sailed for Europe. They made all the photographers and reporters get off the boat, and they put in a special gangway for him to go on the boat. He had dozens of Policemen and Officers to see that no one molested him by even looking at him. Then you will hear some Bonehead say we have no classes in America like they have in England.

Why, if J. P. Morgan was as democratic for just one day as the Prince of Wales is every day, Morgan would feel like he was slumming. He was asked the day before sailing, if his trip had anything to do with the Dawes Debt plan being discussed in Europe now. He said, "no, absolutely nothing at all." No, he is no more interested in that loan than Babe Ruth is in base ball or than W. J. Bryan is in Electric Fans for Chautauquas.

He said he was just going over to Scotland for the Grouse shooting season. Can you imagine what would happen if some one told him he was trespassing during his hunting over there. He would just say to his valet, "Boy, buy this lower end of Scotland for me and send my Secretary the bill; and by the way, Boy, purchase a couple of more million Grouse and turn them loose here. Fix it so that no matter which way I shoot I will at least hit one."

August 10:

We are the only Nation in the world that waits till we get into a war before we start getting ready for it. Pacifists say that, "If you are ready for war, you will have one." I bet there has not been a man insulted Jack Dempsey since he has been champion.

October 19:

I been trying to read the papers and see just what it is in this election that one Party wants that the other one don't. To save my soul I can't find a difference. The only thing that I can see where they differ is that the Democrats want the Republicans to get out and let them in, and the Republicans don't want to get out.

They are so hard up for an issue that Mr. Coolidge has finally just announced his policy will be Common Sense. Well, don't you know the Democrats claim that too? Do you think they will call their campaign "Darn Foolishness?" Besides, Common Sense is not an Issue in Politics, it's an affliction.

Davis announced that his Policy will be Honesty. Neither is that an issue in Politics. It's a Miracle, and can he get enough people that believes in Miracles to elect him?

The only thing I see now that the two old line Parties are divided on is "Who will have the Post offices?" No matter how many Parties you have they are all fighting for the same thing — SALARY. You abolish salaries and you will abolish Politics and TAXES.

November 2:

Well, the publishing of the Income Tax amounts kinder knocked some of the big ones in the creek. It brought out many surprises, Few of us knew before that Jack Dempsey was as rich as J. P. Morgan. They both paid around 90 thousand dollars each. I thought Morgan made that much before breakfast every morning. I see where a lot of the big ones are against publishing the amount. I think it is a great thing to publish them. What's the idea of keeping it a secret?

Don't feel discouraged if a lot of our well known men were not as wealthy according to their Tax as you thought they ought to be. They are just as rich as you thought. This publication of amounts had nothing to do with their wealth. It was only a test of their honesty, and gives you practically no idea of their wealth at all.

November 9:

More Candidates have been defeated after 6 o'clock in the evening than were ever defeated during election day. That's how Tammany Hall of New York has built up its unmatched reputation. They are not strong in point of individual numbers, but in order to belong to it you must be able to live in at least 6 Precincts, and remember correctly your different names in each one, and in case you are put on the inside of the voting booth you must be able to count two for every single vote of your weapon. Ask any Soldier and he will tell you America forgot the War in one year. How was they going to remember the Oil Scandal 6 months? You can't beat an Administration by attacking it. You have to show some plan of improving it.

November 23:

We are able to report much jubilation on the part of the disgracefully rich, or Republicans, element of the entire country. They are celebrating the country's return to Wall Street. Wall Street never had such a two weeks in the history of that ancient and honorable Institution as she is going through now. They had to keep open 20 minutes longer and all the papers made headline stories of the fact. Just think of the inconvenience of the Brokers having to wait until 20 minutes after 3 P.M. in raking in more dough.

It is one of the worst personal hardships that the Exchange Members has gone through with in years. Wall Street men missed golf games that hadn't missed them in years. And stocks, why anything that looked like a stock would sell. People would wire in, "Buy me some stocks." The Brokers would answer, "What Kind?" The buyer would wire back, "Any kind; the Republicans are in, ain't they all supposed to go up?"

Men bought stocks who had never bought even a tooth brush before in their lives. People bought wheat and sent a Truck to the Exchange to get it. Even Moving Picture Companies stock went up, figuring I guess that Pictures will be funnier with Charley Dawes as Vice President than they would have been with Charley Bryan. I can imagine Rudolph Valentino's hair falling out effecting the value of a moving picture company's stock, but I didn't know before that Ma Ferguson being elected Governor of Texas would do it.

It's all right to let Wall Street bet each other millions of Dollars every day but why make these bets effect the fellow who is plowing a field out in Claremore, Okla? Mind you, I am not going to remedy it right now. I will allow Wall Street to run on a few days. Maybe their conscience will hurt them. (What's that you said would hurt them?) But, on the level, it does seem funny these guys can sit here, produce nothing, ride in Fisher Bodies, and yet put a price on your whole year's labor.

You mean to tell me that in a Country that was run really on the level, 200 of their National commodities could jump their value millions of Dollars in two days? Where is this sudden demand coming from all at once.

I am supposed to be a Comedian, but I don't have to use any of my humor to get a laugh out of that. Didn't we have a saying one time something about 100 percent Americans?

November 30:

One night last week we had the War Industries Board, 200 strong, all in one party: They were the famous $1.00 a year men during the War. Now, will you tell me how men who only got a dollar a year could afford the Follies? They still have their organization and once every year they meet and have a kind of a

Reunion, and live over again the old prosperous days. Then, in between they just sit and pine for another War.

They were all Republicans but one. That was Mr. Barney Baruch, the head of it during the war. With all the boasted Republican prosperity they made Baruch buy the Tickets. They keep this one Democrat in there so he can pay for everything.

You see, when President Wilson formed this Board during the war he told Baruch to go out and get all the prominent business men of every line together and see if they couldn't form some kind of Association to speed up supplies for the War. Well, he thought of course Baruch would come in with members of both Political Parties. But when they round them all up, why they are all Republicans!

So Mr. Wilson asked him why be so partial to one Party? And Mr. Baruch told him: "You told me to get prominent men of every industry and I did. Now I can go and get you some Democrats but they won't be very prominent and won't have any Industries with them. Besides, I doubt if you can get a Democrat to work for a $1.00 a year. They are used to getting at least a $1.00 a day."

Well, they decided to use these Republicans and let the Democrats do the fighting. They knew they could do that.

Now you see Baruch took care of all these Political opponents and now that his Party is out and theirs is in, they have not done a thing for him. It is a shame they won't repay him. Why, they even make him pay their fare to these Reunions every year. But he is a game guy and doesn't squawk. He is, you know, the Sight Draft of the Democratic Party.

He come back in my dressing room and sit and talked for an hour, and he complimented me on an Article of mine showing why the Democrats didn't do better in the last election. He said I had it absolutely right when I said that the Democrats had to get rid of the League of Nations Idea and get a Slush Fund in its place, and that if the Republicans had been kinder promiscuous in peddling our Oil, why it only showed that Voters admired personal preparedness in the Public Officials.

So the Democrats should go out and get themselves some slick candidates and not preach too much on their Party's honesty in the Campaign. Shrewdness in Public Life all over the World is always honored, while honesty in Public Men is generally attributed to Dumbness and is seldom rewarded.

December 7:

Well, we were all last week trying to sink our greatest Battleship, the Washington.

Here is a Boat we had spent 35 millions on, and we go out and sink it. And the funny part is that it cost us more to sink it than it did to build it. We shot all the ammunition we had left over from the war into it and those big Guns on the Texas they were using, they only are good for so many shots during their lifetime. So we spoiled the Guns of our next best boat trying to sink the best one.

A great many people don't understand just how this sinking come about. You see we had a conference over here a few years ago. It was called by America. We were building a lot of Battleships and we had plenty of money to do it on, and it looked like in a couple of years we might have the largest Navy in the World. Well, the League of Nations gathering in Paris had attracted a lot of attention and got quite a lot of publicity, none of which had been shared in this country by the Democrats. So, when the Republicans got in, they conceived the idea of a publicity stunt for the Republicans. Why not then have a conference? But what would they confer about? The League of Nations had conferred about six months, and in that time had taken up about every question on the Calendar.

So Secretary Hughes happened to think of an idea: "Let us confer on sinking Battleships." Well, the idea was so original that they immediately made him the Toastmaster. You see, up to then, Battleships had always been sunk by the enemy, and when he proposed to sink them yourself it was the most original thought that had ever percolated the mind of a Statesman. So, when we communicated the idea to England and Japan that we had an idea whereby we would sink some of our own Battleships, why they come over so fast, even the Butler wasn't dressed to receive them when they arrived.

England was willing to tear her blueprints on planned building into half, Japan was willing to give up her dreams of having more ships on the seas than any nation and stop building up to ⅗ of the size of England and America, and Secretary Hughes met that with, "Now, Gentlemen, I will show you what America is prepared to do. FOR EVERY BATTLESHIP YOU FELLOWS DON'T BUILD AMERICA WILL SINK ONE."

Now they are talking of having another Naval Disarmament Conference. We can only stand one more. If they ever have a second one we will have to borrow a Boat to go to it.

You see, we don't like to ever have the start on any Nation in case of war. We figure it looks better to start late and come from behind. If we had a big Navy some Nation would just be kicking on us all the time. Sinking your own Boats is a military strategy that will always remain in the sole possession of America.

December 28:

As I am writing this 2 blocks away the body of Samuel Gompers, the Great Labor Leader, is being viewed and wept over by hundreds of big strong men, who are appreciative of what he had spent his life in doing for them. He was a good friend of mine. Just a few weeks ago he come to see our show and as is customary with any notable in the audience, I introduced him, with: "Our notable Guest has been 40 years at the head of the largest organization of men in this Country. He has done more for the working man than any man living. The reason the Federation of Labor has been so successful is because when they found a good man they kept him. They didn't go off electing some new fellow every 4 years, and the smartest thing that he ever did for them was to keep his organization out of Politics. He makes them work his own way, but vote like they want to."

Well, that introduction seemed to please the old fellow and I then tried this one on him for a laugh: "Mr. Gompers has spent his life trying to keep Labor from working too hard, and he has succeeded beyond his own dreams."

I have before me here in the dressing room a Picture Post Card mailed in Mexico from him, just before he took sick: "Am going to bring you back a new Lariat and some new jokes." He will be missed, and that's saying a lot in these times. All labor stops for two minutes today as a tribute to him. I suppose Capital will take it out of their salary at the end of the week.

And while we are on the subject of labor, I see a lot in the Papers about this 20th or Child Labor Amendment, and I have been asked how I stand on that. If Congress would just pass one law, as follows, they wouldn't need the 20th Amendment: "EVERY CHILD, REGARDLESS OF AGE, SHALL RECEIVE THE SAME WAGE AS A GROWN PERSON." That will stop your child labor. They only hire them because they pay them less for the same work that they would have to pay a man. If Children don't do more for less money, why is it that they want to use them? No Factory or Farmer or anybody else hires a Child because he is so big hearted he wants to do something for the Child. He hires him because he wants to save a man's salary. It's become a habit and a custom that if a Child does something for us, no matter how good and prompt they do it, to not give them as much as we would a grown person, because, I suppose, people think they would just spend it foolishly if they had too much.

CHAPTER TEN

I Meet the Real Bird

1925 — Will tried to find out what a "One Hundred Percent American" looked like. When he couldn't see him on the ground, he took his first flight in an airplane. His pilot was General Billy Mitchell — who had just ceased to be "pilot" of the air policy of the United States. General Billy had been demoted for trying to keep the U.S. first in the air.

Not being able to see what this "One Hundred Percent American" was from the cockpit of a plane, in October Will went on his first lecture tour to meet "the real bird" and not his skeleton on Broadway.

* * * * *

February 15:

Well, I see where Judge Gary, the head of the Steel Trust and Mr. John D. Rockefeller, Jr., head of the Oil Trust went down to

Washington and had breakfast with President Coolidge. They are going to fix up the Prohibition enforcement. They haven't had time to get around to it before. They took down a Pamphlet thanking Mr. Coolidge for his good example in not breaking the law. The Automobile men are going to draw up one now and take it down and give it to him for not stealing a car during his term of office.

They don't have to have men like Mr. Gary and Rockefeller compliment Mr. Coolidge for keeping the law. He has always kept the law. His worst political enemy could never say he ever broke a law. You remember a few years ago this country had to pass a special law called the Anti Trust law, aimed primarily at these two Trusts, the Oil and the Steel. Now if you have to pass a law to curb men like that they are not exactly the men to give confidence to the rest of our Nation in regard to keeping the law. Getting them to arrange our Morals would be like appointing me as Teacher of English at Harvard.

February 17:

We have great fellows back from the War that can show you two Medals for every sack of Flour they have in the House. Heroing is one of the shortest-lifed professions there is. We do something for every fool thing in the World. One time here in New York I played at a big Benefit to get a Statue of Liberty for Russia. Now can you imagine Russia with a Statue of Liberty? We don't even know if they want one or not. If they do want one, we will loan them ours. Ours has got its back turned on us at the present time, showing us what our Liberty is behind us.

February 22:

The last few days I have read various addresses made on Lincoln's Birthday. Every Politician always talks about him, but none of them ever imitate him. They always make that a day of delivering a Lecture on "Americanism." When an Office Holder, or one that has been found out, can't think of anything to deliver a speech on, he always falls back on the good old subject, AMERICANISM. Now that is the one thing that I have never delivered an Essay on,

either written or spoken. They have all had a crack at it every
Fourth of July and Lincoln's Birthday. So now I am going to
take up the subject and see what I can wrestle out of it. Let's get
our rope ready and turn it out, and we will catch it and see really
what brands it has on it. Here it comes out of the Corral. We got
it caught; now it's throwed and Hog Tied; and we will pick the
Brands and see what they are.

The first thing I find out is there ain't any such animal. This
American Animal that I thought I had here is nothing but the big
Honest Majority, that you might find in any Country. He is not a
Politician, He is not a 100 percent American. He is not any organization, either uplift or downfall. In fact I find he don't belong to
anything. He is no decided Political faith or religion. I can't
even find out what religious brand is on him. From his earmarks
he has never made a speech, and announced that he was An American. He hasn't denounced anything. It looks to me like he is just
an Animal that has been going along, believing in right, doing right,
tending to his own business, letting the other fellows alone.

He don't seem to be simple enough minded to believe that
EVERYTHING is right and he don't appear to be Cuckoo enough
to think that EVERYTHING is wrong. He don't seem to be a
Prodigy, and he don't seem to be a Simp. In fact, all I can find out
about him is that he is just NORMAL. After I let him up and
get on my Horse and ride away I look around and I see hundreds
and hundreds of exactly the same marks and Brands. In fact they
so far outnumber the freaky branded ones that the only conclusion
I can come to is that this Normal breed is so far in majority that
there is no use to worry about the others. They are a lot of Mavericks, and Strays.

A bunch of Bobbed Haired men gathered in Madison Square
Garden last Sunday at a meeting of these Reds, or Bolsheviki, or
whatever they call themselves. It was one of their denouncement
meetings. They denounced the heavy snow, Declaration of Independence, 5 cent Street Car Fare, Floods in Georgia, Mayor Hylan's
Bathing Suit, Twin Beds, and the Eclipse. A Kid 14 years old delivered such a tribute to Lenine that he made it look like George

Washington or Abe Lincoln couldn't have caddied for Lenine. Oh, this Boy had got disgusted with America young in life. Incidentally, while he was making this tirade, NORMALISM of his age, at least a million of them were out skating.

Now some say that a thing like that should not be allowed. Why sure it should be allowed! England can teach any Country in the World how to handle discontent. (Maybe it's because they have more of it.) They give 'em a Park, Hyde Park, they even furnish the Soap Boxes (as the former contents of the Box is generally as foreign to the Speakers as his Nationality is to the Country he is speaking in). Give 'em a Hall or a Box to stand on and say "Sic 'em; knock everything in sight" and when they have denounced everything from Bunions to Capitalistic Bath Tubs, then they will go home, write all week on another speech for the following Sunday and you never have any trouble with them.

It's just like an exhaust on an Automobile. No matter how high priced the Car, you have to have an exit for its bad Air, and Gasses. They have got to come out. It don't do any particular harm, unless you just stand around behind smelling of it all the time, but who would want to follow a Car to smell of its exhaust when you could just as well be in the Car riding?

Now sometimes there is a loud explosion, and everybody on the Streets will turn around and see what it is. The minute they see, they will go right on their business. They know there has been no damage done. So that's how it is with this so called Radical Element. Let them have a Park or a Hall as an exhaust Pipe. Then when they have some particular Noted Denouncer, why, you will hear a loud report. You will listen, or read what he said and go on about your business the same as the listeners to a back fire. You know its necessary.

Now I am not much on History but I don't think any of these people were drafted over here, nor that there are any Immigration Laws in Europe against this Country. I have often thought what would happen if the Government sent somebody to one of those meetings and he got up and announced that he was instructed to send every one of them back to the Country where they come from, and had been raving about. Say, there would be such a stampede they would tear down the building to keep from going. You couldn't Shanghai them out of here.

No, sir! This country is too big now. To stop this Country now would be like spitting on a Railroad track to stop a Train. These Reds are on their backs snoring and they ain't keeping anybody awake but each other. No Element, no Party, not even Congress or the Senate can hurt this Country now; it's too big. There are too many men just like those Dog Team drivers and too many Women like that Nurse up in Nome for anything to ever stampede this old Continent of ours. That's why I can never take a Politician seriously. They are always shouting that "such and such a thing will ruin us, and that this is the eventful year in our Country's life."

Say, all the years are the same. Each one has its little temporary setbacks, but they don't mean a thing in the general result. Nobody is making History. Everybody is just drifting along with the tide. If any office holder feels he is carrying a burden of responsibility, some Fly will light on his back and scratch it off for him some day. Congress can pass a bad law and as soon as the old Normal Majority find it out they have it scratched off the books.

We lost Roosevelt TR, a tough blow. But here we are still kicking. So, if we can spare men like Roosevelt and Wilson there is no use in any other Politician ever taking himself serious.

Henry Ford has been a big factor in the Industrial development of the Country. Yet if he was gone there would still be enough of those things left to clutter up the Highways for Years. John D. Rockefeller who has done a lot for humanity with his Gifts; yet when he is gone and Gasoline raises 2 Cents, and all expenses and the Estate is settled we will kick along. *Even when our next War comes we will through our shortsightedness not be prepared, but that won't be anything fatal. The real energy and minds of the Normal Majority will step in and handle it and fight it through to a successful conclusion.* A war didn't change it before. It's just the same as it was, and alway will be, because it is founded on right and even if everybody in Public Life tried to ruin it they couldn't. This Country is not where it is today on account of any man. It is here on account of the real common Sense of the big Normal Majority. A Politician is just like a Necktie Salesman in a big Department Store. If he decides to give all the Ties away, or decided to pocket all the receipts, it don't affect the Store. It don't close. He closes, as soon as he is found out.

So I can find nothing for alarm in our immediate future. The next time a Politician gets spouting off about what this Country needs, either hit him with a tubercular Tomato or lay right back in your seat and go to sleep. Because THIS COUNTRY HAS GOT TOO BIG TO NEED A DAMN THING.

March 1:

It may interest you to know that five of the Will Rogers articles have been read on the floor of Congress and printed in the Congressional Record as representing a typical American view of important public subjects.

When a Gentleman quoted me on the floor of Congress the other day, another member took exception and said he objected to the remarks of a Professional Joke Maker going into the Congressional Record.

Now can you beat that for jealousy among people in the same line? Calling me a Professional Joke Maker! He is right about everything but the Professional. THEY are the Professional Joke Makers. Read some of the Bills that they have passed, if you think they ain't Joke makers. I could study all my life and not think up half the amount of funny things they can think of in one Session of Congress. Besides my jokes don't do anybody any harm. You don't have to pay any attention to them. But everyone of the jokes those Birds make is a LAW and hurts somebody (generally everybody).

"Joke Maker!" He couldn't have coined a better term for Congress if he had been inspired. But I object to being called a Professional. I am an Amateur beside them. If I had that Guy's unconscious Humor, Ziegfeld couldn't afford to pay me I would be so funny.

Of course I can understand what he was objecting to was any

common Sense creeping into the Record. It was such a Novelty, I guess it did sound funny.

And, by the way, I have engaged counsel and if they ever put any more of my material in that "Record of Inefficiency" I will start suit for deformation of Character. I don't want my stuff buried away where Nobody ever reads it. I am not going to lower myself enough to associate with them in a Literary way.

March 29:

Statistics prove that no Vermonter ever left the State unless transportation was furnished in advance. She is what you call a "Hard Boiled State." The principal ingredients are Granite, Rock Salt and Republicans. The last being the hardest of the three.

* * * * *

If Parties are supposed to have to vote together on everything, let each Party only send one man from the entire United States. Why pay these others to just be a lot of Sheep? Party Politics is the most narrow minded occupation in the World. A Guy raised in a straight Jacket is a Corkscrew compared to a thick headed Party Politician.

All you would have to do to make some men Atheists is just to tell them the Lord belonged to the opposition Political Party. After that they could never see any good in him.

May 10:

General Mitchell came and got me and we drove across the river to an aviation field. An assistant handed me a straight jacket, a kind of a one-piece suicide suit and a kind of a derby hat with the brim turned down over your ears. It slowly began to dawn on me that at last there was going to be some flying done in the Army, and that I was supposed to be one of the participants.

There is an old legend that says, "Nine-tenths of the brave things done are performed through fear." Whoever concocted this aforementioned legend certainly had this air voyage of mine in mind. I did not want to see Washington by air. In fact I never had any desire to see anything from the air.

Well, there was so many standing around that there was no way to back out. Right at the moment I thought the fellows who were trying to get this Mitchell out of the air service were right, and I wished they had got him out sooner. He says, "Do you use cotton in your ears?" He seemed to think that I was an old experienced aviator. I says: "No, I only use cotton in my ears when I visit the Senate Gallery." I couldn't imagine what the cotton was for unless it was to keep the dirt out of your ears in case of a fall.

Photographers were there to get our picture. I could just see the picture with this label under it: "Last Photograph Taken of Deceased." But Mr. Mitchell stopped them and asked them if they would mind waiting until we came back. Well, that didn't make me feel any too good. It looked like there might be a doubt in his mind as to whether we would come back. There was a superstition connected with it some way that didn't make me feel any better. Still, it didn't make me feel any worse, because I was just as worse as I could feel. But I never let on. I remembered how nice the papers always speak of a man who goes to the gallows with a smile on his face, and how they laud his nerve.

A man buckles you in so that you won't change your mind after you leave the ground. Mitchell says, "I will point out the places of interest to you." I didn't see him point nor I didn't see what he pointed at. I have always heard when you are up on anything high, don't look down; look up. So all I saw was the sky.

Washington's home at Mount Vernon might have been Bryan's in Miami for all I know. We flew around Washington Monument and if the thing had had handles on it he would have lost a passenger.

Here I was thousands of feet up in the air when you can't even get me to ride a tall horse. I had always figured that if the Lord intended a man to do any flying he would have sprouted something out of his back besides just shoulder blades. He asked me if I saw the Mayflower, the President's private tug. How was I going to see it unless it was flying over us? I didn't come any nearer seeing

it than I'll ever come to riding on it. When we landed and got out
and walked away I was tickled to death. I thought the drama was
all over. But it wasn't.

The most impressive part of the whole thing was in his next few
words. He says: "You have been with me on the last flight I will
ever make as a Brigadier-General. Tonight at twelve o'clock I
am to be demoted to a Colonel and sent to a far away Post where,
instead of having the entire air force at my command, there will
be seven planes." Well, I got a real thrill out of that. To think
that I had accompanied such a man on such a memorable flight.

I had a long talk with Mitchell. He never squealed and he never
whined. He knows that some day America will have to have a
tremendous air force, but he can't understand why we are not
training it now. But it does seem a strange way to repay a man
who has fought for us through a war, and who has fought harder
for us in Peace to be reprimanded for telling the truth. And wasn't
it a coincidence that we had just flown over Washington's home,
the Father of our Country, whose first claim to Fame was telling
the truth about a Cherry Tree! But George wasn't in the Army
then, and the Cherry Tree had nothing to do with our National
Defense.

May 24:

I have worked at affairs for every denomination in the World
here in New York, because one is just as worthy as the other. Old
New York, the so-called heartless city, houses some great people
in every denomination in the world, and I can't see any difference
in them. I haven't been able to see where one has the monopoly
on the right course to Heaven.

* * * * *

Today, as I write this, I am not in the Follies, the carefree Comedian who jokes about everything. I am out in Oklahoma, among
my People, my Cherokee people, who don't expect a laugh for
everything I say. Back home, at the funeral of my Sister.

She and my other sister started in this little Western Town —

Chelsea, Oklahoma — some 35 years ago. They helped build the Methodist Church, the first church there. They have helped every Church, they have helped every movement that they knew was for the best upbuilding of their community. They have each raised a large family of Boys and Girls who are today a credit to their community. They have carried on the same as thousands of Women have carried on in every small and Big Town in the World. They don't think they are doing anything out of the ordinary. They don't want credit. They do good simply because they don't know any other thing to do.

Death didn't scare her. It was only an episode in her life. If you live right, death is a Joke to you as far as fear is concerned.

After all, there is nothing in the world like home. You can roam all over the world, but after all, it's what the people at home think of you that really counts. I have just today witnessed a Funeral that for real sorrow and real affection I don't think will ever be surpassed anywhere. They came in every mode of conveyance, on foot, in Buggies, Horseback, Wagons, Cars, and Trains, and there wasn't a Soul that come that she hadn't helped or favored at one time or another.

Some uninformed Newspapers printed: "Mrs. C. L. Lane sister of the famous Comedian, Will Rogers." They were greatly misinformed. It's the other way around. I am the brother of Mrs. C. L. Lane, "The Friend of Humanity." And all the honors that I could ever in my wildest dreams hope to reach, would never equal the honor paid on a little western Prairie hilltop, among her people, to Maud Lane. If they will love me like that at the finish, my life will not have been in vain.

June 7:

A few days ago there was a man hung somewhere and there was thousands of people to see it. In Sing Sing a few weeks ago there was three young fellows Electrocuted and there was over two thousand applications to the Warden to see them go to their Death. Imagine if you can people who want to see somebody else killed! Sometime they ought to turn around and turn the Electricity on every one of the Spectators that didn't actually have to be there by Law.

Anybody whose pleasure is watching somebody else die, is about as little use to humanity as the Person being electrocuted. There is some excuse for the man being electrocuted. He may be innocent, he may have killed in a wild rage of passion; or not in his right mind, or self-defense. But the people who asked to come there just for the outing — there is no excuse in the World for them. I believe I could stand to be the Victim rather than to see one. I bet if the Warden did turn the Juice on these Spectators, any Jury in the World would set him free.

June 28:

America has a great habit of always talking about protecting American interests in some foreign Country. PROTECT 'EM HERE AT HOME! There is more American Interests right here than anywhere. If an American goes to Mexico and his Horse dies, we send them a Note wanting American Interests preserved and the horse paid for.

We don't guarantee investments here at home. Why should we make Mexico guarantee them? Our Papers are always harping on US developing Mexico. Suppose Mexico don't want developing. Maybe they want it kept as it was years ago. How much do Americans spend in the Summer to get to some places where there is no development — No Street Cars, Elevators, Fords, Telephones, Radios, and a million and one other things that you just like to get away from once in awhile? Well, suppose they don't want 'em at all down there. Why don't you let every Nation do and act as they please? What business is it of ours how Mexico acts or lives?

If America is not good enough for you to live in and make money in, why, then you are privileged to go to some other Country. But don't ask protection from a Country that was not good enough for you. If you want to make money out of a Country, why, take out their Citizenship Papers and join them. Don't use one Country for Money and another for convenience. The difference in our exchange of people with Mexico is; they send workmen here to work, while we send Americans there to "work" Mexico.

America and England, especially, are regular old Busybodies when it comes to telling somebody else what to do. But you notice they (England and America) never tell each other what to do. You bet your life they don't!

Big Nations are always talking about Honor. Yet England promised to protect France against Germany, IF FRANCE WOULD PAY THEM WHAT THEY OWED THEM. They act as a Police Force for pay.

What is the consequence? As soon as Germany gets strong enough so she thinks she can lick both of them there will be another War.

* * * * *

The Lord put all these millions of people over the earth. They don't all agree on how they got there, and ninety percent don't care. But he was pretty wise when he did see to it that they all do agree on one thing, (whether Christian, Heathen, or Mohammedan) and that is the better lives you live the better you will finish.

August 16:
This trip of the fleet to Australia was planned with our Pacific fleet to impress Japan with the size of it. That was not necessary. Japan knows more about our war strength now than either of our Secretaries of War or Navy.

August 30:
I'll tell you about Temperament. Temperament is liable to arrive with a little success, especially if you haven't been used to success. The best cure in the world for temperament is hunger. I have never seen a Poor temperamental person.

October 4:
Well, when you read these immaculate English lines, I may have met some of you personally. I break out into what is advertised as an alleged "Lecture Tour," on the night of October first, at Elmira, New York. If I survive I proceed. If not, they should at least announce to the world what happened to me. We can't

find out what to call it. It's not exactly a Lecture but by the time
you read this it will perhaps have been named. I think we will
get a Title for it from the comment the two fellows will exchange on
leaving the Elmira Opera House. It's a kinder get-together tour
to meet my readers, and I want to meet them personally in my
dressing room, each one of them. Business concerns go over the
country every once in a while to meet what they call their "men in
the field." Now that is the prime object of my pilgrimage. My
readers are the "men in the field" and we want to get together on
what is the best way to remedy the running of National affairs
during the coming year. I do hope I last long enough to reach
your town. If it's got a railroad and a Town Hall we will be there
sooner or later. A Man only learns by two things, one is reading
and the other is association with smarter people. I don't like to
read, and one can't find the associates in New York. I am going
out among the people whom New Yorkers call Rubes. But these
people I am going out among are the people that just look at New
Yorkers and laugh.

October 18:

All I used to know was just what I read in the papers. But that
was when I was "Shanghaied" in New York, because all anybody
knows in New York is just what they read in the papers. But
NOW all I know is just what I see myself. What I see I can understand, but what I read — there is a terrible lot of that I can't
"savvy."

Now that I am looking over America I am going to be able to
tell you something besides "Who Ann Pennington is going with
this season," and "What Millionaire has been in the front row four
nights running." I am out to see how America is living, I mean the
ones that don't go home and brag on what everything cost 'em.
No sir. I have seen him in New York; we have had him out in
front of our footlights for years: he is the one that cusses New York
but still goes there for no reason in the world, and then says, "I
had to on business, or I would never come near the place." No,
he is not the one I am out hunting.

I am meeting the regular Bird — the one that lives in his town; stays in his town; is proud of his town; he offers no apology for not having seen last year's Follies, or any other year's. I wanted to find out what he was thinking about; what he was reading about.

October 21 [*Telegram to Will*]:

WILL ROGERS

FONTENELLE HOTEL

OMAHA, NEBRASKA.

DEAR BILL: I READ WITH INTEREST IN THE WORLD THAT YOU HELD ME UP FOR YEARS. WELL, BILL, I AM WILLING TO BE HELD UP SOME MORE. WHEN WILL YOU START AGAIN?

ZIEGFELD

November 1:

After 20 years, playing your home State for the first time! I have had many a Follies opening night, but the opening night in Tulsa — Well it was the night of nights.

November 15:

I am no believer in this "hard work, perseverance, and taking advantage of your opportunities" that these Magazines are so fond of writing some fellow up in. The successful don't work any harder than the failures. They get what is called in baseball the breaks.

Everyone has deep in their heart the old town or community where they first went barefooted, got their first licking, traded the first pocket knife, grew up and finally went away thinking they were too big for that Burg. But that's where your old heart is.

I have been over 20 years trying to kid the great American Public out of a few loose giggles now and again. Somebody had to act the fool, and I happened to be one of the many that picked out *that unfunny business of trying to be funny.* Now I will tell you why I am happy and nothing don't matter to me now. After acting a

Fool all over the World and part of Iowa, I have been back home, and they seemed glad to see me, and they laughed at me.

They laughed at me MORE than New York or London or Omaha. Now that don't mean anything to you. But it meant something to me. My HOME FOLKS thought I was good. I know lots of Theatre-goers that will disagree with them. But what do I care for them? What do I care for anything? The old home State and the old home Town and the old ranch people I was born and raised with, I got by with them. Twenty years of doubt and expectations as to just what they would think of you.

But one of the things that worried me was, "What's he trying to do; fool us, come here with nothing and get our money just out of old time's sake?" The local manager asked me if I minded if he seated people on the stage. Well, that scared me more than ever. I walked around the building three times before I finally went in the Stage entrance.

They literally had to push me out. I had never seen such an audience in my life. They were packed in, standing at the back, and sitting in the aisles and over three hundred seated BEHIND me on the stage. Two little girls come up and gave me a great Floral piece. Well, I had never received flowers before in my life, and that did stick me. It had been sent by my Home Town. Well, after it seemed like ages, I got started, and they laughed, and they would laugh so long it would give me time to think of another one. Here it was the biggest audience I had ever faced and here it was the Best audience I had ever faced.

Well, they kept on seeming to want more till I did two Hours and fifteen minutes. That's I think a Minor League Record for Monologists. That made all the opening nights in New York I have worried with seem like rehearsals. Just think, back home and they liked you! That was a Kick. It's not the highest type of work, this being a fool, and a Comedian may not excite much envy. But its the best I will ever get, and I felt good enough that night to last me the rest of my life.

Back Home, among the people that I would saw off a leg to make good with. Bring on your towns where they don't think much of you (and we have had some of them since then, they wasn't all Tulsas). But what do I care? I am going to always do my best, no matter where I am, but it was the Home folks that had been worrying me, and its what worries everybody if they will admit it. There is a million Towns in the United States, and a million communities. Pick out a million people and ask them where they would rather be thought well of, and they will say, "Back Home." Gee, I am lucky. I fooled 'em at Home.

December 13:

Now, when I left New York awhile ago, I told you I wanted to get out and find out what was going on. I was tired being like all OTHER BIG Eastern Editors, rewrite something I had already seen written.

Well, when I write you of Texas, I know about it. I have been all through the State. Half of my entire act while in Texas consisted of local things on Texas. I talked with every Editor in each town, all the writers on the papers, Hotel Managers, Ranchmen, Farmers, Politicians, Head Waiters, Barbers, Newsboys, Bootblacks. Everybody I met I would try and get their angle.

CHAPTER ELEVEN

Letters of a Self-Made Diplomat to His President

In 1926 the Saturday Evening Post sent Will to Europe as an unofficial ambassador for President Coolidge (who only knew it by mental telepathy). Will reported his findings in the Post as "Letters of a Self-Made Diplomat to His President" and brought them out in a book by the same name.

Upon his return from Europe Will went to Beverly Hills and was made Mayor with great fanfare. Almost immediately he began his second lecture tour of the United States to get acquainted with "the real bird." He had competition this time from Queen Marie of Roumania who was interested in America — dearly interested to the tune of getting a multi-million dollar loan for her country. Will also fought for space in the paper with "Peaches" Browning, who was getting rid of her "Papa" and with Aimee Semple McPherson, who always made news.

January 3:

Last week I was away up in Boston. Can you imagine me appearing at Symphony Hall in Boston? From the Stock Yards of Claremore, Oklahoma, to Symphony Hall, Boston! Me, with my Repertoire of 150 words (most of them wrong), trying to enlighten the descendants of the Cod. But they were fine. Say, you come right down to it, that Intelligence and culture thing is a lot of Applesauce. Ford Jokes got over bigger there than in Waco, Texas. Just one old boy there that thought we were "desecrating" their temple of Art by causing laughter in it.

We had been out 75 nights all over the country and everybody had been wonderful to us. Hadn't received an adverse notice. So this was our last night of the tour. Well, this old Soul is a Musical Critic. Now, can you imagine yourself raising your son up to be a Male Musical Critic? If one of my boys ever starts shedding off to be a Male Musical Critic the rope that I have played with for life will be put to some practical use. Now you can imagine about how much Humor a man to take up a thing like that must have. His name is Parker. Having a trained musical ear, why naturally my jokes were "Off Key" most of the time. "The diction was poor." My "selections" were extremely bad.

This old Critic learned his first "Criticizing" at Harvard. You know it's been said that "when you graduate from Harvard or Yale it takes the next 10 years to live it down and the next 40 to try to forget it." Well, he thought my "High Register" was on the bum, and my "Low Registered Notes had no roundness to them." Even my "resonance" was in the wrong place.

Dramatic Critics review my part of the show. So I can readily understand your handicap. You were just taking in too much territory. It would be like sending an artist out to look at a Rembrandt for somebody and then at the last minute asking him to stop on the way back and see what Farmer Jones' yearlings look like they were worth.

In short, when you looked me over you were "Slumming." In other words the old Tradition got to working. But you unconsciously paid me a Bear of a Compliment when you said "Will is a small town Actor."

You bet your life I am small town. I am smaller than that. I am NO town at all, and listen, that is what I am going to stay is Small Town.

Bless your old soul, Parker, I bet if I met you we would like each other fine. Because in your own heart you couldn't blame an old Country boy for wanting to finally get into the Symphony Hall of Boston, and I am broadminded enough to see your angle too. It's your pet; it's your life's work. You want to see only the best in there. You have high ideals for it, and I don't blame you. It is beautiful.

Now when I come back up there next year you are the first man I am going to look up, and I bet you we have a good dinner and we will kill off that old Indigestion of yours, and I will have a lot of good jokes against Yale, and maybe Harvard will have won a football game in that time and you will all be feeling good. But give me credit for one thing, Parker. Wasn't that English of mine the Worst that was ever spoken in that Hall?

January 10:

Now, when I tell you that if I was running the Government, there would be No lowering of Taxes, you know now a Comedian is crazy.

President Coolidge says that we are approaching an era of prosperity. Everybody generally admits that we are better off than we ever were in our lives, yet we owe a National debt of almost 30 Billions of dollars.

We owe more money than any Nation in the World, and We ARE LOWERING TAXES. When is the time to pay off a debt if it is not when you are doing well? All Government statistics say that 70 percent of every dollar paid in the way of taxes goes to just the keeping up our interest and a little dab of amortization of our National Debts. In other words, if we didn't owe anything our taxes would only be less than one third what they are today. Well, if two-thirds of what you pay goes to keeping up just Interest, why don't we do our best to try and cut down the principal, so it will lower that tremendous interest? We howl and holler about "Why don't Europe pay?" Why don't we pay ourselves?

Now, here is what I can't savvy. Why is it that one of us, in fact all of us, will work and save, and stint all our lives. For what? Why, to leave something to our children. When we die we want everything we have left clear and unemcumbered. We will break our necks to leave them without a single debt. In fact we won't die if we can help it till we get out of debt for their sake. Now that is what we will do as individuals, BUT, when it comes to COLLECTIVELY, why it looks like we will break our neck to see HOW MUCH we can leave them owing.

* * * * *

You know Americans have been getting away pretty soft up to now. Every time we needed anything, why it was growing right under our nose. Every natural resource in the world, we had it. But with them getting less, and debts getting more, there is going to be some work going on in this country some day. We will have prosperity and get along fine now for a couple of years and then something will happen and we won't be doing so well. Well then they will raise taxes again, but they will wait till we ain't doing very well.

Miami, Florida, February 21:

Grantland Rice was down here to cover the Outdoor Checker Championship of the World. They play in the sun down here, and the game is much faster and open on an outdoor board. Grantland is picking the All American Checker Team of 1926, and also covers the Worlds Series Horseshoe hurling Contests. The Champion Mule Slipper Slingers of the world are at St. Petersburg. They got Guys there that can take a pair of Horses' Pumps and wrap them around an iron stob 40 feet away, when you or I couldn't hit it that often with a shot gun. They can take a pair of second hand Horses' low quarters and hang 'em on a peg more times than a dry Congressman can reach for his hip pocket.

March 7:

I had a great time last week. I don't know of any week I have been out when I got around and saw more old friends and old

places that I wanted to see again, than I did last week. I been on
the stage for 20 years and I love it. There has never been a time
when I didn't like my job. But do you know, really, at heart I
love ranching. I have always regretted that I didn't live about
30 or 40 years earlier, and in the same old Country, the Indian
Territory. I would have liked to got here ahead of the "Nestors,"
the Bob wire fence, and so called civilization.

A lot of old Cowpuncher acquaintances in El Paso wired and
wanted to give me a dinner party. I answered, "There will be
no Dinner. We will go to Juarez and get some Hot Tamales."

April 24:
Well, we have just been everywhere this year. Had the greatest
and most enjoyable year I have ever experienced in all my little
Theatrical career. I have been out all over the country and met
some of the greatest people, and I sure did enjoy playing to them.
They are a great bunch. They don't come to a show to criticize it.
They come in with the idea of having a good time, and they give
you the benefit of the doubt every time. And read? Say, the
audiences in the smaller towns make a monkey out of the big
Cities for knowing what is going on in the world. They know and
read everything.

*   *   *   *   *

Carnegie Hall is where they have all the "Big" Concerts. If a
foreign Fiddler comes here, as soon as he is fumigated they throw
him down and get a Musician's dress suit on him, and put him in
Carnegie Hall for a "Recital." Foreign singers, as soon as they
have lived long enough to learn enough songs for what they call
an Evening's entertainment, go there and give a "Recital." Piano
players are one of the principal commodities that haunt the central
portion of the stage. It seems to kinder be the New York test.
Men who have been let out of regular jobs in Theatre orchestras
form themselves into a gang and add the word "Symphony" and
go in there and play "William Tell" for two hours. It sponsors
every form of artistic graft in the World. You show in there, and
you either go to work after at some useful employment or remain
on the fringes of Art.

Well, this Art thing kinder worried me. I had never by any stretch of imagination been associated with it. So I thought we ought to be playing the Columbia Terrace Theatre on 47 St. instead of Carnegie Hall. I was explaining my predicament to Walter C. Kelly, the Virginia Judge, whom you all know as absolutely America's premier story teller. Walter says, "Well, Will, you have one novelty to recommend you up in that Hall. You will be the only short-haired Guy that ever played that joint."

I know one thing; I am the only one that didn't attempt to try to have on a Dress Suit. I have seen a lot of Artists' dress suits and I knew I couldn't compete with them, so I didn't rent one. I just stuck to the old Blue Serge with the mirror effect in the seat and knees. If it was good enough for Ponca City, and Muskogee it was good enough for Uncle Andy's Temple of Art.

I have tried 'em all here now. I started out in Madison Square Garden roping at a horse, and there is just where I wish I was tonight as the circus is there, and that is just about where I will land up.

Will's trip out to meet the "real bird" in America was just a prelude to a widening of his horizon. In his column on April 15 appeared the following:

I had lunch yesterday at Philadelphia with Mr. George Horace Lorimer, Editor of the Saturday Evening Post, and I am going over to Europe for the Post. I am going all around over there. I am really going to represent President Coolidge. You see, he hasn't a Col. House to run over and fix up things, so that is what I am to be. I want to get away about the middle of May. I want to catch Mussolini while he is going good, and before some better shot gets in their work. I am also to go to Ireland and see what's keeping them so quiet, and if they really are happy, and into Germany and Russia and Spain. I want to see what reason they had for wanting to try to get into the next war by way of the League of Nations.

* * * * *

My trip come at a time when foreign relations are at their most perilous peak; that is, when we were trying to collect money. Any man can fight a war, but it takes a smart man to jar any loose change out of any part of Europe. Especially when they have already eat up the money that was loaned them.

It is much easier for America to whip a Nation than it is for them to collect a dollar from them. I have to go abroad when we are as welcome as rent collectors.

May 12:

My dear Mr. President: There will be a Song hitting you now if it hassent already hit you. Do what you can to keep people from going entirely cuckoo over it. It is in exchange for Yes, We Have no Bananas, and is called Valencia. It was written for Mistinguette, a singer in a Review in Paris. It ain't the Piece — it's all right — it's the amount of times they will play it. Have Ear Muffs ready.

London, May 18:

Lady Astor wanted me to give my ideas to a lot of her friends and fellow M.P.'s. This is not meant for Mounted Policemen, but it's for Members of Parliament. To be a Mounted Policeman you have to stand a very rigid examination both mentally and physically, and serve a very rigid apprenticeship for the position; while with the other M.P.'s there is no requirement necessary.

These M.P. fellows there in the room, they were just about like a bunch of old Nesters elected to congregate at Oklahoma City, or Austin, or Bismark, every two years. They were just about like those old Birds over home. They were just spending this term trying to get back the next. The welfare of the country generally felt a little heavier around their November fourth. But I liked them and I like those over home. We cuss 'em and we joke about 'em, but they are all good fellows at heart; and if they wasent in that, why, they would be doing something else against us that might be worse. For instance, you meeting a Democrat and saying, "I am glad to meet you." Well, that has to be done. It is a custom. But of course, get right down to it, you are not glad to meet him at all. You are just human and wish there wasent such a thing.

Well I am going by Geneva and see this disarmament thing. There will be 21 nations there, and outside of England and France and America, the others will take it serious.

Naples, May 25:

You ought to see the tourists here. Where you haven't seen anything in your own Country, have never been further away from
home than the barn, why those are the people who go see Italy.
It's to the Tourists what Hollywood is to the visiting Iowans.

Pompaei, that was at one time the Beverly Hills of Italy, was
caught in a landslide. It covered the city with a second mortgage.
You should see Pompaei. Philadelphia comes nearer approaching
it than any big City I know of.

I must tell you about Naples, that's the railroad stop for Pompaei. But on our right as we go back there is a mountain, or high
hill rather, looks like somebody had plowed up the top of it.
Well that's Vesuvius. Vesuvius is kinder known in history as being
a sort of local Police or enforcement mountain, when some City
got to putting it on a little too strong in the way of Night life, why
Vesuvius makes a raid on them and its generally so complete that
their mode of living is entirely remodeled. That's why I am going
to move out of Hollywood and Beverly Hills. It just seems an act
of providence, that there is a mountain right back of them the size
of Vesuvius. Now I am not saying this to knock Real Estate values
there. Paris, France and Claremore, Oklahoma, had the right
idea; they built out on the flat not near any Mountain. You can
get away with anything in those two places, without fear of a
moral landslide.

The greatest gag over here anywhere is the Goats they have
driving around the streets in place of milk wagons. I am the last
one in the world to see anything and not see some good in it.
There is no chance of watered stock, the Milk you get may not be
the particular kind of milk that you would like to have but it's
what you ordered, and thats more than you can say at home.
Its Goat's milk, its pure extract of Angora, no pump connection
anywhere. You drink Goats milk steady for two weeks and you
can butt your way into a Bronx local. Three months steady on it,
and you have cloven hoofs and an odor. That's why so many
Singers and Tenors come from Italy. There is no voice advancement in Cow juice. It's the shrill bleat of the Nanny that brings
out all that is worst in a Tenor. If you cant afford to go to Italy

to study why just get a Goat and develop your Soprano at home.

July 11:

Switzerland is the most independent country in the world. They have neither imports nor exports. Its sole commodities are Conferences and Neutrality. When Nations get ready to make peace or war (and generally don't know which they are making), why they always go to Switzerland. Geneva and Locarno are the principal conference towns. It's kinder like Atlantic City is for bathing Contests (without water). It has a corner on all Conferences. It has had fewer wars and has been the starting place of more of them than any Nation that ever lived. They just sit around and remain Neutral during these wars and then collect from all ends. It's the only country where both sides can go and meet and have a drink together during that particular war. Switzerland is a kind of a Speakeasy for any and all sides. There is little private rooms all over and anybody can come and meet anybody else and Switzerland just winks knowingly and says nothing. It's the Blind Tiger of Europe.

Their grandstands were built by nature. All they had to do was to get the hotels ready to take care of the guests or accomplices of a war that are always around but never really in one. They built roads up to the topmost peaks so you could get a close-up of the wars.

They had really what is an all the year around business. The minute a war was over, if there was none booked to start within the next few weeks, why they would hold what they called a "Peace Conference" to prevent other wars. Well now off hand you would think a country wouldn't allow a conference to be held there that would be for the purpose of taking away their means of livelihood. But they were smart. They had made a close study of history for hundreds and hundreds of years back and an old smart one of them told the others, "Don't interfere with them holding these peace meetings here. Let them go ahead. They are held after every war, since Adam first swung on Eve for not having his breakfast Apple there on time. When she came to, her and Adam held a Peace Conference. It was to do away with all wars between

Husband and Wife." Confer or fight; it don't make any difference to Switzerland. They are going to get theirs either way.

July 29 [*First of Will's Daily wires*]:

Nancy Astor, which is the nome de plume of Lady Astor, is arriving on your side about now. She is the best friend America has here. Please ask my friend Jimmy Walker [*mayor of New York*] to have New York take good care of her. She is the only one over here that doesn't throw rocks at the American tourists.

In August Will Flew to Russia for a visit to this "boarding-house hash of Nations." He wrote a series of articles on what he saw there for the Saturday Evening Post *which came out in a book.*[1] *In both he warned:*

Suppose somebody tried to write on the Heart of America. Why, Lord, we can't even keep track of the toe of Maine or the heel of California, much less the heart. Now if anybody could write a Composite Article on America, how are they going to do it on Russia, a country that is so much bigger than us that we would rattle around in it like an idea in Congress.

Will just wanted to see what the place looked like. Particularly, he wanted to see Trotzky. An official refused.

I told him the nature of the visit to Trotsky was to find out just what kind of a Guy he was personally. I just wanted to see did he drink, eat, sleep, laugh and act human, or was his whole life taken up with the betterment of mankind.

Will told the official that what Russia needed was more of a sense of humor and less of a sense of revenge.

The official's reply was: We are a very serious people; we do not go in for fun and laughter. In running a large country like this we have no time for appearing frivolous. We have a great work to perform for the betterment of mankind.

I saw this old boy wasent so strong on me X-raying Trotsky, [*Will said*] I bet if I had met him [*Trotsky*] and had a chat with him I would have found him a very interesting and human fellow, for I never met a man that I dident like. When you meet people, no matter what opinions you might have formed about them be-

---

[1] *Not a Bathing Suit in Russia*, Albert & Charles Boni Inc.

forehand, why, after you meet them and see their angle and their personality, why, you can see a lot of good in all of them.

[*Will let that X-ray mind of his look into corners and nooks as he prowled around.*] The real fellow that is running the whole thing is a Bird named Stalin, a great big two-fisted egg from away down in the Caucasian Mountains. He is the Borah of the Black Sea. . . . He is the stage manager of Bolshevism right now. He don't hold any great high position himself, but he tells the others what ones they will hold. Well, Trotzky is kinder not sitting at his round table at lunch.

There are two main words in Russia, [*he explained*] one is Bourgeois and the other is Proletariat. Now Proletariat means the poor people, or what would be known in America as the Democrats; and the word Bourgeois means the rich people, which in America would be known as Republicans; or if they are very rich, the Conservative Republican Party.

You can ask a Russian any question in the world, and if you give him long enough he will explain their angle, and it will sound plausible enough. Communism to me is one-third practice and two-thirds explanation. . . . It's absolutely impossible for any Socialist to say anything in a few words. You say, "Is it light or dark?" and it takes him two volumes to answer Yes or No; and then you know there is a catch in it somewhere. It's like a Theatrical contract. If one of them tells beyond the Salary and the amount of weeks you are to work, why, you might just as well light a cigarette with it. More words ain't good for anything in the world only to bring on more argument.

If the Communists worked just as hard as they talked, they'd have the most prosperous style of government in the world.

Liberty, [*he warned*] don't work as good in practice as in Speech. You got to figure that bunch of fellows are playing with the biggest toy in the world (and the most dangerous).

Now handling this bunch of fellows [*Russia*] would just be like Judge Gary coming backstage at the Follies and saying, "Here, Will, you and the Girls take over the Steel Corporation and run it." . . . Now you have to have some kind of training to handle something big or else you have to do a lot of practicing on it after you get it, which is generally pretty expensive. Most of those fellows were on little Communist Newspapers. Now America has withstood some pretty rough handling at times, but I sure would hate to see it fall under the management of a troop of our Dissatisfied Newspaper men. Put it in the hands of an old hard-headed Farmer or a small-town Merchant, but deliver it from Editors. They would have more Theories how to run us than the Communists. So you got to give these fellows a little bit of the benefit of the doubt. They are practicing and are trying to do the best they can, but unfortunately they are practicing on 130,000,000 people that have to remain the horrible example till these Guys find out themselves just what it's all about.

This guy Marx, why, he was like one of these efficiency experts. He could explain to you how you could save a million dollars and he couldent save enough himself to eat on. . . . He never did a tap of work only write propaganda. . . . He wrote for the dissatisfied, and the dissatisfied is the fellow who don't want to do any manual labor. He always wants to figure out where he and his friends can get something for nothing. . . .

You know a Communist's whole life work is based on complaint of how everything is being done. Well, when they are running everything themselves, why, that takes away their chief industry. They have nobody to blame it on. Even if he is satisfied with it, why, he is miserable because he has nothing to complain about. Same way with strikes and Revolutions. They would rather stir up a strike than eat. So, naturally, in Russia with themselves, they feel rather restrained, for they are totally unable to indulge in their old favorite sport of going on strike and jumping on a box and inviting all the boys out with them. You make one satisfied and he is no longer a Communist. So if they ever get their country running good they will defeat their own cause. A Russian thrives on adversity. He is never as happy in his life as when he is miserable. So he may just be setting pretty, for he is certainly miserable. It may be just the land for a Comrade to want to hibernate in.

The funny part about it among those American ones you meet over their visiting, they are all so nice and friendly and enthusiastic about it, and believe in it way above our form of government; but they all go back over home. It just looks to me like Communism is such a happy-family affair that a Communist would want to stay where it is practiced. It's the only thing they want you to have but keep none themselves. . . .

Met a big nice jovial fellow from Chicago . . . forgot his name, said he run for President on the Socialist ticket the year Jimmy Cox did. I told him I could faintly remember Jimmy, for he happened to be a good friend of mine, but I couldent remember him. He said he runs pretty near ever year on that Ticket — said, "I may run this year." I told him there was no Presidential election this year unless there was an impeachment.

He said, "Ain't there? Well, mebbe it's next year then; I don't pay much 'tention to what years I am running and what years I am not."

It's just Russia as it has been for hundreds of years and will be for the next hundreds of years. . . . People don't change under Governments, the Governments change, but the people remain the same. Russia under the Czar was very little different from what it is today; for instead of one Czar, why, there is at least a thousand now. Any of the big men in the Party holds practically Czaristic powers (to those down). Siberia is still working. It's just as cold on you to be sent there under the Soviets as it was under the Czar. The only way you can tell a Member of the Party from an ordinary Russian is the Soviet man will be in a Car. . . .

There is as much class distinction in Russia today as there is in Charleston, South Carolina. Why, I went to the races there, and the grand stand had all the men of the Party, and over in the center field stood the mob in the sun. Well, there was Bourgeois and Proletariat distinction for you. . . .

What has all these millions of innocent, peace-loving people done that through no fault of their own they should be thrown into a mess like this, with no immediate hope of relief?

They are at heart just big, simple, kind-hearted, God-fearing people. They try to lead these Russians to believe that all their troubles all these years have been directly traceable to their religion; that if they throw over their devout religion everything will be all right. Course you have to admit that fanatical religion driven to a certain point is almost as bad as none at all, but not quite.

Now they will tell you that the worship of Leninism is their religion. Lenin preached Revolution, Blood and Murder in everything I ever read of his. Now they may dig 'em up a religion out of that, but it's too soon after his death really to tell just how great he was. History has to ramble along a good many years after a man puts some policies into effect till you can tell just how they turned out. . . . You know, there is a lot of big men die, but most of them are not so big that they won't all be buried. Now Lenin may come through right on through the ages, but at the present time they are kinder forcing him on the people. They make the children speak of him as Uncle Lenin. Now it's always best to let the people pick out their own Hero. Don't try to force one on them; it's liable to have the opposite effect sometimes.

Mind you, you can't condemn everybody just because they started a Revolution. We grabbed what little batch of liberty *we used to have* through a revolution, and other Nations have revolutions to thank today. But I don't think anyone that just made a business of proposing them for a steady diet would be the one to pray to and try to live by.

We all know a lot of things that would be good for our Country, but we wouldn't want to go so far as propose that everybody start shooting each other till we got them. A fellow shouldent have to kill anybody just to prove they are right. If the Bolsheviks say that religion was holding the people back from progress, why, let it hold them back. Progress ain't selling that high. If it is, it ain't worth it. Do anything in this world but monkey with somebody else's religion. What reasoning of conceit makes anyone think theirs is right? It's better to let people die ignorant and poor, believing in what they have always believed in, than to die prosperous and smart, half believing in something new and doubtful. There never was a nation founded and maintained without some kind of belief in something. Nobody knows what the outcome in Russia will be or how long this Government will last. But if they do get by for quite a while on everything else, they picked the only one

thing I know of to suppress that is absolutely necessary to run a
Country on, and that is Religion. Never mind what kind; but it's
got to be something or you will fail in the end.

September. 2:

After coming out of Russia and paying some of the prices up there
I was ready to accept almost anything. They had been wanting
me to play in a British-made Picture in London. But I had kinder
held off, but when the Savoy Hotel in Moscow handed me the bill
I immediately wired London to get their Camera ready and have
an extra strong lens on it that they were just about to shoot one
of the most homely but practical faces that had ever registered
Sex Appeal.

British Pictures needed a start, so I thought I just as well go and
help them out. I being the one that started American Pictures.
I was in Pictures in Hollywood away back when some of these big
ones now were just learning to get married. You see Pictures
have to undergo a poor or what Will Hayes would call a "Mediocre"
stage before they can get to be big. Well, there is the stage that I
assisted the great Film Industry through. The minute they commenced to get better, why my mission had been fulfilled. In other
words, I am what you would call a Pioneer. I am all right in anything while it's in its crude state, but the minute it gets to having
any class, why I am sunk. After anything begins to take itself
seriously I have to gradually drop out, sometimes suddenly. So that
is why they sent for me to get the British Pictures through this state.

But I won't last long here because they are a little too far advanced for me now. I was put in to try and handicap Dorothy
Gish, who is the Star in the Picture. You all know Dorothy. She
is one of the three Gish Sisters, the Mother and two daughters.

So I am here in London, uplifting the newest and greatest Art.
It's lots of fun over here making Pictures. Every time you finish
a scene they bring you in a cup of tea, and what makes me sore at
myself is I am beginning to like the stuff. The Picture is the story
of three Vaudeville Actors that are playing in England and they
are not so good. Well, if ever any one was well cast it's me. I have
been in Vaudeville and can fill the Not so good part and also I

remember when I was playing over here one time using a Horse and Buck McKee. Well, it looked like we were going to have to swim the horse back home and hang on to his tail as he did it. So I certainly know how to play a Vaudeville actor that's not so good. If I can just stay natural I will be a hit. If I can just get cast in a Picture now where the part is a Lecturer going around the Country trying to reform all the Politicians, why I will have another natural part on my hands.

Well, you know I told you about going broke and had to go to work in a Picture here in London. I got worse off than that. I had to go to work on the stage too. I was sitting around nights and wasn't doing anything, so I thought I will try my little riddles out on a London audience, so I went on at Mr. Charles Cochran's Revue at the London Pavilion. Well, we had quite a night there the opening night. All the Americans were there to help keep the Englishmen off of me, and were all wondering just how the English would take my nonsense. Well, I want to tell you before we go any further that I never saw a better audience in my life.

All the stuff I had on International affairs they knew all about and they got every Gag I had. When a Gag didn't get much of a laugh it was because it wasn't very funny. So I certainly don't want to hear the old remark when I get back home that the British haven't any humor. They got a lot of humor. Where some of our people have got that idea is because they have come over here and tried to spring a lot of slang expressions. Well, slang is not humor and never will be. Naturally they didn't get it. They could do the same with us. They have just as much slang as we have, and naturally we don't get theirs either.

Dublin, September 12:

This has been a great three days for Germany. They won a foot race and got into the League of Nations. They feel that these two events will just set them right for the next war.

Paris, France, September 17:

France said at the League the other day that she and Germany were old pals again. I guess they are. I floated down the Rhine in Germany all day yesterday and there were so many French soldiers in the way I couldn't see the castles.

October 10:

Well I am back in Cuckooland. I am not going to pull that old gag about America looks pretty good to me. It don't look good — it looks perfect. We are better off than any nation.

But just looking at it fresh, like I am now, after being used to those others over there, why, she looks pretty near good enough to live in.

We blew in here the other day on the Leviathan. My wife and the two younger of our brood, Mary and Jim, and "Lord Jock Dewar." "Lord Jock" is a little white flea hound, one of those new breeds called Sealyham.

Lord Dewar over there is the keeper of the still that makes "Dewars Scotch Whiskey." Not that I was a patron of his brand —. He is the greatest after dinner speaker in England and a very fine old gentleman, and he breeds all kinds of fine horses, chickens, and dogs, and he gave the children this thorobred cur. This old pup has been raised on Scotch, and it's going to be pretty tough to drop him down to Moonshine.

October 11:

President Coolidge,

Dear Mr. Coolidge: Well, I have been gathering up a lot of facts and I am just about in shape to report. I have the biggest news for you that I have had since I have been your little "Shack" in Europe. You know, of course, or perhaps you have had it hinted to you, that we stand in Europe about like a Horse Thief. Now I want to report to you that that is not so. It is what you call at Amherst, "erroneous." We don't stand like a Horse Thief abroad. Whoever told you we did is flattering us. We don't stand as good as a Horse Thief. They knew what you were sore at them for.

Now I have been in all kinds of Countries — about all they have over there, if somebody don't come along with self-determination for small nations and carve out a couple of dozen more. But I have looked them all over. Now you will have people coming back over there tell you that it is not so that we are in bad.

They get their information from people who are trying to be polite to them. But you just get to talking and let an argument start, and you will mighty soon see the old feeling crop out.

But here is what I want to write you about, and the thing that you never hear mentioned or even thought of. Everybody talks about how we are hated — it is to conversation in Europe what Prohibition has been at home. Well, when the discussion would gradually come to the Shylocks, as we had been christened, why, I would just casually, of course, admit that we were a band of highbinders, and were just waiting to get England or France up a back alley and knock 'em in the head and get what little they had left; and while they were discussing jubilantly the subject of our unpopularity I would, in order to keep up the conversation and not change the subject, just nonchalantly remark, "Will you enumerate to me, in their natural order, the number of Nations that you people can call bosom friends?"

Well, they had never thought of that; but when you insist on a count, he finds that he not only could enumerate them on his fingers but he could count them on his fingers if he had been unfortunate enough to have both arms off.

We, unfortunately, don't make a good impression collectively. You see a bunch of Americans at anything abroad and they generally make more noise and have more to say than anybody and, generally create a worse impression than if they had stayed at home. They are throwing rocks at us, but sometimes you think it is deserved. There should be a law prohibiting over three Americans going anywhere abroad together.

It will take America fifteen years steady taking care of our own business and letting everybody else's alone to get us back to where everybody speaks to us again.

I may drop over to see you, as I have lots of stuff that I will have to go over with you personally. I think if you will take my tips I will be able to keep us out of war, and that will be more than any other Unofficial Diplomat has accomplished.

Well must stop.   Hope everything is K.O. with you at the coming election.

Yours Diplomatically at all times,

Willie

P.S.   I certainly want you to know that this is a labor of love that I am doing for you, and I hope to be rewarded in '28.

October 12: [*Published in the* Saturday Evening Post *the following January.*]
On Board Royal Joker Train, Touring America with Object Possible Loan to Oklahoma.
My Dear Constituency:

I had just arrived back home from Europe with 850,000 other half-wits who think that a summer not spent among the decay and mortification of the Old World is a summer squandered.

So I wired Everett Sanders, Mr. Coolidge's very genial and likable secretary, that I was coming down to Washington the next day and I would like to drop in and say hello to our President.

Well, sir, do you know it wasent more than an hour before I got a wire back: Let us know what train you arrive on.   A White House car will meet you at the station, and you are to be the guest of Mr. and Mrs. Coolidge at the White House while here.

* * * * *

Mr. Sanders met me at the train himself and we drove in a White House limousine.   We got to the White House and there sit Mr. and Mrs. Coolidge.

Now there was the President of a Country a third as big as Russia and more than half as big as China.   He and the Leading Lady of our land, waiting dinner on a Lowbrow Comedian.   I had heard so much in Politics about them going to do something for the common people and this was the first practical demonstration I had ever witnessed of it.

Toronto, October 12: [*Will was off on another lecture tour.*]

Have just arrived home after fixing everything up in Europe when White House spokesman dispatched me to look over Canada and make England following offer for it: One doubtful world court seat, "Peaches" Browning, Haiti, All states south of Dixon line. And throw in Al Smith. Deal pending.

Ottawa, Ontario, October 13:

More sentiment here to be annexed by Mexico than America. They know us too well. If we get any nation to join us it will have to be some stranger. We only have one reason for wanting Canada. And modification of the Volstead Act will eliminate that.

Montgomery, Alabama, October 21:

It took two weeks to coach New York politicians how to dress and act to meet Queen Marie of Roumania so they all looked like twins and spoke the same little piece. Americans are getting like a Ford car — they all have the same parts, the same upholstering and make exactly the same noises.

Tulsa, Oklahoma, October 28:

Been riding horseback over my ranch and old birthplace today, and found two stills. That's some stuff I haven't been getting rent on.

Oklahoma City, Oklahoma, October 29:

The South is dry and will vote dry. That is everybody that is sober enough to stagger to the polls will.

November 21:

Annie Oakley is dead. The older generation knew more of her than the present. She was the acknowledged headliner for years of the great Buffalo Bill Show, the best known woman in the world at one time, for when she was with the show it toured everywhere. She was not only the greatest rifle shot for a woman that ever lived, but I doubt if her character could be matched anywhere outside of a saint.

She and her fine husband were great friends of Fred Stone, and I first became acquainted with her there years ago. I had heard cowboys who had traveled with the Bill Show speak of her almost in reverence. They loved her. She was a marvelous woman, kindest hearted, most thoughtful, a wonderful Christian woman.

I went out to see her last Spring in Dayton. She was in bed, had been for months; but she was just as cheerful. I told her I would see her this Fall when I came back, and tried to cheer her in the usual dumb way I have of doing such things. She said I wouldn't, but "I'll meet you." Well she will certainly keep her end of the bargain.

November 28:

Society had been buying dresses and scrubbing behind their necks and ears for weeks getting ready for Marie [*of Roumania*]. The mayor of Kansas City in presenting her said, "It's the greatest day in the History of Kansas City."

Now can you imagine such a statement? Just take it apart and see. Now what is going to make it great because, not only because it was Queen of some minor league Balkan War trap nation, but it would be the same if the Queen of the biggest nation or the King was there. What would that add to the greatness of the city to make it the greatest day of its history?

Why last week when I was there there were seventeen hundred young boys and girls there by generosity of that great paper the Kansas City Star, from over thirty states. They were taking vocational training and had led their various districts back home in the studying of farming and stock raising, and had been brought to see the American Royal Live Stock Show. To see the kings and queens of cattle, sheep, hogs and horses. Real kings and queens that produced something. Real Thorobreds. If there had been a scrawny one and an outcast in the breeding he was discarded at home and not allowed to enter the arena.

New York, December 10:

Every official in the Government and every prominent manufacturer is forever bragging about our "high standard of living." Why, we could always have lived this high if we had wanted to live on the installment plan.

CHAPTER TWELVE

The Doctors Remove my "Bellyache"

1927 — Will talks louder than ever for preparedness. He points out the danger of the Japanese menace. On the humanitarian side he takes up the cudgel for the Mississippi flood sufferers.

Lindbergh makes his flight across the Atlantic to Paris and wins Will's heart. Will sees the great boost this can give to aviation. Will has his gall-bladder operation, to the delight of the politicians. To their chagrin he loses none of his "gall." He is deposed as Mayor of Beverly Hills through the machinations of the California Legislature.

Will gives Al Smith advice on how to be President and not just a candidate. He also establishes his "America Only" Society. "America First" isn't enough — that leaves room for someone to be second. He makes his famous trip to Mexico, along with Lindbergh, to help Morrow get his good-

143

neighbor policy going. Will makes an impromptu speech (on which he worked four days) giving President Calles and other important officials his ideas on what the relationship of the two countries should be.

Hollywood, January 3:

See where America and Mexico had a joint earthquake. That's the only thing I ever heard that we split 50–50 with Mexico.

Gallup, New Mexico, January 4:

In the Mayor's much regretted absence from Beverly Hills, I hereby and hereon do this day appoint as Lieutenant Mayor Charles Spencer Chaplin, who is temporarily out of a wife, and can therefore devote all his humor to the office.

We did not lose an inhabitant by death during the holidays which proves conclusively that the Eighteenth Amendment was strictly adhered to. We can behave ourselves better than lots of more moral towns can.

Ann Arbor, Michigan, January 8:

Am lecturing before University of Michigan tonight on "Better Government by Poorer Officials."

P.S. You will remember this school more readily when I tell you it's the one that Benny Friedman and Benny Oosterbaan are building the new stadium for. Michigan's scholastic standing is a field goal better than any university in the Middle West.

January 16:

We better start doing something about our defense. We are not going to be lucky enough to fight Nicaragua forever. Build all we can, and we will never have to use it. If you think preparedness don't give you prestige, look at Japan. We are afraid to look at them cross eyed now for fear we will hurt their "Honor." Before they got a Navy neither them, nor us, knew they had any honor. Japan or England either would have just as much honor without any Navy at all, but the Navy helps to remind you of it.

All we got to go by is History, and History don't record that "Economy" ever won a war. So I believe I would save my money somewhere else even if I had to work a little shorter handed, around the Capitol there.

Florence, South Carolina, February 19:

Haven't paid much attention to that talk out in Beverly Hills about going to recall the Mayor. I am not afraid of that. They can't let me out. I know too much. Why, I will rock the very foundation of the social strata of screen, oil and realtor business. P.S. If they monkey with me I will undo all the good that Will Hays has done for years.

Hollywood, March 7:

We got wind in the Senate where we had paid to get wisdom.

San Francisco, March 12:

See by the newspapers this morning Secretary Wilbur says there is no danger from Europe from airplanes. WHEN WE NEARLY LOSE THE NEXT WAR, AS WE PROBABLY WILL, WE CAN LAY IT ONTO ONE THING AND THAT WILL BE THE JEALOUSY OF THE ARMY AND NAVY TOWARD AVIATION.

They have belittled it since it started and will keep on doing it till they have something dropped on them from one.

Sacramento, March 16:

Just addressed the California State Legislature and helped them pass a bill to form a lawyers' association to regulate their conduct.

Personally I don't think you can make a lawyer honest by an act of Legislature. You've got to work on his conscience. And his lack of conscience is what makes him a lawyer.

April 3:

You don't know what a Country we have got till you start prowling around it. Personally I like the small places and sparsely populated States. A place looks better before it gets houses on it than it does afterwards. I hit Nevada the other day. I was billed to play Reno, and say she sure is a pretty little town! Its a regular Oasis right there in the heart of the Sage Brush Country, got beautiful homes and Cottages and I am telling you its worth staying there a while to get rid of a lot of husbands that I know.

I had both eyes all cocked to get a peek at the "Divorcees." I was like the little dames from the east when they first visited Hollywood and are all eyes for the Movie Stars. Well I was all set to get a peek at the "Liberty hunters." You know I dident know it, and I bet you dident either (and thats why I have to do all this traveling around and finding out things for you and all you have to do is to stay at home and just learn what it has taken me so much bother to find out for you). Well, there is just as many men come to Reno for divorces as there is Women. So you see Women are not the only things that are dissatisfied with their mates. Some women are failures just as well as men. And you see when some woman comes there to uncouple from the "old grouch" and don't particularly have her mind made up about the next matrimonial accident why you see with all these men there on the same mission, Why she may pick up something worth while right there. The two sexes are just a-setting right there ready to console each other, and a lot of times you can get just as good or maybe better than you are throwing away right there in Reno. You see you got time to write back and investigate each others financial status. But its just a nice little city and outside of Divorces they got a River running through it and a little Zoo in a pretty park with two Buffalo. A mail and a Female and two elk, Male and Female. In fact pairs of several kind of animals and birds and reptiles. It looks like they mated 'em off that way just to show the "Industry" what can be accomplished if they had been born a reptile or animal instead of practically human. It looked to me like an add against their business there in Reno, but I guess they know best. Lawyers meet the trains and line up and holler out the same as Porters do down South at depots for Hotels. They got Lawyers there that can get you loose from an Octapus. They can point out houses where some of the most famous husbands in the world were tied a can to. Lots of them buy these cottages and live in them till their probation is over and then maby sell them to some other "Irreconsible" or lots of them, they tell me, keep their houses there, and then use them when they come back on the next case. Some women have as many as four and five "notches" on the same house, showing they had got their Man.

April 10:

This country is Not prosperous. We got poor people in this country, only they are not the kind that asks for anything, and they are not on the streets where you can see 'em.

Never mind reading bank Deposits. We got a million poor people that live in the Country that never saw a bank. The rich are getting richer and the poor are getting poorer. That's what we better regulate instead of Nicaragua, Tacna Arica, Mexico, and China.

Cleveland, Ohio, April 18:

Al Smith explains that if elected President all Protestants would not be exterminated; that even a few of the present Senators would be retained, including Tom Heflin; that the Knights of Columbus would not replace the Boy Scouts and Kiwanis; that mass would not replace golf on Sunday morning; and, that those that were fortunate enough to have meat could eat it on Friday.

It's no compliment to a nation's intelligence when these things have to be explained.

Morgantown, West Virginia, April 21:

Shakespeare is the only author that can play to losing business for hundreds of years and still be known as an author.

April 24:

Borah debated against Nicholas Murray Butler. They debated "whether something ought to be said about Prohibition in the Republican Platform in 1928." They dident debate whether it would be good or bad for the Country. That never entered either of their heads. They just debated whether it would be good for the Republicans. It was a question of "Will it get votes for us if we put in an Anti-Prohibition plank, or will it get more votes for us if we say nothing." Even the Boston Club that promoted it and run it like a Rotary Luncheon, looking for all the advertising they could get out of it, dident even suggest that they debate on "What was good for the Country." It was always "What is good for the Republicans."

High Point, North Carolina, April 26:

It certainly does pay to have friends. John McCormack heard

that I was giving a benefit performance for the flood sufferers at Mr. Ziegfeld's new theatre next Sunday night, and he called me on the phone just now, from out in Illinois, and said he would come clear in to New York to sing; that "he thought it was the greatest need by the largest number of people of anything that had ever come up."

Now, outside of being a good fellow, he is not a bad singer. So it will be "McCormack and Rogers, those two nifty boys in funny songs and sentimental jokes." But what the whole country has got to do is wake up and give. These people are going to need assistance for months.

Actors will help you in every town to give shows and raise money. They don't fail. And neither do the people, when they know the need.

New York, May 4:

Well, our benefit turned out fine. We got $17,950 and more checks still coming in. Want to try to thank everybody from all over the country that helped out.

Now don't slack on this stuff because New Orleans is out of danger. That doesn't alter the need of those hundreds of thousands of others who will have to be supported till a crop is raised.

May 8:

The poorest class of people in this country is the renter farmer, or the ones that tends the little patch of ground on shares. He is in debt from one crop to the other to the store keeper, or the little local bank. He never has a dollar that he can call his own. City people don't realize the poverty of poor country folks. They can talk all they want about country people being out in the air and in the open, but I want to tell you as a diet and nothing to go with it, I don't think there is a Scientist living that can show any more "Calories" in a few whiffs of Country air over air anywhere on Hestor Street or the Bowery.

And as for the number of children, say the poor in the city would be accused of race suicide if they was stacked up alongside of the poor white family down in the bottom on a cotton farm. The poor man in the city hasent got any dog to feed. Why this first five millions wouldent even feed the dogs that have been caught in this flood. Thats one thing the poor country fellow will always have, his pack of dogs, and no man can be condemned for owning a dog. In fact you admire him, 'cause as long as he's got a dog he's got a friend, and the poorer he gets the better friend he has. Then when you talk about poor people that have been hit by this flood, look at the thousands and thousands of Negroes that never did have much, but now its washed away. You don't want to forget that water is just as high up on them as it is if they were white. The Lord so constituted everybody that no matter what color you are you require about the same amount of nourishment.

What gets my goat is hearing constantly, "Why don't those people move out of there? There are floods every year." How are they going to move? Who is going to move 'em? Where are they going to move to, and what are they going to do when they move there? Why don't you move? Remember these people can't get any relief for themselves until a crop is harvested. We went Cuckoo over the Armenians. We took off our shirts and sent them to the Russians. We give the Poles our socks. Now we have the greatest chance to help our own that has ever been given us, and its needed the worst. Give it to them.

Northampton, Massachusetts, May 10:

Made a speech here in Coolidge's home town last night. He was Mayor here one time.

They all said that my speech was as good or better than what he used to make at the Mayor stage of his career, and the town is no better than Beverly Hills, or Claremore, so they are kinder predicting here that I might get to live off the Government in some capacity some day.

Concord, New Hampshire, May 20:

No attempt at jokes today. An old slim, tall, bashful, smiling American boy is somewhere out over the middle of the Atlantic ocean, where no lone human being has ever ventured before. He is being prayed for to every kind of Supreme Being that has a following. If he is lost it will be the most universally regretted single loss we ever had.

New York, May 22:

Of all things that Lindbergh's great feat demonstrated, the greatest was to show us that a person could still get the entire front pages without murdering anybody.

June 12:

Out in the wide spaces where *Men are Men, and Farms Are Mortgaged.* Where the Government has showed them every way in the World where they can borrow Money and never yet introduced an idea of how to pay any of it back. Where women are women and only get to town when they have to go to endorse a Note with their husbands. If your crop is a failure and you don't raise anything, why you are fortunate. Because it costs you more to raise anything than you can sell it for, so the less you raise the less you lose, and if you don't raise anything you are ahead.

Beverly Hills, June 13:

Look what happens in Russia to the party that criticizes their Government. Over here they are condemned — but not to death.

Beverly Hills, June 14:

Our President left for a quiet vacation with twelve carloads of cameramen, reporters, cooks, valets, maids, butlers, doctors, military and naval attaches. I saw King George when he left Buckingham Palace in London last Summer for his vacation, and you could have put all he and Mary both had in a Ford truck.

We ain't got exactly what you would call a corner on democracy. P.S. A doctor thought I had had a prosperous enough season to call a bellyache appendicitis.

June 15:

As long as they keep their Paving and Light and Water Tax payed, why I don't worry much about how my Constituents live. I just sit at my desk day in and day out taking care of the worth while things that come up for a Mayor of a thriving and growing town to attend to. I have found out that it don't pay to interfere

officially with any kind of Sex problems. I just figure if both sides
was not Slick enough not to get caught, they are too commonplace
for me to waste my official time on.

My constituents, I don't claim that they are all good, but the
most of them is at least slick.

Beverly Hills, June 16:
Here is where the joke writers and everybody get even with me.
I am in the California Hospital, where they are going to relieve me
of surplus gall, much to the politicians' delight.

I am thrilled to death. Never had an operation, so let the stones
fall where they may.

California hospital, June 17:
Right now I can't think of a soul that I would change places
with except Rebecca, Coolidge's pet racoon. Who would ever
thought that coon would get to summer in the Black Hills?
P.S. Well, here comes the wagon. I hope my scar will not suffer
in size with other, older and more experienced scars.

Will was dangerously ill until the twenty-first. He wrote a book,
Ether and Me, *about this experience. Here are some excerpts:*
We were primitive people when I was a kid. There were only
a mighty few known diseases. Gunshot wounds, broken legs,
toothache, fits, and anything that hurt you from the lower end of
your neck down was known as bellyache. There was no such
thing as indigestion then, as everybody worked. Of course when
a bunch was walking and there was quite a sprinkling of girls and
women, why, we did have such a parlor name for it was Cramp
Colic; that was the latin for bellyache.

I don't remember when I first had it, but I sure do remember
one of my dear old Mother's remedies for it. They just built a
fire in the old kitchen stove and heated one of the old round flat
kitchen stove lids — the thing you take off the stove if you want
what you're cooking to burn. Well, they would heat it up — not
exactly red hot, but it would be a bright bay. They took it off,

wrapped it up in something and delivered it to your stomach with a pair of tongs. Well, the heat from one of those stove lids burned you so you soon forgot where you were hurting. It not only cured you but it branded you. You would walk stooped over for a week to keep your shirt from knocking the scab off the parched place.

Well, the bellyache hadn't shown up in years, until one spring on my tour of national annoyances, I hit a town called Bluefield, West Virginia. Now ordinarily when a pain hits you in the stomach in Bluefield, West Virginia, you would take it for a gunshot wound. But the old town had quieted down now and the sharpshooters have all joined the Kiwanis and Rotary Clubs. So I knew it wasn't wounds. Then the pain struck me before the nightly lecture and I knew no one would shoot me before the lecture, unless by chance he had heard it over in another town.

Well, the next time it hit me was just a few weeks later, out at my old ranch on the Verdigris River, in the same house where I was born and where I had previously balanced those flat irons on my stomach years before. My niece, who was living there, she gave me some asafetida. The only thing it tastes like is spoiled onions and overripe garlic mixed. And the longer after you have taken it, the worse it gets. If I was a baby and I found out that somebody had given me that, if it took me forty years to grow up, I would get them at the finish, even if it was my mother.

Just a few nights after that, and my last night on the train coming home to check up on the moral conditions of Beverly and Hollywood, the Sodom and Gomorrah of the West, that night the old pain hit me again. When I got home they called in a doctor. He gave me some powders. The pain just thrived on those powders. I never saw a pain pick up so quick as it did when the powders hit it. Instead of setting around like most people do, I would take a stool or chair and arrange myself over it something like this: My head and arms would be on the floor on one side and my knees and feet on the floor on the other side. My middle was draped over the seat of the chair. Finally, my wife called in Doctor White, a famous physician.

"What part of your stomach hurts?" he asked.

"Practically all of it, Doc."

I almost forgot to tell you that the first part he got to thumping and feeling on was down low on the righthand side, where I had always been led to believe the appendix is. I says, "That's the only part that don't hurt."

Well, that seemed to kind of lick him. An appendicitis operation within his grasp, and here it slipping through his hands. He looked kind of discouraged.

But he was a resourceful fellow. He never, like a lot of these doctors, hung all his clothes on one line. I could see his mind was enumerating other diseases that were not down so low.

He began to take soundings around the upper end of the stomach. When I told him it hurt there, I never had any idea that I was announcing a lead for pay dirt. When I told him where the pain was worse, his face began to brighten up.

Then he turned and exclaimed with a practiced and well-subdued enthusiasm, "It's the Gall Bladder — just what I was afraid of." Now you all know what that word "afraid of," when spoken by a doctor, leads to. It leads to more calls.

He casually inquired if I had had a good season. I told him that outside of Waxachachie, Texas, Hershey, Pennsylvania, Concord, New Hampshire, and Newton, Kansas, I had got by in paying quantities.

He then says, "We operate." My wife says, "Operate?" And as soon as I came to enough I says, "Operate?"

"Where's the phone?" he asked.

I didn't know whether he was going to phone for knives, the hearse the ambulance or what. The wife pointed to the phone kind of dumbfounded.

Well, he phoned for what seemed like a friend, but who afterwards turned out to be an accomplice. These doctors nowadays run in pairs and bunches.

The old fashioned doctor didn't pick out a big toe or a left ear to make a life's living on. He picked the whole human frame. No matter what end of you was wrong, he had to try to cure you single-handed. Personally, I have always felt that the best doctor in the world is the Veterinarian. He can't ask his patients what is the matter — he's got to just know.

Well, after a while I heard a big expensive car coming up our driveway hill. It made it. After years of listening we can tell the calibre of our callers by how many times they have to shift gears on our hill inside the yard.

This new one was Dr. Clarence Moore, the operating end of the firm. He is the most famous machete wielder on the Western Coast. He asked the same line of questions, but before I could get a chance to answer them myself, why, Doc White answered them for me the way they should be answered to show that I had a very severe case of Gallstones.

One doctor was for operating that night, but the next one was more of a humanitarian. He suggested next morning.

Well, the household was up bright and early the next morning to get old Dad off to the hospital. The whole place was what the novelist would call agog. Even the chauffeur — part time — had the old car shined up. This going to a hospital was a new thing to me. Outside of those stove-lid episodes, I had never even been sick a day in my life. I had been appearing on the stage for some twenty-odd years and had never missed a show.

A hospital is the only place you can get into without having baggage or paying in advance. They don't hold the trunk like a hotel does — they just hold the body.

They had a pretty, cozy room for me. Everything was jolly and laughter. The stomach had quit hurting, of course. I couldn't see any use in going to bed at ten o'clock in the morning when I hadn't been out the night before.

Then in came the nurse. Wow! I got one look at her and made it continuous. She was Ziegfeld's front row without a dissenting vote. I got one look at Mrs. Rogers, who was looking her over also, and then she says, "Doctor, is this operation necessary?"

They gave instructions about what to do to get me ready for tomorrow. I didn't think I had anything to do only just furnish the stomach.

The night before they wrapped my stomach all up in a bandage.

I guess that was so no doctor could get at it ahead of them. Then there was a battalion of blood experts. It got so every time a girl would come along with a tray I would start holding out my hands or my ears. I was beginning to think that some of them were keeping a friend who might be anaemic.

The main carver said he had a lot of other operations on that day, but that mine would be first. I asked him if he couldn't take somebody else first — that there might be someone in pain and that I had never felt better in my life. Then I thought his hand might be a little shaky early in the morning. Then we got the signal that we were next.

As I was a-rolling to the operating room with my retinue of nurses and doctors as outriders, I thought I ought to pull some kind of gag when I got in there that would get a laugh.

There was a kind of a little balcony up above the operating-room floor where people with a well-developed sense of humor could sit and see other people cut up. It must be loads of fun. But there wasn't a soul in there for my operation. I felt kind of disappointed.

I thought, "Well, here I am maybe playing my last act, and it is to an empty house."

There were a lot of doctors and more nurses than I ever saw in my life. One fellow had a kind of a hose with a big nozzle on the end of it. Well, I had by this time thought of my joke and was all ready to pull it and set the whole place in a good-natured uproar. I just opened my mouth to utter my comical wheeze when this old hose boy just gently slipped that nozzle right over my mouth and nose both. I certainly was sore. Here I had this last aspiring wise crack and it had been snuffed out before I could give vent to it. And what made it so bad, I can't think to this day what it was. I remember at the time I thought it was going to be a knock-out, but the gas and the ether completely knocked it into another world.

Next thing I knew I heard the nurse on one side and my wife on the other saying, "Lay perfectly still, you're all right. You are fine now. Just relax."

Finally this ether got to leaving me and I sort of remembered what the operation had been for. I asked them, "Did you get any gallstones?"

Yes, they had got some, a couple of sizable dimensions, but nothing in any way approaching what could be used for exhibition purposes. I felt right then that the operation had been a failure.

I would keep seeing the doctors and nurses coming in and looking down on the floor at the side of my bed. I thought at first it was a dog under my bed.

I says, "What's under there that's causing all these mysterious peeps?" The nurse said, "That's the drain from the tubes."

"Drain from what tubes?"

"Why, the tubes that the doctors put in your side."

Well, all this worry of the doctor's was from the fact that I wasn't draining. They had found a rather unusual condition in there. Being in California, it would be unusual. I didn't have sense enough to know it, but I was in pretty bad shape, for this drain was over two days and nights showing up. Things were looking bad for Claremore, Oklahoma's favorite light-headed comedian. If things didn't show up pretty soon, it looked like I had annoyed my last President. Betty was a better actor than the doctors.

Finally it showed up. Doctor Moore got one look and shouted, "If I was a drinking man I would try some of my own prescriptions tonight." He was so tickled that I believe if I had paid my bill then I would have got fifty per cent off.

He tells me what shape I have been in and he sits down and takes a card out of his pocket and draws a blue print of the whole thing. That's one thing any Californian can do is draw a blue print showing you where in six months there'll be three banks, a subway and a department store right next to the lot he is trying to sell you.

You know, the liver is shaped kind of like a boxing glove, and where it's laced up is where the big duct starts in. Just below it and sort of around the corner is what the oil men would call an offset. Near the termination of the wishbone is a small sort of a pocket or receptacle. This receptacle is not very large and you would hardly notice it if it didn't get stones crossways in its main entrance. It's called the gall bladder and is shaped kind of like a hot dog that's been stuffed more at one end than the other.

Well, this main duct that runs from the liver South into the stomach runs by this little hot-dog stand, and there is a detour line that taps into this miniature gravel pit. Now it's this little alley that gets clogged up. Of course he had dug it out, but the main duct line above it was the one that wasn't running. No stone would be up there, for a stone won't float uphill.

Now the Gall goes into this little pocket and remains until needed — that is, until you get sore at somebody and want to use it up on them. That's why it is that good natured people are the ones that have the Gall operations; they never get a chance to use it up on anybody.

The complaint is more common by far among women than among men. Well, that fact didn't please me so much, as I was just bordering on the effeminate as it was. I also learned that it was more prevalent among Jewish people; that's what I get for going to those Kosher restaurants with Eddie Cantor.

Now, as I have so thoroughly and comprehensively explained the location of this, now what causes the stones to form? Well, there are various reasons. Republicans staying in power too long will increase the epidemic; seeing the same endings to Moving Pictures is a prime cause; a wife driving from the rear seat will cause Gastric juices to form an acid, that slowly jells into a stone as she keeps hollering.

Of course I will always believe that mine was caused by no sanitary drinking cups in the old Indian Territory where I was born. We used a gourd, raised from a gourd vine. Not only did we all drink out of the same gourd but the one gourd lasted for years, till Prohibition weaned some of them away from water.

July 10:

So I am just laying and lying. I wouldn't have minded the whole thing so much but they wouldn't let me have any chili, or chili con carne, as you amateur eaters call it. I sure do love my chili. If I could have just bogged down to a few bowls of good old greasy chili, I would have been well in a week. But I got the next best thing that I wanted and that was some real cornbread. Not this old yellow kind made with eggs, but cornbread, real old corn dodger, or corn pone, made with meal, hot water, and salt. But I had to have my sister, Mrs. Tom McSpadden, from Chelsea, Oklahoma, show 'em how that should be made she even had to send back to get the meal, they don't know what corn meal is out here. I mean corn meal. And she showed 'em how to fix some string beans with some fat meat. Not just boiled in old hydrant water, but a real piece of ham or the side of a shoat.

Hollywood, July 17:

Today's best laugh was by my old friend, Will H. Hays, who said films are made in Hollywood by the best thoughts of the real thinking people of all nations.

Mind you, I am not kicking on the statement, for it gives Ben Turpin, myself and Bull Montana about our highest rating.

August 14:

We are the only home in Beverly that has low ceilings, eat dinner at noon, and supper thirty minutes before going to bed, Havent a grecian tennis court, and the hired Girl (I said "THE" hired not "A" hired Girl) says, "Dinner is ready for you all," instead of a Butler bowing low and announcing, "The meal is served, Madam."

Beverly Hills, August 16:

The State Legislature of California passed a law saying that no one not a politician could hold office. And I hereby notify the world that Beverly Hills has left my bed and board and I will not be responsible for any debts contracted by said municipality.

Beverly Hills, August 18:

Herb Hoover is out here among us. He is just waiting around between calamities. When we, as individuals, get sick we send for Hoover. He is America's family physician. He is a great guy, is Doc Hoover, and I hope they don't spoil him by putting him into politics.

October, 1927:

Will wrote "Another Open Letter to Al" in the Saturday Evening Post. *In it he advised Al to write this letter:*

I, Al Smith, of my own free will and accord, do this day relin- quish any claim or promise that I might have of any support or Deligates at the next Democratic Convention. I don't want to hinder what little harmony there is left in the party; I not only do not choose to run, but I refuse to run. But will give all my time and talents to work faithfully for whoever is nominated by the party.

Now, Al, if you will send 'em this letter you will look like you are sacrificing yourself, and in '32 they will nominate you by radio; they can't help it, and you will have a united Party. A half-wit knew you all couldent win in '24. Well, it's the same this year; you couldent put on a revival of Thomas Jefferson and get away with it.

Al, don't let those New Yorkers kid you. You got no Platform, you got no Issue, you can't ask people to throw somebody out just because somebody else wants in. You meet too many Democratic Leaders — that's what's the matter with the Party — these same leaders not knowing any more about Public Opinion than they do. That's why they are Democratic Leaders.

Then, you New Yorkers get a wrong prospectus of things. The outsiders don't care nothing about New York, and if you think Tammany Hall is an asset, you just run and try to carry them with you and you will find you have been overhandicapped. Now it ain't that you ain't strong, Al; you are strong — you are strong — you are the strongest thing the Democrats have had in years. No Democrat could come near you — But it's not a Democrat that you meet in the finals; It's a Republican. Everybody is always asking, "What's the matter with the Democratic Party?" There ain't nothing wrong with it; it's a Dandy old Party. The only thing wrong with it is the law killed it. It won't let a man vote but once, and there just ain't enough voters at one vote each to get it any- where. You can't lick this Prosperity thing; even the fellow that hasent got any is all excited over the idea. You Politicians have got to look further ahead; you always got a Putter in your hands, when you ought to have a Driver. Now, Al, I am trying to tell you how to be President, not how to be a Candidate.

Beverly Hills, Nov. 3:

Bureau of something or other in Washington announced that "America has reached the highest standard of living ever reached by any nation."

Yes, and if they will just cut down on the original payments we have to make from a dollar to 50 cents we will show you some living. It's an injustice to ask a hard-working people to pay a dollar down. It should be 50 cents down and 50 cents when they come to try and find it to take it back.

Course, we don't get meat as often as our forefathers, but we have our peanut butter and radio.

Nov. 6:

Russia has thrown Trotzky out. There is a funny thing about Trotsky. I was over there last summer and found out He is too conservative. This Bird Stalin that is the male Mussolini of Russia, he and Trotsky don't gee together. You see a Conservative in Russia is a fellow that thinks you only ought to divide with him what you have, while a real communist believes that you ought to give it all to him, in exchange get you calling him Comrade. But you notice they don't do any banishing to Siberia, or promiscuous shooting with him. They would like too but they don't dare. You know he and Lenin started in together and while Lenin is dead, the old Pheasants still are strong for Trotzky, so no matter how mad the ruling party might get you can go and bet they will never harm Trotzky. He stands too good with the old farmers. He knows a lot of these things they are trying is apple sauce, and won't work. Communism is like Prohibition, its a good idea but it won't work.

November 13:

Now of course you all have read about Mayor Bill Thompson's Society, "America First," that he is forming. He had asked all the Mayors of the country to join it, and as soon as he gets them in, he will go after some prominent people, and it looks like it might develop into quite a thing. Well, of course, getting my idea from him, I go ahead and form me one "America Only."

There has been a terrible lot of various Societys formed to try and instill Americanism into our lagging Patriots. If you have never formed a Society in your life and don't know what to form one about, Why don't let that worry you in the least. Just start to sponsor "Better Citizenship," or "100 percent Americanism," "America for the Americans," or any of those original ideas. There has been quite an epidemic of these, especially since the war.

It seems that before the war come along, we were really kinder lax in our duty toward declaring just what we were. The war come along and about all we could do was to muster up five or six million men of every breed and color that ever been invented. Now these poor fellows dident know whether they were "100 percent Americans" or "Better Citizens," or what they were, and we started them drilling so fast that they dident have time to go through a clinic and find out.

You see up to then they dident know what all this meant. They thought that as long as they paid their taxes, tended to their own business, went to their own churches, kept kinder within the law, that that was all they was supposed to do. And it was like that in the old days. But you see we was a backwards nation and dident know it. What we had to learn was to be better Americans. Why here was old men that had raised a big family and had never paid a cent of dues to prove to the rest of the World that they were for "America First." Can you imagine such ignorance? How they had ever been able to do this without declaring where they stood was just another one of our lucky blunders. So when the war come along and we found out that all everybody would do was to die, or suffer, or get rich (or whatever the circumstances called for) for their country, why we saw right away that something was needed to instill patriotism. So hence the forming of all these various societies. They come just in the nick of time. For after the war, a lot of young men who had never known much about other men from different parts of the Country, and different Nationalities, during the days in camps and in France had become to know and like and understand each other, and find out each other's viewpoint.

In other words it was just the start of what might a been a bad friendship and understanding. But its like everything else, when the necessity arises somebody always arises with the remedy, so on investigation it was found that a lot of these same boys were not 100 percent Americans at all. We had been kinder lax in who we had let into our war, everything had come up so hurriedly. Why a lot of them couldent even speak English. A lot of them dident go to churches, and worse than all, a lot of them went to the wrong churches. In fact, there was a million things we found out that we should have found out before we associated with 'em. Of course it was all too late now and was all over, and we would just have to charge it off to bad management. But let's get organized and don't let it happen again. We all went in 50-50 in war time, but this is peace now and we got time to see who is who, and why.

So these Societys commenced to be formed and they grabbed our little civilization just when it was on the brink and hauled it back to normalcy. You see in America there was originally just one Society (Well it was really two combined): It was the Declaration of Independence, and the Constitution of the United States. If you was here and belonged to that why you was all members of the same Club. You dident know whether you was 100 percent, or 2 and ¾ percent, or what ratio you was. You dident know whether you was a good citizen, or bad one. All you knew was that you belonged to this club called America, and all you had to do was work for it, fight for it and act like a gentleman, that was all the by-laws there was. As long as you did that, you could worship what you wanted to, talk any language you wanted to, in fact it looked like a pretty liberal layout. But after 150 or more years, it was immediately seen that this plan was no good, that the old boys that layed out the Constitution dident know much, that the country should be divided up in various Societys and cliques. So that brings us down to this generation, who really are showing us just what to do to prove that we are not against the old Fatherland.

We used to think that we were for it as long as we dident do anything against it, but now we find we got to join something and announce daily that we are for it. We have got to weed out these ones that are not 100 percent. We got to get around these Luncheons more, and sing some get-together songs. This old thing of eating at home with the folks is never going to get you anywhere. There is no real Americanism in that. Let's get down to the club and do some shouting and get some spirit into the old land.

"Going to be an election coming along pretty soon and we want to stick by the members of the club against all the outsiders." "There is a lot of these people just sitting around and not doing anything for American spirit and they are undermining the very principals of our Government." So you see its stuff like that that will save us. If those kind of clubs and societys hadent been formed just when they was, this would have been a fine looking country now. So get into a club as soon as you can. I don't care what it is just so its banded together to make somebody else's life miserable and yours great.

Now I have looked over all the clubs and none of them seem to have enough scope, or broad minded ideal. So that is why as I told you a few weeks ago that I wanted to get this Society going. "America First" is all right, but it allows somebody else to be second. Now sometimes a thing second can be almost as good as something that's first. So that's the thing my Society avoids. Its with the whole idea of there being no one else. In other words, I am just taking the spirit and foundation of other clubs and societys and making them broader.

They are against something (They got to be against something or they wouldent be formed). Well, mine improves on any of theirs; its against everything. I can take my "America Only" idea and eliminate wars. The minute we extinguish all other nations there will be no more wars, unless its a civil war among ourselves, and that of course we can take care of right here at home without a shipping board. I am getting a lot of applications already, real red-blooded go-gettum Americans, that have seen this country trampled under foreign feet enough, and they are right out in the open. Why I figure the patriotism in my organization when I get it formed will run around 165 or 170 percent American. It will make a sucker out of these little 100 percent organizations. Its not too late to send your $20 yet. Remember when you belong to "America Only" you are the last word in organizations.

Beverly Hills, November 22:

Mellon, foolishly and unpolitically, saved up a little money out of our national "jack pot." Well, a forthcoming war or a colossal national pestilence couldn't have stirred up half the excitement among entire America as what to do with this little dab of money.

Half of Congress met three weeks early, not to solve the Mississippi floods nor to build Boulder Dam, but to split up the "Jack pot." We owe thirty billion dollars, but we couldn't think of applying it on that; it's too near election.

Hollywood, November 23:

This is Thanksgiving. It was started by the Pilgrims, who would give thanks every time they killed an Indian and took more of his land. As years went by and they had all his land, they changed it into a day to give thanks for the bountiful harvest, when the boll-weevil and the protective tariff didn't remove all cause for thanks.

November 27:

I read the following: "Chefs in London give dinner to visiting Chefs from Paris." And here is what they served. "Sherry wine was the appetizer, instead of cocktails, as they claim cocktails dull the intellect. Pate de foie gras in jelly or Port Wine. English Sole was cooked in Champaign garnished with Brandy, and served on newly picked grape leaves. English Pheasants cooked in Port Wine, Pears stewed in granulated chocolate and smothered in absynthe. The visiting chefs will be entertained tomorrow by the King at Buckingham Palace."

Suppose they come over here and our Chefs give em a dinner. Here is what we would have. For cocktails we would serve denatured alcohol, as nothing dulls your intellect like straight Alcahol. For those French Pot Wranglers we would serve Pat a de Foy Grass (which is really nothing but Alfalfa, unmatured). For the jelly we would just use Corn mash from the still. The English sole, we haven't that. But we could stew em up an English Heel that would be prowling around looking for Wife material. We havent the Champaign to pot boil him in, but we could spread a little home-made "Dago Red" over his form. Now the English Pheasants cooked in wine. We are shy on the Pheasants, but we got some mighty fine young Dominick roosters. We can wring their necks, and spread about a quart of White Mule, or Jack Brandy over their old carcasses and it wouldent taste no worse.

Mexico City, December 3:

Say this fellow Morrow has made a big hit down here. He's going to do some real good. He is a great fellow.

Ambassador Morrow began almost at once his realistic program to make a friend out of Mexico. As a part of his move, he wired both Will Rogers and Charles Lindbergh to come down for a visit. Both accepted. Will not only wrote much about Mexico in his Daily Wires and weekly articles but later did a series of articles for the Saturday Evening Post *on his trip. Although published in 1928, excerpts from these articles are included at the time Will went to Mexico. They follow:*

"Letters from a Self-Made Diplomat to His President"

My dear Calvin: Well, I just got down here as you suggested me doing. You said I ought to go somewhere, so I figured it was Mexico. I kinder kept waiting for my transportation and expense money, but as it dident come I just figured that with Congress there watching you, and you talking so much Economy, that it would naturally look kinder bad for you to be raiding the Treasury just to send another Ambassador where we had already had one. I took a receipt for the fare and will put in a claim, and by the time it goes through all the various departments it will mean a nice little nest egg for my grandch ldren.

We've started in to pay some attention to our neighbors on the south. Up to now our calling card to Mexico or Central America had been a gunboat or a bunch of Violets shaped like Marines. We could never understand why Mexico wasent just crazy about us; for we had always had their good-will, and Oil and coffee and min-erals, at heart.

Of course, as you know up there, Mr. President, some were just for going down and taking Mexico over. Where did this country down here, with no great chains of Commercial Clubs, and Chambers of Commerce and Junior and Freshman Chamber of Commerces, and Rotary and Kiwanis and Lions and Tigers Clubs, and No golf pants, and no advertising Radio programs — where did a Nation like that come in to have Oil anyhow? It was a kind of an imposition on their part to even have to go to the trouble of going down and taking their country over.

But our wiser heads got to thinking, "Well, we picked up the Phillipines and now we got no place to lay it down." Then some that had studied History says, "Look at England! They took everything that wasent nailed down and look at 'em." Then somebody got to figuring out: "We better find some other way."

Now I don't know if it was you, Calvin, or not. I kinder give you credit for doping it out. Well, asking a man to go to Mexico at that time in the interests of the United States was just like saying, "Your tumbler of Carbolic acid is ready, Sir. Would you like water with it?"

You just said, "I wonder if we tried using kindness and common sense would it do any good, or would it be such a novelty that Mexico would think we were kidding 'em?"

That's when I think your thoughts hit on Morrow. Well, I am not kidding you when I tell you you was inspired. You hit on him when nobody else was thinking about him, and here there was a couple of hundred so-called Diplomats laying off that would have even been willing to go to Haiti.

Well, if you remember, when you appointed him he gave up his job with Morgan. That made a hit with everybody, for it showed that he didn't have the least inkling of a Politician in him. For it's not necessary or even customary to give up a side line when taking on any kind of Government work.

But I must get back to myself and tell you how I got down there. I was sitting around Beverly Hills waiting for another screen wedding between old-timers, when your mental message of telepathy come. So I just lit right out.

Somewhere in Mexico on the Presidential Train:

Morrow was the first to show up. I had never met him. But he sure did win me right from the jump. I thought mebbe on account of being such a friend of yours that he would be kinder like you. What I mean by that, he would be kinder stingy with his chatter. But, say, he is the most pleasant fellow I ever saw. He is little, but five foot six of solid personality. We talked about you and he asked me how you was doing, and I made out that you was doing all right.

You know, this Morrow does a lot of things that I imagine are not in the book that tells what Diplomats should do. You know, he kinder figures out that if Calles is the man that he was sent there to deal with, that Calles is the man that he should know and understand. Diplomats, when they get to a Country, they figure they must first meet the rich people of their own Country who are living there, and then the rich ones who belong in the Country. But as far as the Government officials are concerned, why, they will perhaps know them at some time through the exchange of official visits.

You know, the other night on the train I was late for dinner, and when I come into the diner, the President had the interpreter say to me very sternly and with much gravity:

"Mr. Rogers, you are late for dinner. I don't know if you know it or not, but that is a very grave breech of etiquette. In fact, it is an insult to the President for you not to be here to sit down with him when he arrives. What have you to say?"

"Well, I just want to tell the President that I am sorry. I was up in the front cars with some of the soldiers. I have only been in Mexico one week, but you tell him I have learned that it's better to stand in with the Soldiers of Mexico than with the President."

Well, he got quite a kick out of that, and to show you he was there with a Nifty, he said, "You tell Mr. Rogers that that was very smart of him to find that out, but that I found it out years before he did — that's why I am President."

* * * * *

I went in to enjoy the people and the Country and get some Real Chili Con Carne and Tamales, see the Mexican Ropers — the best in the World — see the Senoritas dance, and mebbe, if fortunate, see 'em shoot a Presidential Candidate. For there is a system I

think which has much merit, and could be adopted without serious
loss to almost any country. So you might say that I went in with
no Mind at all.

* * * * * *

I wanted to see how they bred and raised young Bulls that they
use in the Bull Ring. It may not be showing proper respect for a
neighboring Republic's Politics, but a good young Bull interests me
more than any Politician I ever saw in any Country.

Yesterday we had the time of the trip. We spent the day at a big
Ranch, or Hacienda, with some friends of the President.

After lunch everybody piled in cars and on horseback, and out
to the Bull ring. This ranch raises fine bulls that they use for the big
fights. They have their own ring to try them in. It's the most
unique thing, all built out of 'Dobie-mud-walls, and all the corrals are all the same. They had a dandy Grand Stand made up
over it, and used a lot of the young Bulls, about two-year-olds.

Well, this was a bull-fight I really enjoyed, for there was no bulls
to be killed, or horses. And say, what a bunch of Amateur Bull-
fighters we had in our Gang! I thought we had officers and Diplomats and Politicians, but everybody that could grab a cape and get
in the ring did so. The first thing I know, I look, and there is the
President himself in the ring with the cape, making passes and the
bull sailing by him. Can you imagine that? The President, right
down there taking a chance! You know, these Bulls dident know
that they wasent to be killed and that this wasent a real Bullfight.
I thought of you when I saw him down in that ring. I was trying
to picture you down in there with that old Bull a-coming head on; a
speech on economy wouldent have done much good then.

But say, listen! Don't think I am laughing at what you or anyone else might have done. They all kept hollering, "Where is your
American Comedian?" Well, to be perfectly frank and honest, the
American Comedian was up in one of the most comfortable and
highest seats that the arena afforded. That's why he was still a
Comedian, because he had never become quite half-witted enough
to enter the arena with any man's male Ox. Even if they took the
horns off and made a muley out of 'em, that wouldent even tempt
me. I'll bet if a bull was charging down on you, Calvin, you could

name at least a dozen Senators that you would like to have between
you and him.

No sir, I had been butted enough in a branding corral by snorty
old calves to know that Clem Rogers' boy Willie of Oolagah, Oklahoma, wasent carved out to meet any Bull in combat. You know
they had been kidding me about not associating with their Bull.
All at once, when they was all waiting for a new Bull to come out —
from the ring you can't see what is coming out — well, out comes
the real thing — the Stud Bull, a magnificent animal that they had
imported from Spain to breed from. Oh, a great big powerful
animal!

Well, when that door opened and he came charging out there,
you never saw as many capes, hats and even shoes left in one arena
in your life. A raid on Mellon's Treasury by Congress was nothing
to the way Presidents, Generals, privates, Secretarys of State, personal Physicians, vallets, Chapultepec Castle cooks and just Mexicans made for those boards and walls. Men scaled walls that had
come to the ring leaning on a cane and went over them like they
had been one of these Zuave troops. You see, the ring had got so
full, everybody was wanting to fight these smaller Bulls. Some were
fighting 'em with their coats and vests, and even red undershirts.
There wasent enough capes to go round.

But, Boss, when this Male Toro hit that arena he emptied it with
nothing but a glance. No Revolutionist ever cleaned out a place
as thoroughly as that Baby did. He emptied it like a speech on the
tariff will the Senate Gallery. They dident stop to sit on the top of
this wall they had scaled — they just fell on over; and those boards
that they are supposed to hide behind, why, there looked like there
was half of Mexico tromping on each other behind them. The
President was down and two Peons standing on him. A Skunk in
a parlor couldent have more thoroughly disrupted a party than this
lone Bull did.

Well, that's when little Willie had his laugh. I had seen this
animal in the corrals as we come up, and had admired him, and as
I had slipped down to the corral unnoticed during the hilarity, a
few Five-Peso Notes scattered around judiciously among the fore-
men and the Cowboys that was doing the Turning of the Bulls in

the ARENA had sure bore juicy fruit, and I was a-sitting there enjoying the returns of a splendid investment.

Mexico City:

Say, what a City this is! She is a cross between New York, Tulsa and Hollywood, with a bit of Old San Antonio and Nogales, Arizona thrown in. Say, it's clean and well kept too. You ought to see Chapultepec Castle, where their President lives. Why, the White House wouldent make their living room! It's on a high hill overlooking the whole city.

Oh, we went into their Congress. They call it the Chamber of Deputies, and they wear pistols. They are allowed to wear a Gun the same as an officer. I got a great kick out of that. Can you imagine, if we did that, the damage Jim Reed would have done by now? Jim would have exterminated half — the Republican half — the Senate by now, and would have been shooting most of the Democrats just for practice. Can you picture the late Henry Cabot Lodge directing Republican affairs with a forty-five as a Baton? And if Dawes had a gun, we would have to draft a new Senator every morning. I kinder like it. I never heard one Deputy call another a Liar all the time I watched 'em operate. But up home it has become so common that it's almost a greeting.

Well, I must tell you about the dinner. Mr. Morrow give an awful nice dinner to me the other night at the Embassy. He rounded up about fifty — all men — that dident have nowhere to go that night, and we had an awful nice party. I heard the Morrows kinder excited around there one day, and they told me the President had accepted and that he was coming to the dinner. Well, I dident think so much of that concession on his party, as he had been eating with us on the train all that time, and had seemed an awful good fellow. But I come to find out what made all the excitement. It was the first time that a Mexican President had ever been in the American Embassy. That shows you how this Morrow gets along with these people, the ones that he has been sent here to do business with.

Morrow is a dandy impromptu speechmaker, and I had me an impromptu one that I had only worked on steady for four days. I think I got some notes on it here somewhere, and I will jot it down and let you see that when it comes to mixing with these Diplomats, I was going down, doing the best I could.

'Course I knew I stood a chance bringing on a war between the two Nations. But I handled it so diplomatically there may never anything come of it. That's the way Diplomats are supposed to do things, ain't it? — handle 'em so they will just naturally die off without anything ever being done about 'em?

Well, here was my oral note to the President and his Cabinet and our Ambassadors and the others:

"Gentlemen of your word, AND Diplomats: Now that we are all here and no note to open, let's be honest with each other and get the lowdown on Diplomacy. Everybody wonders what I am doing here. I was originally sent here to step in in case the Senate dident confirm Morrow's appointment. They confirmed him, but they hated to see someone get the job that was not a Politician. Some in the Senate condemned him for working for Morgan and Co, but other more thoughtful heads reminded these belligerents that we are all working for Morgan and Co. Now about Diplomacy — Diplomacy was invented by a man named Webster, to use up all the words in his Dictionary that dident mean anything.

"A Diplomat is a man that tells you what he don't believe himself, and the man that he is telling it too don't believe it any more than he does. So Diplomacy is always equal. It's like good bookkeeping. He don't believe you and you don't believe him, so it always balances. Diplomats meet and eat, and rush home and wire their Governments in Code that they fooled the Secretary of State So-and-so. He dident know what I was eating. That's how slick you Babies are.

"The reason I can speak so freely about Diplomats is because there is none here. America has none, and it's a cinch that you-all down here haven't. They are really an ingredient of Europe's — England and France and all those Countries. They really take 'em serious over there. They breed 'em and raise 'em just for that; and due to having such good ones, they are continually at war over there. We don't have diplomats over in this Western World, and naturally we don't have any wars with each other.

"Diplomats are just as essential to starting a war as Soldiers are for finishing it.

"You take Diplomacy out of war and the thing would fall flat in a week.

"A Diplomat and a stage Magician are the two professions that have to have a high silk hat. All the tricks that either one of them have are in that hat, and are all known to other Diplomats and Magicians.

"Diplomats write Notes, because they wouldent have the nerve to tell the same thing to each other's face.

"A Diplomatic Note is like an anonymous letter. You can call a fellow anything you want, for nobody can find out exactly who's name was signed to it.

"England, France and Germany have Diplomats that have had the honor of starting every war they have had in their lifetime. Ours are not so good — they are Amateurs — they have only talked us into one.

"Now about Politicians. The least said about them the best. They haven't the social standing of the Diplomats. All of their damage is internal. Where the Ambassador generally winds up with a decoration of red ribbon, the Politician generally winds up with an Inditement staring him in the face.

"Now, I want it distinctly understood that I dident come down here to try and cement good relations between the two Nations, through these so-called cementers that we are always biting at each other's heels. I am not going to tell you that you ought to wake up and be progressive and trade your Burro for a car. The only thing I can see that you need in this Country is more rain, and if Calles here don't give it to you, I would start impeachments.

"I dident come here to tell you that Mexico needed American Capital. Mexico needs Mexican Capital. Pass a law to make your rich Mexican invest at least half the money he gets out of his own country back into it again. You have more money in this City invested in French dresses and perfumes than you have in the country in Plows. It's not American confidence you are looking for — it's Mexican confidence.

"Make your rich, every time they send a Child to Paris to learn 'em

to talk French — make them send one to Sonora to learn to talk Yaqui.
They are the ones you have to live and get along with, not the French.
You got more imported cars here than you have milk cows.

"The only trouble with this country is, the Verbs have too many
endings. I hope Morrow don't get up and tell you that he come
here to give you all your Liberty. Why should Mexico be the first
Country to have it? It's unusual for a Guest to compliment a Host
at a dinner, but I think you will like this little Guy Morrow. You
are supposed to be kinder rough babies to deal with, so that's why
we sent a fellow down from Wall Street. He looks gentle, but say,
you don't raise 'em down here in this cactus any more hard-boiled
than we do up there on that little Alley.

"There is no reason why we shouldent get on with this Country.
You have lots of things down here that we want, and as long as we
get 'em, why, we ought to hit it off great. I want to thank everybody for their hospitality. I just want to find one thing before going
home — I want to find what makes every Mexican a Guitar
player, Now if I was looking for comedy in Government, I dident
have to come here. I could have stayed at home. I come down
here to laugh with you and not at you. I dident come here to tell
you that we look on you as Brothers. That would be a lot of bunk.
We look on you as a lot of Bandits and you look on us as one Big
Bandit. So I think we fairly understand each other, without trying
to express it. I have nothing in the way of hospitality to offer you
when you come to my country, unless you visit me in Hollywood,
and I will take you out and let you see the Screen Stars get divorces.

"So we will now drink a toast in Mescal: Viva la Mexico, Viva
Estadas Unidas, Bueno Noches, Amigos. Carramba! Yours, Will,
Ambassador, without rhyme, reason or Portfolio.

"P.S. Say, you and Hughes neither one dident make any better
speech than that in Cuba. You spoke on Columbus, I think that
was an old speech you had made when you graduated from High
School. 'Course those Cubans just eat up anything about Columbus
because they think he landed there. They got him mixed up with
Roosevelt. He is the one landed there. But Hughes wasent afraid
to speak about Nicaragua. He told 'em that we were in there
and were going to stay till every one of them voted Republican."

CHAPTER THIRTEEN

It'll Take Two Generations to Sweep Up the Dirt

1928 — Will attended the Republican and Democratic National Conventions. Fred Stone got hurt in an airplane accident. Will took his place in Dorothy's show, giving up a half-million-dollar lecture tour to do so. He advertised the "Democratic Party Franchise" for sale or lease to someone who might know how to use it. He foresaw in the split among the Democrats — Al's Catholicism and wetness against southern Puritanism and dryness — the coming great split in American life. He also foresaw what was happening in the world. "We are at peace," he said, "because the world is waiting to get another gun and get it loaded. Wall Street is in good shape, but Eighth Avenue never was as bad off. The Farmers are going into the Winter with pretty good radios, but not much feed for their stock." Will got his rumblings not from Wall Street's pulse but from the "real birds."

174

Beverly Hills, January 1:

"What do you suppose we are in Congress for, if it ain't to split up the swag?" Please pass the gravy.

Havana, Cuba, January 15:

[*At the Pan-American Conference*]

What a beautiful sight as the Texas steamed into this flag and crowd draped city on a beautiful Sunday afternoon. It made you proud and showed what a friend we could be to the world if we would only let them all alone and run their various countries the way they think best.

Havana, January 16:

The President Coolidge made a good speech. He didn't say that we would do anything for these countries, but, on the other hand, he didn't say that we would do anything against them. So it was what you might call a conservative speech.

Hollywood, January 29:

Somebody at the Havana conference Saturday brought up the question of revolutions, which, when and how to treat 'em. The delegates want to vote to make revolutions unlawful. That is, while they are in, but, when they are out, have them declared legal again.

It's rather embarrassing, for all the delegates are there by grace of a revolution at some time.

Beverly Hills, February 2:

There was a piece in the paper this morning where somebody back home was seriously proposing me for President. Now when that was done as a joke it was all right, but when it's done seriously it's just pathetic. We are used to having everybody named as Presidential candidates, but the country hasn't quite got to the professional comedian stage.

There is no inducement that would make me foolish enough to run for any political office. I want to be on the outside where I can be friends and joke about all of them, even the President.

Beverly Hills, February 7:

America and France signed a treaty that they wouldn't fight each other. Now, if we could just sign one with some nation that there is a chance of having war with, why it would mean something.

Beverly Hills, February 9:

Did you read young John D. Rockefeller's plea to the oil men? He implored them to tell the truth, or tell something, whether it was the truth or not, but to please not just sit there, as that made the whole industry not only look dumb, but guilty. Poor young John D! He is trying to do what is right, but his Bible class should include all his holding companies.

February 12:

This Houston wanted an Ocean and they dident have one, so they just dug one. One man, Jessie Jones, just pulled out his check book when the towns were bidding on the Democratic Convention (nobody had given him any money, there had been no collection taken up before he left Houston) and wrote out his personal check for $200,000; and layed it on the barrel head, and I want to tell you those Democrats pounced on it like a Congressman on a Mellon hard-earned saving. It takes a game Guy in any man's town to do what Jones did. Most towns would have to have Chamber of Commerce speeches and luncheons and drives for a year to dig that up. But that's the way those Babies down there do things. So go to see the town, even if you are not interested in the Convention, and the State has dozens of ones like it, not all as big, but they all believe they are, and they will all surprise you.

Beverly Hills, February 16:

Had visits from two of my "bosses." Mr. Lorimer, who was drumming up subscriptions for his Saturday Evening Post, and Mr. Adolph Ochs, owner of the New York Times.

Aided by Mrs. Rogers, I coyly hinted for a raise from both gentlemen, but even socially they are always the business men. So it looks like I just fed two hungry editors for nothing. Once a sap, always a sap.

February 19:

What should be done with Chambers of Commerce: Let the Secretarys get some other job, and the Members go back to eating lunch at home with their own families.

Camden, Arkansas, February 28:

If I was a coal mine owner and couldn't understand my help any better than they do, I would resign and announce to the world that as an industrial leader I was a "bust." And I would devote my life to seeing that the world burned cow chips.

Montgomery, Alabama, March 4:

I spent the morning at Tuskogee, that living monument to Booker T. Washington.

They have a great idea there that some of our schools are copying. They teach the pupils that they are going to have to work, and how to work. Our old mode of college education was teach 'em so they think they won't have to work.

Albany, Georgia, March 5:

Just read the Smithsonian Institution's explanation about the Wright flying machine. They say the trustees decided Langley's machine could have flown first but didn't. I could have flown first but didn't. I could have flown to France ahead of Lindbergh but I just neglected doing it. I had a lot of other things on my mind at the time.

Orlando, Florida, March 12:

See by today's paper where Senator Borah made an appeal to the country to donate a dollar or more each to save the respect of the Republican Party. I just mailed $5 to make five Republicans respectable. Wish I could afford more, but this continued prosperity has just about got me broke.

Tampa, Florida, March 16:

The elder John D. made no effort to give me the customary dime, whereupon I took out one and gave it to him. He took it. I'll say he took it. I guess this prosperity in big business is overrated.

He is the only man I will watch play golf — there is some excuse for him playing it.

Lexington, Kentucky, April 1:

Today the Governor of Kentucky made me aide on his staff with the rank of colonel. I thought I would get out of Kentucky without being made a colonel.

His name is Sampson, a very strong man. He certainly slayed the Democrats "with the jawbone of an ass." His Democratic opponent ran on "no horse racing in Kentucky" thereby not only supplying Mr. Sampson with the jawbone, but making themselves the whole animal by thinking that Kentucky would vote against horse racing.

So it's Colonel Rogers, suh. Boy, put a sprig more mint in that julep.

Battle Creek, Michigan, April 3:

What a place this is. The home of the sensitive stomach. It's the rendezvous of everybody with an ailment between the chin and the hip.

Everybody is getting along fine. Cheerful and just saturated with sanitarium scandal. Cure you by giving you everything to eat but food. These patients' idea of a wild party is to get their hands on two slices of bacon or just an old lamb chop bone. They can sure overhaul a stomach that's been missing.

Indianapolis, Indiana, April 6:

And don't sell America short. Get some good stock and hold it till it's worth more, and then sell. But don't gamble.

Columbus, Ohio, April 9:

Say, you luncheon clubs, stop eating and singing songs long enough to get you some paint and a brush and go out and put the

name of your town on the biggest roofed building you got. It would
be a tremendous aid to aviators. Lots of towns can't afford an air-
port, but any of you can do this. You Kiwanis's or Rotary's could
do it some day and not miss over half of some speech.

New York, April 16:

I received my $5 back from Senator Borah that I sent him to
clean up five Republicans. I even named the five that he was to
clean up. He wasn't able to raise the fund because people realized
that it was a lost cause. You can't make the Republican Party
pure by more contributions, because contributions are what got it
where it is today.

This was a noble idea of Borah's, but noble ideas don't belong in
politics.

Kansas City, Missouri, April 29:

They are in here now working on ice boxes, sawdust and cuspi-
dors for the Republican Convention.

Chelsea, Oklahoma, May 1:

I got the real kick of my life out of aviation today. Left western
Kansas and flew down to Oklahoma and landed right on the old
ranch I was born on. First machine was ever in there.

I ask you and plead with you again, you luncheon clubbers, will
you please paint the name of your town on top of your building?
I will pay for the paint if you will do it.

Beverly Hills, May 6:

Owing to a shortage of funds I am limiting my offer to supply
paint for names of towns with not more than four letters.

Beverly Hills, May 7:

Paint has been put down to towns of three letters, Ada, Oklahoma, for instance. Mooselookmeguntic, Maine, sent me a bill
for $79. They had to put a letter on each house and borrowed
three houses from Connecticut.

Beverly Hills, May 15:

The only real bona fide indication of prosperity was in the paper today: "Divorces in Reno have increased over 105 per cent in the last year."

Beverly Hills, May 18:

Overestimated my resources when made offer to furnish paint. It was a typographical error, I meant I would send brush to any town who would paint name.

Beverly Hills, May 22:

Big headline in the paper says, "Three newspaper men arrested in connection with horse race betting." In the adjoining column it says, "Wall Street stock market reaches another four million; call money is the highest in its history."

You don't have to look much further in the paper for humor than that. We have one rule: If you can build a business up big enough, it's respectable.

May 26:

We are going at top speed, because we are using all our natural resources as fast as we can. If we want to build something out of wood, all we got to do is go cut down a tree and build it. We dident have to plant the tree. Nature did that before we come. Suppose we couldent build something out of wood till we found a tree that we had purposely planted for that use. Say, we never would get it built. If we want anything made from Steam, all we do is go dig up the coal and make the steam. Suppose we dident have any coal and had to ship it in. If we need any more Gold or Silver, we go out and dig it; want any oil, bore a well and get some. We are certainly setting pretty right now. But when our resources run out, if we can still be ahead of other nations then will be the time to brag; then we can show whether we are really superior.

You know, Cal, you been President at a mighty fortunate time in our lives. The Lord has sure been good to us. Now what are we doing to warrant that good luck any more than any other Nation?

Now just how long is that going to last? Now the way we are acting, the Lord is liable to turn on us any minute; and even if He don't, our good fortune can't possibly last any longer than our Natural resources. So as I look at Mexico, which hasent even been scratched as far as its natural wealth is concerned, I believe they are better off than us in the long run.

It just ain't in the book for us to have the best of everything all the time. A lot of these other Nations are mighty poor, and things kinder equal up in the long run. If you got more money, the other fellow mebbe has better health; and if another's got something, why, some other will have something else. But we got too big an overbalance of everything and we better kinder start looking ahead and sorter taking stock and seeing where we are headed for.

You know, I think we put too much emphasis and importance and advertising on our so-called High standard of living. I think that "high" is the only word in that phrase that is really correct. We sure are a-living High.

Our Children are delivered to the schools in Automobiles. But whether that adds to their grades is doubtful. There hasent been a Thomas Jefferson produced in this country since we formed our first Trust. Rail splitting produced an immortal President in Abraham Lincoln; but Golf, with 29 thousand courses, hasent produced even a good A Number-1 Congressman. There hasent been a Patrick Henry showed up since business men quit eating lunch with their families, joined a club and have indigestion from amateur Oratory. Suppose Teddy had took up putting instead of horseback riding. It's also a question what we can convert these 4 billion filling Stations into in years to come. But it ain't my business to do you folks' worrying for you. I am only tipping you off and you-all are supposed to act on it.

*   *   *   *   *

Do all the farmers vote for the Democrats, so they can get in and cut down the tariff and get cheaper manufactured things? No, just a few in the South that don't raise anything but cotton, and don't have enough to buy anything even if the tariff was cut down. Well, why don't the big farming States of the Middle and Northwest vote for the party that wants to lower the tariff? Because they are Republicans. Well, why are they Republicans? Because they were against slavery. When was they against slavery? In 1861. Well, ain't the war over? Yes, but the North don't know it. Well, ain't slavery over? Yes, it's over for everybody but the Farmer. Well, ain't a Farmer's problem, whether he be in Maine, Georgia, South Dakota, Michigan or Arizona — ain't it the same? Yes. Well, then why don't they all vote together at least, either on one side or the other? Because their fathers dident vote that way, and it's against Tradition. What is Tradition? It's the thing we laugh at the English for having, and we beat them practicing it.

Beverly Hills, May 30:

How would this do as a compromise way to build Boulder Dam? Put California Senators and Congressmen on their side of the river and Arizona's on their side and let 'em start throwing boulders at each other, and in a year there would be enough rocks in the river to make Boulder Dam.

Kansas City, Missouri, June 17:

Here are just a few of the things that I bet you didn't know the Republicans were responsible for: Radio, Telephones, Baths, Automobiles, Savings Accounts, Law Enforcement, Workmen living in houses, and a living wage for Senators.

The Democrats had brought on War, pestilence, debts, Disease, Bo weevil, Gold teeth, need of Farm relief, suspenders, floods, famines and Tom Heflin.

* * * * *

Wow! She is all over, Hoover and Curtis.

Claremore, Oklahoma, June 20:

I am flying tomorrow to Fort Worth, the ranchman's post office. Hurrah for Amon Carter, West Texas, and Dan Moody! Jesse Jones get me some chili rady, and a ticket to the hall where they are exhibiting the New York delegation.

Claremore's got a manicurist. Here's the town for the Democrats in '32, if they meet again.

Fort Worth, June 21:

We are holding a preliminary convention tonight at Amon Carter's Shady Oaks Farm (all of us party advisers). It looks like a dry Vice-President. Then those that are wet can go to the President's dinner and those that are dry can go to the Vice-President's.

Democratic Convention, Houston, June 24:

There is only one thing to do, nominate with Smith a Dry for Vice-President. Well, there is a sure fire laugh, for you then have an animal with a WET head and a DRY tail.

June 22:

H. L. Mencken, the undesirable element of Literature, was sitting by me at the convention and he suggested the singer follow "Dixie" with "Marching through Georgia." I knocked him under the press table, before Captain Hickman, my Texas Ranger Friend, could get out his gun to totally dispose of him.

June 29:

Well, Boys, she blowed up in a blaze of harmony. Joe Robinson of Arkansas got the nomination for Vice President. He comes from the wilds of Arkansas, where they are hard to take. I have had one in my house for twenty years, and there is just no managing them.

Santa Barbara, July 12:

This fellow Raskob, that the Democrats grabbed off for stage manager, took General Motors when it was nothing but a few bent axles and some old carburetors and put it on Wall Street and got away with it. Now, if he can combine all the loose nuts of the Democrats he is liable to repeat.

Beverly Hills, July 17:

This thing of being a hero, about the main thing to do is to know when to die. Prolonged life has ruined more men than it ever made.

Beverly Hills, August 5:

If you ever said a prayer say one for the return of Fred Stone to stage. He has given more people real clean, wholesome laughs than any man that ever stepped on our stage. What a character of a man he is! To see him is to admire him, to know him is to love him.

Beverly Hills, August 12:

Hoover says every man has the right to ask the following question: "*Is the United States a better place for the average man to live in because the Republican Party has conducted the Government eight years?*" If we are privileged to ask the question, I will be the first one to bite. *Is it?*

Beverly Hills, August 12:

Hoover was against poverty and favored education, even if you couldn't get into a fraternity. He said prohibition was a "noble experiment," and he believed in noble things, even if they were only experiments.

Beverly Hills, September 2:

Wouldn't it be great if Mexico started electing by the ballot instead of by the bullet, and us electing by the ballot instead of by the bullion.

LET US PRAY THEY DON'T FIND OUT WHAT'S THE MATTER WITH THE MOVIES

I can't write about the movies for I don't know anything about them, and I don't think anybody else knows anything about them.

It's the only business in the world that nobody knows anything about. Being in them don't give any more of an inkling about them than being out of them.

They, just a few months ago in New York, had a convention to discuss ways and means of regulating them and fixing a few of the things that they thought was worrying the industry. Well, it didn't get anywhere for nobody knew what was worrying the industry.

Everybody knew what was worrying him personally, but there was no two things that was worrying the same person.

The exhibitor said he wanted better pictures for less money; the producer said he wanted better stories and better directors and better actors for less money.

The actor said: "You are not giving me a fair share of what I draw at the box office." Will Hays said: "They got to be cleaner."

The exhibitor says: "If you get them too clean nobody is interested in them."

The novelist says: "What's the use of selling them a story, they don't make the story they buy."

The Scenario Staff says: "It reads good but it won't photograph." The exchange salesmen say: "The exhibitors are a dumb lot, they don't know what their audiences do want."

The exhibitors say: "We may be dumb, but we know how to count up. Give us pictures where there is something to count up."

The so-called intellectual keeps saying: "Why don't they give us something worthwhile in the movies that we can think about."

The regular movie fan says: "Give us something to see, never mind think about. If we wanted to think we wouldn't come here."

The old married folks say: "Give us something besides all this love sick junk, and the fadeout behind a willow tree."

The young folks that pay the rent on these temples of uplift say: "Give us some love and romance; what do we care about these pictures with a lot of old folks trying to show what they do in life. We will get old soon enough without having to see it now."

Wall Street says: "We want more interest on our money."

The producers say: "Look at the fun you are having by being in this business. Didn't we give you a pass through the studio, what do you want for your money?"

The actors that aren't working say: "They don't want actors any more, they only want types."

The actors that are working say: "Thank God they are beginning to realize it's us actors they want and not just somebody that looks like the part."

Everybody is trying to offer suggestions how to regulate the

business and bring it down on a sane basis. They are not going
to bring it back on a sane basis. It will keep right on going just
like it is now. It was never meant to be sane. It grows and gets
bigger in spite of every known handicap.

You can't get a picture so poor but there will be an audience
growing up somewhere that will like it, and you can't get one so
good but what they will be forty percent of the people that see it
that won't like it. If it wasn't that way everybody in the world
would go to see one picture. So they better quit monkeying with
business and let it alone. It's odd now, but it's odd in all of us
movie people's favor.

The exhibitor that says he isn't making as much money as he
used to, means that he is not making as much as he did last year or
the year before but he doesn't mean that he is not making as much
as he was before he got into this business.

The producer who says things are getting tough in the pictures
business, you suggest to him to go back into his original line of business and he will punch you in the jaw.

And the same with the actor, or anyone connected with the business, and the same also with the audience. He starts beefing about
poor pictures, when he was never able to go before and get as much
amusement for twenty, thirty, forty or fifty cents. He can't go into
any other amusement business and better himself. If he could he
would do it. He is is doing better than he ever was in his life before.

  He used to have to go to the gallery and sit in peanut hulls up to
his chin, and come down a long stairs into a dark alley after the
show, for more money than he can sit in a wonderful upholstered
seat that he didn't even know existed till the movie man built his
theater.

It's breaking pretty soft for audiences the same as for movie
actors and producers and exhibitors.

Then the highbrow that says pictures are the bunk, let him try
and find something that will beat them for twenty-five cents. There
is no other branch of amusement in the world that has been
brought right to his own little town, or if in a city, to his nearest
street corner.

They are not bringing opera to your door step, or spoken drama to your neighborhood. You have to go to the city to get them. So don't start yapping about pictures. There is no law in the world that makes you go to them.

No sir, you go to them because there is nothing that has yet been invented that can compare with them for the money.

These fan magazines are always yowling about, "What's the matter with the movies?" Try and get any of these editors to go back into their old newspaper work at their old salaries.

No sir, the movie business is a "cuckoo" business made by "cuckoo" people for "cuckoo" audiences, and as about eighty percent of the world is "cuckoo" anyway they fill a spot that nothing will ever replace unless somebody invents something more "cuckoo."

Everybody is trying to find out what's the matter with them. If they ever do find out they will ruin their own business.

The movies have only one thing that may ever dent them in any way, and that is when the people in them or the people going to them, ever start taking them seriously. That was one wonderful thing about dear Marcus Loew. He made more money out of them than anybody, and he had the greatest sense of humor of any producer of them. But he always said, "I don't know what they are all about, and the more I learn about them, the less I know."

So go ahead, work hard, and do the best you can, but don't try to hold a clinic over the body.

Call them "arts and sciences" but do so with your tongue in your cheek. Everything that makes money and gives pleasure is not art. If it was, bootlegging would be the highest form of artistic endeavor.

So let's everybody connected with them, and everybody that loves to go see them, as we go to our beds at night, pray to our Supreme Being, that he don't allow it to be found out what is the matter with the movies, for if he ever does, we will all be out of a job.

Beverly Hills, September 6:

Politics are receiving a lot of attention because we have nothing else to interest us. We don't have to worry about anything. No nation in the history of the world was ever sitting as pretty. If we want anything, all we have to do is go an buy it on credit.

So that leaves us without any economic problem whatever, except perhaps some day to have to pay for them. But we are certainly not thinking about that this early.

New York, September 12:

Left old Beverly and jumped back to New York to rehearse a part in Dorothy Stone's show. Its the first time I ever did reherse. In all the Follies, I just generally had my specialty and dident have to learn any lines only the ones I would read every day in the papers. But this is a kind of a part. Course its not much of a part as acting goes, but I will have to learn the lines so the other Actors will know when their cue comes.

Its all greek to me. I feel like a kid at his first school entertainment. Old New York looks just the same after an absence of about three years. Course I have played there every year, but only one night just like all the rest. But this will be my first stage engagement with a show since I left the Follies three years ago.

You know I believe a big city changes less than any other place. Its been a many a year since I first went back there, but it dont seem like there has been so many changes. You see it always was so big, that it just dont seem like it can get any bigger. A street can just be so full of houses, and it was full of them when I first saw it. Course they change the houses every few years, but they all look about alike.

New York, September 13:

Been up to see Fred Stone. If the world could see what that man is recovering from it would be worth the accident, just to prove to people what clean living and physical fitness will do for you when you really need 'em.

New York, September 23:

In Omaha Al relieved the farmers, in Oklahoma (near Claremore) he bawled out the Baptists, but in Denver he reached his peak when he told the truth about the power trusts. When you hop on the power trusts you are standing on the very arches of the Republican Party.

I had a joke about the power lobby in the papers and I got so many letters from power magnets saying, "There was no power lobby," that it almost made me lose faith in rich men. So sic 'em, Al. Yours for everybody owning their own river.

New York, September 25:

Al spoke in Montana on oil corruption. That subject can get more applause and fewer votes from an audience than any subject during our time.

Corruption and golf is two things we might just as well make up our minds to take up, for they are both going to be with us.

Springfield, Mass., October 2:

Al Smith unanimously nominated Franklin D. Roosevelt today for Governor of New York.

He is a Roosevelt by blood, but a namesake politically. If he had retained his splendid qualities and stayed with the Republican end of the family, he would have been President. But I doubt if he could have retained those qualities and been Republican.

October 14:

These Politicians would make old David Harum go and burn up his barn. He never saw the day he could pull off swaps these can now. Two thirds of the men in Politics are not "Free born Americans of lawful age and a fair break in intelligence" as the constitution calls for. They was born, but not free; they are of age but it wasent lawful, and the break they got in intelligence was not Fair.

What I mean is they are just a lot of pawns. They belong to their party and mess around and do odd chores, and do all the dog robbing that is handed out to them to do, then a bunch of men meet in a room and start moving these blocks around. The poor Nut don't know if he is to be advanced from an Alderman to Senator or sent back to garbage inspector. These Babies at the head move him and he goes and likes it or gets out. Maybe he has done his work just as well as some of the rest, but he just wasent the type they had picked to advance. Then if he is one that they advance it is somebody that they know the higher they put him the more they can control him.

An Independent Guy with no ties at all couldent not only get to first base but he couldent get a foul off these high ups. There is a hundred things to single you out for promotion in a party politics besides ability.

You can talk all the modesty you want, but its just not one of our major Industries. The old boys like to get their name in the pot. They like to pose as advisers and leaders.

October 21:

You know it just dont seem like we have any game in America where one man stands out so prominently and so far ahead of all the others in his line as Babe Ruth does in Baseball. He is the most colorful Athlete that we have in any branch of sport. Kids are crazy about Ruth, and he is always doing something to keep solid with them. Raised himself in an Orphans home in Baltimore, he has always kept a keen interest and sympathy with kids.

Look what happened in that last game in St. Louis. He had knocked one home run to tie the score and here he was at the bat again and the Pitcher had two strikes on him, and Ruth had turned and was talking to the Catcher and Umpire when Sherdell, the Pitcher, threw one right quick and it was another strike. But they had made a rule before the series started that there was to be no pitch made only when the batter was ready. Well Ruth knew that that was the rule, and he knew that he was in the right. So while the St. Louis players and the Umpires were arguing why he just stepped back and applauded them. Of course they decided in his favor. Then the Pitcher had to pitch to him again, as they dident count that last ball, and as he did why Babe just laughingly smacked one over the whole Grand stand into Grand Boulevard, and waved and kidded with the hooting crowd as he went around the bases. Then two innings later he comes up again amid jeers and just jokingly "putted" into the Mississippi River, his third home run for the afternoon.

In the meantime as he would go to his position out in the field why the St. Louis fans with their accustomed hospitality conferred on him a shower, a good deal as they do a bride when she is about to make the leap. But there was no point lace, or doilies in this.

It was in the nature of Pop Bottles. They had strewn his path with glassware. He just kidded with 'em, and tossed the bottles aside, and then in the very last of the ninth inning when St. Louis had two runners on bases and their heavy hitters up with two out, a long high foul was hit, and even though being crippled, he leaped from bottle to bottle, like Liza crossing the ice. He finally found two bottles standing on top of each other and that give him a little higher lift, so all he was able to do was make a sensational one-handed catch and come down among a case of what had been home brew containers. He is the only athlete that ever rose to the heights with nothing but a foundation of Coca Cola under him. They also shied seat cushions, St. Louis Globe Democrats, and Republicans, and even were mean enough to shy tabloids at him as he ran to catch the ball. But through all this he went right on kidding and laughing at them.

He is the Abraham Lincoln of baseball. It just don't seem right that a Pitcher should be made to have to stand out there in front of him and have to throw baseballs at him and take the chance of being murdered when they come back to you.

New York, October 22:

We have opened up our show. Putting on a Fred Stone show without Fred is about like Ringling bringing in his circus and announcing that he is sorry but that the elephants, clowns and horses were not with it.

New York, October 31:

Well, the "promising" season ends next Tuesday and that same night the "Alibi" season opens and lasts for the next four years.

To show you what campaign promises amount to, can you remember back a few weeks ago when the promise was made on both sides that "the campaign was to be run on a high plane"?

This campaign ends Tuesday, but it will take two generations to sweep up the dirt.

New York, November 4:

Hoover wants no votes merely on account of religion. Smith wants no votes solely on religious grounds. Both would accept

Mohammedan vote if offered.

Hoover would like to live in the White House. Smith is not adverse to living in the White House. In order to get in there either one will promise the voters anything from perpetual motion to eternal salvation.

New York, November 5:

The election ain't over till 6 o'clock tonight, but it's been over since last June.

This is going to be the greatest lesson in geography that New York City ever had. They never knew how many people live west of the Hudson river.

New York, November 7:

FOR SALE — Would like to sell, trade, dispose of or give away to right parties franchise of what is humorously known as Democratic Party. Said franchise calls for license to enter in national elections; said right or franchise is supposed to be used every four years, but if intelligent parties had it they would let various elections go by default when understood they had no chance.

If in right hands and only used in times when it had an "issue" or when Republican Party had split, think it could be made to pay, but present owners have absolutely no business with it. Under present management they have killed off more good men than grade crossings have. Address Raskob, back at Chevrolet workshop.

November 11:

Well, it's all over, and what a relief! What has it proved? What has it profited us? We have gone through the most exciting and bitter election that we have ever held in our history.

Of all the inconsistencies, of all the back tracking, of all the changing opinions, of all the waiting to see what the majority will be liable to do, of all the trading back and forth with each other for support! There is no more independence in Politics than there is in jail. They are always yapping about "Public service." Its public jobs that they are looking for.

This country runs IN SPITE of parties. In fact Parties are the biggest handicaps we have to contend with. If we dident have to stop to play Politics any administration could almost make a garden of Eden out of us. If we were run by the Manager form of Government we would soon be paying so little taxes we would be lonesome. You could transfer the Senate and Congress over to run the Standard Oil or General Motors and they would have both things bankrupt in two years. No other business in the world could afford to carry such deadwood. But we got em, and they are going to live off us someway, so we just as well put long tail coats on em and call em "Statesmen." They are great Guys personally, and they know in their own heart that its a lot of "Boloney," and if they are smart enough to make us feed em, why then we are the Yaps, not them.

Well, all I know is just what I read in the election returns. And from a Democratic standpoint it was some of the poorest reading matter I ever dug into. It really was not only bad composition, but the English was terrible in it. Texas Republican, now thats not according to any English Shakespeare or old Bacon rime ever wrote. Virginia with the Yankees. I bet Jefferson pretty near rolled off that hill.

The everglades of Florida voting the Aligators with Wall Street! I tell you the world is "Cockeyed." North Carolina joining the D.A.R.'s. Whats become of our glorious tradition? Are we leaving the teachings of our forefathers? Where does the fair State of Oklahoma think she can hide her head when she is asked to answer her Ancestors?

December 2:

You know the Democrat at heart is just naturally an amiable fellow. He would rather talk with you any time than make a dollar off you. He just loves politics, not for what he can get out of em, for he never has received much of a dividend on his political investment, but he just wants to be known as a Politician. Now a Republican dont, he wants politics to be known as his side line. He is sorter ashamed of it. He wants to work at it, but he wants people to believe he don't have too. But the old Democrat he is still so old fashioned that he thinks its one of the honored professions.

Just let him head a few committees, and make a few speeches to you every once in awhile and he is in his glory.

When the Democrats get their clutches on a postoffice, why it is a cross between the country grocery store and modern Night Club. They welcome anything in there just so its in the shape of an argument. When they hand you the mail they want to know who its from and Why. The Republicans have been running the Post Office so long that he is as independent as a Bank Vice President. He wont act like you ought to have any mail. The Post Office to him is just a subsidiary of the Republican headquarters. A Democrat is tolerated in there but they dont want him to litter up the place long with his presence.

New York, December 5:

My November message on the "State of the Nation": The nation never looked like it was facing a worse Winter — birds, geese, Democrats and all perishable animals are already huddled up in three or four States down South. We are at peace with the world because the world is waiting to get another gun and get it loaded. Wall Street is in good shape, but Eighth Avenue never was as bad off. The farmers are going into the Winter with pretty good radios, but not much feed for their stock.

December 16:

You have a Budget like you have a limit in a Poker game. You are not supposed to go beyond it till at least an hour after the game has been started. We wont run over the Budget limit till maby as late as August. Its a good thing. It makes another Department in Washington. Then its fun to vote on when its presented.

New York, December 20:

Every time a woman leaves off something she looks better, but every time a man leaves off something he looks worse.

New York, December 31:

Sam Wildoats, farmer (makes a New Year's prediction); "1929 just brings on 365 more days to pay interest to the people who are prosperous."

CHAPTER FOURTEEN

I Take Over the Democratic Party

1929 — Will gave advice to the defeated Democrats and since he saw no hope for them otherwise took over the management — unofficially — of their destiny. At the same time he understood why Cal Coolidge quietly grinned as he went out of office and left the future to "Doctor of Catastrophes," Herb Hoover.

Will finished his Fred Stone theatrical engagement and returned to Beverly Hills where he made his first talkie.

In the late fall Wall Street became "wailing street" and rooms in New York were rented more for jumping purposes than for sleeping. He welcomed broke Eddie Cantor, who'd tried to beat the Street, into the fifth estate.

When Herbert Hoover appointed a commission to find out what the trouble was, and gave them three years to do so, Will announced that he could diagnose the trouble in five minutes.

New York, January 13:

New York is getting like Paris. Its supposed Devilment is its biggest add. The rest of the country drop in here and think if they dont stay up till four A.M. that New Yorkers will think they are "Yokels," when as a matter of fact New Yorkers have been in bed so long they dont know what the other half is doing. New York lives off the out-of-towner trying to make New York think he is quite a fellow.

*   *   *   *   *

On January 19, in "There Is Life in the Old Gal Yet, Al" (Saturday Evening Post) Will gave some more advice to Al Smith:
Dear Al:

I just thought I would take my pen in hand and drop you a few lines. This is not one of those "Too bad, old boy, we will get 'em the next time" letters. This is from an old friend who ever once in a while drops you a line, and tries to be truthful and lay some facts before you as they are, and Not as Political Leaders tell you they are.

Now, I knew you was pretty busy up to around November, and I dident want to bother you, cause this thing of running for President takes up just as much time on the Democratic side as it would on some side where you had a chance. Now you got time to sit down and think it over, I want to run over some things with you — talk over what we might 'a' done, pass over what we did do, and hold a sort of a Clinic over the old Democratic body and see just how much life there is in the old Gal yet.

This fellow Hoover is where he is today because he knew when to refuse something that he knew wouldent get him anywhere. He struggled along for eight years just practically as a Bill of Laden Clerk and a First-Aid Kit to Catastrophes, but look where he wound up. You see, all this is right along the line I wrote you that other letter way back in October, 1927. I was trying to tell you, you got to wait for things till they are ripe; don't just jump into things, just because somebody offers it to you. Look and see if it's going to lead anywhere. Now, after I wrote you that letter, a lot of your own

Party thought I was all wet and dident know anything about it. Now I am not rubbing it in, for you took your defeat in too good a manner. You was a good Sport and dident let out a single Squak. But I repeat, why do we keep on doing things, elections after elections, that we absolutely know won't get us anywhere?

Now, Al, I like you Democrats; you are sorter my kind of people, but I am just sick and tired seeing the whole thing mismanaged. So I have decided to take it over and see what we can salvage out of it. But you all got to take my advice from now on. If I see fit not to start an Entry in '32, why we won't start any. I am tired seeing good men killed off for nothing; I am tired seeing one Party that is not One Bit better than the other, Just Continually outsmart us. Those Guys can be beat, but Not with Jeffersonian and Jacksonian speeches. If a national question comes up, there is no sensible reason why we shouldent be on the Popular side, instead of the Right side all the time. Leave out old Political Leaders in the Senate, where they can't do anybody any good or harm, but hide 'em when a Campaign is on; they been making the same speeches since they was weaned. There is absolutely millions of people in this country who are not even half pleased with the way these Republicans run things, but they prefer 'em to the Democrats' old-fashioned ideas. Now, taken out from under the influence of a lot of these old Mossbacks, you are a pretty progressive fellow, Al, and with you and this fellow Roosevelt as a kind of neclus, I think we can, with a lot of help from some Progressive young Democratic governors and senators and congressmen, why, we can make this thing into a Party, instead of a Memory. Get Raskob back on those Chevrolets again. He may know what Wall Street is going to do, but none of those Guys have got a vote. We don't need a Financier; we need a Magician. And let Norris and Blaine and the rest of them go back to where they come from — wherever that was. That is one of the strictest rules I will have in the future: "Don't let anybody join us unless he is bringing somebody with him."

Now, I will see you around New York during the winter — unless you run onto something. I will write you more about my plans soon. They are all practical; they are not New, but they are new to the Democrats. With four years to work on, we may land Coolidge. Things won't look so rosy when he has to look at them from the outside.

Well, I must close, Al. Good luck to you and all the Smith tribe. Met your Daughter the other night at a dinner over at Mrs. Chas. Dana Gibson's. Now, Al, while you ain't doing nothing will you do me a favor and work on that pronunciation of "Radio."

Yours,

WILL

New York, January 25:

Certainly a great business opportunity showed up in the papers today: "No training, no conscience necessary; all you need is six hundred thousand dollars, but you get it back the first good day."

Wall Street is dividing the kitty with 275 more members.

The farmers ought to go in together and buy one seat. That would relieve the whole bunch.

P.S. Didn't we used to have a word during the war called non-essential?

January 27:

You know a fellow that was out front the other night and come back in my dressing room and we had a fine visit. And funny thing it was the first time I had ever met him personally. I thought I had run onto about all the men that have been mixed up in our National affairs. But here was one that I honestly believe had more influence on American affairs in our generation than any other ten men, and that would include Presidents too. It was Colonel House.

Just think the part that man played during the entire eight years of the Wilson Administration. We had all formed all kinds of opinions and ideas about what kind of a fellow he was, and what manner of man to get this hold on the brain of a man like Wilson. Well from the minute you meet him you know he's got something. He is quiet spoken, but you know he "savvies" what he is talking about. Funny thing about that fellow. You know he and Wilson kinder had a falling out along about the time of one of those trips to Paris to get the League of Nations thing fixed up. The President kinder jarred loose from him. But you notice Mr. Wilson dident do so good afterwards. Nobody knows what all the advice that House give to Mr. Wilson was. But whatever it was, the minute it stopped, you could tell it.

Just think of a quiet little fellow from away off down in those cedar breaks of that wide old State of Texas, holding no office, having no official capacity, yet really controlling the destinies of perhaps not only our 110 million, but the ultimate outcome of millions in other Countries, he alone and single handed talked and negotiated with every European Leader long before we ourselves got into the war. Wouldent his real personal opinion and absolute down to earth knowledge of what happened during those eventful years be the greatest thing we could possibly have? That little fellow knows MORE about the war than any man in America. Well, Sir, do you know I introduced him to the audience, for here was a fellow who I knew that nine tenths of them after all the reading about him had never seen him, and he got one of the biggest receptions I have heard in the Theatre. Pershings was the biggest. I kinder felt like a lot of those people felt like he had never got any too square a deal in the whole thing, and I think they admire the fact that he has never put up a holler or let out a squawk. He has told in his books lots of things that happened, but Lord, what he knows that he never HAS TOLD.

February 3:

Thats a tough Baby that Secretary of State thing. You come in there labeled as a Statesman and limp out headed for the ash can of Political hopes.

New York, February 8:

Every day now stock market "faw down go boom," so tomorrow no session. Called off on account of the "flu." And a funny thing it was on account of the "flu." If it had "flu" up they wouldn't have had to call it off on account of the "flu," but as it "flu" downward, why everybody has to "flu" around Saturday and get ready for not only the "flu" Monday but maybe pneumonia.

New York, February 10

New York can't sleep tonight wondering what the stock market will open at tomorrow. Radio just had its usual amount of static over the weekend, Steel turned out no product or received any new orders during Sunday, Montgomery Ward peddled nothing since Saturday, yet they will all change prices tomorrow.

"Why does this have to happen?" They say, "It's for the good of the country." Now you tell one.

New York, February 20:

It seems to be the nation's pastime now to offer Mr. Coolidge a job. I see today where the Denver Post offered him $75,000. I wonder if Mr. Coolidge wired back, "Is that to read it?"

New York, February 21:

There wasn't any Republicans in Washington's day. No Republicans, no income tax, no cover charge, no disarmament conferences, no luncheon clubs, no stop lights, no static, no headwinds.

Liquor was a companion, not a problem; no margins, no ticket speculators, no golf pants or Scotch jokes, and Tom Heflin hadn't yet read about the iniquities of Rome.

My Lord, living in those times, who wouldn't be great?

New York, March 1:

Mr. Coolidge, you are leaving us, and this is only a comedian's eulogy. But I will never forget what your bosom friend, Dwight Morrow, told me that you said to him on being suddenly sworn in an office that wasn't yours. "Dwight, I am not going to try and be a great President." That's all you said. That will stand in my memory as the greatest remark any office-holder ever made. For no man is great if he thinks he is.

You should be leaving without a single regret. I have told many jokes about you, and this don't mean I am going to quit, for we love jokes about those we like.

Coolidge served his State, town, country and nation twenty-five years and returned home to a rented house; not even a car.

March 2:

This thing of talking about "somebody's life being too valuable to risk in an airplane" is not only the bunk, but it's an insult to the man we ask to do our flying. Where does anybody's life come in to be anymore valuable than anybody else's? Aint life just as precious to one as to another?

We have heard that "can't spare you" attitude till we got a lot of men in this country believing it now. Say, get over that old ego. This country will replace you before your folks get home from the funeral.

If flying is dangerous pass a law and stop it. But don't divide your nation between a class that should fly and one that shouldn't. Aviation is not a fad, it's a necessity and will be our mode of travel long after all the people who are too valuable to fly have met their desired deaths by the roadsides on Sunday afternoons.

New York, March 4:

Mr. Coolidge passed through here this evening and I believe I know what that quiet grin was about. He came into office accidentally and we didn't expect anything. We just thought if this little, inoffensive fellow can keep some of the States from seceding we will all be thankful. But Hoover! Here is just a few things we look to be settled not later than Saturday.

Farm Relief — Now we have never had farm relief in all our history, but we look to him for it.

Prohibition Enforcement — Never had it since it was established, but we expect it from him.

Prosperity — Millions never had it under Coolidge, never had it under anybody, but expect it under Hoover.

And women think he will wash their dishes and look after their babies.

Nothing short of Heaven will we accept under Hoover. Good luck to you, Herb!

March 6:

We got Hoover all set now for four years. After that he will have to hustle for himself. There is an option clause in his Contract, but we will look him over carefully before we exercise it. The night he was inaugurated why Mexico broke out. So this ain't going to be one of those "Let Nature take its course" Administrations.

March 30:

In "Mr. Toastmaster and Democrats" (Saturday Evening Post) Will gave his promised advice to the party:

WE are here gathered in festive array at Chili Joe's Greasy Spoon, celebrating my appointment as Manager and Supervising Director of the great old Democratic Party. In taking over this position I feel that I am replacing no one, or knocking anyone out of work; as it has been years since there has been either head or tail to the party. Now I am not doing this entirely out of the goodness of my heart. I have various reasons; among them is Sportsmanship. I think one of the greatest causes for the early hold that Politics had on our primitive Fathers and Grandfathers, was the fact that it was a real race every four years, and they wagered money back and forth on it. There was even times in its early career that its affairs were so well managed that even-money betting was not uncommon. So it's my ambition and dream to try and return elections to that great speculative stage. As it's been run in latter years, it's a good deal of the same nature as the Stock Market. Betting on the Republicans has been like being a Broker — you couldn't possibly lose. Now that is what the economist will tell you, "is not a healthy condition." There must be some semblance of equality, or where does our whole structure of Government go. Why should the World's Series, Why should the Prize fight, Why should the misguided Greyhound persuing a Rabbit that was sired by Edison, and who's DAm had a One-track mind — why should those things dwarf in speculative value the great National game of "Post Office; Who's got the Post Offices?"

Well, as a young Boy I didn't know a Republican from a Democrat, only in one way; if some man or bunch of men rode up to the ranch to eat or stay all night, and my Father set me to watching 'em all the time they was there — what they did and what they carried off — why, I learned in after years that they was Republicans; and the ones I didn't spy on — why, they were Democrats. For Democrats were loyal that way — they never took from each other. You see, we was on the lower side of the Montgomery Ward line during the Civil War between the Democrats and Republicans.

* * * * *

We got to get out and figure "what's going to happen"; not only figure on it but buy enough votes so it's got to happen. I don't mean to buy all of 'em with money. We will just buy what we can afford to that way, but Buy 'em some other way — with facts, with Issues, with new schemes. No voter in the World ever voted for nothing; in some way he has been convinced that he is to get something for that vote. His vote is all that our Constitution gives him, and it goes to the highest bidder. He jumps the way his Bread looks like it's buttered the thickest. So what I am going to do is to figure out a sales Campaign that will prove to him that we can offer him more butter than the Republicans. Just look at this, for instance: The Republicans have run the Government and made money out of it for themselves. Now what we got to do is to show the people that we can run it cheaper for them. In other words, we got to cut the Republicans' price. It's simply a mercantile business in a town — that's all the Government is. Now the Republicans are established, they got the main store there. We got to come in, open up, and show the people we can give 'em as good or better goods at lower prices. Now, we, in order to do that, might not make as much out of it for ourselves as they are making, AT FIRST, but we have all got to kinder sacrifice immediate profits to what we can get when we really get going good. You see, they are bound to have people in this town that, while they are buying from them now, and have been for years, yet they are not satisfied. They would go to somebody else quick if somebody else had something to offer them. But we can't come in and open up the Store with the same old goods we used to have when we used to run a little Store years ago. We can't sell 'em cotton stockings, button shoes, calico, Horseshoe Tobacco and snuff; we got to sell em scented Cigarettes now. There is not five homes in any town now with a place for a fellow to spit. So we either got to swallow our tobacco juice or change with the times. You can no more sell a man Jeffersonian Principles than you could sell him a Croquet Set. He don't know what they are. If it happened that many years ago, and you have to explain 'em, why, they couldn't 'a' been much good. A jug of Apple Jack and a chaw of Tobacco don't interest him along the hospitality line now. What he wants is a couple of shots of Rye, a niblick and the address of a friend.

Then your Women vote is a-coming in today. So can that old long-Underwear stuff and show em some Step-Ins that are prettier than the Republicans'. You think they are a-buying "Glorious Tradition" at the polls? No, Sir. They want to know what kind of a break they are going to get in Commerce and Industry. If they have to make the living for the family, they want to know what kind of inducement the Government is going to make to them for doing it. They are no smarter than their Mothers were, but they think they are. So what we got to do is to make 'em think we think they are. Somebody humorously told them that they "swung this last election," and they foolishly believed it. So that will just whet their appetite for the next one. But Lord, the last election was won six years before, when Coolidge Just Let Nature take its course.

The Nineteenth Amendment — I think that's the one that made Women humans by Act of Congress; in fact all the Amendments from along about the second or third, could have still been unpassed and Hoover would have made the same trip to Nicaragua. Women, Liquor, Tammany Hall — all had their minor little contributing factors one way or another in the total, but the whole answer was: We just didn't have any Merchandise to offer the Boys that would make 'em come over on our side of the Street. Our Store was open, but we just didn't have any Sale advertised. Our Ads consisted of enumerating the poor quality of the goods of our opposition, but we wasn't offering any longer lipstick for the same money than they was.

Now I don't say for sure that I will start a Candidate in 1932; it all depends. If I am going to coach this lay-out, why, I will go into a Huddle with myself along in the summer of '32, and see what's doing. If there is rust in the wheat, Chinch Bugs in the Corn, Boll weevil thriving off the Cotton, Suckers slack in Wall Street, Price of Liquor less than cost of Production, Mellon declaring he is too old to serve again, Rockne leaving Notre Dame, Peggy Joyce settling down, Oklahoma impeachments at low ebb, Bad year for Babe Ruth, Dempsey refusing to come back that year, as I say, all these above things happen in the spring and summer of 1932, and then I would get a training table ready and send in a Candidate. Mind you, I wouldent do it if all these had happened the year before or in 1931. You can have a Famine, Heel flies, and an Epidemic of the itch, all through the first three years of a Political reign, and then kinder pick up on the last year, and you can walk in. No voter can remember back a year. What happened in the last six months is as far as his mind can grasp. So that's why I couldn't possibly tell you in these next three years just what I will do; it all depends on that last summer.

If I meet you and don't look you in the face, you will know why. Don't think it's because I don't want to recognize you; it's because I am watching your waist line. I will hold a Clinic over the not Body Politic but Body Human and see what's happened just south of the Diaphragm. In other words, along about June or July, 1932, I will put America to a tape-measuring test, and if I find the center section NOT protruding, you will see a real Race in the coming November. But if I tap the public's stomach and it sounds like a Watermelon, we will just crawl back in with the Ground Hogs and won't come out as long as their middle makes a shadow. But the minute we see it receding toward the backbone, why we will pick up hope and be ready. In other words, you just can't beat a Party when the people are reducing PURPOSELY. But you let 'em start getting thin through lack of Nourishment and you can defeat the Party in power with nothing but a Congressman.

Then here is another thing that I have always claimed: You give the Country four more years of this Unparalleled Prosperity and they will be so tired of having everything they want that it will be a pleasure to get poor again. We are a great people to get tired of anything awful quick. We just jump from one extreme to another. We are much more apt to make a whole change than we ever are a partial change.

So I think the Republicans are overdoing this prosperity. You take our rich, now, on their vacations; they like to get away out and kinder rough it and pretend that they are poor again. They like to drive a little cheap make of car around personally. They just love to play poor, like a child loves to play dolls. You know, when you come home at night and find nothing in the Ice Box but Ice Cream

and Cake, it finally gets on your nerves. When a stock market
don't do nothing but go up, and all you have to do is Buy, why
there is not much incentive for a man with sporting blood.

Now, we are all here together at this dinner and there is no use
kidding ourselves; we are just naturally the cheapest of Political
Organizations. We are a happy lot, though; we are in just as good
humor when out of Office as we are in. We are just like a Life
Prisoner who has been made a Trusty; we know we ain't going to
do anybody any harm, and they know we ain't going anywhere.
We are just kinder tolerated for the laughs we hand out every four
years.

There is one thing about a Democrat! He would rather make a
Speech than a Dollar.

Now, the only way we ever learn anything is from somebody's
past experience; so I am in the Market for a speechless Democrat.
That is going to be harder to find than it will be to elect him,
but we will sure keep him quiet during the Campaign. Now, I
can't tell you now what the issues will be — that's too far off — but
one thing I will assure you now; It won't be any of the ones that
have been used all these past years. What we want to do is to
string along with these Republicans in the Senate or House, and
when something accidentally comes up that is good for the Country,
why, put it over. In other words, get in there and act like you was
working for the Taxpayer instead of exclusively for the Democratic
Party. Vote "YES" on something besides widening the Chata-
hoochie. Cut out that balloting on things in private. If you
haven't got the nerve to let the people know how you stand on anything, have a sick friend, and go home and sit up with him on the
day of the vote. But try and be nonpartisan; you would be surprised how quick the people of all Political denominations will find
it out. If the Senate wants to take a secret vote, let it be known
that Democrats were against it to a man. In other words, you got
to shame the Republicans into decency. But in doing so you will
make a rep for yourself.

May 5:
Well, we finished our Theatrical engagement [*Fred Stone Show*]

up in Boston and are moving over to Philadelphia for a couple of
weeks, then one week in Detroit and one more in Pittsburg and then
on the old Plane and out "Where Men are beginning to be heard."

May 12:

I never was much on this Book reading, for it takes em too long
to describe the color of the eyes of all the Characters. Then I like
my sunsets from eyesight and not from adjectives. Congress has got
more fiction in it in a day than Writers can think of in a year.

Beverly Hills, June 5:

England elects a Labor Government. When a man goes in for
politics over here, he has no time to labor, and any man that labors
has no time to fool with politics. Over there politics is an obliga-
tion; over here it's a business.

Beverly Hills, June 6:

The British Ambassador says no more liquor will be shipped in
while he is there. Now here is the catch. He didn't say this until
after his side had lost the election at home, which means that he will
soon be out of a job embassing. By declaring this he gets the next
one in bad by having set a precedent and incidentally not being
entirely destitute of sustenance during the remainder of his short
stay because there is enough on hand by economizing to last.

Diplomacy is a great thing if it wasn't transparent.

Beverly Hills, June 9:

There is an epidemic of towns trying to claim the birth of the
Republican Party.

All they have to do to find where the Republican Party was
formed is find where the first corporation was formed. It was incorporated for the sole purpose of taking over the management and
finances of the United States.

Its slogan is: "Stay with us, we can afford to pay more than our
competitors."

Beverly Hills, June 28:

The tariff is an instrument invented for the benefit of those who

make against those who buy. As there is more buys than there is
makes, it is a document of the minority, but what a minority!

June 30:

Some Professor (I guess it was Harvard, we always look to them
for the freak things) he made the Boys a talk about not aiming too
low. Said instead of marrying the Stenographer aim for the Bosses
Daughter. Now wait a minute. Have you seen ALL the Bosses
Daughters? You look em over and it will take quite a sacrifice to
give up the Stenographer and take The Daughter.

Course when he advised the Boys to be as "Snooty" as possible
and do anything they could to advance themselves, why that raised
a yell that went round the World. Well there was no use howling
about it. It was nothing but "An Old English Custom." Englishmen have been working that system for years. They always aim
above em. What really hurts was that the old Professor really had
about the dope on it. He dident have to tell em to do that, they are
doing it already. Higher education is doing more to teach it to
them than all the professors that would tell them to do it.

Course everybody broke into print and said it shoulent be that
way. But there was so much truth in the old Professors advice that
it had em winging to answer it. Whats the use kidding ourselves?
What makes em high hat any quicker than education? They got to
be high hat to keep up with the rest of their gang, and maby its better that they are. Its pretty tough on us but we just cant have the
children do like we do. We are always drilling into them, "When I
was a Boy we dident do that." But we forget that we are not doing
those same old things today. We changed with the times, so we
cant blame the children for just joining the times, without even having to change.

We are always telling em what we used to not do. We dident do
it because we dident think of it. We did everything we could think
of. We drove a horse and buggy and we dont drive one now. So
we just got to sit and watch em go, and I tell you they got to go some
to keep up with us. If anyone of us has a child that was bad as we
know we are we would have cause to start to worry.

Los Angeles, July 6:

Today I read where a speech that Franklin D. Roosevelt had made just about threw him in the ring as the next Democratic candidate.

Now there is a fine man. The Democratic Party has some of the finest men as candidates that we have in this country and it's almost a shame that they are to be eternally handicapped by being "right but never President."

Beverly Hills, July 26:

Henry Ford is 66 years old today. He has had more influence on the lives and habits of this nation than any man ever produced in it.

Great educators try to teach people, great preachers try to change people, but no man produced through the accepted channels has moved the world like Henry Ford. He put wheels on our homes, a man's castle is his sedan. Life's greatest catastrophe is a puncture, everybody is rushing to go somewhere where they have no business, so they can hurry back to the place where they should never have left.

So good luck, Mr. Ford. It will take a hundred years to tell whether you have helped us or hurt us, but you certainly didn't leave us like you found us.

Beverly Hills, August 10:

The whole financial structure of Wall Street seemed to fall the other day on the mere fact that the Federal Reserve Bank raised the amount of interest from 5 to 6 percent. Any business that can't survive a 1 percent raise must be skating on mighty thin ice.

The poor farmers took a raise from 6 to 10 percent with another 10 percent bonus to get the loan from the banks. It took all that to completely break them and nobody connected with the government paid any attention.

But let Wall Street have a nightmare and the whole country has to help get them back in bed again.

Santa Monica, California, August 14:

The German Zeppelin starts on its round the world trip tomor-

row; the German steamship Bremen broke the world's record in
crossing the Atlantic; their commerce is getting back strong.

These things prove that war is useless. Germany was getting too
strong commercially for some other nations 15 years ago. It don't
do no good to whip a man if he is beating you at anything. When
he gets up he can still beat you at the same thing. You only delay
him. You don't stop him.

August 24:

A Lobbyist is a person that is supposed to help a Politician to
make up his mind, not only help him but pay him.

August 29:

When I write em I am through with em. I am not being paid
reading wages. You can always see too many things you wish you
hadent said, and not enough that you ought to.

Beverly Hills, September 11:

Englishmen live slow and move fast; we live fast and move slow.
Englishmen are the only race of people that never travel for just fun.

Beverly Hills, September 16:

The old bromide about the South "still fighting the Civil War"
don't hold up so good. It was suggested to the Northern boys at
their reunion the other day that they hold a joint reunion with the
Southerners. Well, they just pulled out their whiskers and started
firing 'em at the suggester. Said they would never meet 'em till the
South admitted they was wrong.

So that is one merger that is off indefinitely. The North got all
the pensions and the postoffices. They don't need anything else.

Wichita, Kansas, September 17:

They was opening my first talking picture tonight in Los Angeles
and charging those poor people five dollars. I just couldn't stand
by and be a party to such brigandage. First night audiences pay
their money to look at each other, so if they get stuck tomorrow
night, they can't blame me. It will be because they don't look good
to each other.

Claremore, Oklahoma, September 18:

Back to the old home State. The Governor has just made me Colonel on his staff and I come home to put out a mint bed.

Every farmer in Oklahoma has a picture of the new Farm Board hung right on their wall in between the two mortgages.

El Reno, Oklahoma, September 22:

When you are visiting the beauty spots of this country, don't overlook Frank Phillip's ranch and game preserve at Bartlesville, Okla. It's the most unique place in this country. Got everything but reindeer. He shipped fifty down from Alaska. They stood the Summer fine and all froze to death in the Winter.

Beverly Hills, September 29:

We are all in a lather over lobbying. If a man with no official connection can change a whole conference, it's not him you want to investigate; it's the "buys" that he influenced. If we have Senators and Congressmen that can't protect themselves against these evil temptations of lobbyists, we don't need to change our lobby, *we need to change our representatives.*

Any person that can't spot a propagandist and lobbyist a mile away, must be so blind that they still think toupees are deceptive and can't tell a hotel house detective from a guest.

New York, October 29:

I have been in Washington on Inauguration Day, Claremore on Fourth of July, Dearborn on Edison's Day. But to have been in New York on "wailing day"! When Wall Street took that tail spin, you had to stand in line to get a window to jump out of, and speculators were selling space for bodies in the East River. If England is supposed by international treaty to protect the Wailing Wall, they will have to come here to do it. The wall runs from the Battery to the Bronx.

You know there is nothing that hollers as quick and as loud as a gambler, they even blame it on Hoover's fedora hat. Now they know what the farmer has been up against for eight years.

Waynoka, Oklahoma, October 25:

What does the sensational collapse of Wall Street mean? Nothing. Why, if the cows of this country failed to come up and get milked one night it would be more of a panic than if Morgan and Lamont had never held a meeting. Why, an old sow and a litter of pigs make more people a living than all the steel and General Motors stock combined. Why, the whole 120,000,000 of us are more dependent on the cackling of a hen than if the Stock Exchange was turned into a night club.

And New Yorkers call them rubes.

Los Angeles, October 31:

Sure must be a great consolation to the poor people who lost their stock in the late crash to know that it has fallen in the hands of Mr. Rockefeller, who will take care of it and see that it has a good home and never be allowed to wander around unprotected again.

There is one rule that works in every calamity. Be it pestilence, war or famine, the rich get richer and the poor get poorer. The poor even help arrange it. But it's just as I have been constantly telling you, "Don't gamble"; take all your savings and buy some good stock and hold it till it goes up, then sell it.

If it don't go up, don't buy it.

Hollywood, November 11:

It is something to think that half a dozen men could sit down and casually sign a pact to stop millions of men from killing each other.

If Armistice Day had stopped speeches, it would have done more than to have stopped the war, for speeches is what starts the next war. It's not armament, it's oratory that's wrong with this country.

Beverly Hills, November 12:

Prosperity this Winter is going to be enjoyed by everybody that is fortunate enough to get into the poor house.

All the big financiers and writers are saying "good values are worth as much as they ever were." But that's the trouble, nobody knows what they ever were worth. To make things look prosperous every company is trying to declare a dividend and they will do it, too. If they can sell enough stock to declare it on.

November 13:

This Stock Market thing has spoiled more appetites lately than bad cooking. Some fellow named Rogers Babson a month or two ago predicted that lightning was going to strike the margins, and because it dident do it the day his warning come out why they all give Rogers the laugh and said "This Country is too big and prosperous to have any let up in prices." Well it looked like Rogers had pulled a bone and he had to stand for a lot of kidding. But as the old saying, "He who laughs along toward the finish, generally carries more real merriment in his tones." So as things have turned out why it looks like the whole market has just tried to help Rogers Babson make a sucker out of his detractors.

The Stock Market is just like a sieve (one of those pans with holes in it). Everything and everybody is put into it, and it is shaken, and through the holes go all the small stuff. Then they load it up again and maby hold it still for awhile and then they start shaking again and through the little investors go. They pick themselves up, turn bootlegger or do something to get some more money, and then they crawl back in the hopper and away they go again.

November 17:

It takes years in this country to tell whether anybodys right or wrong. Its kinder a case of just how far ahead you can see. The fellow that can only see a week ahead is always the popular fellow, for he is looking with the crowd. But the one that can see years ahead, he has a telescope but he cant make anybody believe he has it.

Beverly Hills, November 19:

American already holds the record for freak movements. Now we have a new one. It's called "Restoring Confidence." Rich men who never had a mission in life outside of watching a stock ticker are working day and night "Restoring Confidence."

I want to do my bit but you will have to give me some idea of where "Confidence" is and just who you want it restored to.

Beverly Hills, November 20:

Confidence hasn't left this country; confidence has just got wise.

and the guys that it got wise to are wondering where it has gone.

November 24:

Oh it was a great game while it lasted. All you had to do was to buy and wait till the next morning and just pick up the paper and see how much you made, in print. But all that has changed, and I think it will be good for everything else, for after all everybody just cant live on gambling. Somebody has to do some work.

This session of Congress was called primarily to help the Farmer, and then when they all got to Washington why they learned from the Manufacturing State Senators that Industry was in a terrible shape, and that would they mind giving it a helping hand as they went along.

Well that looked reasonable. They dident go to the trouble of looking at Industrys earnings, they just took the Senators word for it.

December 1:

I have been trying my best to help Mr. Hoover and Wall Street "Restore Confidence." You take confidence, its one of the hardest things in the World to get restored once it gets out of bounds. I have helped restore a lot of things in my time, such as cattle back to the home range. Herded Folly Girls toward the stage door near show time. Helped to revive interest in National Political Conventions. Even assisted the Democrats in every forlorn pilgrimage, and a host of other worthy charities. But I tell you this "Restoring Confidence" is the toughest drive I ever assisted in. When I took up the work two or three weeks ago, confidence was at a mighty low ebb, that is so all the Papers and speakers was saying.

Wall Street had gone into one tail spin after another. You would pick up a paper in the morning and read the stock report and you wouldent think there was that many "Minus" signs in the world. Well the effect of it was just like going to Monte Carlo and hearing that everybody was betting on the Black and the Red had been coming up continually for two days. That would just simply demoralize southern France and the whole Riviera. Well thats what this

Market was doing here. It was just taking all the joy out of gambling. If it kept on like that it would discourage Gambling, and that of course would be bad for the country (thats what they said).

Course there was a lot of us dumb ones that couldent understand it. We said, "Well if somebody lost money there, why somebody else must have made it. You cant just lose money to nobody, unless you drop it somewhere and nobody ever finds it." They then said a good deal of the money was "Lost on Paper." That is it was figures but it wasent real money. Well I had done that, I could remember every contract I would get for a seasons work on the stage or screen, my wife and I would sit down and figure out what all we would have by the end of that season. Well at the end of the season we had the figures but we couldent find the money. So Wall Street Men had nothing on us. In fact I dont think it had anything on anybody, for we all can take a piece of paper and if you give us enough pencils we can figure ourselves out a pretty neat little fortune in no time, so when I heard that most of the money had been lost on "Paper Profits," why I felt right at home with them.

But then everybody said it would have a demoralizing effect on the country for so many to have their paper Profits all rubbed out at once. That it would have the effect of making people more careful with their money, and thereby make it bad for speculation. That if people dident trade in stock why Wall Street couldent exist.

So I says what can we do for em so they will keep on existing? "Why restore confidence." And thats what I been doing for weeks, writing and talking. Course I havent been buying anything myself. I wanted to give all the other folks a chance to have confidence first. There is none of the Greedy Pig about me. This confidence was for sale and I wanted them to have the very first chance of buying it.

Course I never could understand what the price of the stock had to do with keeping the company working and turning out their product. For instance if "Consolidated Corn Salve" stock had all been sold, and the company had that money it had brought in and was operating on that, what difference did it make to them if the stock was selling at a thousand bucks, or if people was using the stock to kindle their fire with? Their business was still to keep after

those corns. In other words they should be watching corns instead
of the market. If the shares sold for 564 one day and $1.80 the
next, what had happened during the night to the afflicted toes of
the country? Well I couldent get that.

Course they explained it off some way. Said, "Trading was good
for the country, and kept things a circulating." So I finally went
over to their side. I really did it for vanity, for I could see all the
big men over there, and I felt flattered when I saw that I was one
to join in this great work of getting people back to contributing to
Wall street again. Course there is a lot of them that is going to take
me time to get back. They not only lost confidence but they lost
money, some of them all of their money (and it wasn't "Paper
Money" they lost). So we will have to wait till they get some
money in some other business, perhaps in some business in which
they really have no confidence. Then they will be able to get back
into the market not only with new confidence but new money.
Thats going to take time in some cases.

But I am telling them that the Country as a whole is "Sound,"
and that all those who's heads are solid are bound to get back into
the market again. I tell em that this country is bigger than Wall
Street, and if they dont believe it, I show em the map.

Mr. Hoover called all the Railroad men in and they decided to
do all they could to keep people from riding on Busses. Then he
had all the Bankers there, and they announced what their annual
Jip would be for coming year. They agreed to be more careful in
their loans, and see that the borrower dident buy a farm with it, as
Agriculture was so uncertain. Try and get them to invest in some
business where he could read the paper in the morning and see
what he had. But its a great work, and I am just crazy about it.
Viva confidence.

Beverly Hills, December 1:

These clubs to encourage boys to raise live stock beat all the fraternity pins you can collect in a washtub. Raise live stock instead of
margins, get a farmer some fair prices and these kids will "inspire
more confidence" than a band of financiers.

Beverly Hills, December 7:

With Mr. Hoover pleading with everybody to spend all this money, I wonder what a little gentleman in a rented frame house in Northampton is thinking. The idea of spending will make him turn over in his bed of magazine manuscripts.

Beverly Hills, December 16:

I welcome to our ancient and honorable newspaper profession Eddie Cantor, my very good friend.

We spent our literary apprenticeship in the same school of hard knocks, Mr. Ziegfeld's Follies. We eked out a bare existence among nothing but bare backs. There was diamond necklaces to the right and Rolls Royces to the left of us and costumes of powder completely surrounding us. Those were hardship days, but great training for our journalistic future.

Eddie specializes in Wall Street and financial news. He is another Roger Babson and how I envy him, for my little efforts will always be lowly. I will never get further than just a police reporter on the affairs of Congress.

Beverly Hills, December 19:

There is only one form of employment in our country that I can think of but what has its bright spots and that's coal mining. There is generally an overproduction and they are out of work; if not that, it's a strike. Then when they do go to work, the mine blows up. Then if none of these three things happen, they still have the worst job in the world.

Beverly Hills, December 20:

I always felt there was only one thing that could possibly defeat Mr. Hoover's capable management of our affairs and that was when he run out of practical men to put on commissions and sure enough he is getting short handed. Yesterday's commission didn't have a practical man on it. Every one was a college professor.

It's to find out "what has brought the social changes in our lives here lately." Knowing college professors he gave them three years to agree on an answer.

I could have told him before sundown what's changed our lives: buying on credit, waiting for relief, Ford cars, too many Republicans, Notre Dame coaching methods and two-thirds of the Americans, both old and young, thinking they possessed "it."

Beverly Hills, December 22:

You can't say civilization don't advance, however, for in every war they kill you a new way.

Beverly Hills, December 25:

Passed the Potter's Field yesterday and they were burying two stanch old Republicans, both of whom died of starvation, and the man in charge told me their last words were, "I still think America fundamentally sound."
P.S. What do you know about those Republicans setting the White House on fire, trying to burn up their own records?

Beverly Hills, December 30:

This is our last day of grace. Tomorrow we are obliged to read the usual New Years prosperity applesauce by our same men who are always rich enough to see a great year coming up. And to show you they don't know any more about it than Clara Bow, last year they had their usual hokum predictions, and in October we lost half as much as it cost to put on the war. And yet not a one of these predicted it.

The poor haven't many rights as it is, so let's at least let 'em predict, especially as that's all they are going to get.

Beverly Hills, December 31:

I have read New Year predictions till I am blue in the face, but I have yet to see one word on what 1930 holds in store for the Democrats. And that's the very thing that makes me believe us Democrats may get a break in the coming year. I base my faith on the fact that 98 percent of all predictions are wrong, and on the fact that it's an off year in politics and all off years are Democratic years.

CHAPTER FIFTEEN

There Ain't No Civilization Where There Ain't No Satisfaction

1930 — Will went to the Disarmament Conference at London. Found it was no different from "old Arkansas politics," only the food was a little fancier. He missed a chance to fly back with a woman because he figured his wife would object to his spending the night alone with her out over the Atlantic Ocean.

He finally decided that America was "a nation that flourished from 1900 to 1942" and in their heyday "conceived many odd inventions for getting somewhere, but could think of nothing to do when they got there." He took his stand against success just for the sake of success — or money. Decided that we had plenty of both, but asked "what else?"

When people still couldn't decide what was the matter he bluntly pointed out that it was "the first payment what made us think we were prosperous, and the other nineteen is what showed us we were broke." His answer to

219

that corner of prosperity Hoover kept promising the country was "that war is nearer around the corner than prosperity is." He ended his blunt diagnosis by saying: "We are the first nation to starve to death with a storehouse that's over-filled with everything we want."

January 4:

Xmas is getting kinder like one of our old time western dances. They wait till the dancing is all over and then they sorter sweep out to see how many was left laying around. We are killing off some mighty good citizens with our Xmas cheer and it has been discussed quite openly as to whether the whole thing was worth the tallow or not.

Kids are getting too wise. Why I was a big chuckle-headed Nestor maby ten years old before I really even suspicioned that our old friend of the long whiskers wasent delivering into my stocking every Xmas morning the sack of candy, horn and cap pistol.

The whole Xmas thing started in a fine spirit. It was to give happiness to the young, and another holiday to the old, so it was relished by practically everybody. It was a great day, the presents were inexpensive and received with much joy and gratification, and it was a pleasure to see the innocent little souls as they rushed down to the big room with the fireplace on Xmas morning in their bare feet, and generally the back end of their little sleepers unbuttoned and a-dragging. They remembered right where they had hung their stocking, and they dived into it with great glee and anticipation. No matter what they dug out, it was great, it was just what they wanted him to bring, for they had confidence in him. The merest little toy was a boon to their young lives, and what a kick it was to the parents to have them rush back up to the bedroom and show you "what Santa Brought."

Then the Mother would finally venture down and look into her big-top stocking to see what the sly old Father had deposited during the night. Maby it was just more cotton stockings. Maby it was a new "sofa." Maby it was a new Axe for wood splitting. Maby a hot water bottle. But whatever it was it was the most acceptable thing in the world. It was just what she wanted her man "to get her." Ah! them was the days lads! When you could satisfy em with a squirrell Muff, and a box of five cent cigars practically cinched your friendship with a Male friend for the coming year. Then they talk about Civilization. *Say there aint no civilization where there aint no satisfaction, and that's whats the trouble now, nobody is satisfied.*

New York, January 10:

Since the Wall Street crash, which the Republicans refer to as a "business readjustment," prominent men had done nothing but tell us of the strength of the country. "Steel was strong," "T. and T. was strong," "Radio was strong," "breath was strong."

We have been "stronged" to death in speeches and statements, but last night Mr. Coolidge said, "The heart of the American people is strong," and here over 500 died of heart failure during the late "Republican readjustment." What he really meant was that "the American public's head is strong but his heart is weak."

* * * * *

Well I landed in New York on the Century and made a date to see Winifred Sheehan, the head man in the Fox organization at two o'clock. We talked over a Story that I am to do for my next Picture and found that it would take a little while to prepare it so that there was nothing I could be doing for the next couple of weeks. So I said, "Winnie I believe I will jump over to London to this Dissagreement Conference," and as our Delegation had already sailed We called up the Steamship line and here the Bremen, the newest and finest Boat, was sailing that very night. This was three o'clock and I had no Passport, Visa's or anything.

So we hustled around and grabbed off an Emergency passport, then I had to go get my picture taken to put on the "Suponea," so I rushed to one of those Passport Photo places, got the "Wanted in Oklahoma," then I had to make the British Embassy Offices to get the thing Visayed for their Country or I couldent land, then to get some Boat accomodations, then its knocking right on six o'clock, for this is all away down in the wrong end of New York.

Well I had to have clothes, I dident want a dress or Tuxedo, but I did want an old dark Blue serge that I could get in the dining room on the boat with, so I found a little place open, not exactly second-

hand, but they had been there so long they tasted like it. Then
some black shoes, and a black tie, and I was ready to fool the head
Steward. I was just thinking some people plan for years to go to
Europe and wonder what they will get to wear, and all that Hooey.
But Boy, I had to do it all in just fifteen minutes. Course I looked
like fifteen minutes, but I made it. The whole thing was originally
my Wife's idea anyhow. She had been saying all the time that I
should go to this Conference. I had been to the Washington one
and the Geneva one, and she insisted that I needed some new Gags,
and told me when I left if I had the chance to run over and see what
it was all about, for my Public.

London, January 17:

The American delegation arrived this afternoon and went into
conference at once at the American bar and sunk a fleet of schooners
without warning.

They brought eighteen young typewriters with 'em. That's four
and a half blondes to the delegate, and I can write in longhand,
left-handed, everything that will be done here in the next month.

London, January 21:

Well, the whole thing was nothing but a Democratic convention,
with a silk hat on. The King made the best speech and then showed
his real intelligence by leaving. When speaking he was facing the
American delegation. When he went out he happened to think, so
he sent four men back and they carried the gold throne chair out.
That will go on record as the first lack of confidence shown.

We stood during one speech, sat through eight and slept through
twelve; three solid hours of compliments and not a single rowboat
sunk.

When Mr. Stimson said we will stay here till the world disarms,
his wife says, "My lord!" and the rest of the wives shook hands with
me and bid me farewell forever.

London, January 27:

Mr. Stimson told me, "You go back home, Will, and announce
that one of America's muchly advertised talents has been overestimated. We are not the masters of bunk."

He had just come from a five-hour siege with the whole mess of 'em.

January 30:
Joe Robinson said to me, "Will, the whole thing is no different from old Arkansaw politics, only the food is a little fancier."

Steamship *Ile De France*, February 2:
I have nothing to say and feel in no shape to say it even if I did have. Lindbergh's ocean is as sore at the world as a defeated candidate.

When I hinted that I would fly back if I could, I received a lot of cables offering to take me on, among them Mrs. Keith Miller, one of our best airshees. My wife is not jealous, but she just never did like to have me stay out over the ocean all night with a strange woman or even a friendly woman. If we could have got in before dark she wouldn't have minded. Of course we could have taken a chaperon but not as much gas, and gas is more beneficial on a trip like that than a chaperon.

New York, February 7:
Mr. MacDonald did it today. He proposed to sink all our battleships and all France's submarines. Of course he would sink theirs, too.

Now here is the but. They don't need the big ships. They don't have to go as far for their wars as we do. We have no naval bases. We have to go away off and fight all afternoon and then have enough sandwiches and gasoline to get back on while England's naval bases are as monotonous as speakeasies.

New York, February 11:
I have just come from Fred Stone's opening night. What a triumph! Just think, with everything about him broken and shattered — all but his spirit — yet he never lost faith. He looked forward to this night. Four Stones, all marvelous. Their devotion equals their cleverness.

Now what's worrying me is how are they going to kill him off eventually. If I attend his funeral it will be no surprise to me at the cemetery when he arises and announces that the festivities are called off and then goes into a song and dance.

Beverly Hills, February 21:

On account of us being a democracy and run by the people, we are the only nation in the world that has to keep a government four years, no matter what it does.

Beverly Hills, February 28:

Mr. Taft, what a lovely soul! Just as a man and a real honest-to-God fellow, Mr. Taft will go to his grave with more real downright affection and less enemies of any of our Presidents.

It's great to be great but it's greater to be human. He was our great human fellow because there was more of him to be human. We are parting with three hundred pounds of solid charity to everybody, and love and affection for all his fellow men.

San Diego, March 16:

Every nation must have its legalized form of gambling. We must have our Wall Street. Mexico gives you a more even break. They have "roulette," also a percentage of your losings go to the government. They are a primitive race. They put government above broker.

Folks will take a chance. Old Noah gambled on not getting the "foot and mouth" disease in there with all those animals and old King Solomon bet a hundred women he wouldn't pay 'em alimony and won his bet.

Beverly Hills, March 17:

This is a great country at that. We used to think that "prosperity" was a "condition." Now we find that it is a "commodity." Mr. Hoover has ordered it delivered to us in 60 days, same as you would order a sack of flour or a side of bacon. If "good times" is not laying on our doorstep May 15th, 1930 we can sue the Republican party, get judgment against 'em, along with 123 previous judgments we held against the same corporation.

Beverly Hills, April 16:

You can kid about the old rubes that sat around the cracker barrel, spit in the stove, and fixed the nation, but they were doing their own thinking. They didn't have their minds made up by some propagandist speaker at the "Get Nowhere" Luncheon Club. Yours for more small town rubes.

April 20:

You know one of the most welcome things that has hit us in many a moon is the return of the long dresses. It had to come but it was a long time doing it. You see according to law, fashions must change every year, sometimes every month, and in order to change dresses styles, you have to either go up or down, the crossways change dont count, or show much. So if you can only change one way or the other and you have been going one way for years why it stands to reason that the worm must turn sometimes, even if its a silk worm.

They first showed us their calves. Well that looked fairly promising, and we seemed enough shocked to add spice to our views. But when they just practically overnight yanked another foot off their apparel and we woke up one morning with thousands of knees staring us in the face, why there is where I will always think they overstepped and took in too much territory. A knee is pliable but not what you would call gorgeous. There is 120 million people in this Country with knees, that adds up to 240 million knees, subtracting the He knees, and figuring on a fifty percent male calf crop, that leaves 120 million She knees. It was just old bumpy knees to the right of us, exposed joints to the left of us, volleyed and rattled.

Well to be honest with you the idea just dident get over. Women made a mistake, like everybody else makes the same mistake when they are allowed to much kneeway. So they had to do something radical so some genius conceived the idea of not only covering the knee up but the whole thing again and you would be surprised how much better they look.

Beverly Hills, April 24:

We are just sitting on top of the world. For every automobile we furnish an accident. For every radio sold we put on two murders. Three robberies to every bathtub installed. Building two golf courses to every church. Our bootleggers have manicures and our farmers mortgages. Our courts are full, our jails are full, our politicians are full. If we can't house a prisoner we burn him up.

Truly, Rome never saw such prosperity. "We'll tell the cockeyed world we are going — somewhere."

Beverly Hills, April 27:

Friday night went over the city with some army bombers. Where I stood in there was the place for 4,000 pounds of high explosives.

Millions of lights under you, and hundreds of thousands of defenceless people. Then, they went to London to make cheaper battleships, and not one word was said about restricting the things that you are going to be killed with in the next war. That's why it was only a tax-saving conference and not a humanitarian one.

Beverly Hills, April 28:

Every invention during our lifetime has been just to save time, and time is the only commodity that every American, both rich and poor, has plenty of. Half our life is spent trying to find something to do with the time we have rushed through life trying to save. Two hundred years from now history will record: "America, a nation that flourished from 1900 to 1942, conceived many odd inventions for getting somewhere, but could think of nothing to do when they got there."

Beverly Hills, May 5:

They got Gandhi in jail in India. He preached "Liberty without violence." He swore all his followers "to truth and constant poverty." He wanted nothing for himself not even the ordinary comforts. He believed in "prayer and renunciation." Well, naturally a man that bold couldn't run at large these days. They figured that a crazy man like that was liable to get other people to wanting those fanatical things. The whole thing just gives you a pretty fair idea of what would happen to our Saviour if he would come on earth today. Why, say, he wouldn't last near as long as he did then. Civilization has got past "truth and poverty and renunciation" and all that old junk. Throw those nuts in jail.

You got to sorter give and take in this old world. We can get mighty rich, but if we haven't got any friends, we will find we are poorer than anybody.

Nations are just like individuals. They get mad and fight just like individuals. Their feelings are hurt even quicker than individuals. They do everything just like one person. So thats the way it is with wealth and position.

We might be the wealthiest Nation that ever existed, we might dominate the world in lots of things, but as Nations are individuals, why we are just an Individual, and because we are richer than all our Neighbors or than anybody else, that dont necessarily mean that we are happier or really better off. We dont all envy our Town or State's most wealthy man. We see lots of reasons why we wouldent trade places with him. We not only look at his wealth but we look at all the other sides to him. We may know how he is all wet in lots of ways. So we may say, "Yes he has got money, but what else?"

We are known as the wealthiest Nation of all time. Well in the first place we are not. The difference between our rich and poor grows greater every year. Our distribution of wealth is getting more uneven all the time. We are always reading, "How many men payed over a million dollar income tax." But we never read about how many there is that are not eating regular. A man can make a million over night and he is on every front page in the morning. But it never tells who give up the million that he got. You cant get money without taking it from somebody. They dont just issue out new money. What you got tonight that you dident have last night must have come from somebody.

We have dozens of Magazines that print success articles, but you go broke and see what you can do to get your life story published. Yet the going broke might have made a real man out of you. You may be just starting to live. We do love to talk in big figures. We love to read in big figures. The old boy that dident get the breaks and couldent make the grade we dont care much for.

So thats the way we have become to look on Nations. We are

judging them all by the size of the Navy, or their Territory, but we
dont give a hoot about their character, or maby a hundred fine
things about them. If they dont amount to something in a big way
they are a joke to us.

"What do we care what a tariff bill does to them? Are we in
business for them or for ourselves?"

Chicago, June 24:

Well, they run all the racketeers out of Chicago, and they had no
more than got them out till the Rotarians' convention got in. Now
they are talking about letting the crooks come back. They figure
there is some Rotarians here that could skin the crooks.

You see, that organization only takes the best in each line, so
with all these new lines of commerce we have developed in the last
few years, why they must have pretty slick birds among 'em.

Chicago, June 26:

Rival gangs do not murder each other. They are killed by members of their own gang for "holding out" and at double-crossing.

I tell you this system has a lot of merit to it. Wouldn't it be great
if bankers "bumped off" the crooked ones?

Chicago, June 27:

Why don't somebody print the truth about our present economic
situation? We spent six years of wild buying on credit (everything
under the sun, whether we needed it or not) and now we are having
to pay for 'em under Mr. Hoover and we are howling like a pet
coon. P.S. This would be a great world to dance in if we didn't
have to pay the fiddler.

Minneapolis, June 30:

We are a good-natured bunch of saps in this country.

When the President is wrong we charge it to inexperience.

When the tariff is wrong we laugh it off.

When Congress is wrong we charge it to habit.

When the Senate is right we declare a national holiday.

When the market drops 50 points, we are supposed not to know
it's manipulation.

When a bank fails we let the guy go start another one.

When a judge convicts a murderer that's cruelty.

When enforcement officers can't capture it fast enough to fill orders, that's good business.

Everything is cockeyed, so what's the use kidding ourselves.

Minneapolis, July 4:

This country has come to feel the same when Congress is in session as we do when the baby gets hold of a hammer. It's just a question of how much damage he can do with it before we can take it away from him. Well, in sixteen months these babies have left a record of devastation.

Beverly Hills, July 9:

My genial competitor for the nation's ear, Mr. Calvin Coolidge, in one of his sermonettes advises people to spend more. Now we know that Mr. Coolidge's success *had been based* on personally following that theory, but my advice is the exact opposite. If there ever was a time to save it's now. When a dog has a bone he don't go out and make the first payment on anything. First payments is what made us think we were prosperous, and the other nineteen is what showed us we were broke.

Beverly Hills, July 23:

Well we got the treaty signed now for the limitation of naval vessels. You hold a conference and decide to sink some vessels that would sink themselves if the conference was postponed for another year. England is to sink three battleships that competed against the Spanish Armada. Japan is raising two that the Russians sunk and will resink them for the treaty and the weeklies. We are building two to sink.

Beverly Hills, September 24:

We never will have any prosperity that is free from speculation till we pass a law that every time a broker or person sell something, he has got to have it sitting there in a bucket, or a bag, or a jug, or a cage, or a rat trap or something. We are continually buying something that we never get from a man that never had it.

October 5:

Arthur Brisbane and I have been having a good natured kidding through the papers about Russia. Arthur kinder believes that Russia should be recognized, and me I dont know whether they should or not. Lord, thats a Diplomats business not mine. I am not getting Diplomatic wages. I am only getting acting wages. They are in a position to do quite a little trade with us. So if you want to base everything on a purely dollar and cents basis why we better not only recognize em but go out and look for em.

But then we know that they spend a great deal of money on propaganda to ferment revolution, and that nothing would be so welcome to them as to read some day where everybody that had a clean shave and more than $2.50 cents had been blown up with a bomb, why then you kinder wonder if its good to deal with folks that dont wish you any better than that.

He does know enough about it to know that they are going somewhere and we better watch out while they are on the way. I think on the other hand that he has kinder been Propagandered on em, and he has perhaps got the brighter side, for they were a pretty seedy looking outfit when I visited them in 1926. Course they might have changed a lot. We have. Nobody would have ever thought we would be walking on our uppers to have looked at us in 26. Why we had a gold mine and thought it couldent run out. Now he is a smart man, and I am going to take this advice, and really give a little more serious thought and time to see what they really are doing, for Lord knows we all want to see em make it go, for if they can make it better for everybody, instead of just for a few why they will have practically revolutionized the world.

Beverly Hills, October 7:

Nick Longworth on the air last night hit on a humorous angle that I had never thought of, and I bet none of you had either. He blamed the Democratic Party for the financial depression that is enveloping the world. Its really the biggest advertisement that the Democratic Party have ever had. Why if they was that important, they wouldn't be Democrats. Did you ever notice, there has never been a year when alibis were as scarce.

Camp Richardson, California, October 14:

There is going to be a lot of changes in Washington when the boys gather after the next election. Democrats are going to make some big gains for the people are sore at Hoover because they had to go back to work and couldent just make a living by buying a stock and selling it to the other fellow at a raise. Then him not giving em rain, has hurt him.

Beverly Hills, October 16:

So you think we are doing bad in the U.S. do you? Well lets look around and see what our companions are doing. China is in a mess, not only again, but yet. Russia is starving her own people to feed propaganda to the rest of the world. A guy named Hitler has Germany like Capone has Chicago. France has plenty of Gold, but short on friendship. England has her fine diplomats but no world markets. Spain is trying to get a Republic, they think one is great. That shows their ignorance. Italy has black shirts, but no pants to go with 'em, Brazil has got coffee, but no president, so before you think of giving up your citizenship here, you better think it over.

Did you ever kinder stop to figure it out, this old world of ours as a whole is not sitting so pretty just at the present time. Did you know that there is an awful lot of parts of Europe that is just sitting on what the old time Orator used to call a Powder Keg? Well it is. We cant pick up a paper that from one to a hundred dont prophesy that Prosperity is just around the corner. But let me tell you that war is nearer around the corner than prosperity is.

All this whole mess have no more love for each other than a litter of Hyenas, they either lost or gained territory during the last war, and they feel those that did gain that in another war they could grab off even more, and the ones that lost cant see how they could possibly make that mistake again, and that if given a chance to play the same hole over again they could make it par the next time.

Beverly Hills, October 17:

There is nothing effiminate about this golf thing as played by these champion women. I would hate to beat one of them to a parking space. They just put that innocent little ball down, grit their teeth and swing like a woodchopper, and it takes one of our modern men in mighty good physical condition to even walk where it goes to.

Beverly Hills, October 24:

There has been more "optimism" talked and less practiced than at any time during our history. Every millionaire we have has offered a speech instead of keeping still and offering a job. Our optimism is all at the banquet table, where everybody there has more than they can eat.

October 26:

You know a horse is really from 60 to 70 percent of Polo. Thats about the ratio the Experts figure it. If you cant beat a man to the ball why there is no use going. Its speed, and more speed that counts with those big League fellows. Us Punks can loap around and have a lot of fun on a pack of old Hounds, but if we was among those fast fellows we would get run over.

Most of the Horses that make those big games are Thorough-breds, or three quarters so. An awful lot of them are bred and raised on Western ranches, and lots of them have run cattle. Polo had not only been a recreation or Hobby of a lot of rich people, but has been a God-send to the Horse business. It has done more to establish the breeding of good horse than even races have. Now it is a big business, and there is dozens of men just prowling all over the west buying likely "prospects" for Polo. The game is growing so fast and the demand for horses so great that its a real business now. And you cant always tell the ones you give the more for may not turn out to be the best. Its sorter what suits certain men. No two humans are the same and no two horses either. Nobody can look at a horse and tell what he is worth, he is worth to you just how good he is to you and how bad you want him and how well he suits you.

Beverly Hills, October 27:

To reduce your navy in these times is exactly like a man who is not doing so well financially canceling all his life insurance, figuring it's a dead loss because he hasn't died yet.

Los Angeles, November 2:

Come pretty near having two holidays of equal importance in the same week, Halloween and Election, and of the two election provides us the most fun. On Halloween they put pumpkins on their heads, and on Election they don't have to.

Los Angeles, November 4:

Did you ever figure what constitutes our modern "representative?" The one that can bring home the new Federal postoffice, even if they wasn't using the old one; Federal aid for roads, that nobody may ever drive on, and a government Dam. That's the height of statesmanship is to come home with a dam. Even if you got nowhere to put it. Just raid the national treasury enough and you will soon be referred to as a "Statesman."

Beverly Hills, November 12:

If we pulled together as much to put over a siege of peace as we do a spell of war, we would be sitting pretty. But we can't hardly wait for a war to end to start taking it out on each other. Peace is kinder like prosperity, there is mighty few nations that can stand it.

November 16:

Well all I know is just what I read in the papers, and all I have read in the last week is about the Democratic uprising of November 4th. It was my birthday and the Boys of the party really did them selves proud in my honor. The Republicans were looking for a punch in the jaw, but not for a kick in the pants at the same time. Why there was men beat at this wake that thought they had a deed on their seat.

Joe Robinson is mighty liable to be the Democratic Nominee in '32. It will be between him and Franklyn D. Roosevelt, and they are both mighty fine men. Joe if they want a dry, and Roosevelt if they want a wet. But the wets seemed to kinder swamp everything at this meelee and are gaining strength every day, so in '32 it looks like the wet Candidate will have the edge at the Nomination.

Looks like the Democrats nominated their president yesterday, Franklin D. Roosevelt.

Beverly Hills, November 25:

Russia is a country that is burying their troubles. Your criticism is your epitaph. You simply say your say and then you are through.

Beverly Hills, November 26:

We are the first nation to starve to death in a storehouse that's overfilled with everything we want.

Beverly Hills, December 24:

I got a wish that I believe will have hearty cooperation. Its to leaders of industry, prominent men, please on New Years don't predict prosperity. Don't predict anything. You have had one solid year of being 100 percent wrong, and we just kinder lost our tastes for your predictions. Good times are coming soon, we all feel it, but if you guys say it, it's liable to crab it.

Hollywood, December 29:

You just got two more days now, patriots, to sell your stock and charge it off on your income tax and then buy it back Friday.

Beverly Hills, December 30:

Well the old year is leaving us flat, plenty flat. But in reality it's been our most beneficial year. It's took some of the conceit out of us. We have enjoyed special blessings over other nations. And we couldn't see why they shouldn't be permanent. We was a mighty cocky nation. We originated mass production. And mass produced everybody out of a job with our boasted labor saving machinery. It saved labor, the very thing we are now appropriating money to get a job for. They forgot that machinery don't eat, rent houses, or buy clothes. We had begun to believe that the height of civilization was a good road, bath tub, radio and automobile. I don't think Hoover, the Republicans, or even Russia is responsible for this. I think the Lord just looked us over and decided to set us back where we belonged.

CHAPTER SIXTEEN

We Get Fat in War and Thin in Peace

1931 — Will felt that the country had a responsibility to the people who were hungry. He just wasn't willing to see people starve with granaries and warehouses overflowing. But he thought they ought to work for what they got.

When the government couldn't make up its mind on how to feed them, he went out on his own with Frank Hawks to raise money for the most needy. On October 29, in helping out Hoover, he made his famous radio talk on trying to induce business to put more people to work.

As he had predicted, in the fall elections, the voters started kicking out the Republicans and replacing them with Democrats.

Late in November Will went on his trip to the Far East and on around the world to make a report on conditions there. His reports were again published in the Saturday Evening Post *and were addressed to Senator Borah, because Will wanted to work for the "head man" and not just a figurehead.*

235

Beverly Hills, January 1:

If we could have eaten and digested "optimistic predictions" during 1930 we would have been the fattest nation on earth.

Beverly Hills, January 4:

We havent had such a bad year in comparison to years we used to have, but we have had a disappointing year, for its been a bad year in comparison to the last eight or ten years. We have been just going like a house afire, and we couldent see any reason why we shouldent keep right on burning. We dident see how we could ever run out of fuel. Our tastes were acquired on credit, and we wanted to keep on enjoying em on credit. But a Guy knocks on the back door during the year 1930 and says, "Here, pay for the old Radio or we will haul down your aerial." "Get out of that bath tub we got to take it back." "Get out of that Hoot Nanny, you been driving it without payments long enough."

Well that was sort of a jar. The man talked so nice when he sold it to us, we had no idea he would ever want it back. Why we had kinder got used to all this and took it as a matter of fact. If you never had a fifty cents Cigar why a Nickle one is mighty satisfying, but let you get to puffing on a real one for awhile and the old nickle one is going to be mighty nauseating. It wasent what we needed then that was hurting us, it was what we was paying for that we had already used up. The country was just buying gasoline for a leaky tank. Everything was going into a Gopher hole and you couldent see where you was going to get any of it back.

You see in the old days there was mighty few things bought on credit, your taste had to be in harmony with your income, for it had never been any other way. I think buying Autos on credit has driven more folks to see the Revolver as a regular means of livelihood than any other one contributing cause. All you need to make a deferred payment on anything now is an old rusty gun. I dont reckon there has ever been a time in American homes when there was as much junk in em that dident really belong in em as there is today. Even our own old Shack has got more junk in it that has never been used, or looked at than a storage place. Most everybody has got more than they used to have, but they havent got as much as they thought they ought to have. So its all a disappointment more than a catastrophe. If we could just call back the last two or three years and do our buying a little more carefully why we would be O.K.

Well from now on your going to find some mighty careful folks. A Salesman knocking on our door now with some new fangled Pea knife is going to have to be mighty good to even get in the door much less make a sale. The Lord kinder looked us over and says, "Wait you folks are going too fast, slow up and look yourself over, a year of silent meditation will do you good. Then when you start again you will know you got to get it by working and not by specu-lation."

Hollywood, January 6: [when farmers at England, Arkansas, marched on the town and demanded food]

We got powerful Government, brainy men, great organizations, many commissions, but it took a little band of five Hundred simple country people (who had no idea they were doing anything his-torical) to come to a country town store and demand food for their wives and children. They hit the heart of the American people more than all your senatorial pleas and government investigations. Paul Revere just woke up Concord, these birds woke up America. I don't want to discourage Mr. Mellon and his carefully balanced budget, but you let this country get hungry and they are going to eat, no matter what happens to Budgets, Income Taxes or Wall Street values. Washington mustn't forget who rules when it comes to a showdown.

Beverly Hills, January 8:

Dont get a farmer who is hollering for food mixed up with a Red who is hollering for devilment.

Got a nice letter the other day from Barney Baruch. I had about a year and a half ago, just before the crash, sorter half way decided to get a little dab of some kind of stock. Everybody all around me was just rolling so in profits, that it made my little joke-telling sti-pend seem mighty little. I had never, or havent yet, got a dollar that

I dident tell a joke for, either on stage or paper, so I knowing
Barney mighty well, and having a mighty high regard for him personally and as being the last word in business, so in my little talk
with him I asked him to invest in his own way a little dab that I
thought I could spare.

Well I had to naturally tell him something of my affairs, so I told
him what I owed, mostly on unimproved Real Estate. Well he
liked to have thrown me out of his Wall Street Office. "You owe
that much, and you want to take some of your money and buy
stocks? Say you go home and pay your debts. Lord knows how
long it will take you to do em. But pay what you can on em. You
wont like this advice, no man does. He dont want to pay his debts
as long as he thinks he can make an easy dollar in something else.
I wouldent invest a dollar for you anyhow, things are too high, they
dont look good. Now go start paying on your debts."

Thats the nearest I ever come to owning stock. (I mean outside
of a few Horses, and cattle.) Less than a month from the day I was
in his office the Bust come. So every month he writes me and asks
me how I am making out on the debts, and how much I got em
whittled down.

Washington, D.C., January 16:

Had a long talk with our President this morning. He sincerely
feels (with almost emotion) that it would set a bad precedent for the
Government to appropriate money for the Red Cross. He feels
that once the Government relieves the people, they will always expect it and you have broken down the real spirit of American Generosity and spoiled all that our Great American Red Cross has
worked years to achieve.

No matter what the politicians do, whether its called a "Dole" or
a "Gift"; you cant live on these speeches they are going to make
about it. Oratory is an organic exercise but a digestive failure.

January 18:

If you live under a Government and it dont provide some means
of you getting work when you really want it and will do it, why then
there is something wrong. You cant just let the people starve, so if

you dont give em work, and you dont give em food, or money to buy it, why what are they to do? What is the matter with our Country anyhow? With all our brains in high positions, and all our boasted organizations, thousand of our folks are starving, or on the verge of it. Millions of bushels of wheat are in Granaries at the lowest price in twenty years. Why cant there be some means of at least giving everybody all the bread they wanted anyhow?

But the main thing is we just aint doing something right, we are on the wrong track somewhere, we shouldent be giving people money, and them not do anything for it, no matter what you had to hand out for necessities, the receiver should give some kind of work in return. Cause he has to eat just the same when he is laying off as when he is working. So every City or every State should give work of some kind, at a livable wage so that no one would be in actual want. Of course it would cost the Taxpayers more money. But if you are making it, and all your fellow men are not why you shouldent mind paying a good slice of it for the less fortunate. Course the big mans argument, and all the heavy Taxpayers alabi is that when you take too big a slice from a man as taxes it takes that much more out of his investments and might cut down on money being put into enterprises. But it dident work that way after the war, and during it why Income taxes run as high as seventy percent on every dollar earned, and yet there was more money being made and put into things than there is now.

Now that we got that settled all we have to do is get by Congress and see if the Republicans will vote higher Income tax on the rich babies. It might not be a great plan, but it will DAM sure beat the ones we got now.

Will started on his speaking tour to help the needy, since Congress wouldn't do anything:

San Antonio, January 26:

Spoke before the Legislature at Austin. But a comedian getting up before one of those bodies of men is just lost. I would be like Rudee Valee trying to sing before an audience composed of all grand opera singers. He would just be outclassed. And thats the way I was.

San Antonio, Texas, January 27:

In San Angelo, the real heart of the cow business, today. It's so poor that these old cattlemen are eating their own beef and the bread lines in these towns are composed of independent oil men. They are worse off than the cotton farmer.

Fort Worth, Texas, January 30:

These people in the drouth stricken country aint waiting for the Government to relieve 'em. In Wichita Falls we played to nine thousand one hundred. At Ft. Worth tonight we played to eighteen thousand. At my breakfast matinee yesterday morning at Abilene got sixty-five hundred. Every cent is net.

Fort Smith, Arkansas, February 9:

Say, that Tulsa is a bear — we played there last night to exactly $30,000 at one single performance, making $100,000 the State of Oklahoma paid in one week.

Forrest City, Arkansas, February 11:

A little circus is stranded in Ft. Smith, Ark. The town is feeding the circus people but this elephant and these lions and tigers and all, are about to eat the whole town out of funds, Lots of folks can't seem to get excited over hungry humans, maybe they can over wild animals. This elephant hasn't see a peanut since last summer.

Beverly Hills, February 8:

The government Saturday passed a bill to appropriate $20,-000,000 as a loan to farmers in the drought area but it was to be loaned on security. Now the man and his family that are hungry down there have no security. If he had any security he wouldn't be hungry; he would have already put it up. So this loan has not relieved the people.

February 12 [*sample of what Will said in his relief talks*]:

"Well folks sure glad to be here with you, glad you are starving, otherwise I would never have met you. You have got nothing on the rest of the Country. We are all starving. We havent had a regular meal since the Democrats were in, and if we wait for em to get in again we may never get another one. The Republicans promised us prosperity and we like a half wit believed em. But the joke is on them they aint eating so regular themselves. Starving aint so bad, its getting used to it that is tough. The first three years of a Republican Administration is the hardest. By the end of that time you are used to living on predictions. It seems good to get back in the old South again, for this is about the only old South we got. Prohibition split us in two politically, and the drouth cut the two halves up into quarters, and the Quarters are divided over the Tariff, so that only leaves one eighth of the Party intact, and the Wickersham Report on prohibition killed off those that could read, and the Hoover Democrats have committed suicide. So the old South is solid in favor of anything that aint in effect now. This hunger is not local, its universal.

Senators are drinking corn when two years ago they would have turned up their nose at less than Bourbon. Lobbyists are working on Commission and starving to death, Wall Street Brokers have let their night Chouffers go, Rockefeller Sr. is only playing seven holes. The Rapidan dried up, and the President is using the seine in the Potomac. Coolidge hasent had a new ribbon on his typewriter since Northampton raised its tax rate. Borah hasent issued an ultimatum since Idaho silver mines closed for lack of Gold. I am telling you times are tough.

Beverly Hills, February 22:

Here is what George Washington missed by not living to his 199th birthday. He would have seen our great political system of "equal rights to all and the privileges to none" working so smoothly that 7,000,000 are without a chance to earn their living; he would see 'em handing out rations in peace times — that would have reminded him of Valley Forge. In fact we have reversed the old system; we all get fat in war times and thin during peace. I bet after seeing us he would sue us for calling him "father."

Chick Sale is out our way. I am figureing with him to put me in one up at the Ranch. He is working out the design now. You would be surprised the trade that he has, he has just practically quit

acting, and is specializing entirely. It was too bad; he is a fine
Comedian too, one of the best that ever left the stage. But this new
work is high class, and not hard. Its mostly just consulting, and
working out architectural plans. I wish I could hit on some side
line, that would stop having to just keep digging away day after
day. Its certainly made a fortune for him. You would be surprised
at his prices. He has an office in Hollywood, and is doing practically all Beverly Hills work. You just have to have em done by
Sales or they wont be patronized.

El Paso, April 5 [*on his way to Nicaragua where there was an earthquake*]:
Was going to the bullfight, got my tickets, then saw an old pony
that they was going to use in the fight and I couldn't make it. I
give my tickets to a feller who hasn't been saved by horses as many
times as I have.

Managua, Nicaragua, April 8:
Sitting here in a marine tent writing this and am going to
sleep here. The Doctor is coming around to shoot me for typhoid
and then I am going to learn to cuss and will be a real marine.

Aboard Pan American Airways Plane, April 16:
You have read of the San Blas Indians. You can land and visit
them but you must get away before night. The old chief won't let
you stop after dark. Due to his foresight, they are the only 100
percent pure Indians.

New York, April 24:
Big brokerage firm failed here today and that throws 'em into
another scare. You know funny thing but the rest of the country is
all feeling pretty good but here in New York they are doing more
beefing than all the rest of the country put together. I don't believe New York has got the nerve to stand it like lots of other folks
all over the country. They can be hurting and won't let out a squak.
But this place's nerves are more jumpy . . . but it's a great old town
and I never in my life saw as many new high buildings. But everything is the "Market" with 'em here.

Hollywood, May 1:

Everybody is "beefing" so that you can't tell a Red from a tax-payer.

Old Hollywood has reconciled itself to conditions of the depression better than anywhere. They have just charged off 50 percent of their husbands as a total loss, voluntarily cut alimony, reorganizing with less overhead and going back to prewar mates and conditions.

May 17:

All I know is just what I read in the Moving Picture adds, and say Boy what an education it is! I thought the underwear adds in the magazines were about the limit in presenting an eyeful, but these Movie adds give you the same thing without underwear.

Even I myself appeared in a Nightgown in the Connecticut Yankee, so on the billboards it would add a touch of romantic glamor, to say nothing of a smattering of sex appeal. Mind you you musent let the add have anything to do with what you see on the insides. You are liable to see the wildest stuff facing you on the billboards, and then go inside and everybody is dressed as esquimos all through the picture. In other words Will Hays big trouble is getting pictures that will live up to the pictures on the adds. The big problem of the Movies now is to deliver up to what the Lithograph makers and the add writers have shown on the outside. In other words that branch of the Industry has "Outstripped" the Production end. We just cant seem to get em as wild as they show em on the outside. We got to get wilder people. A lot of these have been out here for years, and they are getting kinder old and tame. There is an awful lot of us out here that just cant arouse the passions in our public like we ought to. And thats why we keep trying to get new blood into this ART. Course my old friend Will Hays still insists that Virtue triumphs, but they keep making you more and more doubtful right up to the end, in fact most of them hold it back till after the final fade out. And I have seen some of em here lately where it looked like it was still in doubt as to whether it triumphed or not. Thats called "Subtelry." All the writers try to be what they call "Sophisticated" or "Subtelry." That means

nobody knows what you are talking about and dont give a D——.
Sophistication means talking all day about nothing. You are both
bored but you have to do something till somebody mixes another
cocktail, we are getting a lot of those kind of Talking plays now.
Titles that if printed on the old silent screen, would have got the
"Rawsberry" now are considered smart; for they apply to nothing
and mean less.

I saw one the other night called "Kiss and Leave each Other
Flat." It was so subtle that it dident say whether you can leave em
flat physically, or financially. They call em drawing room plays,
women with nothing on their minds eat em up, kids hiss em, and
old men sleep right through em. They had em on the stage till they
ruined it. So between "Subtelry" and Gangsters we have run the
old Cowboy trying to save the sherriffs daughter, right back to the
dairy farm. No modern child would want to learn how to shoot a
45 Colt. He wants to know how to mow em down with the old
Browning Machine Gun. But we will live through it, and come out
with something worse. We always do. So we better make the
most of this while its here.

May 18:
Walter Harrison,
Editor, Daily Oklahoman, Oklahoma City, Oklahoma.

Whats this mess over some degree, Bill Estes and his Oklahoma
Chamber of Commerce been wiring me about it. They are as bad
as I am, a degree would read as foreign to any of them as a prescrip-
tion. What are you trying to do, make a joke out of college de-
grees? They are in bad enough repute as it is, with out handing
em around to comedians. The whole honorary degree thing is the
"hooey." I saw some college giving Mellon one, and he is a billion
bucks short. I got too much respect for people that work and earn
em, to see em handed around to every notorious character. I will
let Oolagah kindergarten give me one D A (Doctor of Applesauce).

Yours,

Will

Beverly Hills, May 19:

League of Nations just got started on some big scheme when a Russian gets up and proposes something and the rest of the congregation don't know if he is "kidding" or on the level. Russia dont do as much harm to the rest of the world as they just worry 'em. She just loves to put a thumb in the soup and let the guests see it's in there. The whole world's nerves are "jumpy" anyhow. Right now anybody with a sheet over their head can run the world home and under the bed.

Beverly Hills, May 29:

A couple of years ago no business seemed to be up to date unless it had its "holding company." The title "holding" seemed like you had something so the suckers went for it, but now the stockholders find out that all they were holding was the bag, so that's what the matter with your Wall Street. You can't go out now when your business ain't doing so good and merge with something else that's doing worse and form a "holding company" and issue more stock. What you got nowadays you got to "hold" yourself. The buyers are looking in the bag now before they hold it.

Beverly Hills, June 4:

We used to always be talking and "sloganing" about "back to normalcy." Well, that's right where we are now, and where we are going to stay, so we might just as well get used to it. It's taught us one important fact, that we haven't got as many "big men" as we thought we had. We used to think every head of a big organization was a "big man." And he was, as long as everything was running in spite of him. But when old man "get back to earth" hit us in the jaw, why we didn't have any industry that shrunk like the "big man" industry did. Big men are just like stocks now, they are selling at just what they are worth, no more.

Beverly Hills, June 22:

When some nation wants us to help 'em out they use the same

old "gag" that we should exert our "moral leadership" and we, like a yap, believe it, when as a matter of truth no nation wants any other nation exerting a "Moral leadership" over 'em even if they had one. If we ever pass out as a great nation we ought to put on our tombstone "America died from a delusion that she had moral leadership."

Beverly Hills, June 24:

World ain't going to be saved by nobody's scheme. It's fellows with schemes that got us into this mess. Plans get you into things but you got to work your way out.

Beverly Hills, June 26:

Now when you start telling France something about Germany that's kinder like explaining politics to Calvin Coolidge: it can't be done. France will say "That's fine from an American angle, but we happen to live right across the river from 'em and we know what's going to happen to us soon as they are able again. What are you trying to do, shorten our lives?"

Santa Monica, June 28:

Will you do me one favor? If you see or hear of anybody proposing my name either humorously or semihumorously for any political office, will you maim said party and send me the bill? My friend on Collier's, George Creel (it is he, by the way, that writes that clever "Keyhole column" in Colliers) says that I am taking this running seriously. George, that's the worst statement you ever took against my sense of humor. I certainly know that a comedian can only last till he either takes himself serious or his audience takes him serious, and I don't want either one of those to happen to me until I am dead (if then) so let's stop all this d—— foolishness right now. I hereby and hereon want to go on record as being the first Presidential, Vice-Presidential, Senator or justice of the peace candidate to withdraw. I not only "don't choose to run," but I don't even want to leave a loophole in case I am drafted so I won't use "choose." I will say "won't run" no matter how bad the country will need a comedian by that time.

July 5:

This week I got some interesting letters. One I sure was surprised to get was from Will Durant, a man that has studied Philosophy like Mr. Coolidge has Politics, and both have reached the height in their chosen profession. I met this Durant one time. He is an awful nice fellow. I dont know much about what his "Racket" is, this philosophy Gag.

He wanted me to write him and give him my version of "What your Philosophy of life is? I who have lived philosophy for many years turn now it back to life itself, and ask you, as one who has lived, to give me your version. Perhaps the version of those who have lived is different from those who have merely thought. What keeps you going? What are the sources of your inspiration? and your energy? What is the goal or motive force of your toil? Where do you find your consolation and your happiness? Where is the last resort your treasure lies?"

A copy of this letter is being sent to Hoover, McDonald, Lloyd George, Mussolini, Marconi, Ghandi, Stalin, Trotsky, Tagore, Einstein, Edison, Ford, Eugene O'Neil, and Bernard Shaw, and three or four others that I had never seen in the weeklys. Now I dont know if this guy Durant is kidding me or not. If I got this kind of a letter from somebody less I would say its a lot of "Hooey" and wouldent even finish reading it. But putting me in there with that class, why I figured I better start looking into this Philosophy thing. I think what he is trying to get at in plain words, (leaving all the Philosophy out) is just how much better off after all is an highly educated man, than a dumb one? So thats how I figure is the way I got on the list. He knew that I was just as happy and contented as if I knew something, and he wanted to get the "Dumb" angle, as well as the highbrow.

That education is sorter like a growing town. They get all excited when they start to get an increase, and they set a Civic Slogan of "Fifty Thousand by the end of next year." Well thats the Guy that sets a College education as his Goal. Then when they get the fifty thousand they want to go on to make it a hundred, and the Ambitious College graduates wants to go on and make it a Post graduate in some line, figuring he will just be about as smart as anyone if he can just get that under his belt, and the Town thinking that the hundred thousand will just put them by all the competing towns, not figuring that while they are growing that all the rest are doing likewise and maby faster. When they get to a half million New York will be twenty million, so they are no higher on the ladder comparatively than they were.

And the Educated Guy, he is the same. He finds when he gets his post graduate course that all the other Professors have got one too, and lots of em a half dozen. He begins to wonder if he hasent spent all this time wondering if he knows anything or not. He wishes he had took up some other line. He talks with an old broad minded man of the world of experience, and he feels lost. So I guess he gets to wondering what education really is, after all. For there is nothing as stupid as an educated man if you get off the thing that he was educated in.

So I cant tell this doggone Durant anything. What all of us know put together dont mean anything. Nothing dont mean anything. We are just here for a spell and pass on. Any man that thinks that Civilization has advanced is an egotist. Fords and bathtubs have moved you and cleaned you, but you was just as ignorant when you got there. We know lots of things we used to dident know but we dont know any way to prevent em happening. Confucius perspired out more knowledge than the U.S. Senate has vocalized out in the last 50 years.

We have got more tooth paste on the market, and more misery in our Courts than at any time in our existence. There aint nothing to life but satisfaction. If you want to ship off fat beef cattle at the end of their existence, you got to have em satisfied on the range. Indians and primitive races were the highest civilized, because they were more satisfied, and they depended less on each other, and took less from each other. We couldent live a day without depending on everybody. So our civilization has given us no Liberty or Independence.

Suppose the other Guy quits feeding us. The whole thing is a "Racket," so get a few laughs, do the best you can, take nothing serious, for nothing is certainly depending on this generation. Each

one lives in spite of the previous one and not because of it.   And
dont start "seeking knowledge" for the more you seek the nearer the
"Booby Hatch" you get.

And dont have an ideal to work for.   Thats like riding towards a
Mirage of a lake.   When you get there it aint there.   Believe in
something for another World, but dont be too set on what it is, and
then you wont start out that life with a disappointment.   Live your
life so that whenever you lose, you are ahead.

July 19:

You know those Rascals in Russia along with all their Cuckoo
stuff, have got some mighty good ideas. If just part of em work
they are going to be hard to get along with.   Just think of everybody
in a Country going to work.   I dont mean just the ones that want to
work, but I mean everybody.

What they mean by work is to produce something, to be of some
benefit to the whole community.   Just look at the millions of us
here that tonight we havent done a thing today, that helps the country, or that helps anybody.   We have just gone along and lived off of
it, and we are just "lousy" with satisfaction of ourselves.   Just think
what we could do over here if we ALL worked.   Dont get scared,
I am not putting this in as a Plan.   But we must admit that other
things being equal the Nation that works and saves and dont let the
profits go into the hands of a few thousand or million men, They
are going to be dangerous competitors.   We cant just laugh it off.
We prospered for years on nothing but our natural resources.   Well
they have got twice as much of anything as we ever had before we
used it up.   Its a terrible way to live, and do, but you cant beat hard
work, sacrifice, and unlimited resources.   Its liable, if it does just
even half way work out, to have us winging on our foreign trade.

Beverly Hills, July 28:

I was pretty worried last week.   I am a colonel on Alfalfa Bill
Murray's Oklahoma "Fighting Staff."   I thought he overmatched
hisself.   Take on Kansas till we. get practice, then Texas in the
finals.   When I heard old Bill hisself had hid a long squirrel rifle
under his mustache and gone to the wars "In person," I said to my-

self, "Col. Rogers, you better go into rehearsals." So I got myself
a chemist and we started to work. The only way to lick a Texan
is with bad liquor. Any State that can make worse liquor than
Texas can lick 'em, but it's hard to make worse. That's why Texas
licked Mexico, Texas had the worst. They fattened on Mexico's
"tequilla."

August 2:

You know the other day coming home from the big Claremore
celebration on the Place I either eat something that dident agree
with me, at lunch in El Paso, where we stopped, or it was the general effects of what I had stacked in while at home in Okla. But
anyhow I got home sick.

We always have such good times to eat at my sisters in Chelsea.
Beans, and what beans, kinder soupy navy beans soaked with
plenty of real fat meat. Well when I cant knock off a whole bowl
of those myself, why I am sick before I start. And then the Ham,
fried ham; they cure their own ham. Tom McSpadden my Brother
in Law, he is a prize ham curer of any I ever saw. Smokes em with
old hickory log fire, then salts em away for all this time. Then the
cooking of all this has got a lot to do with it. Sister Sallie has got an
Senagambian Soul there, but she is more for arguing purposes.
Sallie fixes it all up when I get home.

Then the cream gravy. You know there is an awful lot of folks
that dont know much about eating gravy. Why not to be raised on
gravy would be like never going swimming in the creek. They got
their own cows and real cream. Ham gravy is just about the last
word in gravys. Course good beefsteak gravy is good. You know
we fry our beefsteak. Its cut in thin pieces, and say let me tell you
something. Did you know all this eating raw, bloody, rare meat,
like they order in those big hotels, and City people like, well thats
just them. That aint old western folks. Ranch cooks and Farm
women fry steak thin and hard. That old raw junk goes for the high
collars in Cities, they are kinder cannibalistic anyhow.

Well you can get some awful good gravy by putting the old milk
in the skillet after you fried a lot of good beefsteak. Theres an
awful lot of good gravy! A good old home cook can mix up a tasty

batch of gravy just about out of anything. No, sir, the old city eaters missed some mighty fine grub when they dont take advantage of making gravy one of their regular dishes at every meal.

Now then comes the corn bread. Not the corn bread like you mean, I mean corn pone, made with nothing but meal, and hot water and salt. My old Daddy always had that at every meal, said it was only the high toned folks that eat biscuits, and light-bread or loaves like you all eat now. He called that "wasp nest," and thought that was just for the heathen. Well this corn pone is mighty hard to go hungry after. You see I am just a telling you my dishes that they have when I come. I am not telling you of what they have cause they know I would rather have it than to go out and kill that fatted calf, or kill a turkey or some Chickens. Beans, corn-bread, country ham, and gravy and then just raw onions either the young ones if they are in, or the sliced ones. Sallie had some dandy Bermudas that Tom had raised. He has the best garden in that part of the country. Well these wasent strong so she was going to send me some to California. But I dont guess they would let them come in. No, thats one thing about California if you raise anything better than they do, they got a law against it coming in. Thats why its awful hard to get good vegetables and fruits in California. They make you just use home talent.

Then for desert? Dont have room for any desert. Had any more room would eat some more beans.

Oh yes, I started out to tell you bout being sick. Well I have been for a week or so, thought I was going to die, something I eat either at El Paso where the plane stopped for lunch, or the night before at Amon G. Carters "Shady Oak" farm. I had dinner with him and the Gas Sextette, and there was an Amateur Doctor Walker, that mixed up a batch there layed me low. The doctors called it Catarral Jaundice. I was the yellowest White man you ever saw. I never have heard who else died from this Carter dinner. The dish was: Open all the cans of tomatoes you have, all the cans of cove oysters, lots of sliced onions, raw, mix 'em in a big bowl. It's sort of soup salad. It's called "We have scraped the bottom salad."

Beverly Hills, August 19:

The Russians got a five-year plan. Maybe it's terrible, but they got one. We been two years just trying to get a plan.

We will just about have to save ourselves accidentally. That's the way we stumbled on prosperity.

Asking a Democrat [*Owen D. Young*] to feed the country is almost a "believe it or not." Young is in a tough spot. If he feeds 'em through the winter he will only be keeping 'em alive to vote the Republican ticket next fall. Voters can't remember back over two months.

Beverly Hills, September 3:

We got one thing to be thankful for anyhow; the country is not in as bad shape as the rumors have it. If ever a land was rumored to death it's us. There is not a bank in America that is not closed a thousand times a day by whispers. In fact there is no unemployed. We got one hundred and twenty million people working overtime just repeating rumors. If we did pass out as a great nation our epitaph should read "America died from fright."

Beverly Hills, September 4:

The papers today say that illiteracy has decreased. The more that learn how to read the less learn how to make a living. That's one thing about a little education. It spoils you for actual work. The more you know the more you think somebody owes you a living.

Chic Sale was just out to see me; an old friendship we started in vaudeville together many, many years ago. We both wrote a book but I foolishly wrote mine on politics, a subject nobody was interested in.

September 9:

Being President or Leader of any Country during the last two years was just like arriving at the crossing just as the stop signal was against you. There is nothing you can do but just stand and watch your predecessor get through a-flying, and you wait till somebody switches something over which you have no control. I dont suppose there is a leader today who, if he had known what was in store for

him, wouldent have thrown the job right back in your face when
offered it.   Its just an off season for Leaders.

* * * * *

You know Mr. Hoover is sorter right about that "Dole."   He
sees what it has done for England, and he knows what it would do
for this Country.   Of course no Country in its right mind would
ever adopt the method that England did.   That is just give people
money that couldent get work, and not make them do something for
it — just let them sit and draw enough pay to live on.   Its got to
be done by giving them something to do for that money.   Thats
what ruined the whole plan over there.

I will never forget in one of the Arkansaw towns that I visited
with Frank Hawkes last year on our tour.   They had been feeding
something over three hundred in their Soup kitchen, and one night
they announced that they had arranged so that everyone would be
given work the next morning at about (I think it was $1.50 a day).
You could get a real meal in town for 25 cents, and after three meals
that would have left you 75 cents.   Well the next morning there was
less than seventy five out of the three hundred showed up.

You just cant give people something for nothing, you got to do
something for what you get.

Beverly Hills, September 11:

You can't beat that England.   She don't look good till they get
in a hole, then watch her.   They wasn't afraid to put an additional
tax on big incomes.   They forget politics when they are in a tight
place.   Republicans can't tax big incomes over here for they
haven't got next year's campaign budget yet.   Democrats still owe
for their last three elections.

Beverly Hills, September 15:

London has had lots of conferences.   There was enough fuss made
over the disarmament one to fix the whole world for years.   Our
delegates went by special boat.   Dressmakers worked for months
before, but a skinny little fellow with nothing but a breech-cloth, a
spinning wheel and an old she-goat goes there representing more

humanity and with more authority than all the high hats in the world. It's sincerity versus diplomacy. Viva Ghandi.

Beverly Hills, September 17:

Nothing makes a man or body of men as mad as the truth. If there is no truth in it they laugh it off.

Santa Monica, September 20:

Japan has been trying to match a war with China for years; looks like they finally made it. Russia is rehearsing to get in.

Ooloagah, Oklahoma, September 24:

Flying all morning over stopped-up oil wells while Venezuela is shipping it in tariff-free by the shiploads. Now explain that here in my old home section. Bins full of wheat, cribs full of corn, fat steers bring what a fat hog used to. Nobody got much money, but smokehouses all full of meat. Wood piles are high. Bill Murray to look after our troubles so nothing to do this winter but hibernate and listen over the radio to Wall street wailing.

El Paso, October 1:

I am heading down into the wilds of Old Mexico and will be out of touch with what we humorously call civilization. They don't even have a daily lecture on pyrorrhea or know what cigarette will raise or lower your Adam's apple; so primitive they have never tasted wood alcohol or known the joys of buying on credit. They are evidently just a lot of heathens that are happy.

October 20:

Now here we are worrying and reading in the papers about a hundred different problems that they got us all excited and making us believe they amount to something. This country has just got one problem, it's not the balancing of Mr. Mellons budget, (that's his worry not ours) its not the League of Nations, that you read a lot about, it's not the silver question, not a one of these problems mean a thing in the world to us, as long as we have seven million of our own out of work, that's our *only* problem, and to arrange the affairs of this prosperous country, (yes prosperous right now) to so arrange it so that a man that wants work can get work, and give him a more equal division of the wealth the country produces. Now if our big men in the next year can't fix that, well they just ain't big men, that's all. What does all this yapping about disarmament amount too, compared to your own people that havent worked in two years?

What does prohibition amount to, if your neighbors children are not eating? Its food, not drink is our problem now. We were so afraid the poor people might drink, now we fixed it so they can't eat. Now a miracle can't happen and all these people get a job overnight, it's going to take time, so they must be fed and cared for perhaps all winter, everyone of us that have anything got it by the aid of these very people. There is not an unemployed man in the country that hasn't contributed to the wealth of every millionaire in America. The working classes didn't bring this on, it was the big boys that thought the financial drunk was going to last forever, and over bought, over merged, and over capitalized. Now the people are not asking for money, they are asking for a job, but as there is no job, towns and cities can't say they haven't got the money, for the same amount of money is in the country as when these folks had their share — somebody's got it. Last winter we didn't realize the need, but this winter we got no excuse, its been shown to us all summer. I have said for the last two years that things would pick up in 32. "WHY?" Why because its an election year, and the Republicans always see to it that things look good on election years. They give us three bad years and one good one, but the good one is the voting year. Elections are always just a year too late for the Democrats.

Beverly Hills, October 27:

Well, this was Navy Day. We celebrated it this year by lopping off its appropriations. Wake up some morning with a war on our hands then the mad rush will be on to build battleships, give the companies big bonuses to get 'em done quick. Then we will have to go through that silk-shirt-buying period again.

England is a pretty wise old bird. She relinquished her world's financial supremacy but she didn't relinquish any ships. Shows which she thinks the most valuable to a country.

Beverly Hills, October 28:

The Republicans have just got from now till next summer to make things look better or out in the alley they go.

San Antonio, November 4:

Say, what do you know about the Democrats walking away with the next Congress? I am going to try and get out here in the mesquite brush about eighty miles at Uvalde, Tex., and see an old prairie dog, Jack Garner, that is going to be the next Speaker of the House.

Kingsville, Texas, November 5:

Down to the great King ranch, biggest in the whole Southwest, and I did my best acting today trying to look and act like a cowboy on Bob Kleberg's best cutting horse and hanging on by my teeth.

Its just about the biggest Ranch we have in our land. Been in this same family for years, and they are real Ranch folks. Their hospitality is as big as the ranch, and it's a million and half acres. But what I am going to tell you about now is the "Roping," thats the thing I wanted to see, was the Ropers.

Well, Sarah, thats the daughter, and Alice, thats another one, and Bob's wife that the one thats got charge of the cattle, they took us to the "Wagon" where one of their Round-ups were working. They was dragging out calves for the branding, and when I say calves I mean little fellows, kinder scrawny, weigh about seven fifty to eight hundred, just about the size of a horse.

Its brush down there, and they cant miss. They have practiced all their lives. (They are all Mexican Boys that not only them but their Fathers and Grand Fathers were raised on this same ranch). They are a real bunch of cowhands. They use grass ropes, not rawhide, they tie, and not "Dally." They can follow a steer through that thick brush so fast and so close to him that they havent got a chance to throw at his head for the brush, but they put their horse right on his heels, then throw and get his hind feet without swinging, and do it too.

They brand right out on the range. Bob Kleberg wanted me to try it, and I did, but Lord I was in there swinging around and messing the thing all up. I would hit where the calf had been just previously. They had Boys that would rope em out all day, and NOT swing, just pitch away out to the end, and get veal on the end.

Head, hind feet, "Mongano" (Front feet) and they got good horses, and good beans, thats what makes a good Cow outfit, is good beans. Just give me some beans and I will follow you off. I sure wish I was on a ranch. I would like to stay a year on that outfit. But I got to get back and see what Mr. Hoover is doing. But I like roping best.

North Uvalde, Texas, November 6:

I never did go in much for this typical American stuff but this fellow Jack Garner in his career and his home life will come pretty near living up to what we think one is. His only regret — and this is no bull either — in going back to Washington this time, is how he and his wife will miss Nick Longworth.

He is the next Speaker of the House. He has about seven acres right in this beautiful little town of Uvalde, Tex. and he has got his own Cows, and lots of Chickens which he feeds himself every day. Quite a hunter and Fisher, and he had just killed some Deer out of season. He was shooting at some quail when he hit the deer. Course the Quail was out of season too, but he dident hit them. I dont want to eat the deer that night for dinner on account of it being against the law to kill it, but it was all the meat they had and I was hungry. He has a lot of Pecans too. He said they was soft shelled. Aint it funny how a fellow in Politics will just lie, when there is really no reason for it. He could see me clamping down on these Pecans with one of the best sets of Tusks ever swabbed in Pepsident, yet I couldent even make a dent in em. Here I had cracked Hickory Nuts, and old black Walnuts with these Molars, but they met their waterloo that day when I tried to sink em into Jack Garner's SOFT shelled Pecans.

He raises his own Grapes too — and — but as I was saying, its mighty livable life he lives there. His Son and Daughter in law and a mighty pretty little Grand Daughter lives right next door. It was a place I would have liked to stayed longer, but I would have sure wanted a hammer on those SOFT Shelled Pecans. I am going to

Washington to watch him in the Speakers chair, cracking em with
his Gavel.

November 8:

You town Waddies know what a Combine is?

Well here is all it does — just one machine and in one trip over
the ground. On the front end of it is an arrangement that makes a
deal to take over the ground (from the bank that is holding the present mortgage). Then right behind that gadget on this big machine
is a thing that grubs up the Roots and Herbs. Another thing right
behind grinds up the Roots and Herbs into "Sagwa" Indian Medicine, which is sold by a White man who says he is adopted into the
Indian tribe. Then just a few feet behind that, all connected with
the same machine, are the plows that plow the ground. Then
right in the furrow is the seeder, then another plow that plows the
furrow back where it was in the first place. Then comes the ferti-
lizer, and then the sickle that cuts the grain. Then its carried along
a little platform into the Threshing Machine where it is threshed,
then out and into sacks and into a big Grain Elevator that is fastened onto the thing.

Then on near the back end is a stock Market board where a
bunch of men that dont own the farm, the wheat, or the Combine,
buy it back and forth from each other. That is if you have threshed
a thousand Bushels why they sell each other a million bushels of this
thousand bushels which was actually threshed, then they announce
to the farmer that on account of supply and demand, the wheat is
only worth two bits (25¢). Thats what you call a Combine.

Beverly Hills, November 9:

Here is a warning to the world at large; please quit sending me
by either mail, telegram, booklet, volumes or word of mouth
schemes to end depression. Just go ahead and end it without any
aid from me and then you can wire me collect that you have done it.

Beverly Hills, November 10:

I think the only real diplomacy ever performed by a diplomat is

in deceiving their own people after their dumbness has got them
into a war.

* * * * *

*Late in November Will left for the Orient and a trip around the world.
He later wrote this trip up for the* Saturday Evening Post *as "Letters from
a Self-Made Diplomat to Senator Borah." He gave as his reason:*
Dear Senator Borah:

Well, your One-Man mission is on its way: I am getting out of
here in the morning on the Empress of Russia. I just wanted to
drop you a line before I pushed off. There is a few things that
ought to be straightened out between both of us, so we will have it
clear just what I am to do, and why.

As you know, I took this position with you after weighing the
whole thing over carefully. As you also know, I would have gone
over for Herbert on about the same terms that I went over to Europe in 1926 for Calvin. That was, pay my own expenses and split
what I got out of the letters with him. But darn this thing of con-
tinual working for our President — that's what we all are doing.
It's all right if you are in his Cabinet and there is no way of getting
out; those fellows have to stay there and take it on the chin. But
with me it's different. Now, here is a few of the plain reasons that
I dident want to go for the President: In the first place, there is no
novelty to it; you are just another Hoover Commission. Now, that
handicaps you right there; you hand a fellow your card, MR.
WILLIAM PENN ADAIR ROGERS, CHAIRMAN, HOOVER
COMMISSION FOR INVESTIGATING ALL DEPRESSION
WEST OF THE PACIFIC OCEAN. Now, the fellow you hand
it to is going to laugh, for he sees bands of such men every day;
Highways, Railways, and even Oceans are clogged up with Commissions going somewhere to see why somebody else is doing as bad
as they are. They are not all Hoover Commissions, of course —
only about 95 per cent — but it was him that started it. He got
other folks doing it. Of course, it was a good time to do it, for most
of the folks he would appoint was laying off anyhow, and even a
job on a Commission looked better than nothing. He first started

out by only putting Big Men on 'em — that is, what we thought was Big Men then — and they was, as long as everything was going good. But when the blow-up come, nothing went as high and fell as flat as Big Men. Well, the Big Men dident know any more about stopping it than they knew about preventing it before it happened. And, too, the Big Men had run out of Predictions, so middle-sized and Little Men got so they could get on Commissions. They couldent do any more than the Big Ones, but it was a compliment to 'em to be there. Of course, they would not have been there if the case hadent been hopeless anyhow. But lately they draft men to get 'em on Commissions. You can't get one on there of his own free will and accord.

Now the question will be asked, "Why did I decide to go on this trip for you." Well, I am a man that wants to go with the best. What's the use of going all over Europe, or all over Mount Fuji-yama, or Manchuria, or the Walls of China, or that long Barroom in Shanghai, if, when I get back and turn it over to somebody like Mr. Coolidge or Mr. Hoover, or Mr. Smith, or Mr. Roosevelt, or Mr. Baker, they, in turn, can't do anything about it; they have to turn it over to you anyhow. You know, yourself, that all my Coolidge reports had to go right on UP to you. So, I am getting tired of that; I say, "Here, what's the use of my prowling and writing, and then have to have them go first to a mere Supernumiary? — there is a good word, Senator, that was brought over here to Canada by the English."

So I just says, "No more foreign reports to Presidents for me. I am going to work for the Head Man." You, as Chairman of the United States Foreign Relations Committee, are the Guy that does business with everything outside of the United States and Idaho.

They know who has to O.K. any foreign skullduggery that's going on with us. It's Mr. Longhaired Borah.

* * * * *

Excerpts from Will's reports to Senator Borah, as reported in the Post, *which still have contemporary interest and amusement*:

I had heard along the line that Floyd Gibbons, the Worlds Champion Reporter and Radio Announcer was to be on his way to

Manchuria too, but I wasent sure. But when I finally got to Vancouver and they told me it was so, I was tickled to death. Just think of the privilege of traveling and being with him. Here is a man that has been in every nook and corner of the World, knows everybody and everything. I got acquainted with him in Warsaw, Poland, in the summer of 1926, and have been good friends with him since.

It looked like a long trip, eleven days to Yokoma. I am the worlds worst Sailor anyhow. I get sick before the boat unties from the dock, but you know I says, "I am going to lick this, I am going to eat everything they got, drink . . ." Well, anyhow I stayed with em, and do you know I kept waiting to get sick, and kinder looking forward to it, and days went by and nothing showed up, and By golly I begin to believe that maby the old Oklahoma Kid was a Sailor after all.

I'd surprise myself by getting up and going down to breakfast, and then stuck it out till Lunch, and then dinner, and mind you all this time I was packing in the Fodder.

It was about the middle of Mister Balboa's Ocean we hit that Typhoon. This foolishness kept with this Ocean for over two days. It was a Chinese Typhoon, that had run into a Monsoon, that was crossed with just plain Hurricane, and Oklahoma Norther combined.

But I kept eating and HOW! They are always passing something and I was always not letting anything pass me.

Read a lot of books. That old Ghengkis Khan that flourished around over in all this Country around 12 hundred. If you enjoy Jessie James, Al Capone and the Younger Boys, you want to read about this Baby. Oh Lord the World was his Oyster. He ruled everything from all of China clear to the gates of Vienna, and from the North Pole to Africa, and he did it all horseback. There was a real Buckarro for you.

* * * * *

Floyd Gibbons of course was a good Sailor, for he had done nothing but sail somewhere all his life. He was kidding me and telling me to come on and eat a lot, and have another little glass of beer.

Well, we just had another glass of beer, and they were always passing Hors Duervs (I cant spell it but I can eat it). Well I was cramming that in all the time. And three meals a day in addition.

Harbin, Manchuria:

What made this Town famous was the Russians that got out of Russia. It's like Tia-Juana, Mexico. What's made it World-known is the Americans that have escaped over the line and got into the Bars there. Harbin in the "good old days" — you see, these Countrys had "good old days" too — when the Democratic Dynasty was flourishing at home, the White Russian Dynasty was at its top hole here. They say it was the Paris of the Far East. 'Course, that might have been a Chamber of Commerce Slogan. You see, they got those things over here, too; you can't progress without it's accompanying ills.

Well, the Night Life in Harbin is what made the Town livable. You couldent exist there in the day time — you practically had to leave Town till night come on — but when the shadows of the evening broke over the Siberian Stepps, why, the "Scandalousness did begin." Where in our early Western Civilization "every other house was a saloon," why in Harbin every house was a Cabaret. They just Sang, Danced and Drank themselves through two Wars, to prevent wars.

The Russians are a Gay lot, when they got anything to be gay on, and even when they haven't they don't just fold up and holler hard times like the New Yorker does. They take it on the chin, dig up some more Vodka and stand the Fiddeler off for another gazottsky. 'Course, the Bolsheviks have made everybody in Russia serious, but it's taken a Gun to keep 'em from laughing. For at heart they love fun and amusement.

You see, here is a thing you want to get straight, Senator: All these Railroads that this late War is over, that the Japanese are taking Manchuria to Protect, were all built — not by them, or the Chinese either — they were built by the Russians. Had there been no Russians building Railroads there, you would never heard of Manchuria; so the Russians are the real ones that unconsciously made Manchuria worth fighting over. So give the Devil his dues; these Russians spent six hundred million Rubles, on Railroads here alone — that's three hundred million in Mellon's Money. Now, that was a lot of Jack in 1900 to 1904 — that's more than we owed at that time. 'Course, now that would just run us over the week-end. So all these investments that Japan talks about in here was mostly Russian investments. But, on the other hand, Japan put up a tough fight to get it; they waited till Russia got it all finished before they started the War, but they did battle, and they lost about one hundred and twenty-five thousand men, and they feel they paid pretty dear for it. For, you see, Senator, all these other Nations, they don't just go off and have Wars, and then just come back home and claim nothing at the end, like we do — or did. Maby we will be wiser the next time.

'Course, in the Historys, War always starts "for patriotism's sake," but you read on then get down to the Peace Conference and you find that the historian has to write pretty fast and veil things over very cleverly, or the reader is apt to discover what changed hands at the finish besides a mere satisfying of honor. You look at all Wars and you will find that there is more new deeds for land signed at these Peace Conferences than there is good will. Did you ever look on a map and see the Colonies that Germany lost at Versailles? All these Nations that are crying Debt Cancellations, you never hear 'em mention a word about returning Colonies to Germany so she would have a chance to kinder use 'em to help dig up this Reparations. So, you see, in Wars the Slogan is Honor, but the object is Land. They are always fighting for Independence, but at the finish they always seem to be able to use quite a snatch of the defeated opponent's land to be Independent on.

* * * * *

This patriotic business is always the Big Brother is helping the Weak Sister. But I don't care how poor and inefficient little Weak Sister is, they like to run their own business. Sure, Japan and America and England can run Countries perhaps better than China, or Korea, or India, or the Phillipines, but that don't mean they ought too. I know men that would make my Wife a better

Husband than I am, but, darn it, I am not going to give her to 'em.
There is a million things that other people and Nations can do
better than us, but that don't mean they should handle it.

I doubt if there is a thing in the world as wrong or unrealiable as
History. History ain't what it is; it's what some Writer wanted it
to be, and I just happened to think I remember ours is as Cock-eyed
as the rest. I bet we have started just as much devilment as was
ever started against us — maybe more. So far as facts are concerned, the better educated you are the less you know.

* * * * *

It is funny, what a respect and National Honor a few Guns will
get you, ain't it? China and India, with over half the Population
of the entire World, have not only never been asked to confer but
they have not even been notified what has to be done with 'em after
the other Nations had decided. Yet you give India England's
Navy and China ours, and they would not only be invited to the
Conference but they would BE the Conference. Now we gather
to dissarm, when a gun has put every Nation in the World where
it is today. It all depended on which end of it you were — on the
sending or receiving end.

You must get quite a kick out of it, sitting in a reserved seat like
you are, Senator. When you write your Memoirs — That's another Cherokee word; *means when you put down the good things you
ought to have done, and leave out the bad ones you did do — well, that's
Memoirs.* Well, when you write yours you ought to call it, Hooey
as I Have Seen it From the Ground Floor.

* * * * *

Our War Co-respondents that have followed 'em will tell you
that these Japanese will sure fight, and skillfully. 'Course, it's admitted that there was not much opposition, the way the Chinese
were going, and they were GOING.

Then another thing; Where, with the Japs, it's all Cooperation,
United Command and the Heighth of efficiency, with China, just
as they go to shoot, they will find that somebody who was supposed

to have charge of the Ammunition has given them .38 Calibers when their Guns is .44's. They start to send back for it, and they don't know where to send.

A Japanese wants to die for his Country, but the Chinese, he ain't going to let patriotism run away with his life. He wants to live; he loves life; he enjoys it. Life ain't serious with him like it is with the Japanese. The Japanese feel they were put on earth for a purpose, but the Chinese, he feels he was put here by mistake. He wants to get a little piece of land, live on it, die on it, and be let alone. He is, naturally, a compromiser. He wants to trade you; he don't want to fight you. In a lawsuit, they don't want to take the chance of winning it or losing it entirely; they want to have it settled by compromise. If there was some way in a War where you could show him that he would at least get second money — but he knows there is no second money. So why go in there and get your head blown off?

Now, that's all right. It's a commendable thing to be a peaceful Nation. China and India are the two biggest in the World and the most peaceful in the World. How do they stay the biggest? It's not by fighting somebody every day. Your warlike Nations rise to great heights while they are on a winning streak, but let 'em lose a few games, and they not only pass out of the League but sometimes out of existence. You know it's pretty hard for Nations to give advice to China. Giving advice to China is kinder like a Son telling a Father what to do. So it hasent been entirely proven yet but what China has got about the right dope on this war business. I know if I saw a man charging down on me with a Bayonet, I would sure kinder like to talk it over with him first and see if there wasent some way of buying him a drink, or offering him an Apple, or something. Anyhow, fix some way so we could both walk away from the place — not just one of us.

An American was out here trying to sell a Chinese War Lord a Submarine; told him what it would do, that you "could sink any boat out here; just dive down and let 'em have it."

The Chinese said, "You mean it sinks the boats it takes after?"

"Sure," said the Yank.

"Oh, I don't want to sink 'em; I want to capture 'em. How do you suppose I am going to make a living if I sink or kill everybody I meet?"

He had the right idea on war — get something out of it besides a Coffin.

All down through China, Shanghai, Tientsin, and everywhere, there is thousands of these White Russians; the man, lots of 'em, doing practically Coolie work, but it's the Women that have had it tough. These Girls, simply to eat, have had to live under the most degrading circumstances — at the mercy of the lowest class of every race of people under the sun.

It's not Gay in Harbin; there is a semblance of attempted gayety — lots of little cheap Cabarets — but it's just sad. It's not lively, it's not amusing; it's just depressing. They are like any other gathering of Girls or Women — some are beautiful, but their whole manner and looks are just of lost hope, just licked, just whipped. The suicides will run higher here than anywhere in the world. They say they generally hit the dope, and then to the River. The Russians — the Bolsheviks ones — are all getting along fine. They had a big entertainment last night in their big Recreation Hall, which we went into see. They were all well dressed and would compare with such a gathering in any Railway Town at home. You see, there is all these Reds and all these Whites, then two or three hundred thousand Chinese, a good many Japanese and every other Nationality in the World. There is no place like this.

(Say, did I tell you I could tell the difference between a White Russian and a Red Russian — that is, if it's a Girl? If she is pretty she is a White Russian. That's right, Senator; these Reds are mighty hard-looking. There must be something about that "everybody split up what you got with me" idea that makes 'em all look alike. When you got everybody looking alike, that should be the height of Communism.)

Peking: Dear Senator Borah:

Was you ever the Guest of an Emperor in his own Home? I mean a real live emperor, with him in the House, not one of those things where there is a Guide showing you around telling you where the Emporer did live.

The House was not so Elaborate. If we had been putting on an Emperor's Set in Hollywood, we would have walked right by this one without Photographing it.

He brought in some Robes — Mandarin Robes, they called 'em — beautiful things. He asked me to pick one out — all beautiful, fur-lined Kimona-Effect things. Had me try one on. I said, "Ha! This is not for me, is it? This is a Woman's Gown." They assured me it was 90 per cent Male. I said, "Now, won't I look cute prancing in Beverly Hills with this thing flowing and me hollering, 'Whoops, Boys, Mother Rogers is back from China'?" I asked little Tommy Lee which was the best one, and he nodded at one. He had his eye on the same one I did. It was lined with Mink — not Dog Mink but Mink. The Young Marshall said, "That's too small for you." I said, "Yes, for me, but not for Mrs. Rogers." So I Glommed the best one, and Tommy grinned like a Possum, and I grinned more than the rest.

Shanghai:

Mr. Abend, the New York Times Far East main Representative, whom I had met in Manchuria, was home from there for Xmas.

Well, Abend and his Assistant called me up Xmas afternoon. I had just got in the evening before. They wanted to know where I wanted to go or what I wanted to do. Well, I had been in my room writing all day, and I was ready for anything. It was Xmas, the first one I had ever spent away from my Family since committing the Overt Act, and maybe you think I wasent Lonesome. I just thought, "What a Yap! Over here trooping around trying to get something to write about, when Everything Funny in the World that is happening is happening right there at Home." But when Abend come over — and say, there is a fellow that knows the East too; he is an Authority on it. And has the confidence of all sides — when he asked me what I wanted to do, I naturally said, "I want to see this sight of the Far East, the Shanghai Bar."

So the three of us piled into a Cab, and off we went to gratify an

Ambition that I had had ever since I had first heard of it. I just thought, "What a day to do it. Here it is six o'clock on Xmas Day." I knew the place would be crowded with people from all over the World that were away from Home like me. I am not a Bar Connoisseur, but, naturally, in my Rambles I had seen some that, for Length, you could stand in a row about as many friends as you would wish to pay for. Tia Juana, Mexico, has one that, if it was a hundred yards longer, would reach San Diego, California. Some of New York's Speak-easies are only limited by the length of the Block. But this was to be the World's Longest. Time and again I had pictured in my mind the crowd that would frequent such a place. Being in the noted Shanghai, I naturally thought that this place must have been the origin of the Shanghai-ing of Sailors. I could just visualize the Swinging Doors, the Sailors from every Port in the World, the Marines of the U.S., English Tommys, Italian Marines, White Russians, Red Russians, Blue Russians.

Well, we got out of the Car in front of what looked to me like a Bank Building or a City Hall. We went up a long row of steps, into a very imposing Entrance Hall. A uniformed Attendant come and took our hats and coats. Great marble pillows looked like snubbing posts in a Corrall. We then went to a great Book, or Register. He asked me various Questions about my Ancestry, my Fraternities, if any. He finally wrote down "Democrat." From the Answers, I kinder got to doubting if I would get in. Now, all the time I can't figure the whole thing out. I dident ask Abend anything; I just says, "Well, maybe this is not the place; maybe this is some place that he belongs to that we just come by on our way to the Shanghai Bar." Then we are escorted to the Wash Room. Well, I couldnt see any particular reason why it would be necessary that one should be compelled to cleanse oneself before imbibing at this Bar.

Well, we finally enter; it was a tremendous Room, and there is the Bar. It had not been exaggerated; Bobby Jones could have just made it in two. It looked like about a half-mile Straightway. Here was the World's Famous Shanghai Bar. About a niblick shot apart scattered along it, was a Bartender, and standing right exactly in the center on the Purchaser's side was one lone Figure, an Englishman. Well, here stood this lone Englishman, on Christmas Day the very sole Occupant of the famous Shanghai Bar. He had Spats, a Cane, was perhaps sixty, had Sideburns, and, of course, a glass of Whiskey-and-Soda. Here went my Illusion of drunken Sailors from every port, masses of Humanity scrambling for great, foaming Beers; for here stood this lone Figure; he just looked like he was saying, "Prohibition, you shall not pass." Oh, I wish I had been an Artist and painted that picture, it looked just like a One-Man Parade going up the center of Pennsylvania Avenue.

When I saw that there was only one Inmate present, I felt more than ever that I would buy the House a drink. I left Abend and his friend, and ambled over to him and said, in what I thought wasent bad English, "Pardon me, sir, but this being Xmas and my being far from Home, and a spirit of good will within me, would you be kind enough to join myself and my two friends in an Eggnog to the Yuletide?"

He turned on me like I bit him, and said: "I beg your pardon. I don't think we have ever been introduced, sir. Good-day." Well, it wasent a "good day" for me. The World-Renowned Shanghai Bar had been a complete Flop; the only fellow that felt worse than I did was, I imagine, the Chinaman that missed me twenty pounds. I had missed my illusions further than that. I don't even remember now if I even had my Eggnog. If I did, I dident enjoy it. I dident know the thing was a Club, I thought it was a Swinging-Door Joint that took in all comers. They told me that around Lunch Time it was pretty crowded. But they never got me near the place again. I can see that lone Englishman standing there now — "Liberty's Last Stand." So, you see, Senator, you can get fooled with your Foreign Relations.

CHAPTER SEVENTEEN

The "Peanut Stand" Gets a Cop and the
Poor Man a Champion

1932 — Will said that Wall Street could live down the fact that it probably brought on the depression but that it would never recover from Charlie Dawes calling it a "peanut stand." He also pointed out that the bankers were first to go on a dole.

Will got a big kick out of the political conventions ("the clambake of national politics") during the summer, particularly the plight of the Republicans. He gleefully showed that the Republicans were in a tight spot because they could not point "with pride to accomplishments" nor "view with alarm" the mistakes of the Opposition.

When the Democrats just laid down and wallowed in "wetness" and then nominated Franklin Delano Roosevelt, he knew that the Republican monopoly on the Federal Government was seriously threatened. Then when Hoover,

who wasn't going farther from home than the Potomac, got out his time-
tables, Will knew that things were getting back to normal: we were going
to have a political tussle. But when the campaign got to be one of extreme
bitterness with fear *instead of* religion *being thrown into the voters, he*
told the "boys" to go fishing, that the country would get along without either
or both of them — probably better. Nevertheless, when FDR came to
California Will introduced him with "limited praise," telling him that if
he would come back a "President" real oratory would be spent on him.

When Roosevelt was elected — after giving those who wanted something
out of the election to have their say — Will wired him some good advice.

January:

Now, about you Filipinos and your Freedom? Do you really
want your Freedom, or do you just want to Holler? Personally,
I believe a Country can get more real joy out of just Hollering for
their Freedom than they can if they get it. You have always got
Sympathetic Listeners if you are hollering for Liberty, but when
you get it and then start Hollering that you would like to be able
to turn it loose, why, you can't get as big an Audience. You Folks
over there want to realize you lose an awful lot of Alibi's when you
get your Liberty, and no one to lay the Blame on but yourself. I
know I have sat in the Galleries of our Congressional Halls and
heard our learned Lawmakers Hollering for different things that
they hoped they would never get, for if they did, it would cramp
their Style.

But if you Folks out there in the Islands really want your Liberty,
there is really no better way to Get Even with you than to give it
to you. There is nothing that will cure a Nation as quick of wanting Liberty as to give it to 'em. But if you can run your Country
and do a good job of it, why, I am sure in favor of giving you your
Liberty. Then we can copy your Style and maybe do a better Job
of running ours.

Every Administration since Lincoln has promised you Folks
your Liberty, "when you were Ready for it," and you naturally
took that Promise serious, well, that will teach you a Lesson the
next time. Another thing against you Folks getting your Liberty
is the other Nations are against it. If America got out of the

Philippines, why, every Native in the Far East would raise a Holler to have England get out of China, out of India, out of the Malay Straits; France out of Indo-China; Japan out of Manchuria and Korea; the Dutch out of Java. In other words, it would be an example in "Freedom for Determination of all Nations" that would shock the world.

But we will Stall you off and say you are not ready for it. If your Freedom was left to a Vote of the whole American people you would get it two to one. But anything important is never left to a Vote of the people. We only get to Vote on some man; we never get to Vote on what he is to do. A Delegation of Senators and Congressmen will be the ones to decide just how far advanced you are in Intelligence and how many years away from Freedom, it won't be the people that will do that. So until the American People get some Freedom, why, you Folks can't get any. So, no telling when either one of us will be Free.

Singapore, January 6:

You heard about the equator; well, here is a town that is straddle of it. It runs right through my hotel room and in all the beds here they have a long narrow pillow that lays longways. It's supposed to be some aid to you in keeping cool and it's called Dutch wife. This used to be a wild port but this Dutch wife is the extent of its devilment now.

Cairo, January 15:

Today saw Jerusalem, Dead Sea and Bethlehem. Never catch me traveling over here again unless I have read the Book first. These pyramids, Mexico's got bigger, and the Sphinx; Coolidge's got him licked to death.

London, January 21:

I bet you they call the Lausanne reparations conference off, as we are not there. You can't have a picnic lunch unless the party carrying the basket comes.

London, January 22:

See where Congress passed a two-billion-dollar bill to relieve bankers' mistakes and loan to new industries. You can always count on us helping those who have lost part of their fortune, but our whole history records nary a case where the loan was for the man who has absolutely nothing. Our theory is to help those who can get along even if they don't get it.

London, January 24:

Got the dope on these international bankers that are crying for us to cancel. Every American trade commissioner and business man over here tells of the flock of bankers' representatives over in Germany and Europe in the last few years. Hotel lobbies full of 'em offering all kinds of commissions to help put over loans for American banks. The loans were forced over here as much as the sales of 'em were forced over home. Now they want the government to cancel to make up for their mistakes. Now if this is not the real low down on it then Borah is a Republican.

Paris, January 26:

Some queer things going on in the world if you just happened to have been there and seen 'em. Japanese warships are ready to bombard China because China insists on boycotting Japanese goods. England puts 500 more of Gandhi's bunch in jail because they boycott and picket against English goods. Here you have China and India who constitute five-eights of the world's population practically at war because they can't do what they want to, yet signboards all over England say buy British. It's a great world even if you are just looking at it for comedy purposes.

Geneva, February 2 [*At the disarmament conference*]:

This is the hash of nations. There is sixty-five nations represented here. You see this is land disarmament, too, so every nation with railroad fare and a gun is here. The smaller the nation the bigger the delegation. If you disarmed the delegates you would have disarmed over half the countries represented. Turkey is here not to disarm, but to try and book some wars for the coming season. There is lots of nations here willing to throw away two spears and a shield for every battleship we sink.

Geneva, February 3:

Disarmament conference was held up for one hour while we all went to the League of Nations meeting to demand of Japan that she quit shooting while the opening session was in conference. The biggest laugh, of course, was uttered unintentionally by the Japanese when he spoke of Chinese aggression. Well, that like to broke up the meeting. The conference is off to flying start. There is nothing to prevent their succeeding now but human nature.

New York, February 9:

Oh, boy, I was glad to set my old big feet on American soil even if it has got a second mortgage on it. Had the greatest trip I ever had in my life and believe if everybody made it they might come back a little poorer, but better off in the feeling toward our country. I know business is off, they say 60 percent. Well, that still leaves us 30 percent ahead of anywhere I have seen, if we can just let other people alone and do their own fighting. When you get into trouble 5000 miles way from home you've got to have been looking for it.

March 6:

I am glad to get back home and read some papers! A breakfast without a newspaper is a Horse without a Saddle. You are just riding bareback if you got no news for breakfast. Dont underestimate your paper, I dont care how small it is, and how little news you think it might have in it at that particular issue. Lord kiss it, for the news that it does bring you.

Why I have seen times when I would have given $100 for the "Claremore Progress" or the "Claremore Messenger," and thats just two of the smaller Papers of Claremore. Take my ham away, take away my eggs, even my Chili, but leave me my Newspaper. Even if it just has such purely local news as "Jim Jones came home last night unexpectedly and bloodshed ensued," or "Jesse Bushyhead, our local M.D. is having one of the best years of his career practically speaking. But they just wont pay him when they get well."

So no matter how punk you might think your local paper is

getting, why just take it away from you and see how you feel. The old newspaper I think is just about our biggest blessing. Course the car will strike some of you as better, but a Horse and Buggy was a mighty fine substitute for the Ford. But there has been no substitute for the old newspaper.

Never since the oldest inhabitant was born have we lived through such exciting times. The great war was just local. It was all in France. But today news, excitement, is everywhere. Nations are furnishing the news nowadays, and not just Peggy Joyce and Al Capone.

Washington, February 11:

Hoover is worried about this money hoarding and asked me "Write a joke against these hoarders. Humor might show 'em how foolish they are. Now go do that." So after all my kidding about Hoover commissions I am finally on one, "the Hoover anti-hoarding joke commission." So anybody knowing any anti-hoarding jokes send 'em to me. I want to be one commission to make good.

Chicago, February 17:

Spent the day with Mr. Ford in Detroit. When the world is in a hole I go to Ford and ask him. More common sense than all of 'em. Then, too, I know there is more people interested in the new Ford than there is interested in Manchuria; they ain't going to get into Manchuria but they are going to get in these Fords.

He said, "Will, you never was as funny purposely as some of our prominent and rich people are acting these days. This is not a panic, it's a side show, watching folks and seeing how scared they can get."

Chelsea, Oklahoma, February 21:

Out on the Rogers ranch at Oologah, where I spent yesterday, Herb McSpadden, my nephew, had to take a milk stool and beat an old cow over the rear end, she was hoarding her milk.

Beverly Hills, February 24:

You can't get a room in Washington: every hotel is jammed to the doors with bankers from all over America to get their "hand out" from the Dawes commission. And I have asked the following prominent men in America this question, "What group have been more responsible for this financial mess? The farmers? Labor? Manufacturers? Tradesmen, or who?" And every man, Henry Ford, Garner, Newt Baker, Borah, Curtis, and a real financier, Barney Baruch, and everyone of 'em without a moment's hesitation said, "Why, the big bankers." Yet they have the honor of being the first group to go on the "dole" in America.

March 2:

One night out at my little Ranch where I live I was awakened out of my sleep about 2:30 in the morning by a phone call.

You know how that scares you away in the night? You think of the ones that are not there with you. Mrs. Rogers was with my sister in Chelsea (twenty miles from Claremore). She dident fly home from the East with me. She dont mind short flights of a couple or three hours but when they run into days, she believes that old man pullman had a pretty good idea how to cross this Continent, and she has made it so much that she knows every jack rabbit or coyote from California to Kansas. Her being away when the phone rang, and two boys scattered around in schools of which we hadent heard from since Xmas.

But when I am half asleep and nervously grabbed the phone and it was William Randolph Hearst, Jr., in New York. I couldent think what in the world it was. I had just been up to his fathers ranch and I thought maby I did something up there that I shouldent. Maby some of the silver is missing. Maby there is an old William the Conqueror Tapastry missplaced.

This young Bill Hearst, Jr., is a mighty promising young fellow, and looks like he is going to pick up W.R.'S trail and keep the ink smearing over half the pulp wood of Canada. Then when he says, "The Lindbergh Baby has been kidnapped . . ."

Beverly Hills, March 3:

The attention of the world is on a little curly haired baby. Till he is found we can't get back to normal. Never since the two days and a night that this same kid's father was out over the Atlantic has the attention of everybody been centered so completely on one thing.

Roswell, New Mexico, March 4:

Cattle country looks fine, lots of rain, no prices. If Wall street men had these old cattlemen's nerve and "tripe" you would have never heard of this panic. Cattle are so cheap that cowboys are eating beef for the first time in years.

Beverly Hills, March 10:

In one of my little poems I said the bankers were the first to go on the "dole." The "wrath of the mighty" ascended on me. Even the Wall Street Journal (Wall street's house organ) editorially said I should confine my jokes to some semblance of truth. Now I want to be fair, even with the bankers, for they are pretty touchy now. I have had critics come out and say "As an actor old Bill is not so hot." Well, I just wanted to come out and call him a liar, but in my heart and conscience I knew he was right. So I know how you "boys" feel. Now if you will take this money and loan it out to a lot of the little fellows that need it you bankers got a chance to redeem yourselves. People are not "pointing with pride" to your record in this crisis up to now. Will be glad to reprint any alibis.

Beverly Hills, March 11:

Two weeks ago I had two hours with Al Capone. He told me all that I read today he told Mr. Brisbane and more. But there was absolutely no way I could write it and not make a hero out of him, and even as superb a writer as Mr. Brisbane couldn't either. What's the matter with an age when our biggest gangster is our greatest national interest?

Now will somebody please suggest what to do with the story I got bottled up with me and be fair to everybody?

Beverly Hills, March 14:

This depression has lasted so long that it has given the people a chance in all countries to know that nobody can fix it with an idea.

We got some kind of a big overhauling on this tax thing. Different conditions make different taxes. All taxes should be on income and where there is no income either personally, or on your property, why you shouldent pay anything. You should pay on the things you buy outside of the bare necessities.

Get the income tax high. You got to earn big money or you dont pay it, so there should never be any holler about that, but there should be a distinction between earned and un-earned income. For instance a man that earns every dollar by his work or efforts, then another earns the same by having enough money invested to bring him in that much. One has his principal to fall back on, and the other has nothing to fall back on when his earning capacity has diminished.

Beverly Hills, March 23:

We got a long sighted government. When everybody has got money they cut taxes, and when they're broke they raise 'em. That's statesmanship of the highest order. The reason there wasn't much unemployment in the last ten years preceding '29 was every man that was out of a job went to work for the government, state or city. It costs ten times more to govern us than it used to, and we are not governed one-tenth as good.

Beverly Hills, March 29:

No matter what the poor old dumb government tries to do, the "big boys" have a scheme that beats it. Now the big bankers have got a new "racket." Instead of them going direct to the new finance commission for dough, they send the folks that owe them, they gets it from the government and then pays them off. That don't leave a single soul out snipe hunting with a sack but the government. And brother, when one of those "big babies" transfers one of his loans over to Uncle Sam, it's not a "frozen asset," it's a "petrified persimmon."

April 17:

Keeping mighty close to home, riding the old Ponies out in the

hills and looking Nature over and seeing how it was making out
during this long spell of Republicanism.

It just looks like everything is doing fine but humans. Animals
are having a great year, grass was never higher, flowers were
never more in bloom, trees are throwing out an abundance of
shade for us to loaf under. Everything the Lord has a hand in
is going great, but the minute you notice anything that is in any
way under the supervision of man, why its "cockeyed."

And the more men that have anything to do with trying to
right a thing why the worse off it is. If every man was left absolutely to his own method of wrighting his own affairs why a big
majority would get it done. But he cant do that. The Government
has not only hundreds but literally thousands in Washington to see
that no man can personally tend to his own business. They go
there to do it for him, and a mob always gets panicky quicker than
an individual. They hear so much of how bad things are, and that
something should be done, and they immediately feel that its up
to them to do it.

That was one of the great things about Coolidge. Coolidge
never thought half the things that are wrong needing fixing. You
knew that over half the things just needed leaving alone.

* * * * *

We do everything cockeyed. The League of Nations everybody
agreed that we had no business in it, but the first thing you know
we were "advising" with em. The World Court, we wouldent
put on a cap and gown, but we would sit on the bench with em.
We are always doing something through the Kitchen door. We
like the glory but not the responsibilities.

But we are kicking along in spite of our handicaps. The East
and the North have got to get like the South has been for years,
poor and used to it. Us folks down there have had to catch a cat
fish, or kill a possum before we eat for years. So the other part
of the Country have got to learn to look to nature and not to Wall
Street for what goes in the pot. They got to find some other way
making a living besides looking at a list of names in the paper every
day. Stocks and bonds have got so now they dont go up and down

only when there is a reason, not like they used to, go up and down when there was a wish on somebody's part.

Beverly Hills, April 21:

Senate been investigating Wall Street for ten days, and all they found out is that the street is located in the sharp end of New York City, that not only the traders, but the street itself is short, that neither end don't lead anywhere.

Hollywood, April 22:

Morgan kept his German bonds up to ninety, till he got 'em all peddled. Now they are thirty-five.

Santa Monica, April 24:

Wall street will live this down, for the more we find out about anything, the less we ever do about it. But they never will live down Charley Dawes calling 'em a "Peanut stand."

You know it's too bad everybody was so busy getting in on it, that no one had time to investigate Wall street before '29 when the horse was being stolen.

* * * * *

May 1:

We are going to get into a war some day either over Honolulu or the Philippines. Let's all come home, and let every nation ride its own surf board, play its own eukaleles and commit their devilment on their own race. Yours for remaining on the home ground.

Beverly Hills, May 3:

See where two English scientists were able, headline said, "to split the atom." The world is not bad enough off as it was, now they go and split up the atom. That's the last straw. We expect the Democrats to split, the country to split over prohibition, but we always felt that the old "atom" would remain intact. It was certainly a big disappointment to me. Come on boys, let's up and atom.

Beverly Hills, May 10:

Poor Mr. Mellon is just finding out what an Ambassador business to England is. It's to introduce American mothers' daughters to the King and Queen. You ought to hear Charley Dawes tell about his experiences with those ferocious mothers. They drove poor Charley pretty near "nutty." I doubt if a charging elephant, or rhino, is as determined, or hard to check, as a socially ambitious mother.

Beverly Hills, May 12:

In the glorious old State of Oklahoma a rope is not just an implement it's a tradition. Our history has been built on citizens dangling in the air by a rope and some escaped the dangling that would have made better history.

May 15:

A week or so ago I was asked to be master of ceremonies at the opening of that great big Picture "Grand Hotel." Syd Grauman, the manager of the Chinese Theatre in Hollywood, is not only a great showman but a fine fellow. Then Mr. Louie B. Mayer asked me, and I was tickled to do it. I had never been around any of these "Openings," in fact had always kidded about em, for there is plenty to kid at one. The whole thing is the biggest "Hooey" out here.

But its a great "Yokel" show. This was an especially big one for it was the biggest cast pictures ever made. Think of Greta Garbo, the two Barrymores, Joan Crawford, Wally Beery, Jean Hersholt, Tully Marshall, and about half the other pay roll of Hollywood. Well it was a bear of a night, judging by people standing outside on soap boxes, and folks inside with old overhauled ermine's.

But all joking aside they was our best bunch. New York hasent got it on Hollywood for clothes. It was lovely looking out there. And some mighty fine substantial folks. There is some pretty down to earth people in our business, and lots of em have been into it long enough to realize that its a kind of business after all.

My job was to introduce the cast that was in the picture. Now of course you all know about Greta Garbo? She dont go anywhere, or she may go everywhere, for no one gets to her home to see if she had gone anywhere or not. The people in the studio that she worked for have to go see her in the picture when they want to see her. Now everybody out here knows she is not going to be anywhere.

That night, after I had introduced all the principals of the cast except John Barrymore, who was not there, I announced that on account of the importance of the occasion and the prominence that this particular picture had received, that Miss Garbo would break her rule and be there, and that immediately after the picture was over that she had consented to come on the stage and take a bow.

Well Mr. Grauman thinks the later a show is started the better. Syd dont know or has perhaps forgot that all the big first nights in New York are started on time anyhow, no matter when they are finished. Well this one dident start till nine and was over at one fifteen. Now thats pretty late for a country town and after all we are a country town.

Well I had framed up a gag with Wally Beery who I knew would be a big hit in the picture that they had just seen. He got some "dame" clothes and he was Greta Garbo. Sounds kinder funny dont it? Well it wasent to them.

Wally did fine: He even looked like her, but not enough to satisfy that crowd. Now they should have known that Garbo wasent going to be there, but they go and believe it and then get sore at themselves for believing it. I dident mean any harm. Gosh us Comedians must get laughs. But these first nighters dont want us to get em at their expense. They want to be the ones that do all the laughing. I think they got their waitings worth by seeing Wally Beery in skirts. What did they want?

Now about the only way I got making good is to produce Garbo sometime. Course I cant do it, but its a good idea. I got to do something to get back into the good graces of my Hollywood. Maby I can show em Al Capone some time. They all want to see him, but I will never fool the old home town again.

Beverly Hills, May 27:
Bands playing, soldiers marching, orators orating, telling it's

your duty to "buy Liberty Bonds." Fifteen years later, no bands, no marching, no orators, just a patriotic girl, or a broken piece of human frame, trying to sell a "poppy" for a few cents. Made by even a more unfortunate brother in one of our fifty-five hospitals. Given fifteen years to think it over, war has degenerated from the price of a Liberty Bond to the price of a "poppy." Six millions of these boys' regular customers are disabled this year too, and from the same war, so those that have will have to try and make up for these, by buying more. There is only one sure way of stopping war, that is to see that every "statesman" has the same chance to reflect after it's over that these boys making the "poppies" have had.

San Francisco, June 1:

When a Los Angeles guy comes up here to Frisco it's just a country boy going to town, you have to take your spurs off here. You can't explain Frisco, it's just the Greta Garbo of the West.

Chicago, June 12 [*At the Republican Convention in Chicago*]:

A newspaper man spoiled my whole convention by asking me if "I was an alternate." Now a delegate is bad enough, but an alternate is just a spare tire for a delegate. An alternate is the lowest form of political life there is. He is the parachute on a plane that never leaves the ground.

June 13:

Mr. Dickinson of Iowa is the "keynoter," and he has the toughest job any of them ever had. If he points to "accomplishments" he is sunk, and if he "views with alarm" he is sunk, so we are liable to get two solid hours on the weather.

Chicago, June 15:

Bert Snell got to thinking of a lot of things that Dickinson hadent called the Democrats yesterday. He showed those 1100 Republican postmasters seated as delegates that Judas Iscariot was the first Democratic floor leader and Al Capone was one of the last. Then he said that while our Savior had rescued the world in biblical times from the Democrats, masquerading as the Medes and Persians, that Herbert Hoover was the modern savior. In fact, he kinder give the engineer the edge over the Carpenter.

Santa Monica, June 19:

Mr. Hoover says he is not going out an lectioneer for the job. That's kinder like a pitcher saying "I don't need to even warm up against this team."

June 26 [*at the Democratic Convention*]:

They are coming into Chicago by plane, train, Fords, Buckboards and Burros. The Texas deligation arrived on Burros headed by that fearless old Statesman Amon G. Carter, the genial dirt Farmer of Shady Oaks Post Office, Texas.

Amon is national committeeman, deligate, alternate, steering wheel, banker, receiver and wet nurse for the Texas Deligation.

Well, the noise is starting so I better jarr loose and go hear it. I dont know if its a Rube band, or just Amon Carter whispering about Jack Garner to somebody.

Chicago, June 29:

A Democrat never adjourns. He is born, becomes of voting age, and starts right in arguing over something, and his first political adjournment is his date with the undertaker.

Politics is business with the Democrats. He don't work at it, but he tells what he would do if he was a working at it.

It's been a fine convention, nobody nominated, nothing done. But what difference does it make? After all we are just Democrats.

Chicago, June 30:

And did the Democrats go wet? No, they just laid right down and wallowed in it. They left all their clothes on the bank and dived in without even a bathing suit. They are wetter than an "organdie" dress at a rainy-day picnic.

The plank was made from cork wood nailed together with a sponge. I just want to know what all these old dry office holders that went wet overnight are going to tell those Baptist preachers back home. They are going to say, "Father, I can't tell a lie. I saw the votes going and I had to go after 'em."

But wait a minute! Just how much fun is it going to be to drink now when we ain't breaking any law.

July 1:

I am glad Chicago's children didn't come by on their way to school that morning and see how this wonderful system of choosing our country's leaders was conducted. They would never again have asked, "What's the matter with the country."

Claremore, July 3:

Flew down here to recuperate from one straight month of speeches. Heard a mule braying a while ago out at the farm and for a minute I couldn't tell who he was nominating. Roosevelt made a good speech yesterday and he did aviation the biggest boost it ever had. Took his family and flew out there. That will stop these big shots from thinking their lives are too important to the country to take a chance on flying. But it was a good thing the convention broke up. Times was hard. Some of the delegates had started eating their alternates. Cannibalism was about to be added to other Democratic accomplishments.

Claremore, Oklahoma, July 5:

Looks like the taxpayers in the U.S. are the only folks hiring any help nowadays. A private business when it don't do any business don't use anybody, but the less business the public has the more we hire to tend to it.

Vernon, Texas, July 7:

It sure is a lot prettier sight to look at thousands of white-faced cattle than thousands of bald-faced delegates in one corral howling like mad, and milling for nothing. They brand the cattle so you can tell 'em and have to put bandages on the delegates so there's not much difference after all.

Mule Shoe, Texas, July 8:

Down here at the Mashed O. My old friends, the Halsells' ranch, branding thousands of calves. I been roping at 'em all day and they just look around and say, go on comedian and do your stuff on the stage, but don't try a real cowboy's racket. I'll catch one of the little rascals yet if I have to bribe him. Say, I been so interested in real things I just quit reading the papers.

July 10:

You meet some great folks at political conventions. Its the Fourth of July celebration of national politics. Its a clam bake of big politicians. If they cant get on the deligation they come as mere spectators.

But its a show that no American should miss. Its entertainment, and its enlightening. It gives us a kind of an idea that most men that emerge from it with any spoils were more lucky than competent. A good campaign manager can do more than an able candidate. "Trades" make Presidents more than ability. But as bad as we are, and as funny as we do things, we are better off than the other countries, so bring on more conventions. The bigger, the noisier, the crazyier, the better. No nation likes noise and "Hooey" like we do. We are cuckoo but we are happy.

Beverly Hills, July 24:

Our world of "make believe" is sad. Scores of comedians are not funny, hundreds of "America's most beautiful girls" are not gay. Our benefactor has passed away. He picked us from all walks of life, he led us into what little fame we achieved. He remained our friend regardless of our usefulness to him as an entertainer. He brought beauty into the entertainment world. The profession of acting must be necessary, for it exists in every race, and every language. And to have been the master amusement provider of our generation, surely a life's work was accomplished. And he left something on earth that hundreds of us will treasure till our curtain falls and that was a "badge," a badge which we were proud, and never ashamed of, and wanting the world to read the lettering on it "I worked for Ziegfeld."

So good-bye Flo, save a spot for me, for you will put on a show up there some day that will knock their eye out.

Beverly Hills, July 27:

We have a great bunch out here prowling around. It's the National Editorial Association, composed of editors in smaller towns and weekly publications. They are just eating their way around the country, having a good time and getting a lot of pleasure out of it, and giving everyone that meets 'em a close-up of just about as representative a gang of Americans as would be possible to gang together, intelligent, well-read and no national advertising controls their pages. They are not conceited enough to think they "mold public opinion." They just go along serving their community with the most indispensable article that it has. And yet their real power is greater than all of your metropolitan dailies combined. Any person that don't read at least one well-written country newspaper is not truly informed.

July 31:

Say, any of you that have kids in schools, either grammar, high or College, it dont make any difference, but can any of you parents get head or tail of what they are doing, what they are taking, what they are learning? This modern education gag has sure got me licked, I cant tell from talking to em what its all about.

Our schools teach us what the other fellow knows, but it dont teach us anything new for ourselves. Everybody is learning just one thing, not because they will know more, but because they have been taught that they wont have to work if they are educated. Well we got so many educated now, that there is not, enough jobs for educated people. Most of our work is skilled and requires practice, and not education.

But none of these big professors will come out and tell you that our education might be lacking, that it might be shortened, that it might be improved. They know as it is now that its a "Racket," and they are in on it. You couldent get me to admit that making movies was the bunk either. None of us will talk against our own graft. We all got us our "Rackets" nowadays. There is just about as much "Hooey" in everything as there is merit. The heathern live with less effort, and less worry.

Beverly Hills, August 7:

Been telling you for a year what these Republicans would do with that market just in time to knock the poor inoffensive Democrats out of their hard-earned votes in November. Now they are all just buying and selling among themselves.

Here yesterday was a good illustration of how these market boosters can pull a bad one. Yesterday farm machinery went up on the stock market. Now there is not a farmer in the United States that can pay his taxes or his groceries, now how is he going to buy any farm machinery? He has no more credit. If he wanted to he couldn't get a garden hoe, much less a thrashing machine. He can plow with a forked stick and raise more than he can sell. So that raise don't look so hot. That's like Christmas trees going up on New Year's.

Our investigations have always contributed more to our amusement than they have to knowledge.

Beverly Hills, August 12:
Well, he did it. Mr. Hoover held his handkerchief up and saw which way the old "noble experiment" was blowing and joined in the parade. You can talk "morals" and all that, but when the votes lay the other way, why they sho' go with 'em.

Now the question is where are the "drys" going? Both sides are wet and the poor old dry hasn't got a soul to vote for. He is Roosevelt's "forgotten man."

Beverly Hills, August 16:
The farmers are on strike in Iowa. Instead of selling their stuff for nothing, they just eat it themselves, and that saves 'em the expense of hauling it to town. Funny they never thought of that before. I have always claimed that if every farmer eats all that he raised, that he would not only get fat himself, but farm products might "Probably" go up. Course on account of this not being an economists idea it might not work.

Mojave, August 24:
The old desert; the more you see of it the more you can understand folks really loving it. It's a great health-giver to many a disabled soul. It's just like a lot of folks; it never had a chance. The minute you give it any water it grows more stuff than all your

fertile land. Yes sir, when we retire from active life it's the Senate or the desert, and by golly, I believe I will go to the desert.

Bishop, August 30:

California always did have one custom that they took serious, but it amused the rest of the United States. That was in calling everything a "ranch." Everything big enough to spread a double mattress on is called a "ranch." Well, up here is these mountains where there is lots of fishing, why every house you pass they sell fishing worms, and it's called a "worm ranch." Well, I always did want to own a "ranch," so I am in the market for a good worm ranch. I never was so hot as a cowboy, but I believe I would make a good "worm herder." If I can land our Presidents as clients, I could make it sound like England when they sell to the king, "Rogers worm ranch, purveyor to His Excellency, the President."

Bishop, September 4:

I bought my worm ranch. The man is to turn over 2000 yearling worms, 2000 2-year olds, 500 bull worms and the rest a mixed herd. Now I find in these Sierra Nevadas they are fishing with grasshoppers, so got a grasshopper ranch adjoining. Am going to do a Luther Burbank, cross my grasshoppers and worms and produce an animal that if the fish don't bite him, he will bite the fish, so you get your fish anyhow. I am no fisherman and hope I never get lazy enough to take it up. I am in these mountains on an essential industry (ask Bill Hayes) but these loafers up here tell me that the fish are not biting this year. And you would be surprised the votes Hoover is losing.

Beverly Hills, September 6:

Don't miss seeing the building of Boulder Dam. It's the biggest thing that's ever been done with water since Noah made the flood look foolish. You know how big the Grand Canyon is. Well, they just stop up one end of it, and make the water come out through a drinking fountain.

They have only been bothered with two things: one is silt, and the other is Senatorial investigations. They both clog everything up.

It's called "Hoover Dam" now, subject to election returns of

November 8.

The dam is entirely between Nevada and Arizona. All California gets out of it is the water.

Beverly Hills, September 9:

Eighty-two years ago today California entered the Union, on a bet. The bet was that the country would eventually be called California and not America.

We took it away from Mexico the next year after we found it had gold. When the gold was all gone we tried to give it back, but Mexico was too foxy for us. In '49 the wayward sons out of 10,000 families crossed the country, and the roads was so rough they couldn't get back.

Beverly Hills, September 16:

Mr. Hoover, who originally wasn't going further west during the campaign than the Potomac, has started looking at time tables.

Beverly Hills, September 18:

Some guy invented "Vitamin A" out of a carrot, I'll bet he can't invent a good meal out of one.

Beverly Hills, September 20:

Mr. Hoover made a move yesterday, that if I had been one of his advisers I would never have let him make it. He wants "to put more orators *in* the field." I think and hope that it was a typographical error. It should read "we want more orators under the field."

Beverly Hills, September 23:

Mr. Roosevelt, a very fine, high-class man, win lose or draw, is out here shaking the lemon trees to try and bring down some Republican fruit that might fall in the Democratic basket among the oranges.

*   *   *   *   *

[*Will's Speech Introducing Roosevelt*]:

Hollywood Bowl is located between Hollywood and Beverly,

the Sodom and Gomorrah of the Orange Juice Belt. The bowl is dedicated to amusement and rattlesnakes. But the charter is very liberal and doesnt say that a politician cant enter and politic. They will rent it to a nudist convention if they will pay the rent.

Now Franklyn (by the way, are you by any means related to Benjamin Franklyn, the man that I think invented the steamboat?) . . . Then you have taken the name of Delano. That of course was to catch the Italian vote. You cant by any means ring in Goldberg, can you? Well, Franklyn, I can call you that for I have known you for many years, long before your governorship, or even your Secretary of Navyship. In fact, I have known you since babyhood. I knew you since you first started nominating Al Smith for something or other. You have spent a lifetime nominating Al Smith. You used to come to the Follies as a young man — in fact as an old man too — and I would call on you from the stage to say a few words, perhaps in appreciation of Mr. Zeigfelds show, and you would arise and for no reason at all nominate Al Smith for something. But I know Al in the goodness and generosity of his heart appreciates all that and will never forget it and will repay you for it.

Let us hope he does it before election.

But to get away from all this piffle talk and back to fundamentals and the Democratic party. I wont say a word here tonight about your "forgotten man." For every man in America thinks you were referring to him.

We have always been tremendously fortunate in picking candidates in both political parties for President what are men of high character. And this time is no exception.

Our national political conventions, if you have ever attended one or heard it over the radio, are nothing but glorified Mickey Mouse Cartoons, and are solely for amusement purposes. But by the grace of some divine providence they do always give forth two excellent candidates.

Governor Roosevelt — you are here tonight the guest of people who spend their lives trying to entertain. This great gathering is neither creed or politics, Jew or Gentile, Democrat or Republican, whether they vote for you or not and thousands of them wont (never mind what they tell you). Every one of them admire you as a man. Your platform, your policies, your plans may not meet with their approval, but your high type of manhood gains the admiration of every person in this audience.

So we meet not Roosevelt the candidate, but a neighbor from the other side of the Rocky Mountains. This introduction may have lacked logic, and particularly floweriness, but you must remember, you are only a candidate. Come back when you are president and I will do better. I am wasting no oratory on a mere prospect.

October 2:

Ideas? Schemes? Everybody has some scheme or plan to save somebody or the Country. I am just a-gabbing like the usual soap box guy, always trying to remedy something, and not trying to make out with what we got.

Everybody has got a scheme to set the world back right again. Come to think of it, I cant remember when it ever was right. There has been times when it has been right for you, and you and you, but never all at the same time. The whole thing is a teeter board even when its supposed to be going good. You are going up and somebody is coming down. You cant make a dollar without taking it from somebody. So every time we wish for something for our own personal gain, we are wishing somebody else bad luck, so maby thats why so few of our wishes come to anything.

Art is when you do something just cockeyed from what is the right way to do it. When you get to monkeying with art, why you just about left commerce behind. You can make a moving picture that is saturated with "Art" but its liable to not to be even "Diluted" with gate receipts. The mob knows that the old cat has kittens and raises em in about the same way year after year. Occasionally you will hit an old tabby that wants to be unconventional, but she generally winds up on the same back fence.

Beverly Hills, October 4:

Guess who is out here holding a convention, that you never thought would show their faces again?

Yep "the bankers." The Reconstruction Finance Corporation fixed 'em up so they could make the trip.

They are rascals, and now that we are all wise to 'em, and its been shown that they don't know any more about finances than the rest of us know about our businesses (which has proven to be nothing) why they are getting just as human as the groceryman, the druggist or the filling station man. This panic has been a great equalizer. Its done away entirely with the smart man.

So the bankers are here having a good time.

They don't feel that they have any position to uphold. They are just a lot of Elks.

El Paso, October 5:

A man can put a little more into a speech when it means his job. Some men will stand for a lot of things. But you start taking their women or their jobs away from them and you are going to get something besides platitudes.

I'll tell you Al and Franklin didn't make up a day too soon. They made up, going to bury the hatchet. Decided to bury it in Hoover.

San Antonio, October 6:

Been flying, train-riding, automobiling, horseback and buggy riding over Texas for thirty-three years and I've never seen a tenth of it. If it had been in Europe, eighty wars would have been fought over it. There is single ranches here bigger than France. Counties bigger than England. Saddle horse pastures big as Alsace-Lorraine. The lakes of Switzerland would be buffalo wallows in Texas. It's located between Mexico and the United States to keep Mexico from annexing the United States. It's so far to town that the cowboys started in to vote for "Teddy" and arrived in time to register for "Franklin." Its "Vatican" is the town of Uvalde, its pope is John Nance Garner. Its sole industry is internal politics. It's so big that no one Governor can handle it; they have to have a man and his wife. It's the only State where a Republican has to have a passport to enter.

P.S. They would use California for a telephone booth down here.

October 9, 1932:

Los Angeles and Death Valley is two places Frisco folks seldom ever go. To them one is just about as desolated as the other.

* * * * *

Here is the ingredients of a "Pageant." You first pick a cold night, then have plenty of places all over the "Float" for girls to stand. But dont let em have anything on. Thats the first ingredient of a "Float Rider" is to be totally naked. Now she must be able to smile through the snow and sleet. What she is up there doing or what she is to represent must never enter her head any more than it does the man who arranges it. She is just up there to act naked, and hope that she isn't frostbitten by the end of the journey. They are not really "Pageants." They are early stages of pneumonia. They are endurance contests, to see how much a girl can stand before she shivers herself off the pedestal they have her on. You see a thing like that is just right up those old fat Shriners' alley. They sit there in their warm overcoats and delight on betting when the girl will turn to an icicle. A "Pageant" is a collection of bare skin, surrounded by plenty of electric light bulbs.

October 13:

You know Ed Borein, the great Cowboy etcher of Santa Barbara, Cal. Ed makes the best western etchings of anybody. He is a real Cowpuncher, and knows the California "Buckaroo" and the old Mexico "Vaquero" better than any artist living. He has been in Mexico a lot, and in California a lot more. Old Ed swings a pretty mean loop himself and goes to all the Calf brandings around Santa Barbara.

Ed said an Indian told him that the reason a White man always got lost and an Indian dident was because an Indian always looked back after he passed anything so he got a view of it from both sides. You see the White man just figures that all sides of a thing are the same. Thats like a dumb guy with an argument, he dont think there can be any other side only his. Thats what you call Politicians.

You can learn a lot from what that Indian told Ed besides just how not to get lost. You must never disagree with a man while you are facing him. Go around behind him and look the same way he is looking and you will see that things look different from what they do when you are facing him. Look over his shoulder and get his viewpoint, then go back and face him and you will have a different idea.

So lately I been trying to look back over my shoulder like a Wolf and an Indian.

Now for instance I looked back at Hollywood as I left on a plane trip. Now you would be surprised at Hollywood if you look at it from both sides. As you come up to it and its people, you see the movie side, all the pain and glitter and make up, and make believe houses, but as you look back at it, why a lot of those houses have backs to em, and people live in em, and they dont have any make up, and they eat and sleep and fret and worry about work, and about their children, and everything just like any other place. But you got to look back to see it. Yes sir, there is a lot of pleasure in looking back, and peeping around and trying to see the other fellows angle. Every guy has an "angle" on living, and on life, and on everything.

Take the election. Now one side couldent or wouldent want to know really what the other side could do or really thought they could do. Both sides just spent the whole summer hunting up things to cuss the other side on. That the other side might be right in a lot of things never entered their head, in fact they wouldent let it enter it. A Politician is not as narrow minded as he forces himself to be. Nobody is going to spoil the Country but the people. No one man can do it, and all the people are not going to do it, so its going to run in spite of all the mistakes that can happen to it. Any people that can raise more than you can eat and wear is set for life anyhow.

Sure everybody hasent got as much, but everybody dont need as much. Flying along over Mexico, see all the little adobe huts, raising a little patch of "Free Hollie Beans," a little patch of corn to mash up some meal into and make some "Tortillias" (biscuits to you). Now at first you will say "What in the world kind of an existence is that?"

Well now lets look back over the shoulder and see if we cant see a little more than just the hut, and the Mexican Family sitting in the sun. In the first place you never hear of one jumping out of a window when General Motors drops ten points. What the Japs do in Manchuria is no more of his business than it is ours. Only he don't worry about it. A "Burro" in a lope is as fast as he ever went, and he thinks thats fast. A passenger aeroplane at (maby) 140 is as fast as most of us ever went and we think thats fast. But not to Doolittle or Hawkes. You see everything is by comparison. The old Mexican sleeps at night. Nothing bothers him except maby a flea, but he can scratch him off. He knows how to reach him, but we dont know how to reach overproduction, unemployment, second mortgages, poor movies, and a thousand and one things that bite us and keep us awake at nights. And we dont know how to scratch em off for we dont know just where they are biting us.

No, sir, the world has got a million millionaires that would give a million apiece to the old Mexican to have nothing bothering them but just fleas, and other kindred spirits.

Will went to South America in 1932 because he got disgusted at the way Hoover and Roosevelt were carrying on their campaign. He had heard so many things said which weren't true that he couldn't take any more of it.

Antofagasta, October 14: (*Will was on his way to South America*)

This is the heart of the great nitrate region of Chile. We are right at this moment as I am writing this flying over some of the mines. They are not mines, they are right out on a flat prairie desert and they just scrape it almost off the top of the ground. It's just like plowing up potatoes. I can get some mighty cheap and both political parties was needing it mighty bad when I left. Was I talking about rain the other day. Well, we have had 2000 miles of solid desert where it never rains. That's a fact. It was never known to rain.

Buenos Aires, October 17:

Say, had a great trip over these Andes Mountains. Our highest altitude was 21,500 feet. They have oxygen tubes at each seat, but I guess I am so windy anyhow that I didn't use any. I kept prowling up forward and talking and looking with the pilot, an American boy named Wagoner. They are all American pilots on this whole trip. We could see the railroad thousands of feet below winding its way over and through, but high tariffs between each country have killed off the trade and it's not running any more, so that's one way to help the railroads. It's just the starting of spring down here now. Flew over hundreds of miles of checkerboarded green fields like Kansas or Iowa and fattest and biggest cattle you ever saw.

Buenos Aires, October 18:

Say, you talk about a city, this Buenos Aires is as big as Chicago, as live as Paris, beautiful as Beverly Hills and as substantial as Claremore, Oklahoma.

Para, October 24:

Brazil ought to belong to the United States. We like to brag about everything "big." We been flying up the coast line for five solid days and still got another day. If any of you see the Rockefellers kiss 'em for me. There is not a mosquito up this coast. If they can just hear of one trying to get a start down here there is ten Rockefeller Foundation men got him singing the blues before sundown. No, sir, you got to wait till you get to "God's Country" to get eat up by insects. Rio Janeiro is the prettiest city in the world from the air. We are just circling Para, where we land for the night. It's right at the mouth of the great Amazon River. Up from here is where Mr. Ford's rubber plantation is, but somebody sold him all male trees and they are having a little trouble getting them to bear. I bet they wouldn't fool him on carburetors, but he didn't know sex life in the forest.

San Juan, October 26:

Finally got hold of a United States paper. Said I went to South America to buy polo ponies. That must have handed my banker a laugh. Thank somebody for the compliment. Old age and depression hit my polo same year. Type of polo I always played, I could get my horse off a merry-go-round. Besides if I wanted good horses I would never leave America for 'em, and if they will let me race in every State we will have better ones everywhere.

New York, November 1:

There should be a moratorium called on candidates speeches. They have both called each other everything in the world they can think of. From now on they are just talking themselves out of votes. The high office of President of the United States has degenerated into two ordinarily fine men being goaded on by their political leeches into saying things that if they were in their right minds they wouldn't think of saying. Imagine Mr. Hoover last night "any change of policies will bring disaster to every fireside in America." Of all the conceit. This country is a thousand times bigger than any two men in it, or any two parties in it. These big politicians are so serious about themselves and their parties. This country has gotten where it is in spite of politics, not by the aid of it. That we have carried as much political bunk as we have and still survived shows we are a super nation. If by some divine act of Providence we could get rid of both these parties and hired some good man, like any other big business does, why that would be sitting pretty. This calamity was brought on by the actions of the people of the whole world and its weight will be lifted off by the actions of the people of the whole world, and not by a Republican or a Democrat. So you two boys just get the weight of the world off your shoulders and go fishing. Both of you claim you like to fish, now instead of calling each other names till next Tuesday, why you can do everybody a big favor by going fishing, and you will be surprised but the old U.S. will keep right on running while you boys are sitting on the bank. Then come back next Wednesday and we will let you know which one is the lesser of the two evils of you.

Beverly Hills, November 7:

There is only one redeeming thing about this whole election.

It will be over at sundown. And let everybody pray that its not a tie. For we couldn't go through this thing again, and when the votes are counted, let everybody, including the candidates, get into a good humor as quick as they got into a bad one. Both gangs have been bad sports, so see if at least one can't redeem themselves by offering no alibis, but cooperate with the winner, for no matter which one it is the poor fellow is going to need it. So cheer up, let's all be friends again, for one of the evils of democracy is, you have to put up with the man you elect whether you want him or not. That's why we call it democracy.

Beverly Hills, November 8:

If your side lost don't take it too much to heart. Remember there is always this difference between us and Italy. In Italy Mussolini runs the country. But here the country runs the President.

Beverly Hills, November, 9:

Mr. Hoover, the consolation you have from the whole American people is no doubt greater than that ever shared by a losing President.

There was nothing personal in the vote against you. You just happened to be associated with a political party that the people had just "lost their taste for." There is something about a Republican that you can only stand for him just so long. And on the other hand there is something about a Democrat that you can't stand for him quite that long.

We all know that you was handed a balloon that was blowed up to the utmost, you held it as carefully as anyone could, but the thing "busted" right in your hands. Well, there just ain't much you can do in a case like that. No, it wasn't you, Mr. President, the people just wanted to buy something new, and they didn't have any money to buy it with. But they could go out and vote free and get something new for nothing. So cheer up, you don't know how lucky you are.

Beverly Hills, November 11:

I advised 'em all to go fishing. Let the people alone and make up their own minds. Jack Garner was the only one listened to me. He went fishing, made no enemies, had a good time, caught three big channel cats, a seat in the House of Representatives, and the Vice-Presidency.

That's about a record for one catch. He wanted to throw back the smallest of the "catfish" and the Vice-Presidency, and just keep the seat in the House and the other two fish. Garner will be the only man that ever went from "speaker" in the House to "listener" in the Senate.

P.S. By the way, whatever become of the Roosevelts that claimed they was only eighth cousins to this one?

November 12:

The last campaign brought in religion. This one replaced it with fear. This time they tried to scare you into voting a certain way.

It takes a great country to stand a thing like that hitting it every four years. When you figure that you have a system where you make business stand still and people go nutty for three months every four years, why somebody who concocted the idea of elections certainly figured out a devastating scheme. The locusts I saw swarming the Argentine are house flys compared to the destruction to a business by a presidential election. The Candidates are High Typed Gentlemen till the contest gets close then the "Brute" comes out in em. What starts out to be a nice fight winds up in a street brawl. But it all comes under the heading of Democracy. And as bad as it is its the best scheme we can think of. So lets rest up for 36, mow the grass out of the streets, get that disaster out of those firesides, and start another battle over those Post Offices.

November 20:

I'll bet you that Mr. Coolidge would have ducked em if he had been in there under these same conditions. He would have "Not Choosed" right in their face.

Citizens, I am afraid that my administration has not been entirely to your satisfaction (Coolidge would have said), and there seems to be a decided element in favor of a change. I have no alabi's to offer, I have no excuses, I have done my best.

But the "Party" would never have allowed such a sane and sensible course. It would have put them in the hole instead of Mr. Hoover. The "Party" kept hanging onto the idea that "Things" might pick up. They did. Democratic support picked up.

But on the other hand there just seems to be something about running for President that you can never get out of a fellows head. He never seems to figure his chances. It can be an "Off Year" or an "On Year" and just nominate him, and he is perfectly tickled to death. That he will wind up by just being a defeated candidate never seems to enter his head.

Beverly Hills, December 2:

I have heard every kind of reason given for our hard times, but I have never heard the real one. That's that interest is too high. The world, and about everybody in it are broke from paying too high interest. No man should receive more for the "hire" of his money than he could take it and earn with it himself, and for the last three years there has been nothing that he could have made even 1 percent on it, outside of loaning it.

Santa Monica:

Governor Roosevelt, Warm Springs, Georgia.

I dident wire you on your election because I knew you wasent reading any of em anyhow. Now that all the folks that want something are about through congratulating you, I thought maby a wire just wishing you could do something for the country when you get in, and not wishing you could do something for me, well, I thought the novelty of a wire like that, when it was backed up by the facts, might not be unwelcome.

Your health is the main thing. Dont worry too much. A smile in the White House again (by the way when was the last one?) why it will look like a meal to us. Its the biggest job in the world, but you got the most help in the world to assist you. Pick you some good men and make em responsible for their end. If Europe dont pay up, fire your secretary of the treasury and get one that will make em pay. If people are starving and your granaries are full, thats your secretary of Agricultures business is to feed em. If Nicaragua wants to hold an election, send em your best wishes but no marines. Disarm with the rest of the world, but not without it. And kid Congress and the Senate, dont scold em. They are just children thats never grown up. They dont like to be corrected in company. Dont send messages to em, send candy. Let your Secretary of State burn up the notes that come from Europe, dont you have to attend to a little thing like that. Europes not going to do what they "Threaten to do." All those things are just something to give diplomats an excuse for existing. Dont let these State Governors like Pinchot and all those get in your hair. A State is to the Federal Government what an "honery" relation is to any of us. The more you do for em the more they expect. Keep off the radio till you got something to say, if its a year. Be good to the press boys in Washington, for they are getting those "Merry Go Rounds" out every few weeks now. Stay off of that back lawn with those photographers unless you got a Helen Wills. Or your fifth couzin, Alice Longworth. Nothing will kill off interest in a President quicker than "Weeklys" with Chamber of Commerce and Womens political organizations. Now if some guy comes running into your office telling you what "Wall Street was doing" that day, tell him, "Wall Street? Why there is 115 million of my subjects that dont know if Wall Street is a thoroughfare, or a new mouth wash. Its happenings dont interest me." Why Governor you can go in there and have a good time. We want our President to have some Fun. Too many of our Presidents mistake the appointment as being to the Vatican and not to just another American home.

And about people wanting jobs. Just pass them on down to the next in line. And there is so many working for the government that by the time they reach the lowest government employee, why the applicant will be beyond the government age limit. Why you handled more different kinds of people as Governor of New York than you will have in the U.S. and if Tammany comes around telling you "What they did," you just tell em, "Yeah? I know what you did and thats why you better keep quiet." So go in there and handle this thing just like it was another job. Work it so when we see you in person or pictures, we will smile with you. And be glad with you. We dont want to kill our Presidents, but it just seems our Presidents want to die for us. If we are going to blow up as a country lets be good sports and blow up with a smile. Now if you dont like these rules I can send you some more, but you will get the next bunch collect. Just dont get panicky. All you have to do is manage 120 million "hoodlums" and the higher educated they are the bigger hoodlums they are and the harder to manage. The illiterate ones will all work. And you will have no trouble with them. But watch the ones that are smart for they have been taught in school they are to live off the others. In fact this last paragraph is about all that is the matter with our country.

Yours with all good wishes,

Will Rogers.

December 18:

Will got riled up. People kept writing in, particularly Republicans, asking why he was dabbling in politics.

Everybody sure was "Jumpy" during this late uprising. They had a vote in their pocket and a chip on their shoulder, and any insinuation made against their "Hero" was just too bad for you. For instance they would write to the paper, "I read Will Rogers, but why does he have to dabble in Politics. Let him stay on funny stuff where he belongs." Well if they would just stop to think I have written on nothing but Politics for years, you never heard me on a Mother-in-law joke. It was always our National and International affairs.

Well I have been in almost every country in the last few years. I have talked with prominent men of those countrys, our Ambassadors or Ministers, and I would have to be pretty dumb to not soak up some information.

I couldent have done it by staying in Hollywood or in an editorial room.

Still you will read some letters where it says, "Why does Will

Rogers butt into these International problems he knows nothing about?"

Where do these other fellows get all of their vast store of knowledge? I never hear of em going any place. If I write about Mexico, I have been down there half a dozen times. There is not a State in this Country that I am not in every once in awhile. Talk to everyone, get the Ranchers and Farmers angle.

Those New York writers should be compelled to get out once in their lifetime and get the "Folks" angle.

Now I read Politics, talk Politics, know personally almost every prominent Politician, like em and they are my friends, but I cant help it if I have seen enough of it to know that there is *some* baloney in it. Now I am going to be like an umpire, or referee. I am going to keep on doing the same as I have in the past. I am going to call em like I see em. If I dont see things your way, well why should I?

I hope I never get so old that I cant peep behind the scenes and see the amount of Politics thats mixed in this medicine before its dished out to the people as "Pure Statesmanship." Politics is the best show in America and I am going to keep on enjoying it. Why they are missing something.

So on with the Show. We will have many a laugh in the next four years for there is one thing about the Democrats, they never put on a dull show. But always remember this, that as bad as we sometimes think our Government is run, its the best run I ever saw.

Santa Monica, December 18:

The U.S. Senate sentenced the Philippines to twelve more years of American receivership. How can one nation tell when another nation is ready for independence? But our government can do it. Yes sir, there is not a dozen of 'em that's ever been west of the Golden Gate, but they just could tell you to a day twelve years from now, just when the "little brown brothers" would be able to mess up their affairs as bad as ours. Certainly lucky for us we got our liberty when we did.

Suppose the House of Commons in England was holding a clinic over us to decide if we were ready for "self-determination."

Los Angeles, December 22:

This Technocracy thing, we don't know if it's a disease or a theory. It may go out as fast as Esquimo pies, or minature golf courses, but people right now are in a mood to grab at anything. They are sure of one thing and that is that the old orthodox political way of running everything has flopped. There is not a man in the whole world today that people feel like actually knows what's the matter. If there was he would be appointed dictatorship unanimously by the whole world. Our "big men" won't admit they don't know. They just keep on hoping they can "bull" their way through. The case has simply got too big for the doctors, but the doctors haven't got big enough to admit it.

December 26:

The old "Hide Bound" Republicans still think the world is just on the verge of coming to an end, and you can kinder see their angle at that for they have been running things all these years.

Personally I never could see much difference in the two "Gangs." You cant tell one from the other now. Course the last few years under Mr. Coolidge and Mr. Hoover there had grown the old original idea of the Republican Party, that it was the Party of the rich. And I think that was the biggest contributing part in their defeat.

I think the general run of folks had kinder got wise to that. In the old days they could get away with it, but of late years the rich had diminished till their voting power wasent enough to keep a minority vote going.

Big business sure got big, but it got big by selling its stocks and not by selling its produces. No scheme was halted by the Government as long as somebody would buy the stock. This election was lost four and five and six years ago not this year. They dident start thinking of the old common fellow till just as they started out on the election tour.

CHAPTER EIGHTEEN

We're Off to a Flying Start

With the closing of the banks soon after Roosevelt took over, Will saw that this new President was getting action — which was a relief.

As Will began to see America's problems settling out, he became more and more concerned with the world situation. He also began to worry about the way in which the New Deal, with its over balance of brains, was handling things in this country. But the year, all in all, was one to be thankful for. Its results were in the hearts, in the confidence, and in the renewed hope of practically everybody. He considered 1933 as the year of the big switch from "worse to better."

Santa Monica, January 1:

Ten million people have gone without work for three years

306

just listening to "Big Men" solve their problems. I don't know what will be the first commission Mr. Roosevelt will appoint, but millions hope that it won't be the "President of this concern," or "The head of that corporation," but ten men who have been without work; we will at least get an original view point. If the non worker has to go to the dogs, he at least should have a voice on the commission that sends him.

Beverly Hills, January 5:

Mr. Coolidge, you didn't have to die for me to throw flowers on your grave. I have told a million jokes about you but every one was based on some of your splendid qualities. You had a hold on the American people regardless of politics. They knew you were honest, economical and had a native common sense. History generally records a place for a man that is ahead of his time. But we that lived with you will always remember you because you was "with" your times. By golly, you little red-headed New Englander, I liked you. You put horse sense into statesmanship and Mrs. Coolidge's admiration for you is an American trait.

January 7:

Did Coolidge Know the Bust was Coming?

Well we just cant hardly get over the shock of the death of Mr. Coolidge.

I have had many Republican politicians tell me, "Will, you are one of Mr. Coolidge's best boosters." Well I did like him. I could get a laugh out of almost all the little things he said, but at the same time they were wise. He could put more in a line than any public man could in a whole speech.

Here is a thing do you reckon Mr. Coolidge worried over in late years? Now he could see further than any of these politicians. Things were going so fast and everybody was so cuckoo during his term in office, that lots of them just couldent possibly see how it could ever do otherwise than go up. Now Mr. Coolidge dident think that. He knew that it couldent. He knew that we couldent just keep running stocks and everything else up and up and them paying no dividends in comparison to the price. His whole fundamental training was against all that inflation. Now there was times when he casually in a speech did give some warning but he really never did come right out and say, "Hold on there, this thing cant go on! You people are crazy. This thing has got to bust."

But how could he have said or done that? What would have been the effect? Everybody would have said, "Ha, whats the idea of butting into our prosperity? Here we are going good, and you our President try to crab it. Let us alone. We know our business."

There is a thousand things they would have said to him or about him. He would have come in for a raft of criticism. The Republican Party, the party of big business, would have done their best to have stopped him, for they couldent see it like he did, and they never could have understood until a year later.

Later in his own heart did Calvin Coolidge ever wish that he had preached it from the housetops regardless of what big business, his party, or what anybody would have said?

Now here is another thing too in Mr. Coolidge's favor in not doing it. He no doubt ever dreamed of the magnitude of this depression. That is he knew the thing had to bust, but he dident think it would bust so big, or be such a permanent bust. Had he known of the tremendous extent of it, I'll bet he would have defied hell and damnation and told and warned the people about it. Now in these after years as he saw the thing overwhelm everybody, he naturally thought back to those hectic days when as President the country was paying a dollar down on everything on earth.

But all this is what they call in baseball a "Second Guess." Its easy to see now what might have helped lighten or prolong the shock, but put yourself in his place and I guess 99 out of a 100 would have done as he did.

Now on the other hand in saying he saw the thing coming, might be doing him an injustice. He might not. He may not have known any more about it than all our other prominent men. But we always felt he was two jumps ahead of any of them on thinking ahead. Now if he did know that the fire was going to break out and had he warned and warned, and shouted and shouted, he would perhaps been impeached (as Wilson was killed), but he would have gone down as "The World's Smartest Man."

But predicting, or no predicting, the thing was coming anyhow. But no one knows what passed through that wise head of his as he sat for three years on that porch up there and just thought.

My life has got more angles than a cat. You may be one of these Republicans (as most of the Ministers have gone into politics). You may be one that blamed me for electing Mr. Roosevelt, or you might be one of those Democrats who blamed me for electing Mr. Hoover four years ago.

This is kinder the public season to jump on me if anything has gone wrong, everything from a scarcity of skunk hides in the Northwest to a predominating amount of girl babies in Pennsylvania. You see, I think I am as independent as any one writing. I have as many Republican as Democratic papers, as many readers that cant read as can. The editorial policies of these great dailies mean nothing to me, I am going to call em like I see em.

I think I have complimented many a worthy thing in my time, and I have taken a shot at a lot of "Hooey." I am not against it mind you, as it just seems that it takes so much of it in every business. And they are all my friends, I am proud of the fact there is not a human being that I have got it in for. I never met a man I dident like.

I got no "Philosophy," I dont even know what the word means. The Fourth Reader (McGuffys) is as far as I ever got in schools. I am not bragging on it, I am thoroughly ashamed of it for I had every opportunity, everything I have done has been by luck, no move was premeditated. I just stumbled from one thing to another. It might have been down. I dident know at the time, and I dont know yet, for I dont know what "Up" is. I may be lower than I ever was, I dont know. I may be making the wrong use of any little talent (if any) that I accidentally have. I dont know.

I was raised predominately a Methodist, but I have traveled so much, mixed with so many people in all parts of the world, I dont know now just what I am. I know I have never been a non-believer. But I can honestly tell you that I dont think that any one religion is *the* religion.

If I am broadminded in any way (and I hope I am in many) but I do know that I am broadminded in a religious way. Which way you serve your God will never get one word of argument or condemnation out of me. There has been times when I wished there had been as much real religion among some of our creeds as there has been vanity, but that's not in any way a criticism.

Beverly Hills, February 1:

The Reconstruction Finance Corporation is made up of fine men, honest, and mean well and if it was water they were distributing it would help the people the plan was meant to help. For water goes down hill and moistens everything on its way, but gold or money goes uphill. The Reconstruction loaned the railroads money, medium and small banks money, and all they all did with it was pay off what they owed to New York banks. So the money went uphill instead of down. You can drop a bag of gold in Death Valley, which is below sea level, and before Saturday it will be home to papa J.P.

Santa Monica, February 3:

Japan wants a "Monroe Doctrine" now with them playing the part of Monroe, doctoring on China. Not only "doctoring" but operating.

February 4:

The lame duck Congress has been putting us on a mighty inspiring example of just how honery a Congress can be, if they really make up their minds to be honery. We just got about four more weeks of show and then these boys go into what some writer has termed oblivion. Oblivion is a one way ticket down.

We get rid of an awful lot of old rams at this shearing. We has some old big horned babies that had been in that Senate corrall so long their horns were getting kinder twisted, but some likable old animals at that.

Well we are all getting ready for the new deal. We dont know what kind of hand we will get, but we want it even if its just duces.

Beverly Hills, February 7:

One of my broadminded papers wired me, didn't use your article today because you attacked credit and loan. Well, credit means interest, and I will attack interest because interest attacks me and you. Not only attacks us but has what you might call a constant attack. There is not a man that's in the hole today but can look back and wish the first guy had never loaned him anything. Any loan made was better if we had let the first guy foreclose on us, and shrunk instead of trying to expand. Depression ain't nothing but old man interest just gnawing away at us.

Beverly Hills, February 21:

Carter Glass when he told the Senate that the whole Reconstruction Finance thing was bad, told them exactly what every Senator knew in his heart, but didn't have the nerve to say. Every man, every industry in the United States was hit by depression. Before you start dealing out public funds to help, you should have first found out have we enough money to give part of them a sandwich and leave the rest to go hungry. But no, they didn't do that. They just started right in helping the bankers, so every man, woman and child in the U.S. thinks, and rightfully so, that they have got as much right to get some sort of government aid as the bankers, the railroads, and big business got the first U.S. dole, and it will never be finished till the last one hundred and twenty million reach in and get theirs, because they feel they got it coming. No wonder Glass was too smart to be treasurer.

Beverly Hills, February 24:

The budget is a mythical bean bag. Congress votes mythical beans into it, and then tries to reach in and pull real beans out.

Santa Monica, February 26:

All they got to do to stop the war instantly is to agree to not trade with an aggressor nation. meaning Japan, but they won't sacrifice their trade just to save bloodshed. The League has got the weapon to stop war, but try and get the nations to give up that trade. What's a few thousand dead Chinaman compared to Japan as a cash customer.

Beverly Hills, March 2:

'Twas a lovely morning sun shining bright. Arthur Brisbane and the fleet had just returned from somewhere, orange juice was in every glass, cameras were oiled and ready to crank on beautiful screen stars, the birds were singing in the eucalyptus trees. The birds were singing, why? Because they couldn't read the papers. The papers said the bank clerks had worked so hard lately that they should have a holiday, so as we are all on a holiday, let's take it on the chin and grin. The Rogers having laid in no supplies against such an emergency will be living on horse meat as that's our sole product. I love horses, and I only ask, don't let me know which one we are eating today. I hear they have called a moratorium on inauguration.

Bankers, this moratorium you have asked for everybody is joining in good faith and with fine spirit. The ones that had a little money have taken as their example the unemployed who have grinned and took it on the chin all the time. While being the victim of our country the unemployed have been a credit. Now the bankers say if we will bear with 'em they will work it out, and we are going to give 'em every chance BUT (get that but in there with capital letters) if they are handing us the old baloney why then we will know for sure what this country needs. It will need new bankers. Everybody is doing what the bankers ask, but remember they are watching you.

Santa Monica, March 5:

America hasn't been as happy in three years as they are today, no money, no banks, no work, no nothing, but they know they got a man in there who is wise to Congress, wise to our so-called big men. The whole country is with him, just so he does something. If he burned down the capitol we would cheer and say "well, we at least got a fire started anyhow." We have had years of "Don't rock the boat," go on and sink if you want to, we just as well be swimming as like we are.

March 5:
Here a week or so ago I attended my first thing called Symposium. I dident know if it was going to be a circus, burlesque show, or a preaching. Well it was all three.

It seems that this Symposium is a racket. Its carried on by colleges mostly. Its where some given number of men talk on some subject. They get it discussed from different angles. I guess thats about what they are. Thats what this one was anyhow.

All this exchange of talk is a lot of hooey. It changes nobody or effects no opinions, but its kinder like weather talk it does no harm. But a Symposium is pretty good. If one ever travels through your town and plays there, go hear it. Its the old cracker barrel arguments over again.

Beverly Hills, March 8:
It's surprising how little money we can get along on. Let the banks never open, let scrip never come. Just everybody keep on trusting everybody else. Why it's such a novelty to find that somebody will trust you that it's changed all our whole feeling toward human nature. Why never was our country so united, never was a country so tickled with their poverty. For three years we have had nothing but "America is fundamentally sound." It should have been "America is fundamentally cuckoo." The worse off we get the louder we laugh, which is a great thing. And every American international banker ought to have printed on his office door "alive today by the grace of a nation that has a sense of humor."

Santa Monica, March 9:
That is one thing you would have never got a Republican administration to do, voluntarily close a bank. Their theory was leave 'em open till they shut. We can think of the most things

that would benefit the patient, but we never think of 'em till we see the hearse going by.

Beverly Hills, March 10:
Imagine a bank just having to live on interest alone. Removing their security or holding company is like taking the loaded dice away from a crap shooter.

Beverly Hills, March 15:
My bank opened today. Instead of being there to draw my little dab out, I didn't even go to town. Shows you I heard Roosevelt on the radio. Bankers should have over their desks this motto, "God bless radio, and then P.S. God bless interest." But I am telling you that Roosevelt should come ahead of interest.

Beverly Hills, March 27:
Papers all state Hitler is trying to copy Mussolini. Looks to me like its the Ku Klux that he is copying. He don't want to be emperor, he wants to be Kleagle.

You know nobody thought the Democrats could do anything either when our old form of government was overthrown last fall. But the Democrats surprised not only the world, but themselves, and now every country is trying to borrow a good Democrat to come and put 'em on their feet. Mexico has already made me an offer.

March 26:
We're Off to a Flying Start.
You can hear an awful lot by word of mouth nowadays. In fact there is almost twice as much distributed by word of mouth as there is by the written word. Never was people chattering so much. Everybody has got their heads together, but not so many have their heads.

We got the puncture fixed and are headed away. Course I dont know when we may have another one, but its a terrible relief to get this one mended. I never was one of those predictors, for

I never did know what to predict, but we are off to somewhere.

The first move was to close the banks. He beat the depositors by about 24 hours. They would have closed em anyhow. But here is the difference, when a depositor closes one it stays closed, but when the President closed one, it has a relapse and opens later. That was the one big thing that he did that really started the whole "Back to Normalcy."

Thats an old Republican expression. Poor old Republicans, they wasent a bad bunch of fellows but just dumb.

You know a dumb fellow can be the most likable fellow in the world. You can just kinder love em and pity em at the same time. Well what do you think is a Republicans thoughts now? Here they see a guy come in and do everything in the world that they ought to have done years ago, but dident think of it. So its as I say, they meant well, but was just dumb. They dident put the Country on the bum purposely as lots of folks think. They thought they were getting somewhere.

You see a Republican moves slowly. They are what we call conservatives. A conservative is a man who has plenty of money and dont see any reason why he shouldent always have plenty of money. A Democrat is a fellow who never had any, but dont see any reason why he shouldent have some. So the idea of closing a bank of your own free will and accord is as foreign to a Republican as selling stock which you dont own is foreign to a Democrat. Its not the Democrats conscience that would hurt him. Its just that he never thought of the thing.

The Republicans thinks the boat shouldent be rocked. The Democrat says, "Rocked bedambded, why sit here and starve in it? Go ahead and turn it over, maby the bottom side has got some barnacles on it we can eat."

It dident take Mr. Roosevelt long to see that a major operation was necessary. Asparin wouldent do a thing for the patient but prolong the agony. He had had that for years.

You see The Republicans as I say have all the money, and they would much rather be saved by another Republican, but they would rather be saved by a Democrat than not saved at all. You keep a Republican getting interest on his money and he dont care if its Stalin of Russia that is doing it.

Santa Monica, April 3:

Walter Lippman. You all read him. If you don't you ought to, he was a Democrat before the deluge to democracy. But his writings were so fair and impartial that Republicans used to sneak off around behind the house and read 'em. But being Republicans they never profited by his sage advice. But now they read him and weep. Well he was out to our igloo and broke cornbread and chili with us the other day. He thinks the green lights are with us. And the only thing can stop us again is prosperity.

Beverly Hills, April 7:

Well I can't speak with any authority on the condition of the country today, for here it is late in the afternoon and I havent sampled a single glass of the "spirit of rejuvenated America." I have always claimed America didnt want a drink as bad as they wanted the right to take a drink if they did happen to want one.

Santa Monica, April 9:

This Roosevelt knows his human nature. People had been pled with not to hoard. Laws had been passed to stop it. But when Roosevelt said, "Let 'em buy beer," the money come out of hoarding in a high lope. Why out here the first few thousand cases of beer sold was paid for with silver dollars worn so thin they was pasted together like a dollar bill. Every town of course run out of beer Friday but Beverly Hills (always unique and extraordinary). They were the first town to run out of pretzels. Very little intoxication over the country. And what there was, was caused by people using gin as a chaser.

April 13:

I may be all wet, and probably am, but when an American starts telling a Chinese "How to live," why its like a new dude telling an old cowman how to run his ranch.

I would as soon be a heathern and die because the town dident have a sewer, as to be an Episcopalian and get bumped off by a fellow member's Rolls Royce. Always remember that up to the time that the Missionaries arrived in China, and especially up to the time when the Yale and Harvard students arrived back home, China was going great.

If my son is educated at Oxford, I still dont think he can come back home and tell me how to play a hog raiser in the movies. Now you can imagine what a conglomeration of ideas a Columbia Chinese student would go back home with.

China is the only Country in the world that no Nation has to worry about. All the Missionaries in the world cant make China Presbyterian, and all the return students from foreign countries cant keep it from being Chinese.

My theory of the whole Missionary business could be summed up in a sentence. If you send somebody to teach somebody, be sure that the system you are teaching is better than the system they are practicing. Some think it is, some think it aint. A difference of opinion is what makes horse racing and Missionaries.

My motto is "Save America First, then when you get em all saved, save the Portuguese, for the Chinese dont need saving."

Beverly Hills, April 14:

What is the future of the cow business? Well I cant see but one future to it, thats to plow under every third cowman and castrate another third, so they stop breeding any new ones.

I think dude ranching would be a good thing to try. They eat a lot of things that white folks wont eat, and they breed like goats. You can handle a lot of em to the acre, if you put in a bar on the acre. One herder or hazer can handle a big bunch of em. All you got to do is just to keep the males and females parted in the daytime. You can give a hazer a good sheep dog and he can help bring em in at night. Yes there is a big future in Dudes. You got to handle em kinder like a Brahma. If one breaks out you dont take after him, or her, just let em alone. They will run their horse down and he will come dragging in before supper time.

Beverly Hills, April 17:

Every day just shows us what a lucky country we are. We got lots of fleas on us, and everybody is scratching to get em off, but there is one insect that bothers most of the world that we are at least free from, and that is a newspaper press that is not free. Everybody wants to know if the Englishmen in Russia are guilty or framed. Everybody would love to know the very facts of what is going on in Germany. But over here you can write what ever you want to, the only trouble is getting somebody that will read it.

Amarillo, Texas, April 19 [*dust-bowl time*]:

Just flew in here headed west we had to come in mighty high to dodge all the farms and ranches that were blowing around down on the lower strata it aint anything to be hit in the eye with a cow that is blowing with the dust from one ranch to another. But with all her dust and all her drought she is a pretty country.

April 30:

California acts a good deal like a dog pound in any town. It gets the undesirable strays off the street. We are the human dog pound of America. Some of their own communities even go so far as to catch and send out here. But being good humanitarians we just take em right in, and in a week they are as big liars as the natives.

May 7:

Here is a queer streak in me, I am not a hunting man (or fishing either). I wish I was for there must be a lot of pleasure in it, but I just dont want to be shooting at any animal, and even a fish I havent got the heart to pull the hook out of him.

But I do want to make that Alaska. Everybody that went up and come back after that 98 rally, were such liars, I would like to go up and meet the old boys that had the nerve to stick, as they tell me all the yellow ones come back.

Chicago, May 10:

Been looking at the great Chicago Worlds Fair which opens two weeks from Saturday. I am the first "rube" to visit it.

Its exactly what everybody needs, people been sitting at home grouching at each other for three years, now dont think we have outgrown the "fair" stage. In the days when we were a great nation we enjoyed 'em. Now you can see the whole thing for fifty cents, and the way this Roosevelt is going, by then we will have the fifty cents.

Santa Monica, May 14:

I am hereby entering this argument between young Rockefeller and the Mexican artist [*Diego Riviera*], for there is two things that a dumb guy knows as much about as a smart one, and thats art, and inflation. I string with Rockefeller, this artist was selling some art and sneaking in some propaganda, Rockefeller had ordered a plain ham sandwich, but the cook put some onions on it, Rockefeller says, "I will pay you for it but I wont eat the onions." Now the above is said in no disparagement of the Mexican artist, for he is the best in the world. But you should never try to fool a Rockefeller in oils.

Beverly Hills, May 16:

Well lots of war news in the papers today. I knew it was coming when I saw that we had cut down on our army and navy. If you want to know when a war is coming, just watch the U.S. and see when they start cutting down on their defense. Its the surest barometer in the world.

The Democrats have one great failing (that I was in hopes they had lived down) and that is they just want to fix the affairs of the world. Now its big hearted, and its mighty generous, but its just not possible for me (three thousand miles away) to tell you what caliber gun to have in your house. You know your neighbors better than I do.

Sky Harbor, Tennessee, May 18:

Going as a delegation of one from the American Comedians' Association to get some aid from the Reconstruction Finance. No industry has been hit worse than professional humor. There is

too much unconscious amateur talent. We hope to pay off the
R.F.C. (like the bankers and everybody else does) in laughs.

New York, May 22:

The phenominal popularity of the Roosevelt administration
now meets its severest test. They are starting to decide where all
this money they have been appropriating will come from. Now
if he can extract this money and still receive plaudits, then there
can be no doubt of his being a messiah. For taxpayers cheer,
not from the heart, but from the pocketbook.

Beverly Hills, June 7:

Last night Mrs. Franklyn D. Roosevelt finished a transcontinen-
tal flight. There is a real boost for aviation. But here is what she
really takes the medal for, out at every stop, day or night, standing
for photographers by the hour, being interviewed, talking over
radio, no sleep, And yet they say she never showed one sign of
weariness, or annoyance of any kind. No maid, no secretary, just
the first lady of the land on a paid ticket on a regular passenger
plane. If some of our female screen stars had made that trip,
they would have had one plane for secretarys, one for maids, one
for cheffs and chouffers, and a trailer for "business representatives" and "press agents."

June 24:

You know I think I told you over the radio on my last broadcast
about all the Senate asking me to stay on the air, that they enjoyed
it, and they all signed this application. Well do you know it was
one of the most pleasant things I ever had happen to me. Here
was the U.S. Senate that I am always kidding about, and here they
come and do a nice thing like that. Why I never will get through
thanking em, the whole mess of em. Why that petition will remain
one of my most prized possessions, and the next fellow that knocks
the Senate will have to answer to me. Thats my privalege and
nobody elses.

Those old boys watch a lot of stuff that if it wasent for them would be railroaded through. They are really more of a night watchman than the House is. The Senate is kinder like one of these things you have in a kitchen sink to keep the spoons and plates and stove, and all those little things from going on through. We cuss em (and they need it) but they are pretty much doing the best they can all the time. Every one of em is a demagogue if he is a man that dont agree to things we do.

Santa Monica, June 25:

You talk about an earthquake hitting California, that was kindergarten stuff compared to the news that some nut sent over the cables that Sister Aimee (McPherson) had had a baby. It looked like a case of maternity by remote control. Science is so marvelous it is being confused with miracles, and it looked like birth control by electrical transcription. But now that the facts are all in, we find the visit to the hospital was to beautify the present generation, and not to perpetuate the future.

July 2:

On the stage we thought that your talent grew with experience, that if you had had many years to your credit that you had perhaps learned your trade, but in the movies, if you were a good actor 5 or 6 years ago, that means that you have forgot how to act by now, and that some young girl that has just looked well in a bathing suit can outact you, and you must give way to her. Or that if its a boy, and if he has curlier hair and looks nicer why naturally you must pass out.

* * * * *

Walter Winchell, the old boy that tells the stork where to go and when, he was out about ten days ago on our set. Well he is a very surprising fellow, he is small of statue, nice looking, well dressed (as far as I could judge) seemed awful pleasant, very modest, looking for information instead of trying to give out any. I asked him how it was that he could tell the forecoming of a blessed event, and he said it was just second sight he reckoned. That in the early days among all his other accomplishments he studied to be a doctor, and that naturally a Dr had a very keen eye and that he attributed any premonition along that line to his early medical training. Then I asked him how it was he knew when people were going to get married, and when they were going to be divorced. That was not in the regular medical routine.

Well for instance marriage. He said that he watched the divorces first, that was to give him the line on who was to be married. That there never was a divorce without at least a fifty percent marriage being in the offing. So he watched em before they were divorced to see who they would marry after the divorce. He says that marriage is a habit, and divorce is a necessity.

Then of course the minute he finds out who is marrying, it dont take a bit of thinking or figureing on who will be divorced. In fact he seemed kinder astonished at me, that I was so dumb as to not know who would be divorced. "Why the ones that got married." Well as stupid as I am I had never thought of that, but thats just what he does, he just watches the marriages notices, and then announces the divorce from that. You see with the people that he writes about this record is infallible. When they are married you take no chances on announcing their divorce, and when they are divorced you take no chances on announcing their marriage. Course you got to work on a certain class of people to do that, but that is the class of people that he works on.

Now I work on an entirely different class of people. I work on politicians. Well they are not as mechanical as these that Walter works on. My bunch is harder to figure. A politician just figures on a job. How can I make this job last, or how can I get another one. But with Winchells bunch its how long will this wife last and where will I get the next? Ones mind is centered on a wife, and the other is centered on a job.

Santa Monica, July 9:

"Fifteen hundred Americans who have been living in Paris for years have decided to come home on account of the price of our money." There is a bunch of folks will be an awful big help to us.

Beverly Hills, July 11:

Frank Phillips of oil fame, was out the other day, said he was going to Washington, the oil men were going to draw up a code of ethics. Everybody present had to laugh. If he had said the gangsters of America were drawing up a code of ethics, it wouldent have sounded near as impossible.

Beverly Hills, July 14:

The funny part about it, is that all those statesmen really thought they were going to "make History." Well history makes itself, and the statesmen just drag along.

New York, July 16:

I will bet you that this Wiley Post makes it around the world and breaks his own record, I would have liked to have been in there with Post instead of the robot. And I could have if I had known as much as it does.

Beverly Hills, July 26:

By the way Mr. Roosevelt has cut the stock market down to three hours a day. They say they did it themselves, yeah? He just told em, "Now you be good boys. I will give you three hours a day to work on these suckers, and the other 21 hours they are under the protection of the fish and game laws."

Beverly Hills, August 1:

Yesterday before breakfast the U.S. Treasury offered $850 million worth of bonds, and before they had reached the ham and eggs, they were all sold. That means sold and paid for, and salted away, not part paid for and the rest on margins, till you sold 'em over the ticker to somebody else. If industry could interest some permanent buyers like Roosevelt can in his business, then they could truly call themselves industrialists. As it is now they are just manufacturing dice for Wall Street to shoot craps with. Nobody is buying a pair to keep.

Chicago, August 21:

Well the "hillbillies" beat the "dudes" and took the polo championship of the world right out of the drawing rooms and into the bunk house. And she won't go east in years, for the west always

thought you had to have a birth certificate to play it, now every
cowpuncher is herding in the heifers with a corn plaster saddle,
and even the "hay heavers" have changed a pitchfork into a polo
mallett, twenty thousand Chicagoans witnessed Sundays social
massacre. Nineteen thousand of 'em had never seen a horse,
much less a polo game, so from now on west of the Mississippi,
"old dobbin" plows in the fields only till four oclock, and he goes
out on the lawn to cavort in what used to be known as strictly
a social recreation, poor old society they got nothing exclusive left.
The movie folks outmarried and outdivorced them, the common
folks took their cocktails, "near" society took to bridge, now polo
has gone to the buckwheat belt, so poor old society hasent even
been left a code.

Las Vegas, Nevada, August 22:

Going to drop this off here at Hoover Dam hope they don't irri-
gate more land so they can raise more things that they cant sell and
will have to plow up more rows, kill more pigs to keep em from
becoming hogs. Looks like this whole hog destroying scheme of Mr.
Wallaces is a direct slap against my old friend and companion
"Blue Boy." What Wallace is trying to do is to teach the farmer
corn acerage control and the hog birth control and one is just
as hard to make understand it as the other.

*From Will's Speech on Radio as part of the Blue Eagle Drive Program,
Sunday, August 27:*

I tell you folks, I came away from Washington last week with
the idea that the little fellow has got somebody in his corner in
Washington. I don't mean the Administration is against big business. There are hundreds and thousands of big ones entering into
this thing with enthusiasm, and with their money and their whole
hearts; but for the first time in years the big man comes to Washington the same as the little man. If this Administration ever goes
under, it should have written on it's tombstone: "Perished through
trying to give the little fellow a square deal."

Santa Monica, August 28:

I believe that Mr. Moley, chief of the "brain trusters" getting out, is about the starting of the end of college professors in government, a professor gets all of his out of a book, but the politician, as bad as he is, does have an understanding of human nature, and the mob. So we just as well become reconciled to the fact that the old politician is with us, "even unto death." Theorys are great, they sound great, but the minute you are asked to prove one, in actual life, why the thing blows up. So professors back to the class room, idealists back to the drawing room, communist back to the soap box, (and use some of it) but old Congressman "hokum" and old Senator "hooey" are still the Mussolinis of our country.

Santa Monica, September 4:

Give an American a one piece bathing suit, a hamburger, and five gallons of gas, and they are just as tickled as a movie star with a new divorce.

Santa Monica, September 10:

When one nation is big, and one is little, why the little nations port is just like a public regatta. Everybody can come in thats got a boat. The whole thing as I see it all over the world today is, that the little nations has got no business being little.

Beverly Hills, September 12:

Revolutions run in packs, like hounds, or bananas. One revolution is just like one cocktail, it just gets you organized to get ready for the next.

Beverly Hills, September 20:

To inflate, or not to inflate, that is the Democratic question. Whether its nobler in the minds to suffer the slings and arrows of southern politicians, or to take up inflation against a sea of economists, and by opposing, end them. To expand, to inflate, to inflate perchance to dream. Aye there's the rub. For in that sleep of inflation, what dreams may come, puzzle the will, and makes us doubtful whether to bear those ills we have, than fly to others we know not of.

September 23:

We are arranging a picture for the screen now that I think you will remember, David Harum.

I will be a terrible guy to play it, for I am the worlds worst horse trader. I give all the boot and get all the worst horses. But I love to trade.

No sir, there is no kick in the world like a nose and nose finish of the old bang tails. Its universal, its all over the world, anywhere there is horses raised there is horse racing. And there is nothing prettier than a beautiful race track or fine racing plant, or a fine breeding farm. Around Lexington Kentucky is a beauty that cant be surpassed by the Lake Shore Drive in Chicago, Riverside Drive, Yellowstone Park, or Glacier National Park. Thats those wonderful breeding farms, blue grass fields, white fences, scampering thoroughbred colts, and wonderful stables. But its not only the thoroughbred, or high class horses thats coming back. Just the old mongrels are charging toward us with heads up and in increasing numbers.

Then too there is this polo, which used to be looked on as a caviar game, why now its commoner than bridge. You can play it on any kind of an old "Log." I know because I do it. All you have to do is just scratch off a piece of level land, whittle you out some round pieces of wood out of a hickory or bodak tree, take a broom handle and fasten a crochet mallet on the end of it. Get on your old filley and start swinging at it. Cecil Smith, this wonderful Texas player you hear so much of, learned on round rocks, or big pebbles. He used to knock them from Austin Texas clean to Angelo. He dident know for years that it was played with a wooden ball.

Then another thing that I bet you never thought about thats bringing the old horse back is parades.

There is something about riding down the street on a prancing horse that makes you feel like something, even when you aint a thing.

So take that side of the garage where the old Republicans were going to put in an extra car. Remember, two cars to every garage.

Well put in a manger, get you an old plug. The kids will all have
fun, Ma can be kept busy feeding him, and Pa can ride him on
parade days. By the way, I dont by any means want this to be
taken as an add, but I have got some mighty good "All Purpose"
horses, that can be bought, worth the money.

Beverly Hills, September 21:

Put a tax on the New York stock exchange, so they say they are
going to move to New Jersey. There is no industry that could move
easier. All they have to do is change their telephone number, pick
up the blackboard, and tell the loafers where to meet tomorrow.

Beverly Hills, September 22:

Never was a country in the throes of more capital letters than the
old U.S.A. but we still havent sent out the S.O.S.

Santa Monica, September 24:

The farmer deserves a profit, but the guy thats not eating deserves a meal more. The stockholder deserves his dividend, but the
unemployed deserves his job more.

Beverly Hills, September 26:

Ring Lardner died. You can always get better planes, better
trains, but we can't get another Ring Lardner. What a privilege
to have known him since those good old days when he wrote sketches
for Mr. Ziegfeld's Follies. In years to come when libraries put just
books in one wing, and literature in the other, you are mighty liable
to find Lardner's writings right in with the literature.

Beverly Hills, September 27:

I see where the New York Stock Exchange bluffed Tammany out
of the tax. They are going to put it on the street car and subway
travelers.

Beverly Hills, September 29:

There is so many boni-fide colonels of Kentucky that they have formed an association, and have been split up into zones. Irvin Cobb, (who can't return to Paducah) has been commander in chief of the colonels east of the Mississippi River, and I have been appointed to direct all Kentucky colonels west of the river. A war of extermination of Kentucky colonels may be just what the country needs, so nothing would please me better than to meet Irv, and his fat, gouty worn out Negro dialect colonels, with my bunch of young, agile, alert boys that reside on the progressive side of the river. Our men are colonels through achievement and not just through appetite.

October:
Dinner to Marie Dressler:

Now listen, all this compliments and foolishness has got to quit. We got to get some facts into this old ladys life.

They can all get up here and tell you how they love you, but I am not going to lie to you. I cant be up here loving some old woman when dames like Norma Shearer, Joan Crawford, Marion Davies and all those are here.

Whats the use kidding, I am human. Marie is a fine old gal, but I still got my youth and ambition. In fact I havent got much use for old foggies.

Anyhow, why dont they get out and give us kids a chance, then I got no use for homely people.

Sixty-two years ago in Coburg, Canadas oddest looking baby was born. The family retained her because they dident live near a creek, She was born with green eyes, she has got em yet. She has never had her eyes changed or her face lifted, while hundreds of actresses with lifted faces have been strewn by the wayside.

She made her first public appearance at the age of five as cupid sitting on a high pedestal. That was 57 years ago. She was the original flagpole sitter. At the age of fourteen, she got another job in another amateur performance. She was so clever she laid off nine years before she got a chance to work for nothing again, nine years between pictures. She had a bad agent. This second nights work in nine years encouraged her, so that she decided to keep on. She joined an opera co, a light opera company. A light opera company is where 16 singers travel with 4 trunks between em, and as far as receiving any money for her work, she was still an amateur. She never went to school in her life. That accounts for her being one of the most brilliant and best informed women in America. Her mother told her when she left home, to always get the best paper in every town and read it, so she has read Variety all her life.

Roumania had a woman name Marie and because she married a king they called her queen. The United States had a woman name Marie and because of her genius, her accomplishments, and her heart, we call her "Beloved." Thats more than a queen.

October 15:

Well just how is things going. Well the moderately situated ones and the working ones seem to feel hopefil, but the bigger fellows, lots of them, start whining and offering alabi's. They just seem a little scared that the big fellows is kinder undergoing an overhauling, and they dont know if they will fare the same as in the old days, but it is not so much greed, as it is uncertainty.

But all in all, we are doing better than usual. We are trying on everything in the store, and if something dont fit us, well we are just deformed. I was talking to the "Old Economist" the other night, he dont feel so bad about it, so it must look good. Thats Charley Chaplin. Did you know that Charley is just about the one of our best minds on all these deep subjects, well what that little rascal knows will just surprise you.

Yes sir, if you want to get yourself a loaf of economics, with a side car of theories, why Charley can give em to you. He has talked em over with every big wig in Europe, and he knows what the shooting is all about. Course there is one thing about economics and money theories, your theory is always right for its never tried.

We were all down to a mighty fine dinner they gave to Walter Disney. He is the sire and dam of that gift to the world, "Mickey Mouse." Now if there wasent two geniuses at one table, Disney and Charley Chaplin. One took a derby hat and a pair of big shoes, and captured the laughs of the world, and the other one took a lead pencil and a mouse, and he has the whole world crawling in a rat hole, if necessary, just to see the antics of these rodents. But there was more than shoes and pencils and derby hats and drawing boards there. Both had a God given gift of human nature. Well of course they base it all on psychology of some kind and breed, but its something human inside these two ducks that even psychology hasent a name for.

Beverly Hills, October 17:

Yesterday I ran onto a fellow who had hitch hiked his way out here from New York, rather dignified looking old bird, but kinder down at the heels. He give me about the most information I have had, he hopes they won't inflate, in fact hopes they announce they will soon go back on gold, then everybody will know what their money is worth, had optimistic hopes of our future, thought too many people, both large and small, looked too much to the government to fix their troubles, and do nothing themselves. He wasn't sore at the world, and had a good word for everybody, as I let him out of my car to catch a ride with someone else, I asked his name, said his name was Baruch, Bernard Baruch. So pick up all old men you meet, some of 'em are mighty smart.

Beverly Hills, October 23:

Farmers are having a tough time, but they had no idea that they were so bad off till they joined an organization and had some paid leaders tell 'em how poor they were. If ever an industry was having a field day, its the industry of paid leaders in every line, who are explaining to their followers, "what the government owes to them." I havent seen a copy of the constitution in years, (I guess they are out of print) but I don't remember in there anything about what it was to do if you raised too much, or if you bathed in one of your bathrooms too much. In fact, if I remember right we owed more to the Constitution than it did to us.

I was raised on a farm, we had farm hands, farm hired girls, farm horses, farm mortgages (not many), but I never saw a farm that raised farm leaders. This leader thing is a type of growth that has sprung up since everybody started joining organizations, not only in farming, but in everything. In the old days if you was smart enough to be in a business, you was smart enough to tend to your own business, without listening to a leader make a speech. Yours for less leaders and less followers of leaders.

October 29:

I got me a dictionary one time, but goodness it dident last long. It was like looking in a telephone book. I never called up anybody in my life if I had to look up their number. Nobody is worth looking through all those numbers for, and thats the way it was with my dictionary. I could write the article while I was trying to see what the word meant, and thats one good thing about language, there is always a short word for it. Course the Greeks have a word for it, and the dictionary has a word for it, but I believe in using your own for it.

The minute you put in a word that everybody dont know, you have just muddled up that many readers. Running onto a word you cant read, or understand is just like a detour in the road. You cuss it, and about a half dozen of em, and you will take different road the next time. I love words but I dont like strange ones. You dont understand them, and they dont understand you. Old words is like old friends, you know em the minute you see em.

Beverly Hills, November 28:

You can watch it from telling jokes about it. Every once in so often America "goes serious." Get all excited and mad at each other, one of these times is just before election, anything thats said the other side takes offense. Yet all our last Presidents have been elected by millions, showing that all that heat and perspiration was wasted. Then after election is over, you can call the other side a yellow dog, and they just laugh, for they have their sense of humor back. Now we are going into another one of those serious tail spins over this money racket. And its just like the election nothing you can do, nothing you can say, will change a persons opinion. It will all work itself out, without any personal lather from any of us. And in a few months we will regain our sense of humor and balance. Its just a serious spree that we have ever so often to get it out of our system.

December 1:

Everybody likes to make a dollar his way, but if he finds he is not allowed to make it his way, why he is not going to overlook the chance of making it your way.

December 3:

Vodka is fluid, but is what could rightly be classed as a deceptive fluid. Its as harmful a looking thing as a nice gourd full of branch water. But when you start sampling it your eyes begin expanding, and your ears begin to flopping like a mules. Its the only drink where you drink and try to grit your teeth at the same time. It gives the most immediate results of any libation ever concocted, you dont have to wait for it to act. By the time its reached the adams apple it has acted. A man stepping on a red hot poker could show no more immediate animation. Its the only drink where you can hit the man that handed it to you before he can possibly get away. You dont go through that period where people say, "Silas is getting tight." Say brother, when Silas lifts that glass, Silas is not getting tight, Silas is out.

Its a time saver. It should especially appeal to Americans. There is nothing so dull in American life as that period when a drinker is just at that annoying stage. He is a pest to everybody, but vodka eliminates that, you are never at that pest period.

So we havent realized the benefits we got from recognizing Russia, till the vodka starts rolling in.

December 17:

Now I dont want to do anything to bring more "She" condemnation down on me, but out here a couple of months ago, when California put on their lynching, women were the rooting section, and the original encouragement of the thing come from the "She" sex. Many a man has gota licking because his wife has said, "Go on get him John, you aint a going to let him say that, are you?" She will not only egg the thing on, but by golly she will go in and join. Women are not the weak, frail, little flowers that they are advertised. They love to say that women dont want war, and that they have to bear the brunt of it, which of course they really do, but if you ever noticed all their speeches, and denunciations of war, is after its over, they never do it in the making of one. And thats a fine spirit, more power to em. They got more nerve than men.

They enter a thing with more spirit and enthusiasm. You let a woman get up at a recruiting meeting and denounce the whole thing and defy the boys to join up, and I will lay you a bet that the first fifty hands that tore her asunder would belong to the fair sex. No sir the whole thing about the women is, they lust to be misunderstood. They always want you to have the wrong impression about whats in their minds and not the right one. There has never been anything invented yet, including war, that a man would enter into that a woman wouldent too. But here is the thing, you must never let em know but what you think they are just doing everything in their power to prevent war. The wives of the Prime Ministers, Diplomats, and Presidents would only have to say "If you allow war to come to this country I will leave you, so help me."

But history records no record of one having been left for that reason though left for everything else. But when he comes home some day and says, "Honey I guess you saw the extras on the street, I had to declare war." She says, "I know it darling, and we will lick the very pants off that other old mean Nation." And when the recruiting starts, she will make the first speech, and she will work her head off from then to the finish at anything no matter how tiring or dangerous, then when its over, she will say, "We women will prevent war." But thats the way it should be and thats the way we want it.

All the wars in the world even if you won em, cant repay one mother for the loss of one son. But even at that when she says to you, "That's my oldest boys picture. He was lost in the war," there is behind that mist in her eyes, a shine of pride, that could never be there if she had to say he was run over by a Ford.

December 24:

Now here is a funny thing about those Marxes, Groucho can play as good on the guitar as Harpo can on the harp, or Chico on the piano, but he never does. He is really what I call an ideal musician. He can play but dont. In New York when I was playing with Miss Dorothy Stone in "Three Cheers" he even tried to teach me to play the guitar. He would come over to my dressing room before our two shows started, and he would play and I would sing old songs.

Mrs. Rogers and I had dinner over at Grouchos and he played the piano that night. I love to sing old songs, and any time anybody will start one I am the loudest, and if they wont start em, I will myself.

Santa Monica, December 24:

Well there is lots more good cheer this Xmas than last (or the last three) and its not all out of bottles either. Its in the heart, in the confidence, and in the renewed hope of everybody. Course there is an awful lot of folks that are not working, but they have never been the ones that complained, fear has never come from the fellow with no job, or no food. He has stood it wonderful, I doubt if a parallel will be found where millions hung on with such continued hope, and patience as in this country. But I believe even the most down and out, while he might not see a turkey Xmas day, he can see one in the future.

Santa Monica, December 31:

In years to come when all these professors switch from economists to historians, they are liable to label 1933 as the historical years, the year of the big switch, from worse to better. So, so long 33, panics come every twenty years, so we will be seeing you in 53.

CHAPTER NINETEEN

Some of the New Hands Weren't
Dealt So Well

1934 — Will fought actively against having the army pilots fly the air mail. He wanted to keep these boys at their rightful task of making America strong while he advised F.D.R. in the struggle in Europe to say, "Boys, its your cats thats fighting, you pull 'em apart."

When Ireland abolished its senate, he did some wishful thinking about the United States. But the long-haired boys didn't get his mental telepathy.

For relaxation, he took O. O. McIntyre, Irvin Cobb and some of the "weaker sex" for a wild drive on his ranch. They're saved in a nick of time by a quick riding cowboy.

Betty, Bill and Jim, and Will make a trip around the world — from west to east. Will slyly dropped his "wifely" acquired excess wardrobe along the way until he got into New York with his same little red valise and portable typewriter.

After seeing Asia and Europe, he suggested that "about 50,000 airplanes" would be the right number for us. Dopey, great friend of the family, died.

Beverly Hills, January 3:

That Roosevelt handled that congress this morning just like a mother would a fretting baby. Just when any other mother would have told it to hush, and be a good baby, and not cry, he didn't tell 'em a single thing to do. Just slipped 'em all a piece of candy. (The little black republican babies along with the white ones.) And he left 'em feeling that mother had confidence in 'em. And they were all just tickled to death, rolling on the floor, with their toes in their mouth. And goo-gooing at each other.

Beverly Hills, January 4:

Mr. Roosevelt proposed in his speech, that the N.R.A. and a lot of these other government regulated business ethics would be made permanent. Well that was a terrible blow to some business men, they had figured they would only be required to be honest by the government, till the emergency was over.

Riverside, California, January 10:

Did you ever drive one of these "sulkys" in a trotting horse race? Well they got old David Harum sitting straddle of a horses tail out here on the Riverside track, and if you think that hasnt got it on all auto driving you are wrong. I am getting just about old enough, and crabbed enough to take up the grand circuit, so look out Goshen and Lexington, young Pop Geers is coming East. We have our radios, autos, golf, bridge, and a million contraptions, but all of it dont pay, for the thrill missed in stepping out in the red wheel buggy and high stepper. You could be a pretty poor type of lover, but the horse made up for it. Thats how a lot of us were able to go out of our class and get the wives we did.

We are driving the first make of low wheel sulkys. They come in '92. Still they are much higher than the low ones they use today. I want to tell you its quite a kick, trying to drive one of those with pretty fast horses too, and ten drivers on the track at once. There is always a hole big enough for the horse but how about the buggy he is towing along! The only thing I had to recommend me was that I looked as old as a driver. I used to be a pretty good just old common horse driver as a young fellow back home, but I never made the tracks. My father was the best driver I ever saw, though. I have seen him hitch em up when they was really wild and go where he wanted to with em, not where they wanted to. So if I show any driving ability in this my first real effort, it is inherited. Its not from hard work, perseverance, and taking advantage of my opportunities (as the American Magazine used to advise us).

Washington, January 30:
Was talking to a lady congressman and she said to me why do all those men say that a big navy will bring peace, I told her well even if it dont bring peace, it will come in mighty handy in case of war.

February 8:
Bad moving pictures are not made with a premeditated design. It looks to you sometimes like we must have purposely made em that way, but honest we dont. A bad picture is an accident, and a good one is a miracle.

Santa Monica, February 11 [*when mail contracts to airlines were canceled*]:
Whats all the hundreds of aeroplane pilots, and the thousands of people who make an honest living in the aeroplane business, going to do? Its like finding a crooked railroad president, then stopping all the trains. You are going to lose some fine boys, if those army flyers, who are marvelously trained in their line, but not in night cross country flying, in rain and snow, fly the mail. I trust an air line for I know that that pilot has flown that course hundreds of times, he knows it in the dark. Neither could the mail pilots do the army pilots stunts, and his close formation flying. I do wish they would prosecute the crooks but not make a great growing industry, (where 99 percent are hard working, and honest)

suffer. I hope they dont stop every industry, where they find crookedness at the top.

Beverly Hills, February 12:

Papers today say, "what would Lincoln do today?" Well, in the first place he wouldnt chop any wood, he would trade his ax in on a Ford. Being a Republican he would vote the Democratic ticket. Being in sympathy for the under dog he would be classed as a radical Progressive. Having a sense of humor he would be called eccentric.

Beverly Hills, February 15:

Lots of headlines today. "Mussolini's troops camped on the Austrian border," "Hitler says nothing," which means he is too busy moving troops, "England lends moral support," yes and two battleships, "France backs Austrian government," and sends a few hundred planes over to deliver the message. "Japan almost on verge of prostration in fear Russian wont get into this European war." Mr. Franklyn D. shut your front door to all foreign ambassadors running to you with news. Just send 'em these words, "boys, its your cats thats fighting, you pull 'em apart."

Santa Monica, March 4:

Chili is selling nitrates, Europe is fertilizing again.

Beverly Hills, March 13:

Sure the army said they could fly the mails, be a fine army that would say, "No, Sir, Mr. President we cant fly 'em." If my movie Co says, "We are producing Shakespeare, how about it?" Yes sir, I cant do it like the Barrymores, but I will give it an awful tussle. The Romeo part may ground loop me, but I will take old Hamlet over the mountains on the darkest night. And tomorrow if the President calls in the Navy and says, "Can you relieve the farmer?" that Admiral will say, "Yes, sir, the ships will be ready at twelve oclock to take him off the farm."

March 18:

I dont know how I got to reading about the fantastic running of our country, instead of boning up on Shakespeare. But I did, even before I got to making a living by doing a little police reporting on the lawmakers. I am a kind of a slow reader anyhow, and a lot of stuff I have to read was not delivered in what you would call a straightforward or lucid vein, so I have to go back over it a few times to catch the meaning, and then I dont always grasp it.

But I do do a lot of newspaper reading, then at the end of the week I have to do a lot of magazine reading, for it contradicts what the papers have said all week. Then by that time comes the monthlys, and they fog the issue up more than ever. Here is something I have learned that is absolutely true. If you are going to write, talk, comment, or argue over any public question, dont do it by just reading one newspaper. I try to get all kinds, breeds, creeds, and every single different political one. You can tell in a minute a person that only reads one paper. Gosh, you would be surprised how one bit of political news is so differently construed in different papers. Some public man is a horse thief in one paper, and pick up the other and he is just about to be cannonized and made a saint. Then the next paper will say he is a horse thief in the day, but repents at night.

But its sorter fascinating to read a paper clear through, even if you do know before you start about whats in it. But some day when no papers come I am going to get a Dickens book, and see how he stacks up with the Beverly Hills Citizen and the Claremore Progress.

Hollywood, March 23:

Those old Wall Street boys are putting up an awful fight to keep the government from putting a cop on their corner.

You dont hear as much of Senator Bill Borah as you used to, with all the new fangled things they have for breakfast nowadays, you dont hear as much of ham and eggs as you used to either, but its still mighty good eating.

When Mr. Borah says, "when you cut down your wheat production 43 million acres, where are the farmers and people that farmed those 43 million acres going, then its proposed to send 2 million from the crowded cities to the country, how are these two going

to pass going and coming, those professors in the agriculture dept,
are going to have a tough time answering the traffic problem."

Santa Monica, March 25:

Been reading all the Sunday articles by world known writers,
and they all talk war. Well if there is any excuse for anybody
fighting at this time, its beyond me. The consensus of opinion is
that, "so and so has to fight so and so sooner or later," well I believe
if I had to fight a man "sooner or later," I would fight him later,
the later the better. The only legitimate reason I can see why
Germany and France must fight is, they havent fought in 16 years,
and the only reason I can see why us and Japan has to fight is,
because we havent fought before.

Santa Monica, April 15:

On this Sabbath day with a newspaper hid behind my song book,
I saw where the republic of Ireland was about to do away with
their senate. Now ordinarily that looks like a popular move in
any country. But this being Sunday, and having a generous feeling
toward all mankind, (no matter how unfortunate his position) lets
ask our redeemer to not let us act too hastily in following Irelands
example. Thou Almighty, who seeist all things, must know that as
deciples there is not a Saint Peter in the senate, and as for prophets,
there is not a Moses in a carload. They seeist not but neither do
the ones who sent em there see, so lets be charitable. But Oh
Gracious One, if Ireland should be right, help us to see the light
immediately.

Santa Monica, April 19:

In opposite columns appear these two different items, "Lexington, Mass, citizens march to Washington as in Revolutionary days
to protest the government having anything to do with business,"
"Washington, D.C., Secretary Perkins reports 2,750,000 employed
in past year, employment in March was 80 percent of what it was
during peak of 1923–25 average. Weekly payrolls increased
70,000,000 in twelve months, since last March."

So it looks like the boys from Lexington will find quite a few along the line of march to Washington, that will be too busy to join em. I imagine it would be awful hard to ruin a country by paying wages.

Santa Monica, April 22:

Saturday President Roosevelt had at the White House, his graduating class of Harvard, 1904. There was over 300 of em, and all Republicans. I think he was just quietly rubbing it in on em. For the press couldent name a one of em that anybody had ever heard of. I think F.D. with his usual sense of humor, was just in a subtle way impressing on the boys "if there hadent been a Democrat in the class youse guys would never have got to even see the inside of the White House." It only illustrates that every Harvard class should have one Democrat to rescue it from oblivion.

Beverly Hills, April 25:

Mr. Tugwell is just one of the nicest and most pleasant fellows you ever met in your life. All of those brain trust fellows are. But dont let em start explaining something to you. They get you down with theorys, and then stomp on you with phrases. You start to raise up, and they will hit you in the face with a thing called "dogmas." Mr. Tugwell knocked a pretty smart bunch over lately with a "pair of dogmas," called "modernized process," and "experimental approach." Einstein couldnt have had em as mentally goofy.

San Francisco, April 30:

Well San Francisco, I bet that San Francisco was a city from the very first time it had a dozen settlers. Cities are like gentlemen, they are born, not made. You are either a city, or you are not, size has nothing to do with it. New York is "yokel," but San Francisco is "city" at heart.

San Francisco, May 2:

See where the U.S. Chamber of Commerce are gathered in

Washington again. Its the caviar of big business, last time they met I happened to be in Washington, and was the guest of Jesse Jones, (head of the Reconstruction Finance) at their dinner. Now the whole constitution, by laws, and secret ritual of that Orchid Club, is to "keep the government out of business." Well thats all right for every organization must have a purpose, but here was the joke, they introduced all the big financiers, the head of this, that and the other. As each stood up, Jesse would write on the back of the menu card, just what he had loaned him from the R.F.C. (I got that menu card yet), yet they said "keep the government out of business."

San Francisco, May 4:

At the U.S. Chamber of Commerce meeting last time, Mr. Roosevelt appeared (in person) and delivered a lovely talk, this time he just sent the boys a note and told em to quit hollering "Wolf" and go to work, "private business can and must take up the slack. The people will be impatient of those who complain." So the Chamber looked at each other, scratched their heads, and went back to "Passing resolutions."

San Francisco, May 6:

) From all I can read in the papers dated from some foreign capitol, the ambition of their lives seem to be to get us and Japan into war, now if any nation on earth can give any excuse why we should fight Japan any more than they should, they ought to get a prize for thinking of it. Naturally everybody feels sorry for China, but there seems to be concerted plan among the others, to get us to feel so much sorrier for em than they do that we will do all the fighting for em. Besides we couldent go to war with em now, for we just sent our fleet around on the East coast in case we would have trouble with Portugal, or Spain.

May 6:

Had some fun out here at old Uno E Dos Mortgages Rancho [*First and Second Mortgage Ranch*] a couple of Sundays ago. O. O. McIntire and Irvin Cobb and Will Hayes, Bill Hayes wife and Odd's wife and Irvin's daughter (and a bright one too) and Mrs. Billie Burke Zeigfeld.

Well to kinder make O. O. and Irvin feel like Paducah, Kentucky, sah, and Galopolis, Ohio, we hitched up a team of big grey mules to a three-seated hack, I took the ribbons, and Cobb said, "There is where you should have been all these years telling those jokes to a span of grey mules."

This is at heart a dry mountainous country. I have some dirt roads around our patch, but they are so imbedded up against the mountain side that I really have yet to see anybody derive any great enjoyment out of driving around them.

We drove up on a kind of a high lookout. Its our local Pikes Peak. Must be at least 400 feet above sea level. I pointed out Catalina Island, or where I had seen it the day when there was no fog. I pointed distant screen stars homes out. I just had heard they lived within a mile of where I pointed, but there was no place for anyone to argue with a driver. Then I turned my mules down hill and toward the barn. Like a real old stage coach driver I reached for my side break. I throwed her on, but she had jarred loose and she dident connect with the wheel. She had been an awful nice hack in "Atmosphere" tied out in a Western street in a movie scene, but she was a little rusty on mountain work.

Well when the brakes dident work she commenced going up on these old mules heels, those single-trees commenced popping em on the hind legs, and they commenced to hit quite a nice gentle lope. Cobb is in the very rear seat, and cant do the coaching that I figured he would be able to aid me with. He is leaning in toward the mountain side at an angle that must a been about horizontal. McIntire aint on this excursion, or he would a busted a spat, but his wife is, and an 82-year-young aunt of Odd's is sitting up with old Casey Jones Rogers and having the time of her life. A mighty narrow road, a real drop down side into a deep canyon, down hill, mules picking up momentum here and there. Sounds kinder komical now, but not so hot at the time. I got an awful good boy with me, Buddy Sterling, and I kinder suspicioned when we started out that we might need a pick-up man, so he was along on a good horse.

Buddy passed us like a streak and picked em up. Had to reach over one's neck and bull dog the second one too. We got stopped and lost three customers, Mrs. Rogers, wife of the driver of course, Mrs. Zeigfeld, who had never seen anything that wild in the Follies, and Mr. Cobb. Said he dident mind staying in, but he dident like to see the ladies walk down the hill alone as no telling what leading man might attack em. We hobbled one hind wheel to the body and went down in enjoyment. The old Aunt, Mrs. Hayes, and McIntire, and Mrs. Brody, Irv's daughter. I had another (about ten acre patch) that I wanted to show em, but I couldent seem to get anybody interested.

San Francisco, May 11:

These old boys with a pair of specs and a tablet and pencil can sit and figure out how much wheat, corn and oats can be raised each year in order to sell each bushel of it at a profit. Then along come a guy called "elements," this bird "elements" never went to college, he has never been called an "expert," and he has been laying pretty low for quite awhile, but when this guy "elements" breaks out he can make a sucker out of more experts than anybody.

Santa Monica, May 13:

Senate passed the bill to regulate Wall Street, the government is going to put traffic lights on it. Its always been a hit and run street. The red light tells you you better stop and wait before buying. The green light tells you that you are a sucker anyhow, and you just as well go ahead. The yellow light means, put up no more margins, let em sell you out.

May 13:

Congress has just passed the big inheritance tax, and that gets you when you are gone.

I think its a good law. You have had the use of it during your lifetime, so turn it over to the Government and they can do some darn fool thing with it, no telling what, maby something just as foolish as the children of the deceased would.

What is it they say, "Its only one generation from a pick handle to a putter, and one more from a tuxedo to a tramp."

When taxes first started . . . who started em anyhow? Noah must have taken into the Ark two taxes, one male and one female, and did they multiply bountifully! Next to guinea pigs, taxes must have been the most prolific animals.

May 16:

Lowering the price of the money from a dollar to 59 cents dident have quite the effect that the economists thought it would. They had figured that it would raise prices forty cents on the dollar, well it was just one of those theories that worked fine with a pencil, but dident work with money. I can sit in a grandstand with a race programme and a good sharp pencil (I have done it with a dull one) and I can write down the winning horse and what he is thinking about when he crosses the line, but the minute I walk under the stands and reach for a five dollar bill instead of a pencil, that horse just seems to know it, and runs differently. And thats one of the drawbacks of the proffessor, his work is entirely with a pencil, but the minute that pencil is traded for coin of the realm, and the dealings are with somebody else, and not just with a tablet, why life takes on an entirely different outlook.

Beverly Hills, May 29:

Walking Monday afternoon through one of the most famous of the historical California missions, San Juan Capistrano, (half way to San Diego) and who should I find in meditation before a wonderful old picture (depicting the joy of harvest, and the merrymaking at the sale of the crops), it was Secretary of Agriculture Wallace, tears were in his eyes, and he kept murmuring lowly, as he turned to the altar, "Oh What have I done Father that I couldent have been Secretary of Agriculture in days like those."

Santa Monica, May 30:

President Roosevelt is giving Cuba a new treaty, the "godfather" clause is taken out. All their revolutions are to be strictly "home talent." More news down that way, Porta Rica is to be "wet nursed" by the Interior department instead of the army, the

Phillipines are rehearsing for peace, it wont be long now till our army will all be visiting America at one time. Thats the dope, get em all home, add to their number, add to their training, then just sit tight with a great feeling of security, and just read about foreign wars thats the best thing in the world to do with them.

Beverly Hills, June 1:

Among all the big news and headlines of todays news, there was a little item that sure give me great encouragement, it said that some great professor of the Smithsonian Institution, had discovered that a person with a "cowlick" was human, and not like the person who had none and was descended from the ape, as no ape ever had a cowlick. So now instead of having M.D. and P.H.D. after your name (and all those things to publicly advertise your supposed knowledge), why we just take off our hat, show you the old "cowlick," and say "there you apes take a look at a human."

Hollywood, June 24:

We used to think war couldn't last long because one or both sides had no money, why there is no industry under the sun you can get credit as quick for you as you can war.

Beverly Hills, June 25:

The pictures of Hitler and Mussolini are pouring in on us from the press now, and every one of em keep looking more like they are going to bite each other.

Claremore, July 10:

I only had a short time before we were to leave for our trip around the world, so I decided to go on over into Oklahoma and see my sister and folks. Got a little sleep at Wichita, Kansas, that night, then down to Tulsa in Oilman Mabie's plane, a fast Lockheed. He used to trade and sell mules. Now he has more holes in the ground than a gopher, and the funny part of it, the things got oil spouting out of em. They got one field called "Mabie Field." But its not just Maby, its really there.

New York, July 12:

Went on to New York and saw my little co-starring partner, Dorothy Stone, in Marylinn Millers place in "As Thousands Cheer." And was she a hit. Clever girls those Stone Girls, Paula in vaudeville with a great dancing act, Carol a big hit in a new play "The Sparrow." And Fred just walking around beaming. He met me at the Theatre and we all went to Dinty Moores after the show.

* * * * *

Well out at daylight to fly to Maine to see my Mary. Here I had started out just to go to Texas, and wound up in Maine. Good thing there was no other states any further away. Lakewood where they have the theatre and summer stock company and a real one, is a great boon to the speaking stage. They were getting along fine, working hard and happy. I couldent interest Mary in a trip to Japan, so Ma and the two bohunks and I are going to break out.

Lakewood, Skowhegan, Maine, July 13:

Did you ever see a place that looks like it was built just to enjoy? Well, this whole state of Maine looks that way. If its not a beautiful lake, its a beautiful tree, or a pretty green hay meadow, And beautiful old time houses, with barns built right in with the kitchens. Vacationers and everything have improved thirty percent over last year. Roads have been fixed up with federal money. Newspaper advertising has increased over fifty percent. All these things have been done, yet the editorials say that the New Deal is a failure. Its a funny world. You feed a dog and he bites you.

Amarillo, July 15:

On my way to the Halsell ranch at Muleshoe to do some calf roping. Flew all night and got to Amarillo at four oclock in the morning. Its about 100 miles. Well I got a taxi and lit out.

We went by the restaurant to get some ham and eggs, for out West everything you do you must get Ham and eggs first. An old girl and her beau (perhaps) eating in there too about 4:30 that morning, she recognized me. She had on an evening dress, thats mighty late for an evening dress in Amarillo. She wanted me to join her in what she said was a cup of coffee "That had something in it." I told her I was doing mighty well on this coffee I had ordered that had nothing but grounds in it. But she swore she was drinking "Coffee Royal." That sounded awful "Continental" to be browsing around in Amarillo. Why even "Old Tack" never heard of that. Well anyhow she got plum sore at me because I wouldent join her. And when I said "Good morning" as my driver and me went out she turned her bare back on me and muttered, "Them actors are all alike, they are all swell headed, thats what I get for speaking to a ham. He dident know a lady when he seen one."

We drove over a Country where 36 years before as a boy 18 years old I had helped drive a bunch of cattle from that very place to Western Kansas, and there wasent a house or a chicken in the whole country. That plains was the prettiest country I ever saw in my life, as flat as a beauty contest winners stomach, and prairie lakes scattered all over it. And mirages! You could see anything in the world — just ahead of you. I eat out of a chuck wagon and slept on the ground all that spring and summer of 98. (Lot of folks went to the Klondike, but I couldent get any further away from my home in Indian Territory than Texas.) The limit of my "Pay Dirt" was I think 30 dollars a month. Well here I was 36 years later driving out to a ranch, to eat at another "Chuck Wagon," and do a little roping. A good deal had happened to everybody in 36 years. No more happens to one person than to another. Some look bigger, but they are no bigger than the things that look little that happens to the other fellow.

No greater, no happier life in the world than the cattle man. He missed being with the Follies, but so did I miss many and many a great meal from the tail end of a wagon. That coffee is not "Coffee Royal" but brother its coffee.

July 20:

Was getting all ready to make the big hop around the world. Now to get ready for that would take me just about as long as it would most people to get ready to drive to town Saturday afternoon and stay for the picture show that night. I got one little old soft flat red grip, or bag, that if I just tell it when I am leaving it will pack itself. A few old white shirts with the collars attached, and a little batch of underwear, and sox, now all these you can replenish at any store anywhere (I know for I have done it), then throw the old ones away. You dont figure on laundry at all. And its cheaper, for when you start paying excess on these aeroplanes, brother, till then you havent seen any excess. So me and my little red bag and typewriter, one extra suit in it. Its always packed the same, no matter if its to New York or to Singapore.

Well this time it was different, there was women folks along. Ma was going along and she said I couldent be trooping along with her unless I looked the part.

Well it seems that there was concocted a scheme before we all embarked on this present enterprise, that the master ("HA HA") meaning me, should be diked out as never before. They started dragging in palm beach suits to fit onto me when I should have been roping calves. They dragged me in from the polo field where I should be working a green horse to try some white shoes on me.

Well if you just follow this family you could pick up a lot of new unworn things across Manchuria and Siberia, and Moscow, and Finland, and Denmark, and Sweden and Norway. I just slipped one grip full to a bellboy in Honolulu just now. Its going to take a long time to get rid of all of it. But I will come into New York Harbor, with the little red bag, the old blue serge suit, and the typewriter.

July 21:

I was reading an article just now by some smart aleck, and he was giving his solution of censorship, and the movies, and what caused this and that. He happened to mention the "Specialist" by Chick Sales. Well what in the world about that little book? One that every man (especially if he was raised in the country or small town) took home, read to his wife, and to his Mother, and his Dad, for the older you was the more it appealed to you. Then to have somebody speak up that never had enough humor to get the idea that it was a great character study of a man. The story wasent of a building. It was of the mans pride in his chosen profession.

You can make anything you are a mind to out of anything, but that little story that sold over a million copies, and here is a funny thing about it. It was the best people that got it. The dumb guy, the cleverness of the whole thing was lost on him. I wish this bird that wrote that knew Chick Sales, he would get the surprise of his life. He has done for twenty five years the cleanest and most applauded act ever in vaudeville. He is so clean that he is almost a prude. I remember years ago, long before the publication of the book, Chick told me that story, and I rushed home to repeat all of it I could remember, and I could visualize this old carpenter, an artist to his hammered old finger tips.

Chick was the biggest hit with an audience, and the biggest hit off stage with all actors, that I can recall in all my years of stage work.

Gosh that vaudeville, how we miss it. No class of entertainment has ever approached it for real entertainment. The variety, the worlds various collection of talents, the years of practice, to attain perfection in acts of skill. And to have been the outstanding figure in that glorious parade is something Chick Sales can be proud of.

SS *Malolo*, San Francisco, July 22:
[*Will, Betty and the boys leave for trip around the world*]
Just steaming out of beautiful San Francisco Bay putting a bridge across it, they will bridge to Honolulu if the governments don't run out of credit, could wire later in the afternoon but better get this off while I am able as a sailor.

Aboard SS *Malolo*, July 25:
Mr. Roosevelt is out here somewhere on Japans ocean fishing; awful long way to come to fish. I think he come away out here so he couldent hear the Republicans roar and to get away from any new scheme that his own gang might cook up.

Aboard SS *Malolo*, July 26:
Poor old Austria if ever a nation needed to move out and settle

among different neighbors its her they divided her up so much after the last war till there was nothing left but this little game fighting cock Dolfuss. Now they got him. There was a fellow that looked like he was doing a heroic job of trying to hold the few strands together of what had been a great nation. Now its a fresh piece of meat to be thrown to the neighboring wolves.

* * * * *

Honolulu, July 27:

Well we blew in here this morning, on the first leg of our long hop, and imagine who we run into. You wouldent guess in a year. You remember the President we lost just after Congress adjourned, the one that was so tickled that he disappeared, well he is out here at some Japanese Islands in the middle of the Pacific. Just looks fine, same great smile that he used to use on those Congressmen and make em bring sticks out of the water for him. These folks want their sugar quota raised. But he just smiles at em. He is the worlds only man that can turn you down and you go out liking him. The whole of Honolulu is doing the Hula, or riding the surf board for him today. If he dont raise their quota, I will go over his head and take it up with General Hugh Johnson, and get it done for em. For we cant let the garden of Eden be dissatisfied.

Waimea, Hawaii, July 30:

Well they got rid of all the big Democrats now and the Islands can settle down to steady gossip. They cant hardly figure Mr. Roosevelt's visit out, they cant tell if he come to see them or come to get some fish or come to impress somebody. I am not naming anybody mind you that he still would stand for no monkey business in the Pacific anyhow. Whatever he come for it was a big success, that is if it wasnt for fish, the fish didnt bite but everybody else did.

Kulamaui, July 31:

This Island must have the best politicians for they got the best roads. Over home a Congressman is never any better than his roads, and sometimes worse.

Honolulu, August 1:

You don't have to be warlike to get a real kick out of our greatest army post Schofield Barracks and the navy at Pearlharbor. If war was declared with some Pacific nation we would lose the Phillipines before lunch but if we lost these it would be our own fault.

Honolulu, August 2:

The army and navy ought to be flying this hop all the time its like carrying the mail we ask em to do something right now and then blame em because they have had no practice, if we ever had to fly here we would have to ask em to postpone the emergency till we learned it so dont blame the boys, they will have to wait now till commercial lines do it first.

Aboard SS *Empress of Canada*, August 7:

Englishmen out here dont like it because we are giving Philippines freedom, it sets a bad example, it puts freedom into other folks head.

Tokio, August 12:

Had dinner and long chat with Roosevelt in Honolulu and he gave me practically same advice that Calvin Coolidge gave Dwight Morrow on Mexico. The President told me, Will, don't jump on Japan, just keep them from jumping on us. Arrived Saturday, everything peaceful and fine. They want a bigger navy and I think I will let em have it for they are going to build it anyway.

Tokio, August 13:

Japanese Naval Committee announce today going ahead with ship building. If allowed at next conference they will have them. If not allowed they will have them too. Cant beat logic like that.

Hainking, Manchukuo, August 21:

No more monkeyshines in Austria. The Austrian chancellor has been visiting Mussolini and learning a lot. This fellow Benito is running a free school for dictators. They all come to him to learn how to put it over.

You don't have to worry about dictators in America until Rex Tugwell passes his entrance exams at Mussolini's academy.

Irkutsk, August 22:

Nothing in the world's smarter than one Chinaman and nothing dumber than two.

Novosibirsk, August 24:

Wish I had Wiley Post here. This is his old round the world trail. Beautiful country.

They are just harvesting the wheat. Women doing the harvesting and the men are at the depot. You know these folks got some good ideas at that.

Moscow, August 28:

Talk about a town on a boom; this is it. I never saw as many buildings going up in my life. You have heard of equality of sex in Russia. Thats not so. The women are doing the work. They are digging a subway.

Have talked all day with Morris Hindus, Walter Duranty and Louis Fisher. Here are three men that know their Russia from A to Bolsheviki. I am so full of facts and statistics that I feel like a brain truster.

Moscow, August 29:

The Soviet writers are holding a convention here. They are the richest people in the USSR. Maxim Gorkys royalties last year was seven million roubles. I am trying to learn to write in Russian.

Oslo, September 7:

You've heard of Norways beautiful fjords, high walled canyons of water that run back for miles into the land. I took a small seaplane and flew over them for hours. Landed on their lakes and chased herds of reindeer through the snow in the plane.

Minnesota can well be proud of their Fatherland. It's wonderful and substantial. Skol.

Copenhagen, September 9:

Great flight down from Norway. These Danes took nothing but a pig and a cow and common sense enough to stay out of war for fifty years. Today they, along with Sweden, Norway, and Finland, are an example to the world of how to live neighborly and tend to your own business. Theres lots to be learned from these Scandinavians.

Vienna, September 11:

Going to the opera tonight and I will last about one act and then start hunting a vaudeville show.

Bucharest, September 12:

This is a corn country. The only civilized country in Europe that knows what a roasting ear is. They raise lots of hogs and everybody can talk English.

Budapest, September 13:

This is the star city of all Europe. Hungary is a kingdom but got no king, they are looking for one, I believe the old kingfish will fit em. I can fix it for you, Huey.

Aboard SS *Ile de France*, September 21:

I tell you you cant beat England for her justice. Brought some English papers on board and it tells of a man who killed his nagging wife and the judge gave him a year, but apologizes for it. Said he was compelled to do it under the law.

Europe's awful quiet now, dont hear much war talk so I guess that means one will break out. That's when they have 'em when there ain't any reason.

New York, September 30:

Now what might be one classes "Liberty" might be another classes "poison." Course I guess absolute "Liberty" couldent mean anything but that anybody can do anything they want too anytime they want too. Well any half wit can tell that wouldn't work. So the question arises "How much liberty can I get and get away

with it?" Well you can get no more than you give. Thats my
definition, but you got perfect "Liberty" to work out your own,
so get in. And lets get this "Liberty" business settled.

Fort Worth, Texas, October 7:

Last Saturday I was absent from these parts in this paper.
Teacher I cant tell a lie, I wasent sick, or away from a telegraph
station. Friday afternoon after watching Paul Dean almost shut
out Detroit, I rush to the hotel write my piece, and predict that
Detroit was still plenty tough. Then start rushing off to my old
home in Okla and forget to file my telegram. It never happened
before. So I can only plead old age.

But here is what really hurt. The world moved along Saturday
(even better) than any other day lately.

I tell you its surprising how many of us it can get along without.
I dont want to appear rude, but I actually believe it could get
along great without all of us.

Sonora, California, October 22:

Walked into a barber shop in this beautiful and historical little
mountain town. I heard the radio going and somebody raising
Old Ned with somebody. I says "Whos that talking Merriam
against Sinclair, or Sinclair against Merriam?" They says, "Why
no, thats the President giving some folks fits for being against military preparedness." I says "Amen" sic em Franklin, pour it on em.
If they want to show what "Not having a gun will do for you,"
They can point out China and India.

Santa Monica, November 4:

I am pretty sore today, am looking for the ones that reminded
me that 55 years ago today at Oolagah Indian Territory, on Nov.
4th 1879, a boy baby was born. Well anyhow played game of polo
and roped calves all day, so there is life in the old nag yet.

Beverly Hills, November 7:

The Republicans have had a saying for some time. "The
Roosevelt honeymoon is over." They were mighty poor judges of a

love sick couple, why he and the people have got a real love match, and it looks like it would run for at least six years. If theres one thing the Republican Party has got to learn it is, that you cant get votes by just denouncing. You got to offer some plan of your own, they only had one platform, "elect us, and maybe we can think of something to do after we get in, but up to now we havent thought of it, but give us a chance we may."

Beverly Hills, November 8:

You know as all these late precincts keep coming in (where they cant count very fast) the Democratic lead keeps piling up. Its just kinder kicking a fellow when he is down. In the heat of the moment, they have kicked out some awful good Republicans. And then too, too big a victory aint so good. We need quite a few in there just as detectives, or watchdogs. Then too you want to remember that an awful lot of these Democratic voters this time, were really at heart Republicans, and they can revert back to type mighty quick, so dont rub it in boys, for there aint any finer folks living, than a Republican that votes the Democratic ticket. Yours for tolerance.

November 8:

Charley Wagner, my old concert manager, has got the itch again, thinks the Country is ripe for one of those long-winded concert tour talks of mine. No, I am going to let the country alone. Its had enough trouble without me adding to it.

Santa Monica, November 11:

We are mighty proud of our navy, some near sighted folks kick on the cost, but by golly its worth the price to see 30,000 men spotlessly clean, and a "cocky" walk that you dont find on any other animal but a peacock. There is only one whisker, and that on popular Admiral Reeves, he looks more like Robert E. Lee every day. God bless him.

Beverly Hills, November 12:

Well you actors and politicians can have all the race horses and cigars and perfume named after you. But I got some clippings from down in South Carolina that was mighty gratifying to me, WILL ROGERS, an old pot hound, was voted the best hunting dog in the State, and he took another prize for the finest looking dog. So my regards to the champion of South Carolina. There aint nothing better than to ride up on a little hill at night, and stop and hear em running, you dont need to see em, you know who is ahead, whose running second, and third, and just how close they are to old man fox.

Santa Monica, November 18:

Well I was down to Los Angeles Live Stock Show, and I saw these hundreds of farmers boys, that had fattened and cared for a calf, or pig, or sheep, themselves. Its a thing called the 4 H Club. Somebody was inspired when they founded that, its all over the country, by golly they are a great bunch of kids, and dont they have some fine stock, look how young and he is starting in his business, we got the most thorough training in every line of business in this country, but statesmanship and that, you just decide overnight yourself, "I am a statesman."

Beverly Hills, November 19:

The President made one of his best speeches in Tupelo, Miss. Sunday. He told that the people could make their own electric energy cheaper than they were getting it. And say, by Monday morning he had the companies talking "new rates." They all say the government cant do anything toward running any business, but they break their necks to see that it dont try.

November 25:

This Election changed a lot of folks' idea of things. They have kinder become reconciled to the fact that the folks are not so excited about this great debt that is piling up as they thought they were. This thing of worrying about what our grand children are going to have to pay, well most folks say, "Well our children seem to think they are smarter than we are, so if they are the chances are that their children will be smarter than they are, so if they are that smart why maby they can think of some substitute for money that they

can pay off their national debt with, and they will wonder why we
dident have a bigger one. Maby we wont print the money, but
they will, so what difference does it make to us?"

Santa Monica, November 27:

I wrote a little "gag" the other day about "appealing to the President for a guarantee," and I bet a lot of you thought it just to be
writing, well get this headlined in the papers today. C. L. Bardo,
Pres, of the National Association of Manufacturers asks the President the following, "Business must have more definite ideas as to
the direction in which the government is headed." I can just see
Mr. Roosevelt rushing in with a guarantee reading about as follows, "Nobody guaranteed me anything when I took over this job,
no man gambles more than a president of the U.S. so you will pardon me if I am not able to guarantee business that it wont lose."

Beverly Hills, December 3:

Our own Wiley Post went up to break the altitude record, he
drifted from Bartlesville, Okla, to Muscogee. Went square dab
over Claremore. He was up ten miles, just high enough to clear
the buildings.

Beverly Hills, December 7:

Certainly news in the papers today, "Russian firing squad exe-
cutes 200." "Thousands of Hungarians driven from Jugo-Slavia."
"Norman H. Davis gives warning to Japan that ship ratio will not
be changed."

Now there is three separate events, each enough to start its own
war, but time will tell which one of the three proved the most costly.
Two of these are dealing with their own internal affairs, and I just
sorter hate to see us dictate beyond our own borders.

December 9:

The whole world was suddenly slapped in the face with a wet
towel, and told to "Wake up, you are sleeping on your back, and
you are snoring with such satisfaction that you have annoyed the
Gods." And since then the world has just been rolling and tumbling. They cant get back to natural sleep, and they dont know

what to do. Some trying to read, some are counting sheep, and
most of em are walking the floor.

And thats the generation that the new college graduate must step
out in. No job awaits him, no bows await him, he looks out over
the wreck of which he had no making, and says, "So this is the
old folks way. Yeah?" So he starts looking for the keyhole in
the dark, too, and with his young enthusiasm he thinks he can find
it before you can. (Forgetting that you have a little advantage
over him by knowing where it used to be.) His youth will make
him take a chance quicker than we will. He starts fumbling at
everybodys door to see if the key will fit. You holler at him, "Dont
go there, thats not it," and he hollers back, "Well, you dont know
where it is, and so I am going to try em all."

So its not a bright future that we ask them to enter into. They
feel that they are the ones to right it. We feel that we are the ones
that lost it, and that we are the ones that will find it. Its just a difference of opinion, its not a difference of nature. They are absolutely the same as we are. Its viewpoint, human nature dont enter
into it, its outlook, its viewpoint.

We look at it from the old days, they look at if from the now.
We are looking in different directions. We cant help but look
back, they cant help but look forward. But we are both standing
on the same ground, and their feet is there as firmly as ours.

Beverly Hills, December 11:

The biggest news in the papers today was furnished by the Japanese Ambassador, it was pretty strong medicine, he just said that
if England and America made Japan mad enough they would go
and take all of North China.

Well if America is just even half smart diplomatically, they will
laugh the whole thing off, and stall things along till Russia is ready,
and just say "sic em Tige he is your meat."

Hollywood, December 14:

Monday is Aviation Day, thirty one years ago Monday the
Wrights made their famous flight at Kittyhawk. It was a box kite
put together with barrel staves and putty. He sit on a stool out in

front of the thing. Hoping that it wouldent get excited and run
over him. He dident get very high, but he started something that
will change many a map in this world. Aviation is sorter like the
old 45 pistols, which made little men as dangerous as big men, its a
sort of equalizer. You could give little Switzerland enough aeroplanes and she would worry the Old Ned out of the big ones. There
is no end to how many we ought to have. But about fifty thousand,
and take the profits out of war, and you wont have any war.

December 15:

Goodbye to a Great Friend.

We both came from Oklahoma. I went to Madison Square
Garden in New York with Col Zack Mulhall in 1905. Then went
on the stage. He dident come till 1915, ten years later. He come
back with Zack Miller (of the famous Miller Brothers 101 Ranch).
I first saw him at a town in Connecticut, I think it was Westport.
I liked him, and he come home with me, and I think he liked me.
And the whole family liked him, and he lived with us all these years,
up to a few days ago, when he left us, and it made us all sad, very
sad. He was one of the family, he had helped raise our children, he
come to our house the same time Jim, our youngest, did.

I was working in Ziegfelds famous Midnight Frolic (the first of
all midnight shows). We were living in a little home we had rented
across the road from Fred Stones lovely summer home in Amity-
ville, Long Island. We went there to be near Fred and his family.
We had a wonderful time that summer. Jim and Dopey came that
summer. Jim was a baby boy, and Dopey was a little round bod-
ied, coal black pony, with glass eyes, the gentlest and greatest pony
for grown ups or children anyone ever saw. I dont know why we
called him Dopey. I guess it was because he was always so gentle
and just the least bit lazy. Anyhow we meant no dissrespect to him.

Outside of a pony I had in the Indian Territory when I was a
boy, and that put me in the exhibition roping business (he was
called Commanche), and afterwards became very famous at steer
roping contests (in fact Jim Hopkins broke a worlds record on him),
why along pretty near next to him in affection was Dopey.

"Chapel," a bay horse that I owned and used in all my movie

chases down steep hills in the old silent days (and that I know saved my life many times), I still have. He is a free lance, and "Bootlegger" another famous little Oklahoma black pony from the Osage nation, he is also with us. He was a famous roping pony, and afterwards was with me on Long Island where I used to try to play polo. He was little, and had long mane and tail (which is unknown in polo) but became famous through his quick turning.

These and various others that at different times I have become attached too, were all more of my own individual ponies, but Dopey belonged to the family. Our children learned to ride at two, and during his lifetime he never did a wrong thing to throw one off, or do a wrong thing after they had fallen off. He couldent pick em up, but he would stand there and look at em with a dissgusted look for being so clumsy as to fall off. He never kicked or stepped on one of them in his life, and he was a young horse when I first got him from Zack Miller. But he was always gentle, and intelligent.

I used to sit on him by the hour (yes by the year) and try new rope tricks, and he never batted an eye. Then I learned some trick riding, such as vaulting, and drags, and all that. In fact he was the only one I could ever do it on. Then in 1919 we went to California to go in the movies. Dopey and Dodo, another pet poney we had acquired for Mary, rode in the best palace car by express. Then when I would come back to New York to work another year for Mr. Ziegfeld in his Follies, the first thing loaded would be Dopey and Dodo. Then after a year in New York back to the movies again, and back would go Dopey, Dodo, and Chapel, along with any others we had acquired.

One year I took Dopey in a Follies baggage car, on the whole tour with the show, and kept him in the riding academys and practiced roping every day with him. Charley Aldrich a cowboy used to ride him and run by for my fancy roping tricks. He has been missed with a loop more times, and maby caught more times than any horse living. In a little picture called the "Roping Fool" where I did all my little fancy catches in slow motion, he was the pony that run for them. He was coal black, and I had my ropes whitened and the catches showed up fine.

In a private tan bark ring we had in our old Beverly Hills home, all the children learned trick riding on Dopey, standing up on him, running, vaulting, and would use him with Dodo to ride Roman (a foot on each horse), all allowed because I knew they were on gentle ponies. He has been on pasture for four or five years, hasent had a bridle on him. Fat as a pig. When nineteen years of you and your childrens life is linked so closely with a horse, you can sorter imagine our feelings. We still have quite a few old favorites left, but Dopey was different. He was of the family. He raised our children. He learned em to ride. He never hurt one in his life. He did everything right. Thats a reputation that no human can die with.

Goodbye Dopey, from Mama, Dad, Bill, Mary and Jim.

Beverly Hills, December 18:

We had heard of all kinds of likely wars between nations, but this one that Mussolini dug up is a new one. Italy versus Ethiopia. Thats going a long way for an enemy.

Beverly Hills, December 23:

There aint nothing that breaks up homes, country, and nations like somebody publishing their memoirs.

Santa Monica, December 26:

Now comes New Years, and along with it comes New Years predictions of our leading men. This year they will read as follows, all of em, "I am an optimist, and always have been, but we must be assured of no inflation and a fair return on our investment. If the government will just lay off us everything will be fine." Now watch New Years and see how far this misses it.

Hollywood, December 30:

Here is about the best crime prevention news I have seen, "the California Bar Association is to rid its ranks of any attorney found to have connection with the underworld."

The first thing they do now if they are taking up crime as a profession, (even before they buy the gun) is to engage their lawyer. He works on a percentage. He acts as their advance agent too, he picks out the banks they are to rob, Bar Associations invented the word "Ethics" then forgot it.

CHAPTER TWENTY

I Got to See That Alaska

1935 — Roosevelt made the biggest touch in history: "Brother, can you spare eight and one half billions."

Betty and Will had an "old-timer's night" in New York.

Will got more and more distressed the way World affairs were going. "All Gods Children want guns, going to put on the guns, going to buckle on the guns and smear up all of Gods Heaven."

Everything got topsy-turvey so Will went off to Alaska with Wiley Post and they never came back — alive.

Beverly Hills, January 6:

Roosevelt is to send another message to Congress Monday. Its really not a message, its a working schedule.

Hollywood, January 7:

See where Mussolini and foreign Minister Laval had decided to let Austria have a King, you know I didnt know this till I was in Vienna last Fall, but Austria really wants a King, can you imagine that, the nearest we can come to understanding that is an American girl wanting a man with a title. Vienna's a musical city, cafes and a lot of bright colored uniforms, and a King, and some waltzes is about all they want.

Santa Monica, January 8:

Well it exceeded all expectations, President Roosevelt made the biggest touch in history, "Brothers can you spare eight and one half billion?" — Well it goes for relief. And there is nobody can legitimately kick on that. By the end of next year, 36, our per capita debt will be 270.00 each (of course if you think thats too high you got a perfect right to die and beat it). Well England, the country we point out as being the most prosperous at this time, is exactly double that. Why we are just amateurs at being taxed.

Beverly Hills, January 13:

All the "lobbies" are gathered in Washington to see that the tax is put on somebody else's business, but not on theirs.

Congress got all their committees made up last week, and they are composed of two Democrats to each Republican, so what a pleasant year that poor fellow will be in for. Course, there is an awful lot of different breeds of Democrats. I bet you before the session is over President Roosevelt will trade you two or three Democrats for one Republican.

Notre Dame, Indiana, January 15:

Say I am so tickled about Jimmy Doolittle cracking the passenger plane record, you know there is more flyers, (real flyers) that will tell you that Jimmy is the greatest all around flyer there is. Wiley Post told me so last week.

January 20:

I doubt very much if Civilization (so called) has helped generosity. I bet the old cave man would divide his raw meat with you as quick as one of us will ask a down-and-out to go in and have a meal with us. Those old boys and girls would rip off a wolf skin breech-clout and give you half of it, quicker than a Ph.D. would slip you his umbrella. Civilization hasent done much but make you wash your teeth and in those days eating and gnawing on bones and meat, made tooth paste unnecessary.

Civilization has taught us to eat with a fork, but even now if no-body is around we use our fingers. In those days people fought for food and self defense. Nowadays we have diplomats work on wars for years before arranging them. Thats so that when its over no-body will know what they were fighting for. We lost thousands, and spent billions, and you could hand a sheet of paper to one million different people and tell em to write down what the last war was for, and the only answers that will be alike will be, "D—— if I know."

So thats what you call Civilization. Civilization is nothing but acquiring comforts for ourselves, when in those days they were so hard they dident need em. We will strive to put in another bath, when maby our neighbors cant even put in an extra loaf of bread.

New York, January 20:

Left Washington this afternoon. There is two Texans down there that have certainly made good, one is Jack Garner who is vice President and dont care whether you know it or not. After over 30 years of sound common sense, he knows more about the running of this government than any man outside of President Roosevelt. Ask any old time Congressman or Senator what they think of Gar-ner. And this fellow Jesse Jones head of the Reconstruction Fi-nance, I like to hear the big bankers cuss him, for he can loan more money, and collect more of it back than they can. You leave all your assets with Jones.

New Orleans, Louisiana, January 29:

In Louisiana they vote by electricity. Its a marvelous way to vote, but Huey runs the switchboard, so it dont matter which button they boys press, all the answers come out yes. But they are great folks.

New York, January 31:

Headline in the financial page says, "This weeks clearings rise to five billion, one hundred million." So the Roosevelt administrations are not the only ones that are talking in billions. We had been lead to believe that there was no "billions" only on a government "deficit" but there is just as much money as there ever was, nobody eat any during the depression, its just planted deeper in the rat hole thats all.

February 3: Old Timers' Night In Manhattan

About ten days ago, Mrs. Rogers and I were going into New York. It was late Sunday afternoon. We hadent been in N.Y. in a good while. We had nothing to do but broadcast at seven thirty, and that gave us the evening to ourselves. We got into our hotel about six thirty. Dident intend to go and eat till after the wind jamming. Got to the studio, which was a real theatre, with an audience of three floors of people, and a big orchestra sitting on the stage.

Well I hadent any more than walked in the place till I was booked for a benefit performance, there was some kind of a combined charity broadcast by both companies, Columbia and National, for the musicians. It was to be around eleven, so I told em I would be glad to be there. Well then I come from my broadcasting and I hear of another show. Its a big benefit for the Actors Fund, a fine charity ably sponsored for all these years by the beloved Daniel Frohman. Well I was tickled to death to go there. Here I havent been in town over 30 minutes and book myself two shows. You never get so old that somebody dont want you at a benefit, and they have always got audiences, too. I do know that N.Y. people are the most liberal and they always fill a house for a good cause.

You see, Sunday nights are the benefit nights on account of the actors being idle, and they can get the theatres for the show. First actor I met was Charles Winninger, who has become immortal as

Uncle Andy of Zeigfelds "Show Boat" on stage and air. I was with Blanche Ring in a musical show called "The Wall Street Girl" twenty years ago when he and Blanche got married.

Well then out of the theatre and met an old cowpuncher friend, Charley Aldrich, who used to ride bucking horses in the stage show "The Roundup" with Macklyn Arbuckle starring. Then we went to an Italian Restaurant where we used to go and get the best food in the World, "Leones," met the fine old Mother and four sons. You eat so much you cant do much but a short benefit afterwards.

Who should we run onto but Lillian Shaw, the stages best character singer. Played in vaudeville with her for years, and she was a star in my first musical show, one called "The Girl Rangers" at the Auditorium in Chicago. That was in 1907. Wow, 28 years ago! Lillian looked great. John Bunny the first movie comedian, was in that show. The chorus girls were all mounted on horses (that is 12 of them were). Reine Davis was the star. It was a beautiful show, but too expensive. Then who comes over to the old table but Roscoe Turner, and we had to cross and recross India, Persia, Messopotamia, as I had flown that route too.

Where do you think the Actors Fund Benefit was held? At the old Amsterdam Theatre, the one I had spent 10 years playing with the Follies under the showman who will never be replaced, Flo Zeigfeld. Oh, what sentiment! What memories! Some of the same stage hands were there. Gee, if I had just have had as good a jokes as I used to have in those days! Saw Blanche Ring there. She did look great. And Elsie Janis. What a marvel, sing, dance, and imitate like no other human in America and throw the rope better than me!

The grand dramatic actress, Charlotte Walker. All these people I am mentioning we have no one like them. There is no training ground. Where in America is there even a tenth grade Elsie Janis, a Blanche Ring, a Charley Winninger who could do anything ever done on a stage, every musical instrument, a dandy acrobat. No girl can sing those Jewish character songs like Lillian Shaw. And Charlotte Walker in the "Trail of the Lonesome Pine." Saw Heyward Broun back stage, as fat, jolly, and amiable as ever. He must have thought of what those old days were.

Then over the broadcasting benefit. But as we walked out of the stage door of that old Amsterdam Theatre to a taxicab, we both had tears in our eyes. No Amsterdam Theatre, no Flo Zeigfeld. I would never have been as lucky, for no other manager in the world would have let me go my own way and do as I saw fit. At the broadcasting was dear Graham McNamee, who started it, and looks like he will finish it, even if it last a hundred years.

And who do I hear is there of us old timers but Miss Geraldine Farrar. We worked for a year on the same movie lot for Sam Goldwyn in 1919. She was always a remarkable woman, the most pleasant, the most considerate, and the hardest working I ever saw in pictures. Now who can sing like her today?

Then we went up to see our dear friends the Fred Stone Family. Betty says, "They will be in bed." I says, "The Stones are show people they couldent sleep before midnight." Fred has gone to Hollywood on a fine movie contract, and he will make a hit for he can do anything. Where on the American stage, radio or screen is there someone who compared with what he meant to the theatre? They dont develop people like that anymore. They have no place to develop them.

Well as we were driving home mighty late for the Rogerses, Betty said, as we talked of each we had met that night, "Isnt it a shame that not on our whole amusement fields have any of these a successor." Everyone of them today can walk on a stage and show that when they learned their trade it was a profession and not an accident.

People who have spent a lifetime perfecting the art of entertaining people, then to have the whole stage profession snatched from under them, and ship your entertainment to you in a can. Brave hearted people are theatrical people.

Santa Monica, February 17:

See by todays papers Mr. Townsend appeared before the Senate Committee and they had a lot of fun and laughter at his plan, well they can have some fun with the amount, but they cant have much fun with the idea of paying a pension, you see its not just some idealistic cranks, or Bolsheviki idea, all the rest of the world are doing it but us, we thought we had a better idea, we called it a "Poor Farm" and everybody that could afford it, or had any political influence, put their relatives there, now Townsend may have to take only 25 or 15 percent of his original idea, but the Senators are not going to laugh themselves out of paying an old age pension.

Chicago, February 19:

We are always saying let the law take its course, but what we mean is "Let the law take our course."

Beverly Hills, February 21:

Well I was trying to snooze on the ship coming into Albuquerque this morning early and what keeps me awake but some big guy snoring. I look and if its not Wally Beery, he had climbed on somewhere during the night, he is a good pilot himself, and generally flies his own plane. He wasnt so good to look at laying there snoring but he is by far the most popular person man or woman on the screen.

February 24:

Back out here in old Orangejuice Land again, toiling to try and hand a fraction of the folks a laugh on the screen when your beauty has deserted you. When you are getting old you have to resort to pure skill or trickery. I kinder take up the trickery.

Now in the old days just looks alone got me by. I had the men love interest in my pictures stepping out to keep ahead of me. The Lord was good to me in the matter of handing out a sort of half breed Adonis profile. (Well, it was a little more than a profile that you had to get.) Straight on I dident look so good, and even sideways I wasent terrific, but a cross between a back and a three quarter view, why Brother I was hot. The way my ear (on one side) stood out from my head, was just bordering on perfect. That rear view give you just the shot needed. That ear dident just stick out, it kinder protruded just gently. In those old silent day pictures that back right ear was a byword from Coast to Coast. You see all screen stars have what they call their better angles. These women have just certain camera men to shoot them, they know which way to turn em, and how to throw the light on em.

So we toil and we struggle to maintain what is left of our beauty and manliness. Of course the Radio helps us. Any hour somebody is begging and imploring us to go to the drug store and buy something that will take the wrinkles out of our ears, lift our eyebrows, bring back that rudy (thats spelled rudy) complexion. There is as many gadgets on the market to overhaul men as there is women. I doubt if women have got much on men when it comes to trying to outlook themselves.

You watch an old boy in a barber shop and he wants lots of mirrors and a lot done to him besides shearing off his mane. Barbers are awful clever and they have invented a hundred little tricks of theirs when they look like they are trying to get the furrows out, and make your skin look and feel soft. They are artists those fellows. Course I always just wanted a shave, a hair cut and get on out, but most old boys will tarry as long as they will fiddle with him with little rubbing machines and lotions. Your Old face gets back to normal about the time you hit the street anyhow. It begins to hit its original shape, those fancy remedies are awful temporary.

Hollywood, February 26:

Was down last night with Charlie Chaplin, listening to our friend Will Durant, the philosopher, debate on world economics. Charlie has made a study of that. He is the greatest economist in the world. Every nation has lost its export trade, yet stop and think of it, Chaplin manufactures the only article in the world, that hasent depreciated, the world is his market the same as before depression, but he has never let the supply equal the demand. While all the world big industrialists were greedy, Charlie never went in for mass production. Seems odd that a comedian can do what governments are not smart enough to do.

February 27 [telegram]:
The Hannibal Courier, Hannibal, Mo.

I never did write you before because it seemed as redicilous for me to even get my name mixed in with a Mark Twain affair as for all the Kentucky Colonels to be asked to contribute to a war record memorial to Napoleon. Me in your Mark Twain edition would be like Sister Aimee being asked to the Lords Supper. Why I would be a Huey Long in a Supreme Court robe. There is one thing that ought to be eliminated in this country and that is every time somebody gets a laugh of some small dimensions, why he is called the modern Mark Twain. Well you know when the Twain successor will appear in our country, there will be two of em, and they will arrive together, one will be to replace Abraham Lincoln, and the other to replace Mark Twain.

Yours,

Will Rogers

Beverly Hills, February 28:

All you read about Washington is how are they going to spend that four billions. There hasent been even one suggestion as to where it was to come from. It must be marvelous to just belong to some legislative body and just pick money out of the air.

March 4 [*when Gene Howe put on his Mother-in-Law Day*]:

Wes Izzard, Amarillo Globe, Amarillo, Texas

Tell old Tack that I could send him any amount of Hollywood mothers that just with one she, female child, have been mothers-in-law to a dozen. I dont want to strike a note of sadness into what I know is a gay day, but did it ever rain out there yet? Either the Lord or the Democrats one have got it in for you backsliders, and I suspect its the Democrats. Give Ben Turpin my love, he is a fine man, and has done many a charitable deed out here. I know all Muleshoe and Clarendon will be there. I am making one of those fool movies, and my double is sick and I have to stay here and work. Love to everybody.

Will

* * * * *

Beverly Hills, March 4:

Too bad we (so foolishly) split up the old Negro tenth cavalry, we could have loaned them to this King Aba-dab-Ba down there, and Mussolini would have "Shinnied over on his own side."

Beverly Hills, March 5:

I dont know where the money would come from, in fact I dont know where any of all this money is coming from we are spending now, any more than a congressman does, but if Americans are going to stop and start worrying about whether they can afford a thing or not, you are going to ruin the whole characteristic of our people. There wouldnt have been a dozen automobiles sold if that was the case.

Beverly Hills, March 6:

The U.S. Senate may not be the most refined and deliberative body in existence but they got the most unique rules. Any member can call anybody in the world anything he can think of and they cant answer him, sue him, or fight him. Our constitution protects aliens, drunks, and U.S. Senators. There ought to be one day a year (just one) when there is an open season on Senators.

Beverly Hills, March 7:

This thing called money has got the whole mess of em buffaloed, money, horse racing and women are three things the boys just cant figure out.

March 10:

I never have been to that Alaska. I am crazy to go up there some time. I would like to go in the Winter, when those old boys are all snowed in, and I could sit around and hear em tell some of those old tails. They have lied about em so much now that I bet they can tell some good ones. They do a lot of flying up there. There is some crack aviators. Wiley Post went back up there this last Summer to visit one of them that had helped him out, and they went hunting in a plane. Fred Stone and Rex Beach have been up there a lot, but I never did get further north up that way than about a block north of Main Street in Seattle.

Santa Monica, March 10:

Wasnt that a remarkable will that Oliver Wendell Holmes left? Imagine a man giving his money to the government at a time when 120 million people are trying to get it away from the government, or trying to keep from paying em even what we owe em.

At least 80 years of service to his country and he accumulates some money, and is so appreciative of what his country has done for him, that he wants to return it. All we hear is "Whats the matter with the country?" "Whats the matter with the world?" There aint but one word wrong with every one of us in the world, and thats selfishness.

Beverly Hills, March 11:

Paper says the Prince of Wales danced with *a Baltimore woman* in a "multi colored dress of spun glass, and just a single diamond in her hair." If that made international news, what would it have been if he had dropped her in that glass dress? Some day there is going to be a society gal that dident dance with him, then you going to hear of real fame.

Beverly Hills, March 13:

Say did you read about what Mr. Roosevelt said about those "Holding Companies." A Holding Company is a thing where you hand an accomplice the goods while the policeman searches you.

Beverly Hills, March 15:

I have often said that with all our kidding or cussing our public officials that they are as good or better than we who elect them. Well we got a fine example of it in the papers this morning from John Stevens McGroarty, who wrote Californias famous Mission Play. A great writer, a real humanitarian and fine and be-loved type of real gentleman (I expect Los Angeles most universally pop-ular citizen). One of his voters wrote him an insulting letter want-ing to know why he hadnt put trees on the Sierra Madre Moun-tains. McGroartys reply "One of the drawbacks of being a Con-gressman is that I have to receive impertinent letters from a Jackass like you. Will you please take two running jumps and go to H——."

March 16:

Stay out of that Europe, thats a tough game to enter into. Their diplomats are trained, its their life business. Ours makes a campaign contribution and wakes up in Belgium, and dont know which ocean he crossed to get there.

Messing with them over there is just like playing poker with Jack Garner. You will have a smile and a drink and a nice chat, but you will have nothing that you can cash in with when the gathering disbands. Now if you want to get in just for the smoke, and the drink, why go ahead. Not these old diplomats you see sitting around here, they dont look much, but they out dealed foreigners all their life. What they had to contribute was from their head not their purse.

March 17:

The N.R.A. at the time of launching looked like it would do the work, but it fell from its own complicated structure. I wrote a little gag at the time and said that the whole N.R.A. plan should be written on a post card. Nobody can work a man over a certain number of hours (without extra pay) and nobody can pay anyone under certain sum (no matter what line of business it was), nobody can hire children. There was the whole N.R.A. in those few words. No codes, no lobbying, no running to Washington. You dident say a man had to hire more men, you said he couldent work the ones he had over a certain number of hours, and that number applied to all industries.

Then if he said well I have to have my place open longer than that, well he automatically hired more men, not by Government compulsion but by necessity, let all the prices, and all that can take care of itself, the same as it had all our lives. If a man undersold another man it was done by good management, and not through low wages or long hours. It was because he just was a better business man.

There was enough money spent by everybody running to Washington on codes to pay off the depression, and then all business got sore. All was looking for the best of it in their codes, and they went home and closed up their shop. This other way, everybody would have been on one footing. You dont get kicks when you know that everybody is treated like you are being treated.

The minute a thing is long and complicated it confuses. Whoever wrote the Ten Commandments made em short. They may not always be kept, but they can be understood. They are the same for all men. Some Industry cant come in and say, "Ours is a special and unique business. You cant judge it by the others." Well no committee come pullman-carrying-it into Jerusalem looking for Moses and saying "Ours is a special business." Moses just went up on the mountain with a letter of credit and some instructions from the Lord, and He just wrote em out, and they applied to the steel men, the oilmen, the bankers, the farmers, and even the United States Chamber of Commerce. And he said, "Here they are Brothers, you take em and live by em, or else."

Well thats where Moses had it on Hugh Johnson. Hugh had as good intentions, but Hugh Moses Johnson went up on Capitol Hill and come down with 24 truck loads full of codes. He just couldent come out plain and say, "Thou shalt pay so much. And thou shalt work thy men only so much, and if thou canst not gettith thee some more, but payeth them likewise." Hugh should have been born B.C. (before codes).

Course that is not all our troubles. It wouldent have solved everything any more than the Commandments have solved human weaknesses, but they did stop all arguments as to whether they were good and fair to all was concerned, and they left no argument as to whether they would work if you kept them. I expect there is a lot of lessons in the Bible that we could learn and profit by and help us out, but we are just so busy doing nothing we havent got time to study em out. But in Moses time the rich dident gang up on you and say, "You change that Commandment or we wont play."

Santa Monica, March 18:

Democrats in Congress, want to get the President to abandon all his humanitarian schemes, and center on just the old age pensions. In other words the kittens have arrived at such an age that its time to pick out the one that will be the biggest and strongest by November 36, and drown the others. They would drown some fine helpful

brotherly love schemes, but the one thing that I would stake my
life on that Mr. Roosevelt has learned since he has been in there, is
that the people are willing to co-operate, but they are not going to
willingly pay to do it. You can bet that his faith in human nature
has had quite a jar.

Beverly Hills, March 22:

I was shooting off the other day about holding companies, Mr.
Roosevelt and lots of folks may think they are uncalled for, but the
folks working for em think mighty well of em, its the old fault of
not calling your Shots, by naming the bad ones, and not shooting
into the whole covey.

I tell you another argument a fellow wants to keep out of, and
thats this printing money thing, its a subject where nobody knows
just exactly what it would do, and every person thinks he knows
exactly what it would do. All I know its easier to print than to
make by work. But please dont write or wire explaining it, if you
know all about money you are awful lucky, and its a secret you
should cherish and not let even your grandchildren know about.

Santa Monica, March 24:

Just been reading Mr. Hoovers message to the underprivaleged
Republicans. It look like he was bringing out some stuff that the
Democrats would like to keep buried in the ash can. Mr. Hoover
is a mighty honorable and respectable citizen. And his parables
should be given mighty serious consideration. For he is about half
right. There is some schemes that havent exactly percolated for the
Democrats. Anyhow its good to hear that we have again after a
relapse returned to a two party system.

New York, March 28:

Flew through these dust storms last night with the pilot flying
entirely by instrument. Where in the world is it going too, its a terrible thing, and its going to bring up some queer cases of law. If
Colorado blows over and lights on top of Kansas, it looks kinder
like Kansas ought to pay for the extra top soil, but Kansas can sue
em for covering up their crops, now this weeks wind has picked up

Colorado which was in Kansas, taking Kansas with it, and thats whats in the air looking for a new place to light. In the middle west now you got to put a brand on your soil, then in the Spring go on a roundup looking for it.

March 31:

Seeing the Presidents headline about em, why I said, a holding company is like a fellow handing the other fellow the swag while they search you. Well I dident figure that little half witted remark would upset the whole holding company business. But I forgot that a remark generally hurts in proportion to its truth. If its so untrue as to be rediculous why nobody pays any attention to it. And on the other hand I dont want to get any remark that will be so true that it hurts, I mean really hurts. So I was in wrong both ways. Now I dont know what it is, but right or wrong, there must be some little teeny weeny bit of underground connivance connected with the idea of holding companies, or is there?

Now be honest. In a straight forward legitimate business, a farm, a store, a little manufacturing concern, or any business, what makes the holding company necessary? Dont it have something to do with shifting the responsibility over to another company that are liable only for so much?

You see here is something that any of us that write have found out, if we write or say something that agrees with you, why then we become quite a smart guy in your estimation. But if we should write or say something that dont agree with your idea of the same subject, then we become a "Menace" and should be eliminated from the public prints. So we are only good as long as we agree with you.

New York, March 31:

Here is New York City where all the money in the world is. And where every guy with a dollar is doing better than he was a year ago. "Say whats this country coming to. I tell you this income tax is terrible." "My business is picking up every day, but I am scared." "I am doing better than I have since 29, but when are we going to get back to the good old days?" Well the old days with most of us was when we dident earn enough to pay an income tax.

Tulsa, Oklahoma, April 2:

Government loaning farmers enough to get teams, seed oats or corn and a milk cow. That don't seem such a terribly nutty scheme. Everybody that is making money has it in for Roosevelt. You will have to explain that one yourself.

Beverly Hills, April 4:

Well today Austria says they want a gun. Yesterday it was Germany. Englands got a gun, France has a gun, Italys got a gun, Germany wants a gun, Austria wants a gun. All Gods children want guns, going to put on the guns, going to buckle on the guns and smear up all of Gods Heaven.

Beverly Hills, April 5:

California had a bill to investigate lobbying, and the lobbyists bought off all the votes and they cant even find the bill now. Putting a lobbyist out of business is like a hired man trying to fire his boss.

Beverly Hills, April 8:

Girl aviator teaching stronger sex to fly, he froze controls and was about to crash. She picks up fire extinguisher and used it in a way that would do the most good, just casually bent it over his head, causing temporary unconsciousness. As my good old native son of Florida Arthur Brisbane would say, "There is a lesson in that. Man is not as mighty as he thinks he is, the gorillo is mightier, and a woman with a fire extinguisher is not only mightier than the man, but we all know a lot of em even without an extinguisher that can worry a gorillo till he says, maybe I am wrong."

Beverly Hills, April 9:

My boss is dead, my friend is dead. Adolph Ochs owner of the great NY Times is the first man that I ever wrote for, and it was him personally that got me to try it. Think of being lucky enough to break in at the top, for that paper is tops. He was a fine friend, and a fine citizen.

Beverly Hills, April 12:

I am suggesting that postmasters deliver no mail to anyone of Republican faith. Why should hard working deserving Democrats take up their valuable time handing out what is no doubt anti-Democratic propaganda, and I am so advising em.

Beverly Hills, April 16:

Dorothy Stone my little pardner in Freds show one time, why she opened here as the big star in "As Thousands Cheer," and while I went myself, I plum forgot to send either wire or flowers. Now I meant well, but I get off to talking to some old guy about the N.R.A. or some cowpuncher about who won the roping at Ft. Worth at their big show, or maby knocking the ball around the field, or roping at some old gentle calves that are trained to stick their heads in the loop. I get to doing all this foolishness, and plum forgot to do what I ought to do. I sometimes wonder if the Lord is going to make the proper distinction between the fellow that means well, and the ones that does well. I dont believe he will blackball us just because we dont remember.

Now some people are so wonderful about things, and they remember, and they do and say just the right things at the right time. My desk right here before me now is piled higher than Jim Farleys with letters from friends, and folks that should be my friends if I would show them the least courtesy of answering. But do you know I will keep putting it off. I carried some of them clear to N.Y. and back. Now I knew in my own heart darn well that I wasent going to sit down and write any letters while I was on the planes or in hotels, but I meant well I intended to answer em, but I knew darn well I wasent going to. There aint a thing in the world to lay it onto but laziness. I could have quit talking and boring somebody long enough to answered a lot of them. I could have stayed up an hour or so later and answered a dozen or so, but no I was too darn lazy, and I get sleepy early, and then the darn reading. I want to read everything in the world thats in the paper. No sporting writer ever wrote anything that I dident read it all.

Why you know what I do, and I bet you I am unique. I even read the editorials. Yes sir, now you cant beat that for missolaneous reading. Thats what you call exploring in reading. Course I forget everything I read. I havent got any more memory than a billy goat, and I forget about nine tenths of what I read, and get the other tenth wrong. But it makes me think that I am sorter doing something when I am reading. Then too, I can fall to sleep and never drop a paper. My closest friend cant tell when I am reading or sleeping. They are pretty near always wrong. They say, "You read a lot," and I say, "No, I sleep a lot over my reading." If they would just quit printing newspapers for about a year, I could get some books read, but by the time the daily papers are read I am sound asleep. They send me books, they autograph em to me, sometimes with some very kindly and much more than fair inscriptions, but do you know that I am that lazy and honery that I dont acknowledge em.

Now that is terrible, but I just get out of it by letting the impression go around that I am just so busy that I havent the time. Well I havent got the time because I am out on a horse somewhere, or asleep somewhere. If it wasent for riding, and reading newspapers and dozing off I bet you I'd be writing to more people than Mrs. Roosevelt. Now here lay all these important letters here tonight, and I could answer at least a tenth of em, but here comes the mornings papers. (They come out the day before). Now will I answer these letters and maintain my friends. No I will take the papers and go to bed, and go to sleep holding it out at arms length, the light burning, and the glasses on.

April 17:

Can you imagine Our Saviour dying for all of us, yet we have to argue over just whether he dident die for us personally, and not for you. Sometimes I wonder if his lessons of sacrifice and devotion was pretty near lost on a lot of us.

* * * * *

Its kinder as I heard a very learned American man one time say, "Dictatorship is the greatest form of Government there is, provided you have a good Dictator." Well ours is doing better than a lot

of folks think. They accept everything he does for em, but they
dont think he does enough.

April 21:

I just got a kind of a hunch that things are going to pick up all
around. Everybody hollers about all this big new batch of money
that is to be spent, but (in spite of what the Republicans and part of
the Democrats say) Roosevelt must know certain things by this time
that will bring results. You cant possibly spend that much money
without giving a lot of people work, and you cant give a lot of people
work without them spending it. They cant hold it, they cant bury
it, they have to spend it. The man they spend it with, the store-
keeper and the butcher, he has to spend it. Its bound to have a
beneficial effect all around, and the big ones that are hollering so,
its bound to reach them, and fix them so they can pay higher income
taxes.

I am like everybody else. I could sit down by the hour and tell
of plans that has been tried in the last couple of years that havent
worked, that have maby not only looked foolish, but were foolish,
but darn it all that criticism wouldent do any good. It would just
add to the yell of the pack. It would be just another howl in the
wilderness. I could sit down from now till morning and tell you
what he should not have done, but if you give me five minutes continuous time, I couldent tell you what he should have done, and
neither can any of the rest of em. They can view with alarm by the
hour, but they cant point with pride to something else for a minute.
All they can say is "Let Business Alone."

Well that all sounds fine, and it looks like a good thing to do, and
it would be a good thing to do, but it was done. It was already
done. Mr. Hoover certainly let it alone, right during this same
depression. There was not one sign of a handicap put on it. There
was no hollering about usurping the rights of the Constitution.
The Constitution was a-going wide open, and business had the
same leeway. Then what was the holler? All you have to do is
remember back.

"Why dont the Government do something?" "Why dont they

put out five billion dollars?" Dont you remember the first five billion that we were hollering for the Government to spend? This is not the first time this sum of money has been asked for. Its however the first time they ever got it.

We are in a hole and we are just running around in there looking for someone to lay it on. Big business wasent entirely responsible for getting us in there, and they are not going to be entirely responsible for getting us out as lots seem to think. They can help naturally, for they are a tremendous influence.

I think this fellow Roosevelt saw that there was a lot of ills connected with the way businesses were run, and he started in with idealistic plans as to how they should be remedied, and he has found that any business wont work with you when its not paying. He has persuaded, he has coaxed, he has tried but you cant make you or I invest our money if we are afraid, and he has kept em afraid. But maby the minute that this gigantic expenditure starts showing some results business will join in with him, and that will assure the whole plan's success.

We can talk all the politics we want, but business rises above politics in this Country. The South has gone Republican, and the North has gone Democratic. Why, both have done it because it looked like there was money in it. Let Roosevelt start showing some results with this new money, and it will have a lot of outside dough join it. There is not a Country in the World that can change our outlook as quick as we can. Just a dollar in our pocket makes a different man out of us. So lets dont thumbs down on this thing till we see, and the minute any of that dough commences reaching us, we are going to think its a pretty good place.

Beverly Hills:

I bet any Sunday could be made as popular at church as Easter is, if you made em fashion shows too. The audience is so busy looking at each other that the preacher just as well recite Gunga Din. We will do anything, if you just in some way turn it into a show. They say children in kindergarten must play in order to get em to learn. What do you mean children? Cross word puzzles learned grown folks more words than schoolteachers. And what arithmetic the women folks know they got at a bridge table. Our splendid English comes from attending the movies. My geography comes from an aeroplane window. Yes sir there is 120 million in the American kindergarten.

April 28:

Wiley Post, just about king of them all, cant break records getting to New York in a six-year-old plane, no matter if he takes it up so high that he coasts in. Equipment and engines change too fast. That Winnie May should be right in the Washington Museum, along with all the other historic planes. Its already done more than any plane in the World. Twice has it broken records clear around the world, broken altitude records. He has thrown off his wheels and has forced landings on his "Belly." And she never breaks a thing. Six years; thats the greatest advertisement for aeroplane safety the world has ever seen.

So when Wiley gets ready to put her into the Smithsonian we all want to give him a hand. Its his own plane, you know. Thats all he got out of two hazardous trips around the world was the old ship. Lord, last Summer when the family and I were days and days and days by train crossing Siberia we would come to towns with great long names, and they would remind us of places where we remembered Wiley had landed at on his crossing of Russia. All alone, couldent speak a word of Russian, land at a field, and he couldent tell em a thing in the world. What ever he wanted done in the way of some minor work on his ship he couldent tell em. He would have to do it when he hadent been asleep for a couple of days.

One place he wanted a drink of water. Said he never was as thirsty in his life, but they couldent understand, and from his motions and actions, they thought he wanted liquor, or vodka. Well they had the welfare of his trip at heart and wanted to do all they could. (And he says they were wonderful to him on both trips across there. They are great aviation enthusiasts, the Russians.). So he was sleeping out in a shed at the hangar, and they left a soldier on guard to watch him, and wake him for an early start. Well he was dying for a drink, and he kept making signs, and the soldier kept saying and motioning "No, No!"

He was trying to tell him that liquor would not be good for him. Finally the soldier seemed to get so mad that he left, and it must have been miles to town, but finally he come back with two quart bottles. Well Vodka looks like water, and Wiley grabbed one and started in on it. Naturally thinking it was water, and it was vodka (the poor soldier had perhaps said to himself, well if you are going to holler for it all night I will give it to you.) Wiley got up, warmed his plane up, (he dident have to take it out of the hangar, as the planes all stand out over there. Thousands of em in a field winter and summer with nothing but a canvas sheet over the engine) and he took off, and flew 1800 miles on to another place, just to get a drink. I tell you I think the W.C.T.U. or some good temperance society ought to take that true story and make something out of it. Left two bottles of vodka and flew 1800 miles for a drink of water, and the Russian got sore naturally, after walking all that distance to get em for him. Course I guess when Wiley was gone and the Russian got good settled down into about the second bottle he dident cuss Wiley so much. Course if it had been me I would have poured one bottle in my engine and the other in me, and I would have been in New York by sundown. That vodka really sends you places.

Santa Monica, April 28:

Never in our history was we as willing to blame somebody else for our troubles, America is just like an insane asylum, there is not a soul in it will admit they are crazy. Roosevelt being the warden at the present time, us inmates know he is the one thats — cuckoo.

Beverly Hills, April 30:

The one thing these old boys with a big navy are scared of and thats submarines. They are always claiming they are inhuman, and not a civilized mode of warfare. It would be rather interesting to see published the names of the weapons that are considered a pleasure to be shot by.

May 12: [*Broadcast of Gulf Refining Company's program on Mother's Day.*]

This is Mothers' Day. It's Mothers' Day. Of course it's pretty late in the evening now to remind you of it. If you didn't know it before, there's not much you can do about it now. Unless you might possibly be ashamed into going or phoning to a florist. They're keeping open this evening just to accomodate late consciences.

Of course, florists — they got mothers, too, florists have, but they've got more flowers than they've got mothers, and — and they have a great organization the florists have. They, they have led us to believe that no matter how we have treated our Mothers during the last year that a little bouquet of hyacinths or verbenas will square it, you know — not only with mother but with our conscience too; when, as a matter of fact you don't need to be square with your mother. She knows you better than you know yourself.

A mother is the only thing that is so constituted that they possess eternal love under any and all circumstances. No matter how you treat them, you still have the love . . . I was telling that to my wife today, and I was telling her a little thought that I wanted to use in there, and I said — you know, Betty — I says — a mother and a dog is the only two friends that has eternal love. No matter how you treat 'em. And my wife makes me cut the dog out. Said it — well, it didn't sound very good, and it might sound disrespectful to a mother, but I certainly didn't mean it that way, but it's the only thing that really is. You know what I mean.

So the poor old dog he'll have to go. I can't use it on account of my wife made me leave the dog out, but it still loves you just the same — just as much as a mother did. Some day we may have a dog day too, or something, and I can use that on the dog day. I hate to leave the dog out. My wife runs this outfit.

Well anyhow, they both, they both certainly — no matter what you do to them — they all love you.

May 20:

One night on the Radio I was yapping about all these people who are criticising Mr. Roosevelt and saying he was spending too

much money, yet admitting that the Government was the only one
who was spending money, and that if that was the case that everybody that was making any must be indebted to the President for
making it, for it was evidently Relief Money that we were in a
round about way getting, and that a person to really be consistent,
he should refuse to take any of it, that is if he was so critical of the
Government policies.

Well there was a little too much truth for that to set very good.
I guess I brought it out a little too crude and bare faced, folks dont
like to be told they are living off the Government, but thats about
what we are all doing.

* * * * *

Los Angeles, June 2:

Well sir a forlorn looking gentleman come to my house this Sunday afternoon. Said he was one of Roosevelts Cabinet, and he
looked it. It was Mr. Roper, Secretary of Commerce. I try to
make it a point to never turn anybody away. First one of the New
Deal I had seen since the Supreme Court took their matches away
from em. But he was a game Southern gentleman. No kicks, no
squawks. He and I searched around through the burned embers,
to see if any little New Deal object might be salvaged.

We decided that big business operating under the old "Dog eat
dog" plan, so many dogs would eventually get bit that parts of the
N.R.A. would look like a halo by 1936.

Santa Monica, June 19:

At the great San Diego Worlds Fair yesterday, Mr. Hoover received a tremendous ovation. There is no country in the world
where a person changes from hero to a goat, and a goat to a hero, or
visa versa, as they do with us. And all through no change of them,
the change is always in us. Its not our public men that you cant
put your finger on, its our public. We are the only fleas weighing
over 100 pounds. We dont know what we want, but we are ready
to bite somebody to get it.

Beverly Hills, June 24:

See there is bill in congress to do away with tax exempt bonds, thats the best bill of all of em.   The way it is a man could have a million dollar income from tax free bonds, own no property or nothing else, and not pay one cent of tax.   And its all lawful.   If they can make all these bonds pay tax they will be doing one of the most fair share the wealth plans there is.   It was put in so that a town or a state, or the government could sell more bonds than it ought to.

Beverly Hills, June 26:

The first battle of the next war was fought in N.Y. City Tuesday night, big Italy met little Abysinia and Mussolinis first spring drive was halted in its tracks.   General Joe Louis head of the Etheopian forces met El Duce Carnera (the biggest Roman of them all), and treated him like a Christian of Gladiatorial days.   Now there is a movement on to send "Lion" Louis to Abysinia to meet Mussolinis whole army, his trip is being gladly paid for by several American philanthropists (new friends of Abysinian liberty), a Mr. Braddock, a Mr. Baer (not Bugs), and even a German, a Mr. Schmelling, has contributed to make Mr. Louis trip to Africa more permanent.

Beverly Hills, June 27:

One thing you got to say for an administration that try out a lot of plans some of em are apt to be pretty good, now this one that broke out yesterday where they help out these young folks, that sounds awful good.   Course I look for bountiful editorial condemnation, for its going to cost money.   But if you help out the young folks up to twenty, and the old ones over 60, that only gives a fellow a little stretch in between of about 40 years where he has to do any worrying for himself, (or herself as the sex may be).   If we can keep the young happy, and the old satisfied, why all the middle aged have to look out for is women automobile drivers.

June 30:

A fellow can't afford to die now with all this excitement going on.

July 2:

Anytime a slick salesman meets a ten dollar bill there is a deal made. All it has to be is on the installment plan. There is something about American folks that they think it must be on the level or the company wouldnt trust us to pay the other payments, its never entered our head that the first payment more than pays for it.

July 2:

Brotherly Love Is Having a Boom. Mussolini sent his Army down into Africa for a training trip hoping to annex some loose territory in route. Thats your next war. England has strongly remonstrated with Italy and told em of the text in the Bible where it says, (I think its the third chapter, third verse of the Book of Dutyrominy) which reads "They shall not covet thy neighbors territory, nor thy neighbors prospective oil wells, or thy neighbors natural resources." Thats what England told Mussolini and Mussolini broke out laughing, and Englands representative dident know what Mussolini was laughing at, and he finally asked him, and Mussolini said, as follows, "Where was the third verse, of the third chapter of Dutyrominy when you boys was coveting India, South Africa, Hong Kong and all points East and West?"

Well for a minute there wasent any reply. The El Duce had the Englishman stuck, but not for long, for the Englishman replied, "Well I guess thats in the New Testament and it wasent written when we grabbed Gandiland, and those other little Knick Knacks."

You see Mussolini is just native shrewd enough to know that about all the big Nations of this globe live in glass houses, and when they start throwing stones of criticism about coveting some outside range, why its liable to catch em on the rebound, even as moral old Christian Nation as "The land of the free and the home of the brave" has gnawed off a little here and there during its short span of life. Grabbing off the Phillipines was not exactly by popular demand of all concerned. Course we are going to give em up, but not till just about two jumps ahead of when somebody would take em away from us anyhow. We are really dropping the candy just because we see a big bully coming around the corner to take it away

from us. Had he got out the day we got in we would never have
been humiliated. We did it pretty good with Cuba, only we never
did really get plum out. We always had some sort of a bill where
we was still to be the big brother, as long as the sugar lasted. So
both individually and nationally we are just living in a time when
none of us are in any shape to be telling somebody else what to do.
Thats why your League of Nations wont hold water is because the
big ones run it, and the little ones know that the big ones have only
turned moral since they got all they can hold. I can come in with
a full stomach and advise the rest of the gang not to rob the fruit
stand. That it aint right. The big ones would like to sorter stick
together. They say its to protect the little ones, but its to protect
themselves. There is no Nation laying awake at night worrying
about a little Nation, unless the little Nation is one where somebody
can march across to get to them. Who would have protected Belgium if Germany had been marching through Belgium, going
nowhere.

Its not what you are doing to the little Nation, its what you going
to do to us after you get through the little Nation. It would be
a wonderful thing if it did. But brotherly love has never crossed a
boundary line yet. If you think it has why dont somebody protect
China? China has never bothered anybody. They have been a
friend to the World. They are having their Country taken away
from em, but nobody says a word for she is so far away that they
hope no Nation can march clear through her and get to them.
Yes sir geography has more to do with brotherly love than civilization and christianity combined.

July 3:

I have been working pretty hard (laugh) on some movies. It
just happened that I almost had three right in a row. Now that
dont mean that they will be released as fast as we made em. They
only come out about every four months, but we got a couple ahead
already made and that means that I will have little time off to do a
few things I been planning on, and that I wont look like I am trying
to get in front of every camera that is grinding.

We run one the other night called, "In Old Kentucky," and its got a lot of laughs. Had a lot of awful fine people in it, and they sure made good. You know the old idea of one person trying to be the whole thing in a picture is all washed up. Pictures are like a ball team, the pitcher cant do it all. Its got to be the whole team. You just watch pictures close and see how well done are just small parts, or what they call "Bits." Its because they are done by real actors, actors that anyone of them could go in and play the leading part. They may only get two or three days work out of it, but they do it like it was a star part, and you never hear em whining either about the part not being in keeping with their ability.

No sir, I believe there is more real nerve and gameness under the most discouraging circumstances in the picture business than any other place on earth, course the stage is not far behind, its a heart breaking racket but they dont sit and tell you about it. Their heads are always up. They keep neat, they hide a lot with a great smile.

Well after I finish a long seige I sorter begin to looking up in the air and see what is flying over, and Mrs. Rogers in her wise way will say, "Well I think you better get on one. You are getting sorter nervous." Well this time the Fourth of July was a coming on. I had had a lot of invitations to a lot of places where I would have liked to have gone on the Fourth.

So I went to a real cowboy reunion in Texas on one of their most famous ranches. Not a professional rodeo like you see everywhere else, but a real celebration in a real cowtown by real old timers. I wouldent have missed it for anything.

Stamford, Texas, July 3:

Cowboy sports and contests are about the most popular thing there is, especially where they know what its all about, I had often heard of the great time this little city holds every year, its called a cowboy reunion and it is, its put on by real ranch hands, this is the heart of the old Texas ranch country, the outfits send in their chuck wagons and they have a great time, lots of good horses and lots of good ropers, grass is high and cattle are a good price and everybody feeling fine. If Mr. Brisbane dont want to use his old slogan any more I will take "Dont Sell America Short."

Beverly Hills, July 4:

Well breakfast in Ft. Worth this morning did kinder want to go on and see what the boys in Congress was doing as there was a plane standing there that would have put me there this afternoon another leaving for Brownsville Texas and Old Mexico I looked longingly at it, another leaving for Tulsa and Claremore, I did want to go on it, but finally settled on the one for California, as thats what I should do, come on home, in here at four oclock this afternoon, fifteen hundred miles, it dont take you long to go a long distance and get back nowadays. Lot of hollering among the rich and near rich. We are living in a great time, something to get excited about every minute.

Santa Monica, July 5:

That liberty that we got 159 years ago Thursday was a great thing, but they ought to pass a law that we could only celebrate it every 100 years, for at the rate of accidents yesterday we wont have enough people to celebrate it every year, and the speeches? Did you read them? Never was as much politics indulged in under the guise of "Freedom and liberty."

They was 5 percent what George Washington did, and 95 percent what the speaker intended to do, what this country needs on July the Fourth is not more "Liberty or more freedom" its a Roman candle that only shoots out of one end.

Santa Monica, July 14:

California has been lucky. We escaped the winds, the floods, the droughts and the heat, but pestilence finally caught us, the bo-weevil descended on us, in train loads. Thirty-five hundred law-yers of the American Bar Association are here eating us out of house and home. They are here, they say, "to save the Constitution. To preserve state rights."

What they ought to be here for and that would make this con-vention immortal, is to kick the crooks out of their profession, they should recommend a law that in every case that went on trial the lawyer defending should be tried first. Then if he comes clear, he

would be eligible to defend.   As it is now, they are trying the wrong
man.

Beverly Hills, July 15:
Pat Hurley called me up last night, remember Pat, Sec of War
during the time when we had no trouble with the Constitution but
had it with everything else.   Well sir there was a cheerful and in
fact an arrogant ring in Pats voice, you know Republicans voices
are changing, they are not whispering any more, you meet one now
and he hollers across the street, "Hello, hello, did you know that our
free American institutions are in greater danger today than ever
before, did you know they are going to take our Rolls Royces away
from us and make us ride in a mere Cadillac, did you know that six
months ago there wasent a Republican Presidential candidate in a
car load, and now there is over a million, happy days are here
again."

Vermejo Park, New Mexico, July 26:
This sure is a beautiful country up in here, lakes, streams, mountains, fish, deer, elk, everything, everytime we would see a good
looking ranch and a little meadow down in the canyon Wiley Post
would set his Lockheed down in it, visited our old friend Waite
Phillips first, he has a marvelous place, and three hundred twenty
five thousand acres of pretty country, now we are at the famous
Vermejo Ranch, the greatest fishing and game place in the whole
Southwest.   Wiley is fishing, and I am out looking at cattle.

Durango, Colorado, July 28:
Towns are like people they are proud of what they have, Trinidad Colo., with enough coal to melt the North Pole down till it
runs, then Wiley hit a beeline over the tops of the mountains to
Durango, a beautiful little city, out of the way and glad of it, gold,
silver, and Mesa Verde Cliff Dwelling Ruins, where civilization
flourished before it started to go backwards, today Wiley is flying
over Brice Canyon, Zion Canyon, over, down, and through the
Grand Canyon, Hoover Dam, New Lake, no wonder American

people are filling roads, trains, and air, there is so much to see, what we lack in reading we make up in looking.

Beverly Hills, July 29:

Say did you read about Mussolinis army being camped on a stream, and the Abysinians went above em, and diverted the creek, and left em with no water, (thats a dry country down there). I cant imagine anything any more disconcerting to an army than to wake up in the morning and find the river hid from under you.

Modern armys have everything. But there is just something about a native in any country in the world, where he seems to have more sense than any general army corpse. Our old Apache Geronimo drove 19 sets of U.S. army officers "Nuts," the Boers hid the Englishmens tea for two years. Cortez great, great, grandchildren in Mexico are still trying to whip the Yaquis. If I was going to fight somebody I would pick out the most civilized one I could find, cause they are the dumbest.

Beverly Hills, August 1:

Here is rather an amazing statement. It dident get much publicity in the press. But it was in there. It was made by the President. (Who has access to the records and must know) "58 of the richest people in the U.S. paid no federal tax on 37 percent of their incomes." This soaking the rich has got two sides to it. Roosevelt gets him a pack of humorously called "Brain trusters" to help him devise ways and means of trying to get at this extra 37 percent. And the rich get them some lawyers that are just as smart as Roosevelt tribe, and their job is to cook up an antidote. So up to now most of the soaking has been done in the papers and not at the cash register.

Santa Monica, August 2:

Well havent got much time to do any editorializing today, tomorrow (Saturday) the big worlds championship cowboy contest starts, and I am busy setting on the fence blathering with em, (which is about all I can do along cowboy sports line) some of em are right from my home range in Oklahoma, and I think learned to rope on some of my stock, its like baseball, its a sport you can attend and not know that its not "in the bag," you cant put a calf or bucking horse in a bag, its not like prize fighting or wrestling, where the loser gets a big slice too, nobody is paid a nickle but the winners, depression hit everything but horseback riding, there was never as many people riding, and interested in ranch life.

I been just messing around doing this and that and not much of either. Get an old "Soap Suds" and ride off up a little canyon I got here with running water in it. Dont mean a thing to you all in most of the places where you might unfortunately read this, but to us folks out here in California, or in any of these arid states I tell you running water is just about the last word.

August 5:

The banker, the lawyer, and the politician are still our best bets for a laugh. Audiences havent changed at all, and neither has the three above professions.

August 6:

Away here a week or so back I went out to the flying field at midnight in Los Angeles to catch the plane for Seattle. I was off on a little sight seeing trip with Wiley Post. When my wife knew it was with Wiley, it dident matter where it was we was going and she was mighty fine about it.

Well she is about everything. You cant live with a comedian long without being mighty forgiving.

Juneau, Alaska, August 7:

Well that was some trip thousand mile hop from Seattle to Juneau was going to stop at Ketchikan for lunch but mist and rain and he just breezed through never over 100 feet off the water and talk about navigating there is millions of channels and islands and bays and all look alike (to me) but this old boy turns up the right alley all the time nothing that I have ever seen is more beautiful than this inland passage (by either boat or plane) to Alaska. You know I just been thinking about things at home you know who I bet would like to be on this trip Mr. Roosevelt.

Juneau, Alaska, August 9:

Bad weather not a plane mushed out of Juneau yesterday had a great visit last night. Rex Beach a mighty dear old friend arrived from Vancouver, Alaska. Welcomed him like an old brother. He did more to popularize it than anyone. The first movie I ever made was in 18, an Alaskan story by Rex called Laughing Bill Hyde. Tourists still arriving not much news of Congress and what we do get is mostly bad. Guess its about the same down there.

Nothing could be more appropriate to end this selection of Will's writings than with his introduction done to his good friend Charley Russell's Trails Plowed Under:

I bet you hadn't been up there three days, Charley, until you had out your pencil and was a drawin' something funny. And I bet you that Mark Twain, and old Bill Nye, and Whitcomb Riley, and a whole bunch of those old joshers was just a waitin' for you to pop in with all the latest ones.

And I bet they are regular fellows when you meet em, ain't they? Most big men are.

Well, you will run onto my old Dad up there, Charley, for he was a real cow hand, and I bet he is runnin' a wagon; and you will pop into some well-kept ranch-house, over under some cool shady trees, and you will be asked to have dinner, and it will be the best one you ever had in your life. Well, when you are thankin' the women folks you just tell the sweet lookin' little old lady that you knew her boy, back on an outfit you used to rope for, and tell the daughters that you knew their brother, and if you see a cute little rascal runnin' around there with my brand on him, kiss him for me.

Well, can't write any more, Charley, damn paper's all wet, it must be raining in this old bunk house. Of course we're all just hangin' on here as long as we can. I don't know why we hate to go, we know its better there.

From your old friend, WILL.